Theatre Stuff: Critical Essays on Contemporary Irish Theatre

Edited by Eamonn Jordan

The Arts Council
An Chomhairle Ealaíon

A Carysfort Press Book

Theatre Stuff: Critical Essays on Contemporary Irish Theatre

First published in Ireland in 2000 as a paperback original by Carysfort Press, 58 Woodfield, Scholarstown Road, Dublin 16, Ireland.

Typeset by Carysfort Press

Printed and bound by Colour Books Ltd, Unit 105, Baldoyle Industrial Estate, Dublin 13, Ireland.

This book is published with the financial assistance of The Arts Council (An Chomhairle Ealaíon), Dublin, Ireland.

CONTENTS

Acknowledgements

When it comes to this book, there are many people to thank. First of all, I would like to thank all of the contributors for their response to my request for articles and I would like to acknowledge their support for this project. Thanks to the Arts Council for its moral and financial backing. I am indebted to Christopher Murray for his support and advice over the years. I would like to thank my former colleagues at the Drama Studies Centre, NUI, Dublin, especially Hilary Gow. I would like to say thank you to Redmond O'Hanlon for all of his keen insights and provocations. I am grateful for the support I received from colleagues and staff at the Sligo Institute of Technology; Eamonn Fitzpatrick, Dermot Layden, Francis O'Regan and Pat Scanlon, with whom I share an office, and especially Michael Barrett, Diarmuid Timmons, Dermot Finan, Perry Share and John Kavanagh. I would like to acknowledge gratefully the backing of Lilian Chambers and Cathy Leeney. Thanks to Dan Farrelly for his substantial contribution to the proofing and preparation of this text. Likewise, a huge debt of thanks is due to my family, friends and relations. Finally, for my own part, I am indebted to the students with whom I have discussed many of these issues and with whom I continue to share a deep passion for Irish Theatre.

Introduction

Eamonn Jordan

Irish Theatre has never been so successful, yet at the same time never more in need of rigorous evaluation. Many of the plays by Brian Friel, Hugh Leonard, Thomas Kilroy, Thomas Murphy, Frank McGuinness, Sebastian Barry, Anne Devlin, Conor McPherson, Bernard Farrell, Martin McDonagh (London-Irish), Marina Carr, Billy Roche and Marie Jones have won substantial awards. The much praised and lauded directors Garry Hynes, Patrick Mason, Ben Barnes, Lynne Parker, John Crowley and Conall Morrison have worked at some of the best theatres in the world and with some of the best theatre talent available. Likewise, Irish administrators, actors and designers have had numerous successes. Overall there is evidence of increased urgency, focus and professionalism. These need to be encouraged and celebrated.

It was a privilege to be able to bring together such a range of critical and dynamic voices from many different countries and backgrounds. We have contributors from Ireland, England, France, Canada, Japan and America, comprising playwrights, directors, journalists, theatre practitioners, critics and academics. Most are not confined to any one single field. On offer is a range of essays with no unifying coherence or argument, and no attempt was made to establish that. Each contributor takes an approach which is passionate, idiosyncratic and refreshing. Astuteness is the hallmark of all of the work. Little is taken as given, and most things come under the critical spotlight. The insistence in the writing is consistently to challenge, provoke, position and to connect. The assessments are not about congratulations and back-slapping; neither are they exercises in begrudgery. All of the essays, in one way or another, hints at the magic, urgency and ephemeral qualities of good theatre.

Irish Theatre has changed both fundamentally and radically on so many fronts. Funding has always been a huge issue, but there was never so much money available to the Arts Council and this has liberated the theatre sector. Infrastructurally, huge changes have come about over the last number of years with new theatres springing up all over the country. The Abbey Theatre, Gate Theatre, Rough Magic Theatre Company, Passion Machine, Field Day and Druid Theatre Company to name but a few, have all toured internationally with great success. (The Abbey Theatre itself, under Patrick Mason's stewardship to the end of 1999, has had a relatively stable period.) In addition, the need for professional theatre training has been given a more substantial base, and, academically, a number of theatre departments have sprung up around the country, encouraging a vast quantity of quality undergraduate and graduate research that remains substantially and unforgivably unpublished. Rapid changes in printing have affected the publication of plays, by making it easier and less costly to do so. The demise of *Theatre Ireland* was one of the great losses to the Irish Theatre sector and it is great to see the *Irish Theatre Magazine* emerge as an influential forum for debate and analysis. Definitely, there is a small but significant move away from text-based theatre to improvised scripts, a shift away from verbally driven productions to a greater conscious emphasis on the visual dimension, a switch from what is perceived to be formal theatre spaces to less formal ones. But again what is totally new in that?

These essays are not so much about the intellectualising of theatre practice as about encountering theatre in different, passionate ways and about the challenges facing those who make meaning in theatre. As well as this, some of these essays confront the lip service paid to the role of the director, designer, theatre space and performer in the making of meaning within theatre. Long gone are the days when drama and theatre were just a component of English Literature and this is something that the new Leaving Certificate Syllabus is attempting to address. Clearly, today's audiences are more sophisticated and demanding in their encounter with a performance. In addition, these essays remind the reader of the gender challenges facing theatre practice. The slow emergence of women writers, unlike the advancement of women in theatre administration, production and performance, is part of the ongoing troublesome debate. Not everything could be covered, not every invitation to writers to contribute was accepted and, occasionally, what was promised was not delivered for numerous reasons. Nevertheless, there is no perfect balance and not everybody will be comfortable with certain absences, but the objective with this book was never to be all-inclusive; instead the intention was to be somewhat representative of what is going on now.

Watching some daytime television recently, I saw two programmes that fascinated me. Jenny Jones' show offers men and women the opportunity through DNA testing to establish the paternity of a child. DNA testing is as accurate as can be. The results were announced "on air" and the viewer could bear witness to the instant responses of the panellists. The other programme was Ricki Lake's. A mother and daughter were on this particular show. Communication between mother and daughter was fraught. (Guests hardly ever hide their identities behind a screen as you might find on a RTE or BBC programme.) And in order to address the difficulty, the young woman had agreed to take a lie detector test off camera; the findings of which would be related to her mother, who posed the questions to be answered.

The polygraph test would measure heartbeat, pulse, breathing rates and the conductance of the skin in order to distinguish between what is true, what is false and what is inconclusive. What is truth, what is fantasy and what is fabrication? Despite the voyeurism, and taking into account the performative opportunity afforded to guests on the show and the chance to realise some escapist fantasy, there is a belief that television is the court of appeal and that "truth" can be ascertained and verified publicly, by the spectacle of the chat show. Is there some ultimate truth that a heightened pulse or an escalated blood pressure can somehow confirm? And can in effect, physiological feedback or DNA testing be equated with truth. What is the relationship between fact and truth? Is there any need to establish one? Most of all, what has social class got to do with it all? I make some of these comments in light of Prime Cut's recent production of *Problem Child* by the Canadian playwright, George F. Walker, which dealt with some of these issues.

What once was the ritualisation of truth in theatre and performance becomes the spectacle of truth, voyeuristically framed by the perverse quest for verification and authenticity within the chat-show format; a quick fix in both meanings of the word. Neither the resolution of issues in private nor the recourse to expertise beyond the frame of television is enough. The transaction is a complicated one, but the guests, though not victims in a narrow sense of the word, still perform some act of self-laceration. Often on such shows, the pain is spectated, made spectacular and numbed by the presence of the camera and made offensive by an intrusion that is invited from the studio audience, which often attempts to determine the value and worth of an individual's pain and of his/her behaviour. It becomes a show-trial by (the usually female) chat-show host and her studio audience. (It is unknown, in my experience, for the host and audience not to share relatively similar responses, and as such the guests are judged according to some common value system that is without complication and driven by nostalgia and sentiment.)

The bigger deception, however, is the lie of compassion promoted by programme makers in the name of ratings and profit. It seems as if there is no emotion and no feedback accommodated, without the presence of the camera and no substance or validation of identity without the intervention of the public. What does it mean to play to the public gallery?

A specific type of television is selling us one reality and what are our playwrights peddling? Written texts are funny things. What is a text's status? What is the relational dynamic between a production and a written text? Who makes meaning and who controls meaning? These are hard and serious questions. All writing emerges from specific contexts and to any observer the society from which Irish writing has sprung over the last forty years has been a swiftly altering one. This not only impacts on the content of the writing but also on form; what stories are told and how are they told? New ways of telling must be continually sought. Fundamentally, the concerns, ideas, dramatic practices and audiences' expectations have altered substantially since Brian Friel, Hugh Leonard, John B. Keane and Tom Murphy began to work in the theatre. The references, allusions, modes of understanding and of relating have all adjusted radically. The values of one generation are certainly not those of another; the concerns of one specific group fail to impact on another. That said, for comparative purposes it is impossible to say that there are no continuities. Only the innocent or the naive would prompt that. Within a vastly altering Ireland new relationships are the governing reality. That is both the task and dilemma facing the administrator, writer, designer, director and performer.

From here there is a broader question. What is the standing of contemporary writing practice? Why have Irish plays abroad been so successful, especially since 1990 with the acclaim granted to *Dancing at Lughnasa*? Clearly, we cannot deny the huge success of Irish drama of late. But what is the truth of it? How do we evaluate that success? Is it the number of awards garnered, by playwright, production or performer, is it the length of the run and the scale of the audiences attending, is it measured by the substances of critical responses, or by the translation of texts into other languages and contexts? Is it too immediate to assess or is a play truly of merit, only after it has been through many new productions and many interrogations before a broad spectrum of spectators? The answer to such a series of questions is complex.

From a late-nineties perspective, many of the major cultural aspirations and much sought-after freedoms of the recent past are now taken as given. Much has happened economically, politically and socially, including Church scandals, new social legislation, the growing force of feminism, two women Presidents and a slackening of the propensity to include Britain in the evaluation of Irish identities. The heightened productivity of technology alongside labour and technological alienation, new concerns about ownership and belonging, a growing redundancy of faith, an increasingly assertive intercultural penetration and a previously unknown dynamic economy have all led to a society in serious transition. Effectively, the confusions and confidences delivered by a period of social liberalism, the collapse of political difference with the demise of left-wing alternatives, the apparent confluence of political thinking and the influence of politically correct ideology have ensured that difference has been submerged and the impact of oppositional energies diluted. We have modified through a period of accelerated history and an accumulation of intensities that have changed radically the structures of Irish society. These changes have impacted on the writing. So the social and political shifts, new dramaturgical influences and the complicated intersection between the post-colonial and the postmodern have all resulted in intricate and elaborate writing practices. Tom Kilroy argues in his essay in this collection, written in the early 1990s:

> It is only in the past decade that Ireland has become truly urbanised in the late-twentieth century meaning of that term, in other words, characterised by great mobility, using highly complex, far-reaching systems of communication, with increased secularisation and the break-down of the old bonds of familial, tribalistic society. We have yet to have a theatre of this Ireland because it is as yet incompletely formed but we are getting plays that reflect the confusion attending those changes.

Change is fundamental to a dramatic practice and the challenge facing all of our present dramatists is to match and map the experiences, confidences and demands of a changing society. Kilroy raises a number of substantial issues in his essay. First are aspects of a tradition that still shape his own writing and the writing practice of his own generation that grew up in a "virtually cashless society", with a "containable, endurable poverty everywhere". It was a situation marked by "isolation, repressiveness and dreariness". How different is Kilroy's description of his economic reality to the one presently on offer to a substantial part of the population? For Kilroy, out of the dour circumstances of 40s and 50s Ireland emerged a "new writing" and a "new sensibility", a writing practice which profited from aspects of "distancing", "self-consciousness" and "artifice", as were laid down by playwrights mainly from the Anglo-Irish tradition. It was a writing style that was "alive to the dislocating perspectives of the mid-century and the fluidity of expression possible on stage with modern lighting, design and direction". Yet it still took his generation, according to Kilroy, to bleed dry certain forms; namely, the "Irish peasant play", the "Irish Religious play", the "Family Play" and the "Irish History play". Kilroy delivers a warning, stating that "Within the metropolitan centres there is always a nostalgia for cultures which are untouched, untainted by the ennui, the busyness, the crowdedness of the centre". Finally Kilroy ends with the statement that "nostalgia may no longer be enough, indeed it may not even be necessary as Irish drama begins to locate itself more in the present".

Nostalgia is the note upon which Kilroy ends, and is also the concept against which Declan Hughes rails. Hughes charges against a tradition and the expectation of a tradition that inhibits and in a way paves a space for the distinctiveness, integrity and originality of his own generation. Hughes' essay is a moral and visionary one, versed more in the cultural practices of America than that of an Irish tradition. For him, an overly cosy consciousness of being "Irish" is suffocating in its own right, even if it seems as if the world wants to be "Irish too". People are too satisfied in "being Irish with themselves". He wonders why "does contemporary Irish Literature ignore contemporary Ireland" in the main. Instead Hughes argues that we are still processing in our writing an "Ireland that hasn't existed for years", perhaps even an Ireland that never existed in the first place. The Irishness for which we once generally opted, as much out of an oppositional defiance perhaps as anything else, has been substantially eroded. Moreover for Hughes we have to acknowledge the impact of popular culture on both our consciousness and on how our writing is now being increasingly shaped.

This popular cultural impact has been significant of late. A blatant model of contrast would compare the wild dancing in Friel's *Dancing at Lughnasa* to the beat of the traditional *Mason's Apron* to the dancing inspired by the sound of *Bullet with Butterfly Wings* by the Smashing Pumpkins used in Hughes' own *Halloween Night* (1997) (both dances were partially performed on top of tables), would oppose the operatic influence on the structure of Murphy's *The Gigli Concert* (1983) with the effect of the television soap opera format on McDonagh's work and would differentiate between the significances of the King James' Bible, Shakespeare or Mikhail Bakhtin's underworld of the carnival to McGuinness' writings and the influences of Quentin Tarantino, Irvine Welsh and *The Simpsons* on the work of Alex Johnston.

Hughes perceives very clearly the fetishisation of authentication and views that to be a dangerous cul-de-sac of sorts. For Hughes, "What used to be creativity, inspiration, energy has congealed into tradition. What is tradition anyway? Habit in fancy dress. An excuse for thought. A mindless worship of the past". He ends his essay with a question, if the Celts never really existed, and if the versions of Irishness we feed ourselves are an illusion, a fabrication, how liberating might that be? How much easier it might be to resolve certain tensions, but perhaps it is this confidence trick that has prompted the freshness and vision of what has emerged in so much of the writing of late.

Hughes sees a need to fend off tradition and elsewhere he has written of placing an embargo on the writings of an older generation, in order to allow a new generation space to prosper. To me, there is more boldness, recklessness and provocation in that statement than real desire. Essentially, as an emerging post-colonial society, we are still locked between village and city. Hughes states that: "The village is no longer the objective correlative for Ireland: the city is, or to be precise, *between* cities is. That space between. That's not to say that people don't live in the country any more, or that rural life isn't 'valuable'; it's that culturally, it's played out. It no longer signifies. Mythologically, it doesn't resonate any more".

There are three traditions of translation/adaptation in operation in Irish drama, the translation of modern European classics (McGuinness, Friel and Kilroy), the adaptations of Irish poetry best seen in the work of Bolger and MacIntyre and the re-working of Greek classics. The consistent modification of Greek classic drama is a re-invigoration of tradition, a cross-cultural absorption and adaptation of form, content and context, and an attempt to interrogate the present by appropriation. Marianne McDonald's essay maps that vigorous approach towards the classics at a particularly sensitive time both socially and politically. McDonald notes that:

> Each of these Irish playwrights has a particular approach towards Ireland's history and political situation, some more overtly than others. Field Day Theatre first performed Tom Paulin's *The Riot Act: A Version of Antigone* by Sophocles at the Guildhall, Derry, on September 19, 1984. It uses the language of the Irish North to place us in its modern locale, and the ideas expressed translate well into the issues which divide Derry.

80s Ireland was in part a world of suspicion and little compromise. *Antigone* was the obvious attraction here. Through this text, distance, insight, repudiation and the processing of fears and anxieties are available to the writer. Moreover, it is not just a recent Irish passion for the classics. Yeats' attempts to appropriate the classics are duly noted by McDonald. Moreover McDonald escorts the reader from the world of politics into a specific post-colonial context, something that most definitely needs articulation.

McDonald argues that literary classics not only provide a "heightened mode of communication", but that they can also be used to "filter personal terror, such as fear of death". The fact that the playwrights opted for *Antigone* more than any other text gives an indication that the concerns are "on human rights more than on fate and identity". A version of *Oedipus Tyrannus* is striking by its absence. So, in re-writing or re-working, adapting, translating, and transposing the classics, McDonald argues, the main function is to create a "literature of protest". Justice is the quest and justice is the obligation. Overall for McDonald, "The result is not simply a political tract protesting abuse, but a passionate expression of hopes and fears".

Towards the end of her essay McDonald quotes Seamus Heaney's lines about the need to believe in "miracles" and in "healing wells and cures". Such is his optimism and such is the role of the writer to step outside of the brutality of fact and into mystery and parable. The Greek connection fulfilled that in part, where curses, revenge and the bond of blood were commonplace and resolution problematic on many fronts. Irish versions of Chekhov and Ibsen in particular fulfil a not too dissimilar function.

Obsession, the process of change and the intense and lacerating bonds of family seem to be the attraction, apart from the need to resist the demands and imperatives of British versions of the same plays.

If tradition is problematic on a number of fronts, then Lionel Pilkington complicates it further by determinedly tracing what is perceived as being tradition and more importantly what is excluded from that. Such exclusion then impacts in a number of ways, not least of which is the relationship between tradition and institutionally formal theatre and more importantly, what is marginalized, repressed and excluded from our contemporary definitions, something which ties in with later essays by Caoimhe McAvinchey and Victor Merriman. Pilkington draws on John Harrington's work in which he claims that even the Irish melodramas of the 19th century "functioned as an important counterweight to the misrepresentation of Irish character on the English stage and thus helped to prepare the way for the possibility of a somewhat more independent Irish theatre".

Pilkington invites us to evaluate critically the origins of our National Theatre project and by so doing refute the narrow version of it, once held so dear by so many, and perhaps still is by some, to this very day. Foundation assumptions like that no indigenous Irish theatre existed prior to the Irish Literary Theatre is fatally flawed. Historical exclusion has led to canonical exclusion. Likewise, the insularity of definition of the National Theatre project either ignores or downplays folk drama, the mumming tradition, working-class-based theatre practices and also the popular theatre tradition. According to Pilkington, the National Theatre project was a riposte to the representation of Irishness on English stages, yet the newly emergent theatre project was "so compromised by Anglicisation as to be incapable of being described as indigenous".

For Pilkington, "the Irish Literary Theatre functioned as a means by which the social and political leadership role of a section of the southern Irish landlord class could find expression as champions of modernisation rather than stand out as colonial anachronisms and remain vulnerable to the now much expanded, increasingly confident, and predominantly Roman Catholic, Irish electorate". Pilkington goes so far as to say that:

> For both groupings the theatre was thought of as an ideal form, dissolving political conflict in the context of an overarching national ideal and reinforcing traditional structures of authority. In the theatre — or so it was hoped — spectators would behave not like a crowd, but like individual citizens, maturely suspending their personal circumstances and vested interests within the context of a national ideal.

Clearly, nationalist practices had very strong anti-colonial initiatives, but the theatre that emerged was owned and administered by "Ireland's traditional ruling elite" and financed by an Englishwoman, Miss Horniman. Such anomalies and contradictions go a long way towards the fuelling of Irish drama. For Pilkington, the project began by "portraying those features of Irish culture that were perceived as recalcitrant to modernity", which is often a charge levelled at some of our younger writers today.

Anna McMullan's essay looks at issues of gender, authorship and performance in plays by Marie Jones, Emma Donoghue, Marina Carr and Mary-Elizabeth Burke-Kennedy. McMullan argues that it is not so much that women don't write for the stage, but that for many reasons, including the "lack of resources, alienation from traditional working practices and forms of authorship in the theatre", and she adds "Irish women playwrights in the past have had no place in the selection of playwrights and texts that the culture has endorsed as being of significance and value". Despite under-representation, women are active on many fronts, especially in the areas of education and community work and in "non-literary and popular theatre". More importantly, women playwrights are willing to work with specific audiences rather than general ones, deploying "a variety of modes of theatrical authorship, where members of the company and the community may have input into the text through improvisation sessions or collaborative creation". But things are changing. McMullan argues that:

> there is a growing interest in the perspectives on identity, sexuality and the legacies of myth and history which Irish women playwrights have presented. The playwrights... contest traditional stereotypes of women as a-sexual self-sacrificing mothers, powerless victims, or sexual comforts. Women are centre stage, propelling the action, and forcefully articulating their subjectivity and their sexuality. These playwrights present a range of theatre languages and often exploit the corporeal medium of performance to destabilize traditional concepts of gender.

Fintan O'Toole in his article accounts for three substantial shifts in writing practices over the last hundred years. Synge, Yeats, Lady Gregory and O'Casey form the first band, writers who were capable of dealing with a nation on the move. Despite differences in lifestyles, religion and class, in the writing of the early Abbey writer "there is a substratum of nationalism: Irishness is what defines the cast of characters, 'Ireland', a single thing which does not need to be spelt out, is the oil that makes the plot run". For O'Toole, the first phase as he identifies it, moves towards a decline as "the society became complex and became "no longer definable as a single reality". Thus, old dramatic practices, especially a naturalistic style of theatre could not be sustained. A naturalistic theatre "in which every effect has a cause, in which every action has a motive and in which every character has a fundamental substratum of coherence, became virtually impossible".

The singularity of vision gave way to doubleness and with the arrival of Friel and just as importantly, "the doubleness begins to be internalised, to infiltrate the borders of personality itself.... Doubleness is characteristically located in the notion of exile, but equally characteristically, even that very notion of exile itself is double", according to O'Toole. This doubleness is captured in *Philadelphia, Here I Come!* in terms of character, in terms of the permeable border between fantasy and reality in *A Crucial Week in the Life of a Grocer's Assistant*, and between past and present, and between the living and the dead in a play like Leonard's *Da*. It is not that doubleness was unique, if as O'Toole reminds us, we go back to *The Silver Tassie* or back to Wilde's *The Importance of Being Earnest*, where doubleness, impersonation, multiple identities are prevalent. But that doubleness began to filter through with enormous consistency from the late 50s and early 60s.

The third identifiable phase which begins to emerge in the late 80s, argues O'Toole, builds on the second, retaining the "disintegration of personality, the permeability of character, the discontinuity between cause and effect", but moving further on by adding a lyrical evocative quality that at the same time downgrades conflict, character and action. It is a theatre that works through "evocation rather than dramatisation". For O'Toole this new writing practice delivers plays that are "all extraordinarily linguistic creations, concerned to evoke or conjure up a world rather than to create one. They have to do so because the worlds they are concerned with are so particular, so angular, that an audience cannot share in them through naturalistic conventions".

Bruce Arnold, Chief Critic with the *Irish Independent* approaches some of the concerns marked by O'Toole, but from a very different vantage point. Arnold's approach is to pose serious and provocative questions. Indeed the intention is rightly and justly argumentative. Arnold suggests that Irish Theatre "has limped its way through the whole of the twentieth century trying to assert a purpose and a meaning. Essentially, that purpose and meaning has been the nature of Ireland. Who are we, what are we, where do we come from, why do we exist"? For him,

> Unlike theatre elsewhere, they were persuaded of the nationalist rather than the socialist purpose in what they did. In the hands of Ibsen in Norway, and later throughout Europe, or in the plays of George Bernard Shaw in London, there were social and moral objectives to be achieved on the stage. But in Ireland the essential purposes were directed at the framing of a programme designed

to create and define the national spirit. Within this broad objective lay both the glories and the banalities of Irish theatre.

And if the history of Irish theatre is interrogated here, then the present activities come under additional scrutiny. Arnold states that for him, "Theatre is increasingly seen now as a marginal art form. It has lost its political power. It no longer provokes much argument or debate". This statement in a way encapsulates what the contemporary playwright is struggling with.

If the national theatre proved to be an unambiguously problematic project, then the drama that emerged from Northern Ireland is just as difficult. Northern dramatists of distinction to have emerged over the last forty years include Friel, McGuinness, Anne Devlin, Bill Morrison, Martin Lynch, Christina Reid, Graham Reid and Stewart Parker. And of late a new group of writers has emerged, with Gary Mitchell, Daragh Carville and Owen McCafferty the more prominent. Young companies like Kabosh, Tinder Box and Prime Cut (formerly Mad Cow) are making a huge impact. The diversity and complexity of these writing practices in Northern Ireland are tackled by a number of our contributors.

Ashley Taggart in his expansive essay looks at the ingredient of conflict that a violent and belligerent social atmosphere generates in Northern Ireland's dramas. Political and military disturbances add to this. Despite the recent political changes, for Taggart nobody still "could fail to see this as a place riven by ongoing tensions and unforgiven grievances". While the Northern situation offers plenty of conflict he argues that how you deal with that ingredient is altogether different. "The danger", Taggart suggests, "for the writer is that he or she may become overwhelmed by the scale of events and fall into naked polemic. Each of the playwrights examined here has side-stepped this temptation in a different way — by challenging the established political agenda, widening the focus of debate, or taking it into another historical arena".

While Marianne McDonald pointed out the distancing realised through the re-working and re-coding of Greek classics, Taggart goes for the space given to the writing by relocating plays in the past; Friel is the specialist at this, McGuinness likewise. Christina Reid's work, especially *Tea in a China Cup* operates within the same type of territory. Yet if the past is the safer reality, then humour is a force of travesty and inversion. Marie Jones' *A Night in November* is a particular case in point. Humour brings with it another series of problems, something the recent Lyric Theatre's production of McGuinness' *Carthaginians* made obvious. I had seen three different productions of this play prior to its Belfast run. At each, the audiences went along with the trajectory of the humour. During the Belfast run and on the day I saw the play, it became clear to me that a section of the audience could not handle the irreverence of the piece. A celebration of the dead, as McGuinness desired it to be, was not tolerated by a small sector of the audience.

For Taggart, Northern politics needs to find a way around stereotype, sloganeering and myth making. Drama offers obvious possibilities here and the better of the writing achieves these. And the admission of a strong feminist voice adds immeasurably to it. Both Devlin and Christina Reid, create "a feminist viewpoint which reminds us how far the Northern Irish conflict is prosecuted, chronicled and controlled by men", he suggests. While many of the playwrights turn to major historical events, figures and celebrations of these incidents and people, other writers, notes Taggart, are just as successful when turning towards the "domestic arena, the small canvas", so as to "attempt to, if not evade, at least humanise the ineluctable political slant given to life inside the six counties". Ultimately, Taggart argues the saving grace is the "mordant humour which informs even the simplest daily transactions, and which pervades the work of all its writers".

Caoimhe McAvinchey comes from an academic and practical background and both are given due emphasis in her article as she wonders about the future of theatre. Without serious change she warns that theatre "as a contemporary cultural medium, might have a limited shelf life". She monitors some of the more recent developments in Irish theatre, specifically the site specific work carried out in Belfast. Performance art and installation work have not fully caught on in Ireland yet. And in general there has been a reliance on theatre festivals, especially in Galway, Dublin and Belfast to radicalise performance in this direction. She sees these festivals as "vital laboratories of the imagination, where ideas can be sparked and fertilised in response to productions which work in a totally different style than an Irish audience can expect to see". But increasingly more Irish theatre companies are moving in this direction.

McAvinchey notes the magic, frustrations and privileges of working in a contemporary theatre environment. The specific re-location of theatre practices offers a different type of licence, which has to be incorporated in a more formal way in traditional theatrical practices. For her, "By taking the audience and the theatre activity out of the theatre building you are automatically playing with the audience's sense of expectation and allowing them to engage in a different way than they would in a more traditional environment". It is vital to have the freedom to re-invent spaces whether it is the *The Wedding Community Play* at the 1999 Belfast Festival at Queens or the street theatre work of Macnas. For McAvinchey:

> Theatre is a nebulous term that covers everything from the actual building that houses the event to the action itself; from Kabuki's

highly codified performances to Geese Theatre Company's work in prisons; from Niall Tobin's one man show to Théâtre de Complicité's epic ensembles; from regional rep theatre productions of the classics to the Wooster Group's presentation of reworked texts from the canon; from Macnas, who parade their theatre through the streets with the help of a town's local inhabitants to the student drama companies busying away in campuses across the world.

Joseph Long's essay on the practices and developments in the independent theatre sector traces the impact of a changing society and of new work and rehearsal techniques on both drama and dance practices. Long recognizes that "Dublin has become a cosmopolitan city, attracting young visitors from all over Europe and beyond. It is expressed with increasing coherence and energy in the practice and policies of the many new and emerging performance groups of the nineties". He concentrates on many of the younger companies that have been supported by the innovative policies of places like the Project Arts Centre. Likewise he maps the emergence of companies in Cork, Clonmel, Kilkenny, Waterford, Belfast, Derry and Galway. Long's assertion is correct that "The present generation has widened its concept of theatre and is exploring new forms of expression, across the full range of the performing arts. Its horizons are international and its aspirations innovative. It is no longer the case that a transfer to one of the established theatres would be seen as the ultimate accolade for an independent production". Despite all the changes, Long argues that there remains nonetheless, "if not a crisis of arts management throughout the country, at least an endemic unease".

If many things have changed in the making of theatre, other matters have remained relatively unchanged. The reviewing practices of most newspapers are outmoded. If increased professionalism is demanded from the production side, everything from costume to marketing, then these changes must surely be met with increasing professionalism in theatre reviewing. Jocelyn Clarke's trenchant and perceptive essay focuses particularly on this. Clarke distinguishes between "reviewers" and "critics" and this is a valid point. Moreover he confronts how theatre reviewing is linked to the attitude of newspapers towards theatre in general. When you add to this both the absence of training and class and gender biases within the reviewing community, it seems as if the practice needs many adjustments.

Clarke states: "Theatre criticism is an act of engagement", that brings with it responsibilities of "describing and analysing, interpreting and evaluating". "Consideration and generosity" must be the hallmarks of such criticism, concepts prompted by Jim Nolan's expectation that his "ideal critic is someone who comes to see a production, wanting it to succeed". No doubt Clarke's convictions pose severe challenges for reviewers, especially since funding applications are often supported by reviews of previous work. For Clarke, dialogue must be encouraged between the theatre community and the critics. No doubt for reviewing to be of any substance the reviewer must embrace contemporary writing and performance practices and, just as substantially, a vocabulary adequate to the circumstances and status of the theatre.

Bernice Schrank offers a potent analysis of Friel's *The Freedom of the City*. Her emphasis is on the relationship between text and reality on a broader level and on the relationship between the play itself and the specific incidents of Bloody Sunday and the Widgery Tribunal that investigated the event. For Schrank, the play is not propagandistic in the narrowest meaning of the word. It "is a positive (and, given the circumstances, moderate) cultural intervention, not a rallying cry to people the barricades", according to her. She adds: "The resemblances" are "unmistakable", but "it is not a political play in the narrow agit prop sense of advocating a specific doctrine or party platform".

Friel retains some level of distance through many different devices, which Schrank deliberates upon at length, including language, staging and theatricality. There is a failure of translation, in the broadest meaning of the word; a failure of objectivity. "The claims to objectivity (RTE Commentator) and/or privileged understanding (Priest and Professor) prove either false or of insufficient relevance", claims Schrank. For her, "Through the repeated use of monologues, Friel implicates the theatre audience in the politics of the play, encouraging them to move from passive spectatorship to active engagement". In terms of stage space, Schrank notes that "separate stage spaces correspond to the sectarian, national and class divisions of Northern Ireland. The divisions are maintained by force of arms as well as by filtering of words; in short, by the ability of the language of power to voice over and erase dissent from public discourse".

Redmond O'Hanlon offers a substantial assessment of Friel's brilliant *Living Quarters*, a play whose complexity may well be one of the reasons why it is not produced with much frequency. O'Hanlon puzzles over "Friel's addition of 'after *Hippolytus*' to the title since its relation to Euripides' play seems somewhat oblique". O'Hanlon states that "a closer reading suggests that there are certain formal elements in *Living Quarters* which remind us of its Greek antecedent and which seem to allow Friel to move beyond a naturalism, and even melodrama, which could so easily have engulfed his play". In both *Living Quarters and Philadelphia Here I Come!*, he argues that "the passion is anger against the father", whereas "in Euripides it is Phaedra's all-consuming desire for her stepson".

The complexity of the play demands that an encounter with the play is way beyond the conventions of naturalism: "the characters are free, in their imaginations, to make minor adjustments to the eternally fixed facts of that fateful day, but they are prisoners of the irreversibility of time and of the consequences of what they did and did not do". The only thing worthy of note in *Living Quarters* is the Sir figure. O'Hanlon sees Sir as "aesthetic distancer", who is "very reminiscent of the Chorus at the end of so many Greek tragedies". He is "a fascinating creation, an amalgam of Greek Destiny, Prologue and Chorus as well as of the modern director and stage-manager", according to O'Hanlon. Furthermore, he suggests that in Friel's work "homecomings are fraught events and they are often transmogrified into funerals. Archetypically, homecomings generate the freedom/determinism, change/no change *Agon*". *Faith Healer* is another example of this. The play captures the tension between determinism and freedom. "Sir tells us, the characters are still haunted by the possibility that they can escape from the deterministic frame in which the action is set", but for O'Hanlon "there's no future in repetition". The argument is stretched to suggest similarities between Frank and Sir and in that way the play becomes a haunting of sorts. "Can it be that Sir is so trapped in a male narrative and in a male repression that we have to read his amnesia as a sort of psychic murder of the feminine", O'Hanlon wonders. And if so what is the value of this question when applied to Friel's other work.

Declan Kiberd's article on Murphy goes back initially to George Bernard Shaw and Oscar Wilde and he claims that they are the two "who did most to clear the way for this conception of drama as musical performance". Kiberd quotes Patrick Mason who states: "Tom Murphy hears sound as character or he expresses character as sound. All his characters make individual sounds — they have individual sound patterns". For Kiberd, music is vital, "not just because it has charms to soothe the savage breast, but because it affords a more sensitive, less invasive way of reading and defining a self". And in a way the music is deployed to console, to name aspirations, to use the imagination and to move beyond the apparent limits of the possible. Murphy's central characters, initially an Irishman and later JPW King, will not rest until they sing like Gigli, or until they are possessed by the spirit of Gigli. Kiberd moves from this notion of soul-play on to the notions of shadow, the divided self and the doppelganger, where fears and "pathological self-absorption" are countered by the dynamics of possibility. Kiberd adds that in *The Gigli Concert* "the self is not presented as a fixed, unitary entity so much as a provisional complex at a point in time. The nature of that self may best be revealed, and most usefully defined, in performance". There is a substantial connection between role as performance or play, and music, itself, as play.

Into this debate on the riven self, Kiberd brings the character Mona. He argues that:

> The repressed feminine principle is never so easily denied: and invades the room in the shape of Mona, the vulgar trollop and faithless wife, who is to King's world of facts as his idealized Helen is to his world of values. His endless skulking in his room is a symbolic portrayal of his refusal to face the world as it really is. Mona, however comes repeatedly in from that world, bringing news of it, as well as practical help.

In addition Kiberd reminds us that Richard Kearney sees the Northern Mona as "a sort of neglected go-between: the woman victimised by the male-dominated struggle for power". But ultimately Kiberd argues that by the end of the play Mona "has cured him (JPW) by her offer of a love without conditions. She penetrates his self-absorbed exterior and, at that moment, it is possible for the Shadow, An Irish Man, to disappear for good". Such a clearly argued reading is both fresh and confrontational and along the way builds on and rejects some of the earlier interpretations of the play provided by other commentators.

Kiberd's interpretation is as valuable as Anne Kelly's. She offers a timely re-reading of Tom Murphy's plays specifically from a feminist perspective. The great strength of Kelly's piece is to challenge some of the received wisdoms regarding Murphy's work. She specifically queries the position of women in the plays, taking her initial prompt from Lynda Henderson's essay which suggests that the women characters, unlike the male ones in Murphy's work, have no access to the life of the spirit. Kelly looks "at the representation of women and their role as bearers rather than makers of meaning" and thus as such are "excluded from the abstract spiritual dimension". In contrast to Declan Kiberd's reading of *The Gigli Concert*, Kelly argues that the success of the play is in part due to the fact that the play "affirms the patriarchal imagination that is at the heart of the cultural process". For Kelly most of Murphy's work either idealises or disembodies the female characters. She identifies the fact that masculinity is problematised by the colonial experience and that this, in itself, is part of the problem. Kelly concludes her article with the statement that in *Bailegangaire*:

> The traditional severing of head and body in the ancient Celtic warrior tradition is continued in our representations where the 'source of spiritual potency' is represented as male and is dominant while the body — the physical — is represented as female and is repressed. Further reconciliation is needed than Mommo's achieved level: the reconciliation between spirit and body for the individual characters themselves and the reconciliation between male and female sexuality and spirituality.

Such a movement towards wholeness in Murphy's characters might also disclose the holiness that he craves.

Terry Eagleton's essay deals with Seamus Heaney's version of Sophocles' *Philoctetes* called *The Cure at Troy*, which was toured by Field Day in 1990. Eagleton argues that the play is "an oblique allegory of the "Troubles", and Heaney's explicit allusions to hunger strikers and police widows in an appended Epilogue are meant to leave no-one in doubt about the bearing of ancient Athens on contemporary Ulster". For Eagleton "Resolution, as Heaney's naturalising imagery intimates ("tidal wave", "sea-change"), arrives as miraculous gift rather than as political construct, inarticulable epiphany rather than political strategy". Eagleton concludes his essay with the following:

> Right at the play's end, then, the allegorical use of myth releases an *unintended meaning*, which is only possible because the conquest of Troy has been distanced and stylised to a sort of metaphor of Philoctetes' own personal regeneration. The play thus "unwittingly" inserts into its reconciliationist (Catholic-Protestant) mode the very confrontationalist (Ireland-Britain) model which a good many Northern writers, including Heaney himself, would rush to disown. Paradoxically, in displacing the focus from the political to the personal, from outward to inward warfare, *The Cure at Troy* breeds a political implication which outruns its author's personal mastery.

Akiko Satake's very fine essay looks at Stewart Parker's play *Northern Star* and she discusses how Parker brings his own unique touch to the history play. The fact is that "although Parker was extremely meticulous in the way he pieced together historical details, he makes no pretence that what is being presented is an objective representation of what actually took place". Encountering such a play, "we participate in the very formation of history" argues Satake. She reminds us that Parker's Seven Ages of Man, is "The shape he gives to his life" which is:

> A morality-like heading going from the Age of Innocence, through Idealism, Cleverness, Dialectic, Heroism, and Compromise, to the final Age, which he may have intended to call the Age of Shame (this is the only Age without a clearly defined name). Each age, moreover, is set up in the characteristic style of representative Irish dramatists in chronological order (from Farquhar, Boucicault, Wilde, Shaw, Synge, O'Casey to Behan and Beckett), so that overall this kaleidoscopic procession gives rise to an impression like that of a series of medieval pageants.

In Parker's work "The mediator of history, moreover, is appropriately a fool figure, whose outsider's view can provide a frame from which to look at what is enacted on history's stage".

Deirdre Mulrooney delivers a substantial essay on the work of Tom MacIntyre. She indicates the vast array of influences on MacIntyre's work from Grotowski to Kantor and from Pina Bausch's Tanztheater Wuppertal to "the writings of Jungian depth psychologists James Hillman, and Marie Louise Von Franz".

The article appropriates a necessary vocabulary in order to come to terms with the work of MacIntyre. Mac Intrye's first work for theatre goes as far back as 1972 and he is still highly active with *Cuirt an Mhean Oiche*, directed by Michael Harding, his latest offering in 1999. Mulrooney points out that MacIntyre's theatre not only resists a "pre-ordained Aristotelian mindset", but has also influenced how theatre is written, but more importantly how it is made, and more substantially again, how it is received by the spectator. (The influence of MacIntyre on McGuinness' *Mary and Lizzie* is obvious.) It is vital to note how the collaborative work between writer, director (Patrick Mason) and actor (consistently Tom Hickey) has shaped the working arrangements in Irish theatre in a way that moves away from a primarily writer and text based theatre. For Mulrooney:

> MacIntyre's idiom at its best is characterised by this anarchic, traumatic feel of raw experience, yet un-told. His theatrical language is incantatory, and three dimensional. It is parole, the spoken word, which lives in the ephemeral moment of performance, as opposed to in the residue of written literature. His is the poetic vision of a true theatre-poet.

Mulrooney quotes Patrick Mason, who states that the task was to forge a new theatre language, where "every word and act of theatre is both real and metaphorical".

My own essay is on the notion of metatheatricality in three of Frank McGuinness' plays. Declan Kiberd in his article on Murphy sees this spirit of play as being of great substance, Eric Weitz looks at play in terms of the work of Barabbas, Akiko Satake pursues it in relation to Stewart Parker's *Northern Star*, Bernice Schrank devotes a section to play in her article on Friel's play *The Freedom of the City* as does Redmond O'Hanlon in his essay on *Living Quarters*. The importance of play in an Irish context is gaining increasing recognition as an alternative strategy in the comprehension and experiencing of performance. With regard to McGuinness' work, I note that the energy of artifice or of play "runs the whole gamut from self-conscious performativity to impersonation, from trickery, contrivance or the confidence trick to misrule, from the generation of co-operative narratives to masquerade, parody and the burlesque, from mimicry to multiplicity, from drag to re-enactment and from storytelling to play-within-a-play, features that have been loosely labelled metatheatricality". I conclude with the following:

> Play is about make-believe, about release and about the establishment of a space of transition, of working out and of recognition, most of all a protective and insulating strategy. Through play anxieties are worked through, blockages negotiated with and adjustments and change prioritised. Memory, history and myth prove to be both the playground and the battleground.

Christopher Murray approaches the work of Billy Roche from three different points of view, "Setting, Place and Critique". The huge phenomenon of Irish plays on English Stages can be traced back to Roche as the pathfinder of sorts. It is not that Irish plays went unperformed in England, it is just that these were mainly productions which toured to places like London and Edinburgh. Irish playwrights began to have previously unperformed work produced on British stages. Moreover, a number of these writers were not well known.

Murray acknowledges that "Irish writing in general is saturated with a sense of place". He posits the notion that Roche does something different. "The interesting thing about Roche in this regard is his theatricalizing of place so that it becomes *lieu* in a double sense. On the one hand there is the actual place in mimesis; on the other hand there is place in the theatrical sense *qua* space". Murray pursues this further, arguing that: "Roche plays variations on the two meanings until they interlock in irony, compassion and defiance, interrogating and celebrating small-town life at the same time". "In short", for Murray,

> Roche proposes social criticism by astute manipulation of synecdoche: the setting within the setting, the part for the whole, the pool hall for the town and the town for the nation" as "the distance required for detachment was supplied by the actual ("real") setting of the plays in London: their popularity in London is bound up with their neutrality there.

In *The Wexford Trilogy* Roche sets his plays in a pool hall, Bookmaker's Shop and in a Belfry. For Murray: "This move away from the family as setting is significant. To be sure, Tom Murphy, Brian Friel and Tom Kilroy all at various times have forsaken the familiar Irish setting of kitchen, tenement or drawing room, but never without transforming the location into a version of the home". He continues: "The disjunction between home and world is far wider in Roche's work than in any preceding Irish playwright. To that end he chooses settings which are in their ways anti-family: places of gambling, male preserves, places hostile to domestic values". What is more, that instead of the plays being naturalist and mimetic, Murray argues that "by accumulation and focus of images" they become "metaphoric and even symbolic". Murray goes on to say that the betting shop setting in *Poor Beast in the Rain* is "a metaphor for play, gaming, or chance".

Of the younger generation of writers, Sebastian Barry is seen by many to be the most accomplished. Fintan O'Toole has championed the work from many perspectives, stressing above all the move away from a theatre of conflict and towards one of evocation, through language and image, a renewal of a poetic theatre of sorts. Barry's range of influence is broad; "He has learned it at the hands of other dramatic craftsmen, from Yeats and Beckett back to Sophocles. Most of all, from Shakespeare, he has found how imagery in speech and action can explore and extend the resonance and richness of the worlds he creates", according to Fitzgibbon. When it comes to *Prayers of Sherkin*, Ger Fitzgibbon argues that "The lyrical Utopianism of their vision, their chasteness of style and honesty of toil does nothing to assuage that contradiction or avert its consequences. As a community, they therefore face a crisis of extinction or absorption". Interestingly, Fitzgibbon rates *White Woman Street* above *Prayers of Sherkin*: "Through its structure, its poetry and its fable, *White Woman Street* becomes a more complete theatrical achievement, a more satisfying marriage of the poetic, the dramatic and the intellectually provocative than any play Barry had written before".

Of all of Barry's plays to date, only *Boss Grady's Boys* has any immediate relationship to contemporary Ireland. Barry, like McGuinness, in some respects has continued on the tradition of the Irish playwright obsessed with the past. Fitzgibbon refers to the impulse to "retrieve a lost past, picking out figures who are representative of the more occluded or wayward areas of Irish social and political history, and offering them for contemplation to the young cubs of the Celtic Tiger". (In addition, Fitzgibbon duly notes that *Our Lady of Sligo* "is almost a gender-reversed version of *Steward of Christendom*".) Like one of the brothers in *Boss Grady's Boys* who sleeps in the "dip" of the bed shaped by his father, likewise many characters in Irish theatre sleep and dream in the "dip" of history. In a way, the past has been an obsession. History and politics have ensured that in part. But there is a movement away from the past in the most recent work from a newer generation of writers. For Fitzgibbon, Barry's plays deliver "a kind of familial archaeology, drawn from his own ancestral connections", but this "does not affect the fact that in the writing he is reincorporating these lost figures and what they represent into Irish history". "Barry generates a form of theatre that has the aimless fluency of dream. Yet it is not a theatre of pathos or nostalgic escape", so argues Fitzgibbon.

The appropriation of history, through either the history or memory play, results in acts of capitulation, recovery, distinction and in the attestation of difference. In *Prayers of Sherkin*, according to Fitzgibbon, despite losses, frustrations and a need for change, Barry "lingers over the images of the Sherkin community as an integrated, childlike, unproblematic past where work is pleasure and fulfilment and where lives of frugal comfort, permeated by intimations of immortality, are conducted with calm and wisdom". Fitzgibbon views Barry as "an unique voice in Irish theatre", that his work is "distinguished by considerable craft" that "he has an ear for quirky and idiomatic speech which he can combine with a sophisticated capacity for poetic evocation" and that throughout the plays, there is "a long, vigorous negotiation between the narrative and dramatic demands of theatre and the lyrical impulses of the poetic voice".

Martine Pelletier offers an insightful reading of Dermot Bolger's work, positioning him well outside a bland social-realist context. She quotes Fintan O'Toole who reminds us that Bolger is "the champion of those "new places,… places without history… where sex and drugs and rock'n'roll are now more important than the old totems of Land, Nationality and Catholicism". For her, *The Lament for Arthur Cleary* is one of the seminal texts of Irish Drama over the last few decades. Indeed it is the theatricality of the piece, inspired by the workshops guided by the director, David Byrne, that infused a potent theatricality into a piece of work which started out as a translation of an Irish poem. Pelletier places Bolger, like Joyce, firmly within a Dublin and urban tradition. Yet it is a Dublin very different to that of Declan Hughes or that of Paul Mercier. The world of Arthur Cleary is almost Yeatsian, a "dreaming back" of sorts. The presence of ghosts is consistent across a range of Irish plays and no more so than in Bolger. For Pelletier:

> Through the presence of ghosts, life and death, past and present become interrelated in ways which can be either tragic or ultimately liberating. Ghosts are also symbols of incompletion, as is, in a sense, the sterility of various characters. In such images we may find a sign of Bolger's overall concern with continuity and rupture, both in a personal and in a cultural sense.

Like Anna McMullan, Riana O'Dwyer questions the relative absence of women playwrights on the major stages. She focuses her argument on the quality of the writing produced by Christina Reid and Marina Carr. Across a range of Reid's plays O'Dwyer argues, "There is a sense that the plays speak from within the confines of both patriarchy and of political identification with the loyalist tradition". Of Reid's work O'Dwyer notes, "The women prided themselves on being strong and on keeping the family together. Under the stress of the Troubles, these sustaining certainties begin to crumble, and both the family bonds and the political allegiances are called into question". While Reid's work has a strong social dimension, it is not without ritual and celebration. For O'Dwyer, Reid, "Having represented the sustaining aspects of such rituals, political and personal", then "allows her plays to question them from a position of understanding and belonging". But "as long as you remain within the tribe, and conform to its expectations, you will be supported, but step outside the invisible boundary and you forfeit the right to be so considered", suggests O'Dwyer.

If there is one playwright more written about than Friel then it has to be Marina Carr. Obviously Carr is a terrific writer. *Portia Coughlan* and *By the Bog of Cats* have made a huge impact. Moreover, Carr bears the burden of being the one southern Irish woman playwright who is consistently produced at the Abbey Theatre. O'Dwyer notes that "Her recent plays have been more conventional in their staging: houses and kitchens have featured as settings and also as symbolic places of detention". Yet located as such, the "plays go beyond realism into a symbolic realm, where explanations are not to be found in common sense or psychology, but in mythic reference, poetic language, the presence of ghosts and the telling of stories", argues O'Dwyer.

Melissa Sihra focuses almost specifically on Carr's Medea-inspired *By the Bog of Cats* and she correctly locates Carr within the tradition of Irish theatre and aligns the work with the consciousness of Synge. The common bond between Synge and Carr is the relentlessness, the darkness of the vision and the carnivalesque, almost absurd consciousness that slowly accumulates.

The other substantial influence on Carr, apart from the Greeks and Synge, is of course Henrik Ibsen. Both *Little Eyolf*, as Sihra points out, and *John Gabriel Borkman* run riot across *By the Bog of Cats*. Women in Carr's work are given substantial power, whatever about choices. (It is interesting to view Carr in the light of Anne Kelly's essay on Murphy for instance.) Sihra argues, "The mother-figure in Irish theatre has traditionally been viewed as a personification of the nation. Carr presents the myth of Big Josie Swane as an alternative to the romanticised literary Mother Ireland figure.... This is Yeats' *Cathleen Ní Houlihan* re-imagined". In addition, Sihra suggests that the positioning of the woman as outsider, "outlaw", "deviant" and located either outside or at the margins is a common feature of Carr's work.

For Sihra, "The conceptualising of space and property in *By the Bog of Cats* is unstable and indicative of the nature of identity. Hester crosses spatial boundaries more radically than in Carr's previous work (The Mai remains indoors, while Portia flirts with the threshold)". Space becomes one of the keys to any understanding of theatre performance; the works of Murray and Sihra suggest that. "The bog, a place and a non-place (hovering somewhere between the actual and the imaginary), transcends what Beckett viewed as the aesthetic reductivism of specific geographic allusion", argues Sihra. Ultimately, "Carr's *mise en scène* has the best of both worlds. While on the one hand it is recognisably Irish, it belongs as much in the domain of Greek tragedy, Gothic horror, Absurdism and Grotesque surrealism", according to Sihra.

Barabbas... the Company, comprising Veronica Coburn, Raymond Keane and Mikel Murfi, has been one of the most substantial companies to impact on the Irish theatre scene. Gerry Stembridge collaborated with them on a number of productions. Eric Weitz tackles the notion of play in Barabbas' reworking of Robinson's *The Whiteheaded Boy*, which "first saw the light of a stage in autumn 1997". For him: "All theatre can be seen to spring from a spirit of play, of pointedly reworking the world under a licensed dispensation" from social realities. He adds: Barabbas uses the "theatre as the plaything itself" and further he argues, the company's performance style "also suggests that such a spirit of theatrical playing, while sharing a private joke with the audience, serves to open otherwise unused windows for the perception of life". The essay proves to be detailed not only on the rehearsal and performance techniques of the company but is an example of how writers/commentators can respond in such a precise fashion to a play in performance. On some levels Robinson's play has severely dated, but Barabbas' imaginative intervention more than compensates for that. For Weitz:

> Under their diligent guidance, people are drawn nightly to contemplate some of the things that still press upon adult psyches 80-odd years after *The Whiteheaded Boy* was born, questions about appearances and truth and humankind's little blemishes. The performers invite collusion in a world tuned risibly to these issues, its building blocks open to the same healthy disrespect, and from the stage they can feel the recognition in our laughter. That, of course, is a factor one can lose sight of amid the admiration for theatre's magical spaces: the ability to view something in a spirit of play also happens to be a defining condition for laughter, and it does tend to make the occasion quite a lot of fun. Now is that the crowning bonus or the most important feature of all?

Victor Merriman's essay on Calypso productions not only broadens the range of what can be defined within the parameters of Irish theatre, but also lays down serious challenges to those involved in theatre practice. The work of Calypso productions varies from specific "Educational" work to "site specific and street performances". Merriman stresses Calypso's commitment not only to the development of educational programmes, but also to the provision of "resource materials", which are "circulated widely, and especially to legislators, to whom they are intended as a challenge". The company is about exposing double standards, about raising awareness, about change and the provision of an "ethical framework". In a play like *Rosie and Starwars* Calypso "stages the invisible power of racist discourse to structure and marginalize a people", according to Merriman. Merriman argues that with *Rosie and Starwars* "The project is specifically and overtly pedagogical. In its commitment to including travellers in audiences for the play, and as participants in workshops and discussions arising from it, Calypso extends its cultural project in important ways". Likewise, Calypso states that the genesis of *Farawayan* was "in opposition to the emergence and proliferation of racist discourse in Ireland". For Merriman, "Since 1995, Calypso Productions has exposed the local elaboration of the new international paradigm in its focus on intranational betrayals: of travelling people, refugees and asylum seekers, and a poor, criminalized 'underclass'". We must see this in the context of other attempts by the likes of Martin McDonagh, Paul Mercier and Dermot Bolger to appropriate, interrogate or re-contexualise the marginalized. When it comes to marginalisation and the political and dramatic implications of it, Merriman states that:

> The world appears in these texts as a statement of fact, a space which exists to ratify and legitimise existing social relations. It stages the life experiences of marginal persons and groups as departures from the norm. Such departures exist only to facilitate the triumphant return of that norm in the plenitude of narrative closure.

Two playwrights give rise to most of the contemporary debate: Martin McDonagh and Conor McPherson. Both have risen through the ranks at a phenomenal speed. Scott Cummings tackles the issue of monologue and the significance of storytelling in McPherson's work. McPherson's *The Weir*, at the time of writing, is still playing on London's West-End, having originally opened in the summer of 1997 at the Royal Court's Theatre Upstairs before transferring to its main stage in the spring of 1998. Clearly, Friel's *Faith Healer* has had a huge impact on McPherson's work. The narrative structure of this Friel play teaches a budding playwright so much about storytelling and how the story must seduce, manipulate and draw in an audience. Think also of the characters in McGuinness' *Someone Who'll Watch Over Me* who are obsessed by terror and driven to find consolation in any narrative performance or the performance demands on the actor playing Mommo in Murphy's *Bailegangaire*, where storytelling is substantial and essential.

Cummings identifies in McPherson's early monologues an "immediacy and a roughness", where the "immediacy comes from the simplicity of the monologue form: an actor stands onstage and talks directly to an audience for an hour or more. The total emphasis on narrative verges on the anti-dramatic. There is no theatrical fiction, no pretence that the stage represents an imaginary elsewhere. The time is now and the place is right here — in the theatre". Cummings notes that in the case of *This Lime Tree Bower*, all the characters do is tell stories, "without impersonating other characters or engaging in other physical histrionics". That is a vital distinction. McPherson requires something different from his actors to the demands placed on the single actor in Marie Jones' *A Night in November* or somewhat similarly, the energy and exuberance displayed by Dónal O'Kelly in performing his text *Catalpa*, where O'Kelly uses props, sound effects and impersonation to telling effect.

For Cummings, "In McPherson's stories, getting out of a predicament is tantamount to getting away with something, an indiscretion, a sin, a crime or just the obnoxious bravado of a drunk". While a "devil-may-care attitude masks a brooding conscience", there still exists "a smouldering mix of self-pity and self-loathing" which surface "at moments in a way that activates an odd compassion", argues Cummings. Even in the more "conventional *The Weir*", McPherson "demonstrates how stories create community and provide consolation for loss, loneliness, and regret" and ultimately storytelling restores to the characters "a measure of lost innocence that can be had no other way".

While Mcpherson has been hugely successful with *The Weir*, McDonagh's *Leenane Trilogy* has been just as potent. *The Leenane Trilogy* is set in the west of Ireland, was produced initially by an Irish company, Druid, and written by a Londoner of Irish descent. There are seriously divided opinions as to the merit of McDonagh's work. More than anything else people have linked the work of McDonagh to Synge, despite the fact that McDonagh denies any knowledge of Synge at the time of writing his own plays. For Karen Vandevelde: "The imitations and echoes of literary precursors are so apparent throughout the trilogy that the playwright's self-reflexivity becomes ironical, if not subversive". In that way she argues: "… this double edge makes it perfectly possible to read the trilogy as either a canonical or a radical text".

But there are certain anomalies that need to be pointed out. For Vandevelde: "Contrary to the expectations of a new play at the radical cutting edge of the nineties, McDonagh's trilogy does not feature drugs, pop music or trendy lifestyles, but members of a rural community who are victims of loneliness, depression and economic progress". She goes on to argue that "The fusion of a grotesque style inspired by Tarantino, and a melodramatic mood reminiscent of many contemporary soap operas bring about an unusual juxtaposition of opposite emotions, actions and temperaments".

Christopher Murray in his article on Roche notes that the current generation of playwrights is "creating new narratives of Ireland's shifting place in the world" and further, he adds, this generation "is bored stiff with Mother Machree, Kathleen Ní Houlihan, her four green fields and all the rest of it. Their appeal is to audiences, equally young and disaffected, who can respond to a search for new ways of regarding experience". This new generation of writers is partially addressed in this volume. Today they can validate differences and divisions in terms of gender, race and class like no other time previously. While the older generation of writers continue to write, plays like *Philadelphia Here I Come!* or Murphy's *A Crucial Week in the Life of a Grocer's Assistant* could no longer be written.

Inferiority, marked by aggression and defiance, has made way for assertiveness and as a nation we are all the better for that. The older distinctions between urban and rural, freedom and repression, inside and outside, civility and barbarity, industrial and agrarian, local and foreign, primitive and sophisticated, home and exile, male and female, and master and servant have been re-imagined. (The obvious dialectical tension between feast and famine is replaced by the comfort of the "Happy Meal".) New ways of making theatre, new ways of making meaning in one's life and new ways of connecting are linked in some way. New affluence and a new resilience that confidence brings are more visible, yet they hamper drama in a curious way. Likewise, dramas set in bourgeois locations with middle-class characters seem to be increasingly ineffective, because there is a perception, rightly or wrongly, that existential angst within a bourgeois frame is un-dramatic. Effective bourgeois settings are to be found only through a historical time frame or within the confines of monologue. Think of the relative failings of Murphy's *The Wake* and *Too Late for Logic* or Friel's *Wonderful Tennessee* or *Give Me Your Answer, Do!* There are additional reasons why these plays did not work fully dramatically, apart from the circumstances being relatively bourgeois; language was one of them and poor editing and structuring are others. (The utterly overwritten final wake scene in Murphy's play by that name is a case in point.) There has been some critical resistance to anybody who questions the merits of Friel's latest plays, but for me they will not be regarded as his better ones, not matching the quality and intensity of say *Aristocrats*, *Faith Healer* or *Translations*. (Striking plays have emerged over the last number of years, some of which are not documented sufficiently here — ranging from Kilroy's *Double Cross* to Declan Hughes' *Digging For Fire*, from Pat McCabe's *Frank Pig Says Hello* to Enda Walsh's *Disco Pigs*, from Dónal O'Kelly's *Catalpa* to the devised work *True Lines* and *Double Helix* overseen by John Crowley for the Kilkenny company Bickerstaffe and from plays like Paul Mercier's *Studs* to *At the Black Pig's Dyke* by Vincent Woods.)

Today we move in a world increasingly motivated perhaps on one level by the hormonal, genetic self, not one driven by conscious or unconscious tensions, not one driven by a quest for authenticity, and not one driven by a belief in change. The mentality of difference at the core of Friel's and Murphy's work, the oppositional forces on social, political and psychological levels have more or less collapsed. The fundamental energy created by a post-colonial consciousness struggling to assert change and recovery is now perceived to be a residual one. What has stepped into its place?

For me, *Faith Healer* and *Dancing at Lughnasa* by Friel, Frank McGuinness' *Observe the Sons of Ulster Marching Towards the Somme* and Murphy's *Bailegangaire* would be the plays that best exemplify a move towards an ending of a specific era. Tom Kilroy talks about the "distancing" and "artifice" devices deployed by traditional Anglo-Irish playwrights and for many of the post-war generation, these effects were achieved by the reflex of play, set in historic or memory contexts. For the contemporary generation things are very different. The dramaturgical conventions of an older generation seem less and less appropriate. For me, the substantial shift in the framework of play is the serious crisis. Play has moved from a post-colonial context to play within an increasingly postmodern one.

These above mentioned five plays are history or memory plays that focused on issues of identity, place, home and authority. All five have play as their driving force, in terms of performance, storytelling, re-enactment and disguise. The impetus of play was used — to borrow Homi Bhadha's phrase — to establish "the menace of mimicry", a subversive and transgressive consciousness that had defiance, articulation and confrontation at its core. These were plays of protest, interrogation and exchange. Kilroy's opening stage direction to *Talbot's Box* states that the performance space is a "primitive, enclosed space, part-prison, part-sanctuary, part-acting space", an environment that brings together, confinement, comfort, consolation and the exhibitive nature of play. *Bailegangaire*, with its story-telling and laughing competition, establishes a framework of both play-within-a-play and carnivalesque underworld. Without going too much into the details, magic, miracle and a destructive mimicry are common to all five plays and common to so many plays from *The Playboy of the Western World* forward, where both the theatricality and perversity of power are noted. Likewise in *Juno and the Paycock* a temporary carnivalesque inversion of order emerges with the announcement of the fake will that proves to be only a temporary abeyance of tragedy. In *The Freedom of the City* Schrank notes that Skinner, from the Guildhall, calls his bookie, bets on a horse, plays the radio, dances and sings with Lily, drinks whiskey, smokes a cigar, stubs out the cigar on the desk, dons the ceremonial robes of the Lord Mayor, bestows on the others the freedom of the city, pushes Lily to call her sister in Australia, fences with an imaginary opponent using the ceremonial sword, stages a mock meeting of City Council, sticks the sword into a picture of one of the city's dignitaries and signs the Distinguished Visitors' Book. This extravagant naughtiness is bright and often very funny; but it is also idiosyncratic and self-indulgent, a gesture against prevailing orthodoxies rather than an effective action.

The substantial warning in all of this is that although play is a vital component of Friel's dramaturgy, play must never be fetishised in the same way that the temporary inversions of carnival must not cater for nostalgia. The meeting of the archaic and the anarchic has always been a source of a substantial playful energy. The plays of an older generation veered towards release or exorcism or, at a minimum, possessed the trajectory of release. Irish dramas of an older generation used the history play, intertextuality, carnival and fantasy as devices that substantially accessed play, in order to re-configure a consciousness. More importantly the relationship between text and reality is a complicated one. The mirror is not natural, more a fevered, fractured and fragmented one and is always manipulated by the obligations of dramatic rhythm and form. The relationship thus is always tangential, nearly always a betrayal and always the correspondence is no more than a trace.

But the perception of play has changed in the latest writing. That something new I think is a shift from the "menace of mimicry" to the "mimicry of menace". This is how the gift and the horror of postmodernism come into play. What is new is how play is framed within the dramas and the implications that follow on from that. Once excess was a trope of opposition; now excess is normalised, especially as violence is performatively eroticised. Parody and spectacle have downgraded the ritual dimension of drama. Within a postmodern frame, the notion of play becomes imitative, simulated, ungrounded and absent. While identity is complicated, there is no real space for the validation of choice or for an insistence on opportunity.

As part of the contemporary dramaturgical complications, some things crop up again and again. Suicide as a resolution is one feature. Imagined, fake or bizarre offspring are other patterns. The tension between fake offspring and mock death motivates Wilde's *The Importance of Being Earnest*; Carr's *Low in the Dark* is an example of fake offspring and in McGuinness' *Carthaginians* mock death is essential. Additionally, the growing reliance in the accessing of emotion through either the presence/absence of a dead child is difficult not be identified as a worrying configuration. The fact that the child is usually male, leads to the masculinisation of memory. The list is lengthy; from Carr's *Portia Coughlan* to Barry's *Our Lady of Sligo* and *Steward of Christendom*, from McGuinness' *Mutabilitie* and *Baglady* to Friel's *Faith Healer* and *Translations* and from Hugh Leonard's *Love in the Title* to Murphy's *Bailegangaire*. Even Mark O'Rowe in *Howie The Rookie* relies on the dead child to partially propel his text. Bolger's most recent play *The Passion of Jerome* is haunted by the ghost of both a young boy, who hanged himself in a Ballymun flat and a baby girl who died soon after she was born.

So many Irish plays are motivated by death. With the death of the child serving multiple functions, it is difficult to generalise. A number of things are happening simultaneously. In part, the child as an emblem of possibility is denied through death. There is never the sense that the death of a child is sacrificially enabling in any way. Mommo in *Bailegangaire* mentions children found in shoeboxes and as the play progresses we learn of the fate of her children and of her grandchild, Tom. In terms of the laughing competition in *Bailegangaire* it is possible to link up death and laughter and in *Carthaginians* McGuinness does likewise. And yet, the figure of the dead child does not seem to allow for this type of carnivalesque connection, even if McGuinness links the death of Maela's daughter from cancer with the deaths of the men who died on Bloody Sunday. The graveyard as both carnivalised marketplace and playground cannot be appropriated when it comes to children. In this way play is stillborn.

Instead the absence of the child is more a comment on the unreasonableness of a reality that cannot accommodate its presence. In a way there is a cyclical incompleteness in operation. Think of Friel's use of the pattern of christening and death of a child in *Translations*. There is a critique of a reality that cannot give new life, and this is not to take away from either the complications of childbirth or the reality of infant mortality. Feminist critics, will ask whether male playwrights are connecting unconsciously dead babies and the feminine?

It is almost as if pain only becomes nameable under the circumstances of a dead child. The death of a child is in a sense about the end of a certain type of possibility, about a denial of a future. Maybe that is what we have been doing for so long, with the recurring need to deal with the past and the figure of the child seems to be a way of stalling that progress to the future or maybe it gives substance to the unrealization of the future? Is it birth or re-birth that remains the "unfinished symphony"? Carnival gives access and recognition to the body, so is it time to decrown the past and crown the future? Infertility is another prominent part of the consciousness, as is the presence of imaginary/ghost children in

Murphy's *The Gigli Concert* and *Bailegangaire*, and McGuinness' *Innocence*. In terms of dead children McGuinness' *Innocence, Mutabilitie* and *Dolly West's Kitchen* do very interesting things. In the first play, the second act of the play is a nightmare suffered by Caravaggio, in which his sister's ghost arrives to tell of how she died giving birth, in order for her child to survive. In the second play, the File's child, whose sex is not identified, dies in unclear, but violent, circumstances, yet the child of an English couple is adopted within the tribe. The third play concludes with the end of the Second World War and with the arrival of a child. The paternity of the child is not clarified and, in a way, is not in need of clarification. But the arrival of the child suggests some sort of mature resolution for the people involved or not involved. Likewise there is an exploration of the consciousness or symbolic substance of children, with adult-children or adults playing the parts of children being increasingly prominent. There is a closing down of public spaces of the adult kind.

Above all, the monologue structure is the most substantial focus in contemporary writing practice. In some ways the memory plays of Murphy, Friel, Kilroy and McGuinness provide the templates for the monologue. Monologue is a response to a certain type of cultural remoteness and to a new concept of sanctuary. Subjectivity is precarious, where the self is a sort of stand up (erect) self, manipulator, entertainer, terrorist, scapegoat and performer. The storyteller serves multiple functions, but the substantial one is to structure the spectator's illusions by tracking the tensions between confession and compulsion, bonding and detachment. On top of that we have the relationship between the anecdotal and the archival self. Any response to narrative is a complex one. There is projection, transference and a voyeurism involved that are balanced by a curiosity, fascination and a trust, ensured by the distancing provided by the act of mediated storytelling, by the capacity for demonstration, re-enactment, mimicry, impersonation and substitution. But the narrator is not on trial; the audience seldom serves a judicial function. (The chat-show confessional format is given a different twist.) On one level, the monologue form is a closing down of public interpersonal spaces and still the audience is re-constituted and re-appropriated as community as part of the transaction. As such, monologue often delivers the spectacle of memory. Monologue establishes between spectator and performer liminal spaces or spaces between text and reality, a sort of textualised/performative reality. Monologue and its attendant interiority (something which for me is often an internalisation of protest) is another feature. Conor Mcpherson spoke at a conference in 1998 about the strength of Irish writing. He suggested that Irish writers wrote from the inside out and that many contemporary British playwrights wrote from the outside in. It is my contention that we can look at it from an alternative point of view; for me, it is more from the outside out and from the inside in. Thus play is reconfigured on the level of public and private spaces.

If play was a distancing and dialectical feature of an older writing practice, now monologue with its absence of judgment, through its drift towards and encounters with surreality, achieves a somewhat similar effect. At its best, the blatancy of narrative blurs or rather complicates the distinctions between role and identity, unconscious and conscious and at its worst collapses those distinctions and tends towards an unhealthy type of interiority. In the main, the earlier generation of writers wrote protest plays of sorts. Today's writers cannot do the same thing, given the perceptual collapse of difference and given that the body politic cannot be penetrated on a certain level. In a way the invisibility of power within present society is balanced by the dilution and impact of power or by the dispersal of power in many contemporary scripts. McMullan argues that when it comes to Emma Donoghue's *I Know My Own Heart*, she sees the play as exploring "female sexuality and the performance of gender roles from a lesbian perspective". Overall many women playwrights deploy "performative strategies such as cross-dressing to unsettle traditional gender positions, presenting gender not as destiny, but as subversive performance". Women playwrights still possess the capacity to use play for powerful subversive purposes, whereas the male playwrights seem increasingly to be unable or unwilling to access the same thing. (What are the implications if it were to be the case that it is *Women who run with Wolves* and men who dance with words?)

The other aspect worth noting is the use of extremely seedy situations in which to set plays, giving rise to drug prompted realities. The connections between extremes, marginalisation, underclass and voyeurism are complicated. Violence is prominent in these situations. Yet it is a violence that is increasingly performative and sensational on one level; ultimately there is a blurring of the distinction between pleasure and pain. Neither pain nor pleasure offers any acknowledgement of right or wrong and no means of validation off-stage, even when rape is used as a dramatic propelling device. We are heading in a direction where surface is the key and little can be validated. David Cronenberg's film *Crash* or Mark Ravenhill's *Shopping and F***ing* are examples of this shift. Recent plays like Daragh Carville's *Observatory*, Chris Lee with *The Electrocution of Children* and Dermot Bolger with *The Passion of Jerome* are headed in the direction of drug-induced realities, but as yet without the postmodern ring of Ravenhill or Cronenberg. In Bolger's play the ghost of the dead child asks the stigmata-marked Jerome to: "Play Jesus for" him. How does one play Jesus? At this instant the request is deliberately loaded with ambiguity, on the one hand an interrogation of religion in a society which is increasingly secularised, and on the other, it gives an emphasis on the power and responsibility of intervention, while at the same time sounding like some refrain from a country and western song. Ultimately, we are approaching a stage where there is less and less distinction between the world of play and the real. The shift in emphasis in terms of violence from a post-colonial to an increasing postmodern one is best captured by McDonagh's work.

When it comes to his writing, I am not so much interested in establishing dramatic precedents; I am more interested in establishing points of reference. When I consider *The Lonesome West*, I think of the work of the Coen brothers, Ethan and Joel, in the films *Fargo* or *Raising Arizona*, of the theatre work of Joe Orton, especially *Loot*, or of the crazed reality inspired by the two characters in the television series *Bottom*. *The Lonesome West* is in a sense the *Addams Family*, Irish style with two brothers home alone. Sam Shepard's *True West*, a play about the battle between two brothers, is another appropriate correspondence point in understanding the compulsion and disorientation of the characters. In an Irish context, Pat McCabe's novel *The Butcher Boy*, even the comic series *Fr. Ted* or the comic duo *D'Unbelievables* are appropriate points of contact. The stage version of *The Butcher Boy*, titled *Frank Pig Says Hello*, directed by Joe O'Byrne is one of the great texts of the last twenty years.

What all of this type of work offers is a certain strained, filtered consciousness, a certain way of encountering reality. In a way this type of work delivers alienated characters on the edge of a normal society. It is a world where the characters are violent, impetuous, retaliatory, obsessively self-centred, and spiteful. They are concerned with ownership, revenge and the serial re-enactment of past incidents. They endeavour to deprive, exclude, to defy and to intimidate one another.

There is a strange casual openness that comes from such characters; yet an inherent voyeurism and simultaneous distance on offer for the spectator. There is no mental focus, no moral or conscious filter, no pattern of socialisation through which the characters' deepest thoughts can be screened and they are unable to offer empathy or insight in anyone else's lives. Their thoughts shift with ill discipline from one idea to the next, displaying a sort of moral attention deficit disorder. They are wild, unmonitored, and chillingly childlike in many ways. No continuity is to be found in either behaviour or thought and no serious focus is in operation. A moral value system is seriously misplaced and the Priest-figure does his best to "peg" it in to the mix. Despair and sacrificial fantasies are part of his motivation. Does his suicide have any merit or value?

In *The Lonesome West*, the references are to popular culture; to films, women's magazines and cop shows such as *Hill Street Blues*. The brothers pass the time bearding up photographs in Women's Magazines, collecting coupons, consuming Tayto crisps and drinking alcohol. In the play Girleen uses the perfectly apt phrase "Kings of odd" to describe the brothers, Valene and Coleman. In a way it is a world upside down, where there is no political correctness, where animals get human names, where a young girl jokes about condoms with a priest and suggests that the brothers might use the condoms "on a hen", where the brothers go to extremely violent means to make a point, where characters are troubled by "vol-au-vents" and not the death of a father, and where offspring kill parents over minor conflicts. Think of Tarantino's hit men in *Pulp Fiction* discussing quarter-pounders and foot-massages before an assassination. Thus the world in which McDonagh sets his drama is a darkly comic, sordid and bizarre reality, where expectations are breached on every front. And like Synge, McDonagh offers consistent snippets of grotesquery, by peppering his plays with stories that account for extremes, mutilations and murder.

Many have been quick to confront the work on a number of fronts, from its lack of empathy to its incapacity to subvert clichés and stereotypes of what it might mean to be Irish. There is shorthand for a type of Irishness, that includes usage of crucifixes, hearths, shotguns, Guinness or poteen bottles to which many take offence. But to accuse McDonagh of this is to miss the point somewhat. "Just like real life", was a New York spectator's comment which was broadcast by RTE to mark the success of McDonagh's *Beauty Queen of Leenane*. This statement remained unquestioned by the report. This is surely a fundamental failure, for the world of stage and reality cannot meet so directly headlong. On one level, one cannot assume anything about the present day West of Ireland from this play; no more than one can extrapolate, from the health professionals who take part in the docu/soap *Ibiza Uncovered*, the state of the Health Service in Britain or the standing of contemporary British youth culture. Yet both pieces give angular access and insight into a certain consciousness.

In this way, *The Lonesome West* maps violence, even tribal violence and the difficulty of the journey towards compromise. The attempted reconciliation scene is wonderfully written, tracing the co-operation, apologies, admissions, confessions and forgiveness, while all the time hinting at the pleasure taken from revelation and retaining the competitive edge that exists between the two brothers. (The connection between memory, performance and confession is interesting in the light of recollection and memory in *Dancing at Lughnasa*.) Coleman concludes that fighting shows that they care about one another. And their ways of resolving issues have been read, as Karen Vandevelde points out, as a parable about the Northern Peace Process and about decommissioning. What form of external intervention can take place, whether it is religious figures, Americans, Canadians or South Africans, all of whom have offered help in Northern Ireland? Can McDonagh's characters move from stalemate, unconscious antagonisms and vengeful impulses to a position where some optimism can be found in compromise? And then, is there any chance of them ever entering the more complex, mature, rational, adult world of obsession, calculation, re-enactment, revenge, prejudice and compulsion? Play, violence and adult-child come together. If this is one take on play in contemporary writing practice, then it is vital to consider one other approach, that of Brian Friel from the early part of the decade with *Dancing at Lughnasa*.

In *Bailegangaire*, Murphy rails against a process of national memory, in which by association and by tacit agreement many people are implicated. There is a serious need to revisit what might be called a memory of pain and Murphy dramatises the process of purgation that relies in part on a carnivalesque subversive consciousness, both in Mommo's telling of how the town Bochtán came by its new name, Bailegangaire, and in the disturbing topics of conversation that inspired the laughing competition. *Dancing at Lughnasa* was first performed in 1990, yet the memory moment of the narrator takes place in the 1960s. For a playwright whose major intellectual and dramatic strengths are dominated by the elusive, the unreliable and unverifiable shape of memory and fact, it is surprising to find people accusing him of sentimentally settling for a concrete male-dominated and female subjugated memory.

Throughout Friel's plays memory is loose, incalculable, indeterminate and fluid. Indeed in part, memory has the ephemeral and magic qualities of good theatre. Thus the play dramatises the process of memory itself; is about the act of remembrance, yet the need to forget and the need to prioritise something (a dance sequence) that is in the overall scheme of things not entirely substantial. And by so doing, something else is let in. Memory is not monumental, even in the face of a spectator's tendency to believe it to be the case. In a way the drama is about the impossibility of fully accessing, resuscitating, processing or purging memory.

Memory and dancing co-mingle, and this connection is elaborated upon further by the setting up of relationships between pairs such as religious/pagan, Donegal/Ryanga, Ballybeg/Glenties. Ryangan ritualistic practice and the festival of Lughnasa substantiate a pagan value system, but it works only as an alternative value system that interrogates the conventions and imperatives of what is validated, induced and implored by a generally repressed society that the Mundy's find themselves in back in the 30s. Only the naive would suggest that Friel is attempting to superimpose the pagan world of the back hills onto the Mundys or that Fr. Jack's tale of marital relations is a practical amenable, alternative. Likewise, there can be no equivalence between the Africa and Donegal of the play. Layering and cross-referencing are possible; one can inform the other, but there can be no integration or superimposition. This fraught, fragile and transitional world is given temporary alleviating substance by the subversion of dancing. It is this defiance which Michael identifies with, not their energy of the grotesque, of subversion, and of caricature. The temporary, wild, exuberant and excessive energy of carnival may be a temporary inversion of order, but its marker of difference and its marker of confrontation stand out. When does inversion and playful defiance become abandonment? Dancing, although grounded in the real, moves to the level of fantasy and will-fulfilment and it shifts from the sentiment of the collective or of community to an unconscious acknowledgement of impending disaster.

The conventions of the play in performance require the spectator to consider that the central memory is summoned up and this cannot be altered despite the best attempts of Michael to mediate or intervene. Michael cannot control the central memory, but what he tries to do is to articulate its meaning, significance and substance.

Michael almost implores the spectator to see things as he does, to interpret and record the way he does, to spectate in the way that he has. Furthermore, Friel allows Michael a kind of suggestive and incantatory tone, which the spectator must resist. In most of Friel's plays the battle cry is "no surrender" to memory; here he plays a different game, as he assiduously invites surrender, tempts an audience in, but defiance is the truer obligation. The blatant contradictions between the dance and Michael's eloquent descriptions of it should be blatant and not lost in a haze of nostalgia.

The memory is a male one, as Michael generates it. Michael is not there to tame or distort the memory; he is not at his wit's end to keep them at bay, yet they come to him in an almost surreally casual manner. There is the suggestion that the masculine is more than a guardian of the feminine, that the masculine is about colonising, ordering, controlling, manipulating and repressing the feminine. While at times there are suspicions that Michael is idealising and romanticising, Friel manages to pull the dramatic rug from underneath him on many occasions. The tyranny of memory is most obvious.

Certainly, the spectator is not to trust Michael's account. Michael as a child was at the edge or borders of the experience, (the film centres him in a way), and through the act of memory he attempts to push himself centre stage, to give himself some control and impact over its re-enactment. This has less to do with mastery fantasies and more to do with his desperate need to have some impact on a situation of impossibility. Memory here has nothing to do with him being a control freak and everything to do with desperation on a huge scale.

There is an attraction in the belief that memory is enclosed, frozen, inanimate and suspended in time, but through mobility and through the spirit of play or dance/play there is release; there is energy of momentum of transgression of distortion, fracture and inversion. That is the great strength of *Dancing at Lughnasa*. Memory is mediated through the spirit of playful transgression. Memory and fantasy conspire with failure and poor opportunity to deliver the strange, surreal, omnipotent endeavour of Michael's memory.

Michael cannot believe his eyes on seeing the real Jack. There is a huge gap between the photo of Fr. Jack that fell from Kate's prayer book and the person in reality, and as Synge prompts us, there is a huge gap between the gallous story and the dirty deed, between the gallous, sacred memory and the dirty otherness of reality. In McGuinness' *Carthaginians*, Dido addresses the audience and invites the spectator to speculate as to what he or she has witnessed. "What happened? Everything happened, nothing happened, whatever you want to believe, I suppose". The onus is on the spectator. The final invitation made by Dido is to "Play". Memory is everything and nothing, so is play.

That the sisters fought, disagreed, contained and sustained antagonisms, compromised, co-operated and cared should be duly noted. There is humanity in their judgements of one another, a leniency even in the most vicious putdown or accusation. They are characters at an extreme, in pain and they find some succour and confidence in the bond they share between them. Life did not grant the women a level of freedom or of subjectivity. Did it grant most men much more? Kate after two year's unemployment ends up tutoring Austin Morgan's children and Chris works at what she despises. But to survive, to give one's live some substance, there were no radical alternatives; nothing pagan and nothing romantic to be appropriated. But to say that there was nothing more creative than "Eggs Ballybeg" is far from the mark.

The dance scene is not the single big moment for the sisters, (there are huge moments of collective care, intensity and courage elsewhere) but it is the largest expression of their capacity for life, displaying high energy, high commitment and a high emphasis on a community celebrating its bonds, temporarily outside of a masculine frame and outside a social reality that was soon to doom them all to very different ways of life. This is why the urgency and blatancy of dance or dance play is such an apt appropriation.

What Friel does is to capture how people make the most of trauma, how they invest enormous substance in things that on one level are very much insubstantial in a broader social context. Michael gives more time over to the description of the dance than he does to the emigration of his aunts. He wants desperately to idealise it, but Friel denies him his wish. Yet through displacement and refraction, Friel, like Chekhov, lets in entirely different sets of recognitions that work best because they go almost unacknowledged, as they are not blatant. We are still waiting on a production that will acknowledge the formidable intellectual challenge that Friel places in his text. Its success of course up to now points to the fact that the play in performance has tapped into many of these forces, but for me, the best is yet to come.

Language and atmosphere, memory and dance, fabrication and fact, Donegal and Ryanga, the pagan and the secular all conspire, but nothing is drawn close together to achieve synergy or synthesis. Disharmony and disjunction are only credible for his dramatic community at that time. Misreading, mismatching, mistranslation and inappropriateness are the dominant energies of the play. Memory cannot be re-enacted, memory cannot be pure and memory cannot be recuperated, instead it can aid recovery, prove to be a point of rest, a device of assessment and the impetus to move on. It is an act of self-preservation. In that way the play celebrates not wholeness but incompletion, not a golden moment but the flaws, fractures and cracks in memory (and in the mirror). Michael is possessed by memory and fantasy and he is dispossessed by the reality of the dance.

In the initial monologue, Michael uses words like "spontaneous", "laughing", "screaming" "excited" "deranged" to describe the mood and the dancing, by the final monologue his description relies on words like "floating", rhythmically", "languorously", "hushed rhythm", "silent hypnotic movement", and in between, "grotesque", "aggressive", "raucous", "erratic", "caricaturing" and "parodic" are some of the words Friel employs to describe the central dance. The gap between Michael's words and Friel's stage directions is where the brilliance of this play lies. Friel is as manipulative as Michael endeavours to be.

Poverty, the absence of choice and agency that belonged to one world, seem to be very different for a substantial part of the population today. Under liberal capitalism, benign democracy is the defining feature. As such the ritualism of difference at the heart of theatre, seen within the realm of defiance, courage, heroic gesture, has in some ways fallen flat. Akin to this is the manner in which, at least within first world countries victimisation has in many ways begun to lose its status, in every sense of the word. Anti-Government protest plays, which were the staple of post-war British Drama, have, for the moment, had their day. In a crude sense, New Labour, under Tony Blair's leadership, has led indirectly to the absence of precisely demarcated alternative politics, the dilution of oppositions and the unsatisfying postmodern concept of substitution rather than an older concept of definite difference. In Irish writing the tensions of colonialism have fed into many plays from *Translations* to

Murphy's *Famine*. Again McDonagh is a point of contact. In *The Cripple of Inishmaan*, two characters, Helen and Bartley, play "Ireland versus England". Bartley stands still while Helen breaks eggs against his forehead. In a sense the national conflict has been ironically reduced to a game, and the family game of the brothers in *The Lonesome West* to the level of ruthless historical conflict perhaps. This is the radical dichotomy existent in contemporary writing practice.

So instead of viewing contemporary Irish drama as either being substantially postmodern or post-colonial, it is the interlocking of the postmodern and the post-colonial that in part accounts for the huge successes in recent years of Irish plays elsewhere. The cultural context of present day Ireland is uncomfortable with a post-colonial consciousness and still flirting with a postmodern one. A postmodern one, pushed to its most severe limits, has little to offer. Recent films like *The Matrix*, *eXistenZ*, *The Fight Club* (Think of the Carney family in *A Whistle in the Dark*) and *The Truman Show* query the whole notion of being locked into roles or how the impact of role shapes reality. Part of contemporary cinema practice is grappling with something that Irish theatre has struggled against for such a long time.

My fear is that we will be overburdened with station dramas in the Strindbergian sense or that there will be an increasing absence of exchanges in public spaces between characters. Fortunately, the monologues at present still avoid in the main angst ridden expressions of trauma and are shy of introspection.

Is it good to talk? Will the chat room be increasingly the space of public discourse? (I am thinking of Patrick Marber's brilliant play *Closer* here, a sort of "find yourself" on-line.) If play is driven inward, then it will lose its capacity to contest and will have no grasp of otherness. The notion of a self, whether on-line or main-line must not be driven by self-absorption. Impersonation must have a relationship with otherness. Recently I wrote elsewhere, "Will it be the blur of drugs, the slur of comedy and the lowest common denominator of tragedy that will be available as dramaturgical models"? So how do you write about the present? An earlier generation answered this by writing mainly about the past. But we can no longer process the present in this way. Indeed we peddled to ourselves the notion that "this is then, that was now". The past and present cannot be recreational versions of one another. What we need now is an ability to imagine purposefully the future.

A Generation of Playwrights*

Thomas Kilroy

We were children of what Patrick Kavanagh called the Hitler War years, growing up in an Ireland that now seems as remote as the last century. The next decade, the fifties, became part of our imaginative landscape when the unreality of the war years gave way to the enforced reality of isolation, repressiveness and dreariness. An Ireland, then, that was a self-isolating place, timidly holding itself inwards while the modern century rushed by, headlong and frantic, outside. In retrospect it seems to have been virtually a cashless society with a minimum of material needs, presided over by that ascetic icon, de Valera. Boots were repaired, often on the home last, with heavy studs and steel tips and sometimes sandals were worn through the winter with insoles of newspaper padding. There was a smell of containable, endurable poverty everywhere and everyone rode the bicycle, often on huge journeys that would now be worthy of the peleton. And yet out of this dispiriting world came the stirrings of what would be the first significant shift in sensibility in the Irish theatre since the early days of the Abbey Theatre.

An Irish playwright even remotely concerned with tradition is faced with a tri-furcated past with such tenuous connections between the three strands that the very notion of tradition becomes questionable. Firstly, there are the Irish born playwrights of the eighteenth and nineteenth centuries who turned to London, writing for the English stage, or imitations of it in Dublin. Secondly, there is the small group of playwrights around Yeats who set out to weld the fracture between the Anglo-Irish and Gaelic Ireland from a largely Anglo-Irish perspective. Thirdly, there are those playwrights, predominantly of Catholic background, who came to dominate the Irish theatre through the thirties, forties and fifties. Yeats was unhappy with the naturalism of these latter writers and their efforts to write a poeticised drama didn't seem to register with him. For Yeats the playwrights of Catholic background (he had in mind Colum and Martyn but his views would equally apply to their successors) were "dominated by their subject" whereas playwrights of his own, Anglo-Irish background "stand above their subject and play with it" (Wade: 1954, 464). In each case, whether by Catholic or Protestant playwright, "their subject" refers to Catholic Ireland and, more specifically, to the peasant play. The Anglo-Irish playwrights, with the possible exception of Denis Johnston, never really created a significant drama out of their own social material.

In part, Yeats' distaste for naturalism was a distaste for sociology or rather the sociological burden of a writer working closely to his material.

Art should never try to compete with history, otherwise it would never come into contact with mystery and what lies beyond the limits of logic. Yeats called for a kind of freedom from subject-matter or what he described as a "victory" over one's material, a distancing from it, as it were, although he does not use this particular term. The playwrights of Catholic background who followed Colum and Martyn, writers like T.C. Murray, Paul Vincent Carroll, Brinsley MacNamara, ensured that this line of naturalistic drama flourished into the forties and fifties. One unkind but accurate joke suggested that the Abbey Theatre never had to change its set for decades; all that was needed was a fresh coat of paint. This was the Irish theatre as we knew it as youngsters and one could understand what Yeats was complaining about. For my own part, born with a Protestant mind in a Catholic body and soon secularised, I have always regretted the disappearance of the Anglo-Irish imagination. I have always greatly admired its drama, its elegance and wit, its high style and, above all, its intellectual and moral passion.

But is this matter of tradition of any interest any more? Certainly, younger people in the Irish theatre today find it a bore. There is even the eerie sensation of watching some of the work of one's contemporaries and, worse still, of one's own, becoming historical while one is still alive. But that, precisely, is why the question of tradition is important at this time. The writer who is born into a traditional culture and lives to see it undergo massive change has a peculiar problem in bridging the present and the past. My own may be the last generation with such a sense of continuity with the past, particularly the immediate past. But it is also a generation of originality and that originality is the most interesting thing about it.

The two productions which ushered in contemporary Irish drama, Hugh Leonard's adaptation of Joyce, *Stephen D* (1962) and Brian Friel's *Philadelphia, Here I Come!* (1964), will illustrate what I've been trying to say. The imagery of Ireland in both plays is traditional with many of the stock situations and characters that had appeared in other plays before but the sensibility of both writers is what is striking: modern, alive to the dislocating perspectives of the mid-century and the fluidity of expression possible on stage with modern lighting, design and direction. Leonard was drawing upon Joyce, of course, but he brought his own very considerable technical inventiveness to bear upon the Joyce texts, the cinematic lay-out of differing planes of action and time-scales. The Friel play is set in the kitchen-home of a county councillor. One might be in any number of kitchen farces, comedies, tragi-comedies of the preceding decades. But not quite. The play calls for a split stage and a generous apron which is, as the playwright puts it "fluid", a place to be occupied by the imagination of the audience (Friel: 1984, 27). These, then, are plays which impose a new kind of theatrical imagination upon traditional material and this mixture of traditional material and formal inventiveness came to typify the work of some, at least, of my contemporaries over the next quarter of a century.

To speak of traditional material in this context is to speak of a rural village or small town ethos and I am using these terms descriptively and not pejoratively. Leonard's Dalkey is as village-like as Friel's and, indeed, Joyce's Dublin has all the intimacy and shared codes of a small, provincial town. It is only in the past decade that Ireland has become truly urbanised in the late-twentieth century meaning of that term, in other words, characterised by great mobility, using highly complex, far-reaching systems of communication, with increased secularisation and the break-down of the old bonds of familial, tribalististic society. We have yet to have a theatre of this Ireland because it is as yet incompletely formed but we are getting plays that reflect the confusion attending those changes.

What I'm suggesting, in effect, is that the typical Irish play of the sixties, the seventies, the eighties, is something of a hybrid, reflecting the suspended condition of the writers themselves. These are plays written by agnostic believers and uneasy patriots, reluctant farmers and local cosmopolitans, incredulous parents and recalcitrant, elderly children, citizens of a country not always identical to the one of their imaginations. If we were to crudely label many of the plays they fit the conventional types of times past: the Irish Peasant Play *(Bailegangaire)*, the Irish Religious Play *(Talbot's Box)*, the Irish Family play, the Irish History Play *(Making History)* but could anyone make the mistake of placing these plays in pre-war Ireland? In each of the plays the material is being used for effects that transcend the material itself. There may be fidelity to the material but it is not the slavish fidelity of mere naturalism. We are constantly being reminded that what is being represented has slipped or is rapidly slipping out of view. The present tense of the plays, as it were, is occupied by the viewpoint or perspective of the writer and it is this self-consciousness, finally, that distinguishes the work of my generation from that which preceded us.

The problem of writing about a world which has already passed away or is in the process of doing so, is a problem of creative distancing. Nowhere is this better exemplified than in the fate of that most durable of all Irish theatrical genres, the Irish Peasant Play. It is arguable that from the beginning this type of drama had a high degree of artifice and that playwrights with an authentic experience of peasant Ireland, like John B. Keane and M.J. Molloy, for example, were the exception. With a sophisticated artist like Synge what you got was a highly wrought artefact as much about the intense, personal pre-occupations of the artist as about the portrayal of a peasant community. The Anglo-Irish playwrights, including Synge, who wrote about peasant Ireland, were themselves socially, politically, culturally removed from their material and their distancing of the material, their shaping of it into an aesthetic shape is the effect, the mastery of the material, which Yeats so admired. For an Irish playwright today to write about the forties or fifties requires a similar act of distancing, of occupying an angled perspective, if you will, of finding a way of framing, of indicating or acknowledging the fact that we are in the past but that we are looking at it from the present.

The controversy over John McGahern's *The Power of Darkness* (1991) had to do, partly at any rate, with the fact that McGahern makes no such concession. He presented his peasant material with a frontal immediacy that was well nigh intolerable to his Dublin audience which angrily denied the possibility of such scenes in their hinterland, at this point in time. Part of this outrage was due to the fact that most of the audiences were but one or two steps removed from rural Ireland and the sensitivity within this new, gauche metropolitanism was acute. McGahern knows perfectly well that there are still pockets of primal, peasant savagery in rural Ireland but he made no attempt to translate this experience for an outside audience. Quite the contrary, he employed an old-fashioned melodramatic style which seemed to enrage his audience even further. It was an instance of an audience refusing to accept a work on its own terms out of a desperate need to obliterate those images on stage out of existence and out of memory. It is one way of looking at the end of the peasant play on the Irish stage but there are other ways as well.

In 1987 the School of Education at Trinity College Dublin produced a remarkable report on the relationship between creativity and education in this country. Eighteen poets, twelve prose fiction writers, twelve playwrights, seven painters and sculptors and four composers were interviewed and the whole was accompanied by extensive analyses, some of them, unfortunately, of a heavy-handed kind. But the interviews are extraordinarily revealing. The published report, *Education and the Arts,* contains only a selection of the interviews. Five playwrights are included: Hugh Leonard, Tom Murphy, Eugene McCabe, Sean O'Tuama and myself. The interviews of the other seven playwrights, including Brian Friel and John B. Keane, are presumably lodged in the School archive. These interviews offer a composite portraiture of the generation that I've been talking about and, in particular, they offer an account, often vividly, of the way in which the Ireland of the forties and the fifties has been refracted into the imaginative life of these writers.

Life bounded by the country kitchen. The drama of family and of neighbours and the very occasional stranger. The language of the people, that troublesome richness which has been as much a liability as a resource, not only to the playwrights but to the people themselves. And everywhere the iron regime of the Church. In many ways, the interview of Tom Murphy is the most lively on how an imaginative youngster came to cope with these narrow confines and how he transcended them. Here he is with his friend Noel O'Donoghue (who collaborated with him on his first play, *On The Outside*):

> One Sunday morning we were standing in the square in Tuam after the last Mass. This was the usual thing to do, generally talking about football. We felt infinitely superior to the plebs. O'Donoghue said to me, "Why don't you write a play?" I said, "What would we write about?" And he said, "one thing is fucking sure, it's not going to be set in a kitchen". That was the most progressive thing anybody had ever said to me (Murphy: 1987, 173).

Over the years that followed, plays continued to be set in the kitchen, by Murphy as well as by other playwrights, for the very good reason that Ireland continued to act out her dramas there. That minor rebellion on the square of Tuam had, nevertheless, its own significance. The peasant play and its cramped setting had come to stand for everything that was outmoded in the Irish theatre and yet it required two exceptional plays, *Translations* and *Bailegangaire*, to finally exhaust the form itself and put a seal upon it.

There is a distinct sense of an ending with each of these plays. Each is a theatrical elegy for the life which it acts out. Both begin with strong emplacements of traditional Ireland. Murphy: "The room is a country kitchen in the old style" (Murphy: 1984, 43). "The hedge-school is held in a disused barn or hay-shed or byre" (Friel: 1984, 383). The point about each of the locations on stage is that it is being used for a function for which it is not intended. Friel's school in a byre (however historically accurate) and Murphy's bed in the kitchen are jolting images for a modern audience, particularly for one with little sensitivity to the fate of traditional Irish customs. There is a jumble here, a displacement and as the plays proceed, a dehiscence, as Beckett once observed memorably of O'Caseyan farce, in which the suffering of individuals stands in for the shifting of the floor of a whole civilisation (Beckett: 1975, 167).

Both plays are very knowing texts not least in their echoes. Friel recalls Boucicault's redcoats and peasants and the love across the divide, O'Casey's chassis and even Synge's fugitive to the Erris Peninsula. There is Murphy's extraordinarily resonant re-echo of *Riders to the Sea* in Mommo's enumeration of her own bereavements. These are not simply modish references. They are evidence of a larger awareness in the writers, an ability to lift the purely personal onto a plane of wider implication.

Murphy's play is built upon the image of the bed, the domestic centre, the place of fertility, but now the nest (as in Jonson's *Volpone)* becomes the place of decrepitude with the voice of that tormented old woman trying to complete the telling of her story. It is a remarkable image of Irish *seanchas* at the end of its tether. What makes the basically untheatrical situation theatrical is, firstly, the histrionic figure of the old woman herself and secondly the fact that what she is recounting is itself a deadly, grotesque piece of theatre, the laughing competition which ends in death and the re-naming of a place.

The contrast with *Translations,* where the central metaphor of profound, historical change is map-making, is obvious. And yet if these two playwrights illustrate something of the sophisticated use of traditional material in contemporary Irish theatre, no two playwrights could be less alike. Murphy's method is a kind of excavation, a burrowing down into incoherence or near incoherence where the identity of the single person melts into some common fodder. Friel, on the other hand, is a highly formal artist who shapes his material in this play through a single, controlling idea of history, that the fate of a doomed civilisation becomes manifestly tragic at the point where the fate of its language and the fate of its territory intersect and inform one another. So infusing is Friel's tact that virtually everything in the play refers to everything else. Dismemberment of the house, of the school, of the countryside, of the race itself, this is the most comprehensive enshrouding of peasant Ireland in the modern Irish theatre. But the final effect of the play is of a fullness to the brim, a ripeness, even while the stage action reflects despoliation, defeat. This is truly a "victory" over the material, as Yeats would have it.

There is, finally, another aspect to all of this and it has to do with non-Irish audiences and their expectations of Irish plays. Within the metropolitan centres there is always a nostalgia for cultures which are untouched, untainted by the ennui, the busyness, the crowdedness of the centre. This has always been so in human history and no doubt the planners in the future will create reservations to satisfy this need. In our century this has taken the form of a persisting interest in the primitive, the provincial, the remote even while the main expressions of the centre would appear to be a rejection of the values offered by the periphery. In our century this has taken the form of incorporation of primitive elements into modern art itself or the creation of a neo-primitivism as a severe alternative to the art of the centre.

A place apart, a place retaining some of the innocence of the pre-modern, a kind of literary environmentalism, a version of greenery, some Irish writing has always answered this appeal, sometimes shamelessly, from readers and audiences outside Ireland. Certain stereotypes of Irish writing and the Irish writer have thereby become entrenched, the Irish writer as roaring boyo, for example, or as un-tutored, natural genius and Irish writing as a pure, natural flow of words, untouched by a contaminating intelligence. As traditional Ireland fades into the past these stereotypes become even more absurd and are best consigned to pulp fiction. And as it does, nostalgia may no longer be enough, indeed it may not even be necessary as Irish drama begins to locate itself more in the present.

*This article first appeared in the *Irish University Review*, 1992. It is kindly re-printed with the permission of the Editor, Dr. Anthony Roche.

Works Cited:

Beckett, Samuel, (1975), "The Essential and the Incidental", in *Sean O'Casey: A Collection of Critical Essays,* ed., Thomas Kilroy (Englewood Cliffs, N.J.: Prentice Hall)

Friel, Brian, (1984), *The Selected Plays* (London: Faber and Faber)

Murphy, David, (1987), ed., *Education and the Arts: A Research Report* (Dublin: Published on behalf of the school of Education by the Department of Higher Education and Educational Research, Trinity College)

Murphy, Thomas, (1988), *After Tragedy* (London: Methuen)

Wade, Allan, (1954), ed., *The Letters of W.B. Yeats* (London: Hart-Davis)

Who The Hell Do We Think We Still Are? Reflections
On Irish Theatre and Identity
Declan Hughes

1

You don't live in Ireland; you know nothing of the country but the last thirty years or so of its literature. And then, one cold morning, you arrive in Dublin in 1999. You're going to be very confused, aren't you? Why didn't anyone warn you about all this? The cranes, the plate glass, the extremes of wealth and poverty, the corruption, the vulgarity, the new slapped gaudily on the old like bright paint on a crumbling facade. What were those writers *doing*, obsessing about the Nineteen Fifties, stuck down the country being Irish with themselves? Who the hell do we think we still are?

2

Why does contemporary Irish literature ignore contemporary Ireland? Yes, there are exceptions, but that's what they are: cranks, objectors, loons with the preposterous notion that literature should, in Mr. Trollope's words, reflect The Way We Live Now. For the most part, Irish writing is still based on an Ireland that hasn't existed for years.

3

In an introduction to a collection of plays a couple of years ago, I wrote the following:

> The experience of growing up in Dublin in the sixties and seventies was not unlike the experience of growing up in Manchester or Glasgow, or in Seattle for that matter. The cultural influences were the same: British and American TV, films and music. You read Irish literature, but mostly for the past; to discover the present, you looked to America. Irish writers flicked through the family album; American writers looked out the window. You knew you would go to America one day, to work, or for a holiday, or just to get the hell away from home, or maybe you lived in California or New York already, in your mind. You were People Like That, and if you felt your cultural identity dwindling into a nebulous blur, well, you believed that what you had in common with others was more important than what set you apart, and you knew there were millions like you all over the world, similarly anxious to be relieved of the burdens of nationality and of history. You were tired of hearing about those who didn't learn from history being condemned to repeat it; you

sometimes felt the opposite was true, that those who were obsessed by the past were doomed never to escape it, to replicate it endlessly, safe and numb within its deadly familiarity.

I use America in that passage as an idea; America as New Found Land, that which we all seek: the opportunity to put the past in its place, to stop answering the question "Who Are We?" with "This is who we used to be — this is how we got here". To reinvent ourselves for the future, to stop defining ourselves in terms of the past. Identity is inchoate: it's up for grabs, it must be constantly reinvented: like theatre, made new every day.

4

In the late seventies, I was a regular reader of the *New Musical Express*, which at the time dealt with an extraordinarily rich mixture of music, film, literature and politics: a kind of learned journal of popular culture. It was fantastically pretentious: a review of a Rip Rig and Panic gig invariably contained references to Derrida and Lacan. It was also the first publication I had come across which suggested that there was no contradiction in listening one minute to the Ramones, the next to Steve Reich, or in reading Don DeLillo *and* the X-Men; indeed, it suggested that if you didn't investigate the range of culture, high to low, then you were seriously out of touch. The policy was: Not only but also, as opposed to Either/or.

It was relentlessly secular, hedonistic, politically correct, foul-mouthed, internationalist. It understood that the 20th century had been, and would continue to be, for better or worse, the American century, and that culturally, again for good or ill, we had all been colonised irrevocably by the first beam of light Hollywood had shone on us, by the first notes of music we'd heard the descendent of an African slave play.

The *NME* at the time came as cultural manna from heaven to a gloomy suburban teenager who could find absolutely nothing in Irish culture, official or unofficial, that resonated in any way. Irish culture then was obsessed in every respect with the past; that has changed to some extent, but unfortunately, nowhere near comprehensively enough.

5

> **RORY**: I thought you were busy embracing the chaos in the biggest burgh in burgerdom, Danny, what's wrong, does it scare you when you see it in your cherished little homeland?
>
> **DANNY**: No, what I'm saying is: the chaos *is* here — wannabees and weirdoes on the airwaves, brains fried from T.V. and video and information overload — so acknowledge it, don't pretend there's some unique sense of community, that

Ireland's some special little enclave — things are breaking down as fast here as anywhere else.

BREDA: You just don't understand, talk radio here — even if people feel isolated, lost in the suburbs or something, they can tune in and feel a part of what's going on — it's like they're living in a village, and they want to keep up with the gossip.

DANNY: And what about the people who don't want to live in a village? The people who left before their village suffocated them? Is village life supposed to be the most authentic, the most Irish?

BREDA: It's also about having a sense of place —

DANNY: And what happens when you don't have a sense of place? When I arrived in New York for the first time, and as the cab swung past that graveyard and around the corner and I got my first glimpse of the Manhattan skyline, I felt like I was coming home. The landscape was alive in my dreams, the streets were memories from a thousand movies, the city was mine.

RORY: Well you have a sense of place, Danny. It just happens to be somebody else's place.

DANNY: No it doesn't, it's as much Ireland as Dublin is; millions of Irish went out and invented it, invented it as much, probably more than any ever invented this poxy post-colonial backwater.

BREDA: So what's the problem? You don't like it here, fine, you don't live here; you feel at home there, great, you live there. What's the big deal?

DANNY: The big deal, the big deal is, that *there* is as much *here* as *here* is... and I don't believe the *here* you're describing exists here. To me, *here* is more like... *there.(Pause)*

EMILY: Danny, are you on drugs? (From *Digging For Fire* (1991), in *Declan Hughes: Plays: 1* (London: Methuen, 1998))

6

I work in a profession whose practitioners are famed for their loquaciousness. The joke about actors of a certain age entering their anecdotage is well known, but like so many jokes, it makes us laugh because it's true, and it's true for profound reasons. If you've ever seen a film of a theatrical performance, you'll have remarked on its oddness: the timing, the rhythms, even the acting seem out of kilter, somehow skewed, at once too obvious and curiously opaque. Photographs can't capture it, sound recordings won't do it justice. Theatre is written on the wind. As we tell our friends, speaking of some great night they missed: You had to be there. The only memory is an anecdote, a rambling story that can't quite capture the magic. We trust that it was magical, but we can't quite figure out how. And as some old actor rambles on, we begin to wonder if it was as ever as good in the past as we know it to be now. There was a legendary Olivier "Othello", (legendary because everyone said so) which was filmed. I watched the film in incredulity, as a blacked up ham gives the most preposterous display of vainglorious preening and bombastic declaiming. They said it was a legend, but it looked like a load of old nonsense to me. Maybe Olivier wasn't all they said he was. Maybe all those old guys were overrated, maybe what counts, all that counts, is what we're doing right now. Making it new. But if I'd been there, at the Old Vic all those years ago, I'm sure I would have been enthralled.

Written on the wind. This is the essential purity of theatre as an art form. It's created out of air, and vanishes into it. All the accretions of the past, all the *tradition* counts for nothing. Howard Brenton has said, of working for one of the large English institutions — you know the ones, they have Royal or National in their names — sometimes, rather greedily, both — that as soon as anyone starts talking about "the traditions of this theatre", you know you are in trouble. What used to be creativity, inspiration, energy has congealed into tradition. What is tradition anyway? Habit in fancy dress. An excuse for thought. A mindless worship of the past.

7

There are two ways of reacting to the perceived collapse of cultural identities in the modern world. One is, literally, to react: to insist on national and regional identity, authenticity, to stress more and more the need to be Irish against the swirling and chaotic global forces, to employ a national culture as a kind of nostalgic bulwark that stresses, and eventually fetishises, the differences between Ireland and everywhere else. The irony is that, by and large, those things that make us different are those which tell us least about ourselves today, but hark back to the past. The country kitchen, the rural pub, the farm, the nineteen fifties; this is a form of perverse nostalgia: nostalgia for the time when we think we were Irish, when we had an identity.

8

Nostalgia is in many ways the Irish disease, and it corrodes at every level: at its most extreme, it becomes the savagery of war: as Don DeLillo says in *White Noise*:

Nostalgia is a product of dissatisfaction and rage. It's a settling of grievances between the present and the past. The more powerful the nostalgia, the closer you come to violence. War is the form nostalgia takes when men are hard-pressed to say something good about their country.

9

The village is no longer the objective correlative for Ireland: the city is, or to be precise, *between* cities is. That space between. That's not to say that people don't live in the country any more, or that rural life isn't "valuable"; it's that culturally, it's played out. It no longer signifies. Mythologically, it doesn't resonate any more. Despite the fact that the overwhelming movements and changes in Irish society in the last thirty years have been urban, global, technological; that in every other area, we divest ourselves of the past like the good little I.T. loving global capitalists we're becoming; culturally we persist in defining ourselves by the ethnic, the pastoral (and that qualified form, the tragic pastoral). Even if we do it in an iconoclastic way, the iconography remains powerfully the same: half door, pint bottle, sacred heart.

We make a show of ourselves as we think we were in the past, because we don't, or won't confront ourselves in the present. Because, correctly, we fear the set of identities we have for ourselves won't add up any more. And foolishly, we think that fear is better avoided than embraced. And the rest of the world colludes in this because they want us to be Irish too; hell, they'd like to be Irish *themselves*.

10

I read a piece in *The Guardian* recently decrying the film *Waking Ned* for its paddywhackery, and attributing its box office success in the UK to racism against the Irish. I thought that it was quaint these days to see racism and the Irish being used that way round, and I thought it was a bit over the top devoting an entire column to what is a bog-standard piece of shamroguery. But then I noticed that the author, Lawrence Donegan, was flogging a book. Mr. Donegan, a Scotsman, had spent a year in an Irish village, and the book, published by an English publisher, would be a hugely charming, meaningful testament to how bloody marvellous we "Irish" are. I resisted the temptation to write in, because I'm saving for a later and madder chapter in my life the role of The Man Who Writes Letters To The Newspapers.

But I thought: almost as bad as being discriminated against because you're thought inferior is discrimination in your favour because you're thought *marvellous*. And I thought, spending a year in an Irish village in 1999 is about as useful as living on a Scottish croft would be as a way of assessing the contemporary character of the two countries. And I thought, the more people agree on who you are and are not, the more your identity is fixed by others, the less easy it becomes to investigate who you really are — investigate whether an identity defined by nationality, or geography, has a meaning any more. And I thought of David Mamet's line from *Speed-the-Plow*, a line that sometimes seems as if it was written with Ireland in mind: "I wouldn't believe this shit if it was true".

11

I'd like to see Irish theatre embrace the profound change that has occurred: that we are barely a country any more, never have been and never will be that most nineteenth century of dreams, a nation once again; that our identity is floating, not fixed. I could live a long and happy life without seeing another play set in a Connemara kitchen, or a country pub. I think it's significant that in contemporary theatre and cinema, so much attention gets paid to the nineteen fifties, the decade before Ireland opened for business, the time when we *were* a "special little enclave". And of course, as a form of pastoral idyll, that's attractive to audiences from countries who were by that time heavily industrialised and urbanised. But I don't see any mythological resonance in it: all I see is a marketing strategy: this is our special, uniquely Irish past: isn't it funky? Isn't it perversely exotic and thrillingly *other?* Well, no actually, it's just a miserablist equivalence of Merchant Ivory costume drama: the bourgeois fallacy that art is always set in the past.

Too often when I go to the theatre, I feel like I've stepped into a time capsule: even plays supposedly set in the present seem burdened by the compulsion to... well, in the narrowest sense, be Irish. It sometimes feels like Stephen's Night, listening to a bunch of aged relatives reminisce: it's comforting, sad, gently amusing and not a little dull. That's not even enough for Stephen's Night, let alone a night at the theatre. I'm not suggesting that drama should be "relevant': I'm never quite sure what that means. Or that it somehow act as the artistic wing of journalism, getting yesterday's headlines onto tomorrow's stages (although there can be a certain exhilaration when that occurs). But Irish drama needs to show more guts: the guts to stop flaunting its ancestry, to understand that the relentless dependence on tradition collapses inevitably into cannibalism. The village will eat itself.

I never again want to see an Irish play set in a community where everyone talks and thinks the same and holds values in common. Because that is not truth: that's nostalgia: the illusion that there is something that still binds us together. Increasingly, there isn't. This has formal implications, of course: on a simple technical level, plays are easier to construct if everyone on stage follows the same rules; if we all know who we are. But we don't know who we are any more. There's a fair possibility that we never will again. That's an exhilarating notion to take into a new century.

12

The novelist Hugo Hamilton has spoken about his generation being the last of the Irish, that under the twin influences of Europe and America, the Irish identity will soon disappear. He seemed to think this was a good idea, and I agree with him. I was reminded of it when I saw Warren Beatty's film *Bulworth*, wherein the splendid theory is expounded that the solution to the problem of race is mass miscegenation, until there's only one race left: the human race.

This brings me to the second way of reacting to the collapse of cultural identity in the world: to reflect it, to embrace it, to see it as liberating. It's the condition. Simple as that. Not only but also. The future, not the past. Bring it all on.

13

Depressingly, the only other people at present who seem to relish the idea of abandoning the past, ignoring history and welcoming the future are businessmen, modern incarnations of the fumble-in-a-greasy-till-merchants who have always been, revoltingly, with us. (No prizes for guessing why they might relish a valueless, ahistorical, individualistic work force.)

And since the values of the culture are now almost overwhelmingly business values, what we need more than ever are clear-eyed writers who will take the trouble to view the world as it is, in all its complexity, and will then speak the truth: nostalgia is cold comfort; the truth is what we need.

14

We have had an explosive thirty years in Ireland. Fortunes have been made, crimes have been committed, democracy has been abused, politics has been debased, greed has been glorified, character has been derided. And in the main, we look in vain to the theatre, or indeed anywhere, to see these events transformed imaginatively into art.

Journalism has done part of the job we should have been doing. But journalism will not last. And journalism cannot mythologise. While the nation still exists, it is there to be imagined. And after that... there is a world elsewhere.

15

My favourite modern parable was outlined by Neal Gabler in his great book *An Empire Of Their Own: How the Jews Invented Hollywood.* Gabler describes how these men, Cohn and Fox, Warner and Mayer, Zukor and Laemmle, the sons of Eastern European Jews forced from their countries by anti-semitism, came to Hollywood and created the great dream factories of our age. They were discriminated against by the WASP establishment, who wouldn't let them into their American country clubs and dining clubs. In response, they founded their own. Meanwhile, they were producing the stories that, round the world and in their own land, would depict, define and eventually stand for, America.

They came to America and thrived, but were not considered a part of America. So they invented their own America, one in which they could be kings. AND that's the America everyone recognises. It's the America that in many respects exists. I thought of this recently when the theory emerged that the Celts had never actually existed, that they were a fabrication. All that Celtic art, and literature, and *ethos*... all made up in order that besieged and insecure peoples of these islands might feel they had some identity, some roots, some tradition.

I got very excited. I hope it's true. Because, if the Celts never really existed, then we must have made them up. And if all we did was make the Celts up, then we don't have to be them any more. We don't, in the sense we have understood it, have to be ourselves any more.

> Weightless and free.
> Who will we be then?
> Whoever we like.

Classics as Celtic Firebrand: Greek Tragedy, Irish Playwrights, and Colonialism

Marianne McDonald

Classics have often been used to further the cause of imperialism. Nevertheless, classics can also provide a literature of protest. Since 1984 we have seen more than thirty adaptations of Greek tragedy by more than fifteen Irish playwrights including: Tom Paulin, *The Riot Act: A Version of Sophocles' Antigone*; *Seize the Fire: A Version of Aeschylus' Prometheus Bound*; Aidan Carl Mathews, *Antigone*; *Trojans*; Brendan Kennelly, *Antigone: A New Version*; *Euripides' Medea: A New Version*; *Euripides' The Trojan Women: A New Version*. Seamus Heaney, *The Cure at Troy: After 'Philoctetes' by Sophocles*; *Euripides' Medea*, trans. Desmond Egan; *Sophocles' Philoctetes*; Derek Mahon, *The Bacchae: After Euripides*; *Racine's Phaedra*; Marina Carr, *By the Bog of Cats....* (following Euripides' *Medea*); Frank McGuinness, *Sophocles' Electra*; Euripides' *Orestes* by Greg Delanty; a film by Pat Murphy (*Anne Devlin*, whose heroine resembles *Antigone*) and a television play, *In the Border Country* by Thaddeus O'Sullivan, a version of Aeschylus' *Oresteia*.

It is noteworthy that four of these are based on Sophocles' *Antigone*, three on Euripides' *Medea*, two on *Trojan Women*, and none on *Oedipus Tyrannus*: they are plays that focus on human rights more than on fate and identity. The result is not simply a political tract protesting abuse, but a passionate expression of hopes and fears. The literary classic provides a heightened mode of communication. In the same way that the classic can be used to filter personal terror, such as fear of death, and allow the audience to confront this fear, so can it explicate social and political atrocity so that the audience can finally see what in many cases it would prefer to ignore.

Does there come a time in a nation's history — a crisis of identity, of cultural and political consciousness — when recourse is made naturally to that literature which most radically investigates and establishes national identity: fifth-century Attic tragedy? Ireland's history shows the imprint of English imperialism to the point that by 1703, the Catholic Irish themselves owned only 14% of their land. Perhaps now the self-scrutiny which was the background for Jean Anouilh's *Antigone* in Nazi-occupied Paris is apparent in contemporary Ireland and the Irish are now redefining themselves in the terms provided by the Greek dramatists.

It is especially fitting that the Irish turn to, and appropriate, the literature of civilisation: the Greek classics. To justify their colonisation, the English felt it was ideologically necessary to construe the Irish as barbarians. They drew the analogy that, just as the Romans had civilised them, they were in turn carrying out a sacred duty to do the same for the Irish. The pattern of subjection that they used in Ireland (seizure of lands, and de facto enslavement of the indigenous population to work the lands) was also followed in America, India, Africa and elsewhere. In our times the Irish writers have been using the very texts which are considered the epitome of civilisation to give literary expression to and aid their own drive for freedom and justice. Besides being inspirational, these texts are a refutation of the ideology which continues to prevail in British newspapers and literature. The Irish as a civilised people with their own unique culture and language are now demanding their justified rights.

With their genius for adaptation, the Irish make full use of the power of Greek tragedy, not only for the expression of personal feelings, but beyond that, as a vehicle for the expression of the Irish people and their public concerns. Each in his own way addresses "the Irish question". Ireland becomes England's Trojan women; its Medea exploited by Jason; its Antigone, who in the face of insufferable odds, does not falter, but retains a sense of justice. On the other hand, there is Seamus Heaney's *The Cure at Troy*, after *Philoctetes* by Sophocles, which espouses reconciliation between enemies.

Irish involvement with the Greeks is not new. One might compare the profound and peculiarly Irish interpretations of the classics by Yeats (particularly his translation of Sophocles) and Joyce with Brian Friel's classical meditations in his plays: in 1977 he wrote *Living Quarters* after Hippolytus. In my *Ancient Sun Modern Light: Greek Drama on the Modern Stage*, I point out the parallels between Tom Murphy's *The Sanctuary Lamp* and Aeschylus' *Oresteia*. There are other classical influences on Irish writers, including J. M. Synge, Oliver St. John Gogarty and Sean O'Casey. Pádraic Pearse made the revolutionary connection explicit when he spoke of the need for "The divine breath that moves through free peoples, the breath that no man of Ireland has felt in his nostrils for so many centuries, the breath that once blew through the streets of Athens that kindled, as wine kindles, the hearts of those who taught and learned in Clonmacnois".

Many have noted the political relevance of classical plays to contemporary issues. Mary Holland wrote of a performance of Sophocles' Electra in Derry: "At one level, last week was an awesome vindication of those who believe that this is what the arts should be about, and where they should be — close to the cutting edge of political argument. Fiona Shaw said: 'I do believe we must use the theatre to debate these dangerous issues — justice, retribution, violence'".

Each of these Irish playwrights has a particular approach towards Ireland's history and political situation, some more overtly than others.

Field Day Theatre first performed Tom Paulin's *The Riot Act: A Version of Antigone* by Sophocles at the Guildhall, Derry, on September 19, 1984. It uses the language of the Irish North to place us in its modern locale, and the ideas expressed translate well into the issues which divide Derry. Field Day was established to give a Northern voice to a number of divisive issues. Like Greek tragedy, Field Day speaks the unspeakable and makes visible the invisible. The first play that Field Day performed after its founding in 1980, did just this: Brian Friel's *Translations* was performed in Derry and dealt with the existential sense of the loss of Irish identity that came from the arbitrary British renaming of Irish locales. In Paulin's play the Northern accents shape the classical text, and the particular is joined with the universal. The theme is often justice: who has power over whom.

The words have resonance in the modern political context: Tiresias sounds the theme: "Now so much blood's been spilt/ there's none can call a halt /to those thrawn and jaggy hates /deep-rooted in your state". This idea of strife lasting for ages suits the Irish landscape. When Creon makes a speech he sounds like many a politician and Anthony Roche in 'Ireland's Antigones: Tragedy North and South' in *Cultural Contexts and Literary Idioms in Contemporary Irish Literature* (ed. Michael Kenneally) rightly noted the Northern accents: "We hear a verbal medley of the two reigning powers in Northern Ireland, Westminster and Unionism". Westminster stands for England, which since 1972 has been dominant in Northern Ireland, and Unionism is the movement led mainly by Northern Protestants to keep Northern Ireland linked with England as a part of Britain. Roche narrows the field further by seeing Ian Paisley (the vociferous Northern Irish Protestant and Unionist) in this role, since Creon is introduced by the chorus as "The big man". Roche sees Paulin as rewriting Conor Cruise O'Brien's heavy-handed endorsement of Creon's role in this play as a justified representative of conservatism: status quo *über Alles*.

Paulin's Creon switches to a prose that is more prosaic than the Greek and could fit a handbook for the "political speech". He says, "However, let me say this, and say it plainly right at the very outset, that if ever any man here should find himself faced with a choice between betraying his country and betraying his friend, then he must swiftly place that friend in the hands of the authorities". The padded rhetoric adds humour, if it weren't so tragically apt. One remembers the "supergrasses", those people suborned by the authorities to turn in their friends. The speech concludes, "Thank you all for coming, and any questions just now? We have one minute" (*Flashes stonewall smile*). This is hardly Sophocles, but Paulin giving us a politician. The parody reduces Creon's authority and his position as a valid counterbalance to Antigone. In Paulin's play, right is expressed in Antigone's words. The dialectic of Antigone's right (personal, familial) confronting Creon's right (social, political) — which Hegel and others have noticed in Sophocles' play — is destroyed by reducing Creon to a cardboard politician. But the tragedy returns as we realise the accurate portrayal of "Creon's" power in the North of Ireland. Seamus Deane in his *Preface* to *Selected Plays of Brian Friel* notes of the "official" language in Brian Friel's plays:

> Yet its official jargon represents something more and something worse than moral obtuseness. It also represents power, the one element lacking in the world of the victims where the language is so much more vivid and spontaneous.... The voice of power tells one kind of fiction — the lie. It has the purpose of preserving its own interests. The voice of powerlessness tells another kind of fiction — the illusion. It has the purpose of pretending that its own interests have been preserved. Antigone refuses to play the game, and dares to say the truth, so her words must be stifled.

Roche sees Antigone's loyalty to the family as parallel to the loyalty of Republicans (Catholic Irish who work towards a unified Ireland with equality and freedom for all) imprisoned and abused for their beliefs. Other Republicans who have suffered are like a family. He cites a Maze prisoner, "I am one of many who die for my country", adding, "Finding no point of sustained identification with the formal body of laws encoded in the North, Republican prisoners apprehended under those laws turn in a self-consciously ritualised and dramatic way to the extended family of those who have preceded them". Creon's laws are those of the city and state, and in Paulin's play those of Northern leaders; he lets us glimpse the city and state following the leader "whether right or wrong" (*Ant.* 667). Creon sows seeds for his own destruction, and we see the rot in his stated principle.

Three plays and one film by the Irish about Antigone were done in Ireland in 1984 by Tom Paulin, Brendan Kennelly, Aidan Carl Mathews, and Pat Murphy with his film *Anne Devlin*. In the same year Athol Fugard's *The Island* was performed at the Gate, another play based on Antigone. It shows two prisoners playing Antigone in prison to keep their sanity in the midst of the insanity of Apartheid, an unjust system of government in South Africa which deprived an entire segment of the population of their human rights. Anthony Roche and Christopher Murray have chapters on the 1984 Antigones in Ireland in two important books dealing with Irish literature and theatre. 1984 was important for human rights, and the rights of women in particular. This was the year the divorce referendum was rejected, just after abortion rights had been rejected, and the year when the Criminal Justice Bill gave increased rights to the police.

Paulin begins *Seize the Fire: A Version of Aeschylus' Prometheus Bound* with a quotation from Marx: "Prometheus is the foremost saint and martyr in the philosopher's calendar". He goes on to illustrate this and marries Aeschylus to Marx; the marriage is uncomfortable at some points, powerful at others. His play is a paean to liberty. Prometheus was purported to be the creator of man — and stole fire for man after Zeus took it away to punish this audacious race. Prometheus is the freedom-fighter who opposes tyranny; Zeus is the overweening tyrant. Paulin transforms Zeus into an imperialist, the capitalist who will use men as tools for his own self-aggrandisement. Zeus is also the England that devours Ireland for its own pleasure. Prometheus stands for all who oppose such barbaric acts. "Seizing the Fire" is a metaphor for regaining one's country, by the use of arms if necessary. It is a metaphor for gaining freedom not only from the tyranny of occupation, but the tyranny of dogma, and, of course — faithful to Marx — class. Prometheus calls himself one who loves man too much (*Pro*: 122). Paulin communicates the difference between Zeus the tyrant and Prometheus the democrat: "Zeus said Exterminate! /I said Miscegenate!" (Make love not war?) Power breeds hatred, or as Aeschylus has his Prometheus say, "There is a disease in tyranny that makes one distrust all one's friends", (*Pro*: 226-227). Paulin turns this into the biting line: "Power, it clamps like a frost on those that get it".

It is ironic that Prometheus is the healer who cannot heal himself, as the chorus point out (*Pro*: 474-5). Paulin transforms this by having Prometheus say he cannot free himself, although he brought freedom to man. This shows us the new emphasis with the disease being slavery as a legacy of imperialism. Zeus is shown to be a tyrant who tries to bribe Prometheus, sending Hermes with awards for Prometheus if he should reveal the secret only he knows: a threat to Zeus is about to be born. Other gods carry out his dirty work. Paulin's Hermes tries to bribe Prometheus with a medal, a post, and a title, "First Intellectual of the State". The chorus chime in, "The state's approval, /recognition — /that's what they'll give you!" Prometheus answers, "Just a contradiction! /They'd let me free /but freeze my mind". Hermes offers more bribes: a chateau and a place for writing, with the leisure time to go along with it (most writers' dream). It is the insidious bribe to an intellectual to sell himself to the state, what Julien Benda called, *la trahison des clercs*. When bribes do not work, Hermes adds the threat of torture. But for the hero and freedom fighter the sops are not enough when a feast is possible. Hermes asks Prometheus to sign, like Michael Collins, "It's there you'll sign /two public texts — /a recantation /and a treaty". We think of the present peace negotiations.

Paulin's Prometheus takes images from modern Ireland to make his points. Oceanus tells Prometheus, "I'll see you're freed". Prometheus answers, "More likely you'll get kneecapped". The tyrant Zeus excelled in a prison system, "a killing zone, /a meatgrinder". Paulin's Prometheus adds, "Had I not stole the fire /every last human body would be stacked up dead here". We see that Prometheus' fire might be the importation of arms to oppose the occupier. Prometheus goes on to describe a revolution that will force Zeus to come to him: "Tanks on the lawn, new blackouts, /locked doors and panic — /those empty sinister blocked roads...", and immediately the North of Ireland comes to mind. Paulin continually uses the past to interpret the present, and vice versa: he interweaves the strands of history to make his tapestry.

Aidan Carl Mathews is also overtly political in his *Antigone: A Version*. For instance, the audience was handed copies of the Criminal Justice Bill (mentioned above) at the first performance in Dublin's Project Arts Centre, 1984. It is obvious that it represented a violation of human rights, and the *Antigone* serves to remind one that in the face of such violations, human beings always possess the power to express their discontent. The text of this Bill was read at the end of the first act, and during the intermission, so the lines between past and present, audience and stage, were purposefully blurred. Mathews' *Antigone* is a quiet one, who lets others rant and rave about her, exercising their various forms of power. Her power is in her silent indictment, which she is able to articulate indirectly through her own life. One thinks of the many hunger strikers in Ireland who joined the "family" of others who gave their lives for Ireland.

Mathews' *Antigone* paints the letter P on walls, and for defacing the walls — and trying to stir memories — she is executed. In this play one brother is called Peteocles and the other Polyneices, so when she writes P, it can refer to either brother. Antigone underlines the similarity and a Marxist message is apparent in her actions. She does this to counter the fascist, who must maintain difference as his *raison d'être*. As in all of these plays, freedom of speech and the suppression of words are important issues. This is vital for the Catholic Irish, whose own speech, whether Gaelic or political, has so often been suppressed, rewritten, or distorted. Even political figures in Sinn Fein had their real voices dubbed when they spoke on public networks. Stifling the voice is well known in Ireland as a form of censorship.

Kennelly's *Antigone* shows us Creon as *Cromwell*, the man responsible for murdering what is thought to be one quarter of the population of Ireland in the 17th century. Kennelly has written a book of poetry called *Cromwell* and we find echoes of the earlier poetry in this play. Roche noted this and refers to the chorus in the Antigone saying to Creon, "You have the power to turn your words to action". He adds, "This same 'power' is attributed to Cromwell in Kennelly's poem". We also see

Jason as Cromwell in Kennelly's *Medea*. Jason is cut from the British mould, using self-righteous words that suit Cromwell, and Kennelly staged a version of *Cromwell* in 1986.

Another theme that sets Kennelly's *Medea* clearly in Ireland is that of exile: "Exile is the worst form of living death". So many Irish were exiled, either because their land was confiscated, or because of their poverty. Jason throws in Medea's face: "our savage language has guaranteed your exile... /Exile is hard". The British would often call the Irish savage, and imply that they had earned their exile, whereas the civilised language of the British themselves created true savagery.

Marina Carr's *Medea* (*By the Bog of Cats*) also is an outcast, and one of the "tinkers" ostracised by those better off. Her solution besides vengeance is suicide with herself and her daughter. How often the Irish solution is a living suicide in drink, or other forms of self-destruction. Self-hatred and self-mutilation can result from an internalisation of the coloniser's negative construction of the colonised. In Carr's play death is a refuge for the mother and daughter, a place where they can be free from patriarchy.

Kennelly's *Antigone* says that she has more love for the mistreated noble dead than for the ambitious living. We remember the words of Pádraic Pearse, "The fools, the fools, the fools, they left us our Fenian dead". They inspire the living to fight to make Ireland free. Antigone's acts lead to the downfall of a tyrant, and she also was inspired by the dead of her past. McGuinness' *Electra* is also one who, through memory of the past, fights back against present oppression

Money in Kennelly's *Antigone* is seen as problematic: "Money is the greatest evil men have known. /Maddens men from their homes /Money destroys cities /Twists decent souls till they /will do any shameful thing". During the potato famine (ca. 1846-50) the Irish starved because they had to pay exorbitant rents. Grain stored in towers for export rotted, and a Quaker gift of grain was diverted from the Irish needy to English merchants. The English landlords went unscathed, and reports from Ireland were said to be "greatly exaggerated". Undeniably, Ireland's history is one of poverty. The Irish were not imperialists, but victims of imperialism. As one sees one's child starving, betrayal of one's country becomes possible, and the English, like many other imperialists, knew this. Kennelly's words resonate, as Marxism did for many of the people. Sophocles' reference to money in Creon's speech is expanded to a lamentation, and the Irish understood.

In Kennelly's *Medea* there is not only the rage of woman towards man, but parables of another rage: just as Jason exploited and victimised Medea, England exploited and victimised Ireland. Medea is the Aisling (a typical Irish spirit that often represents Ireland) that hates and destroys. She gave everything to Jason, but he was unworthy because he lied and cheated. In vengeance she killed her own children, and Ireland, until recently, was killing her children in her own agony of vengeance.

Kennelly talks about betrayal as "the ripest crop in this land". The betrayal is not only found among the enemy, but worse, among friends — the informer co-opted in the service of the enemy. Mahon in his translation of Racine's *Phèdre* shows us betrayal and lies once again. The Catholic church colours much of the language in Kennelly's plays, as it does Mathews', Heaney's, and Mahon's. Gods become God, and prayers, curses and blessings resonate from antiquity to modern times. Jason is said to have violated Heaven's laws (*Med.* 33), and whereas Euripides has Jason mention prayer once in his reply to Medea, Kennelly expatiates on prayer. Jason tells Medea: "Pray to make sense of the swirling world". She answers:

> Your prayer for sense —
> the commonest of common sense —
> is an insult. Prayer is not
> a way of coping with fools.
> Prayer is for dealing with the injustice caused by fools...
> Prayer, my plausible friend, is
> anger at what is, and a longing
> for what should be.
> Prayer is a bomb at the door of your house.

Prayer returns us to the Irish question. Prayer can lead to acts. As the nurse says, "Medea knows the meaning of prayer. /She knows the meaning of revenge". In this play we find the opposite of Heaney's *Cure at Troy*, which urged the cure of the wound: "Believe in miracles, believe in healing wells and cures". Here Medea/Ireland takes poison from her wound so that she can get her revenge.

In Mahon's *Bacchae: After Euripides* we also find the Catholic Church, and here, as it did during the Crusades, it sanctions a Holy War. Politics and the church have always had an uneasy alliance in Ireland, as elsewhere. Dionysus also is associated with Christ, with his title, "Lord of the Dance". One remembers the popular Irish song describing Christ coming to earth to save mankind and to lead them in the dance of salvation.

Brendan Kennelly's *Trojan Women: A New Version* is a play about suffering. Captive women are hauled off to slavery, and when they feel they can suffer nothing worse than the loss of their country, they learn there is more: they can lose their lifeblood — their children. This is a story for Ireland: it is well understood there because they have lived it.

The history of Ireland validates many observations:

> Freedom is like health -
> you never know it until you've lost it.
> People of my heart, do everything you can
> to banish war
> from the lives of women, men and children.
> But if war comes to the land
> like a murderous brute into your house
> and you find that you must fight
> then fight like people who have found
> their special light,
> there's no evil in that fight.
> There's nothing more dangerous to a winner
> than one seed of hope in the heart of the loser.

Seamus Heaney's artfully crafted *The Cure at Troy* proceeds from, and ends in, optimism. It is a version that truly urges and believes, and hopes "for a great sea-change /On the far side of revenge/... that a further shore is reachable from here".

The chorus at the beginning and end of the play places us in the middle of the Irish problem:

> Heroes. Victims. Gods and human beings.
> All throwing shapes, every one of them
> Convinced he's in the right, all of them glad
> To repeat themselves and their every last mistake,
> No matter what.
> People so deep into
> Their own self-pity self-pity buoys them up.
> People so staunch and true, they're fixated,
> Shining with self-regard like polished stones.
> And their whole life spent admiring themselves
> For their own long-suffering.
> Licking their wounds
> And flashing them around like decorations.
> I hate it, I always hated it, and I am
> A part of it myself.
> And a part of you,
> For my part is the chorus, and the chorus
> Is more or less a borderline between
> The you and the me and the it of it.

This is an exposition that not only locates the chorus in its mediating function, but lays out the theme of the play: a focus on the wound, rather than the cure. The play is about a man with a wound, and he will be cured at Troy. But Troy is a place only discussed in the play: Philoctetes' intent is finally to go there, but the wound and Lemnos are what is shown. It is obvious that this is Ireland and the Irish who have suffered.

Heaney's optimism shines at the end in a speech delivered by the chorus leader. These words are not in Sophocles, but in modern Ireland:

> Human beings suffer,
> They torture one another,
> They get hurt and get hard.
> No poem or play or song
> Can fully right a wrong
> Inflicted and endured.
> The innocent in gaols
> Beat on their bars together.
> A hunger-striker's father
> Stands in the graveyard dumb.
> The police widow in veils
> Faints at the funeral home.
> History says, Don't hope
> On this side of the grave.
> But then, once in a lifetime
> The longed-for tidal wave
> Of justice can rise up,
> And hope and history rhyme.

The sufferings on both sides are mentioned: the hunger-striker is a Republican who dies in protest while imprisoned by the British or Unionists. The police widow mourns her dead husband who supported the Unionist regime. The hope is for a peaceful settlement, and a healing of the wound of hate. We can see Yeats' image from 'Easter 1916', "Too long a sacrifice can make a stone of the heart", in Heaney's "Human beings suffer, /They torture one another /They get hurt and get hard". All these images derive from Ireland's history.

Derek Mahon's *Bacchae: After Euripides* is also a parable suitable for Ireland. Dionysus can be regarded as a force of nature, the force of a people who are fighting to reclaim their rights — a people who are laying claim to a land that has been taken from them. This simple act of reclamation harbours the potential for great violence. There is a chorus in his *Bacchae* in which the Asian Bacchantes describe the pleasure of holding one's hand over the head of a conquered foe:

> What pleases best, what grand
> gift can the gods bestow
> more than the conquering hand

over the fallen foe?
It's still the same old story,
a fight for love and glory,
and every heart admits that this is so!

Mahon places this appeal within his play in a position corresponding to where Euripides placed it, but it also concludes Mahon's play, so the final note is one of vengeance in contrast to Euripides' more formulaic conclusion attributing power to the gods and the unexpected. Part of the tragedy in these Irish reworkings is history itself, and Mahon's lines beat with the lifeblood of passion.

Aeschylus' *Agamemnon* was directed by Michael Scott in Dublin. Agamemnon was faced by the terrible dilemma of paying for a war with the life of his child, Iphigenia. This leads to vengeance by her mother, who murders Agamemnon, and so the bloody cycle continues. Euripides' Iphigenia is sacrificed by her father for political expediency; she is a symbol of all children sacrificed in wars. The mother who is deprived of her child, however will fight back.

Now Irish poets exaggerate and excise in accordance with their dreams. Some poets seem to urge restraint, and avoidance of the horrors that have just been seen on stage; others, whereas they may not advocate imitation, stress the nobility of the passions depicted. It is a measure of the Irish civilisation that it, like the Greek, completely integrates art into society and politics, that it is a true *polis* where all important issues are defined in art as well as in the forums of power.

Words indeed shape the future, and since they have been used long enough against Ireland, perhaps now Ireland can reclaim them as its own weapons. The world can arm itself with words that communicate, educate and enthral: an entertaining play works. An informed future must be modelled on lessons from the past, and drama provides the impetus for change.

Theatre History and the Beginnings of the
Irish National Theatre Project
Lionel Pilkington

One of the surprising features of Irish theatre history and criticism is its apparent immunity from the changing conventions of historiography in general. If history writing in Ireland has been dominated for the last 30 years by 'revisionism' — an intellectual movement that defines itself as an objective critique of the orthodoxies of pietistic nationalism — it is odd that no parallel movement may be detected in relation to the Irish theatre. Indeed, the very opposite is the case: for most Irish theatre anthologies and theatre history the focus is exclusively on the national theatre tradition of the 20th century. Beginning with accounts of the first productions of the Irish Literary Theatre on 8 May 1899, historians and anthologisers start their discussions with assessments of the work of the principal contributors to the early Abbey Theatre, W.B. Yeats, J.M. Synge and Augusta Gregory. In all of this, Brian Friel's 1972 claim that no Irish theatre existed prior to 1899 remains the foundational assumption.

Notwithstanding recent scholarly work by John P. Harrington on Dion Boucicault's Irish trilogy, Stephen Watt's and Cheryl Herr's consideration of nationalist melodramas performed at the Queen's Royal Theatre in the 1880s and 1890s, and Adrian Frazier's excellent pioneering study of the extent to which the cultural agenda of the Abbey Theatre between 1904 and 1909 was constrained by its patron, Annie Horniman, and her virulent *opposition* to nationalism, the narrative of Irish theatre history and criticism operates with its nationalist assumptions firmly intact. Irish theatre history and commentary is, on the whole, a story of the establishment and development of Ireland's official national theatre project — the Irish National Theatre Society, Limited — at the Abbey Theatre. In this brief essay I want to consider some of the implications of this emphasis in terms of what is thereby excluded from the Irish theatre canon, and in terms of its implications for theatre history.

Perhaps the most obvious consequence of the presumption that indigenous theatre in Ireland begins in 1899 is the imposition of an artificial insularity on Irish theatre history and the exclusion from the Irish dramatic canon of a working-class and popular theatre tradition. From the 1860s, for example, plays such as those performed at Dublin's Gaiety and Queen's Royal Theatre routinely included melodramas that were both sympathetic to Irish nationalism and were also part of an extensive touring circuit that included provincial English cities and, in some cases, North American venues like New York and Montreal.

Despite the Gaiety's still prominent Vice-Regal box and its continuing support for charity performances in aid of the victims of anti-government outrages and despite the flagrant loyalism implicit in the very name of the Queen's Royal Theatre, the growing popularity of plays such as Dion Boucicault's *The Colleen Bawn* (1860), *Arrah na Pogue* (1864) and *The Shaughraun* (1874) or J.W. Whitbread's *Lord Edward, or '98* (1894) and *Wolfe Tone* (1898) attest to the prestige and currency of an emerging nationalist cultural discourse.

What was taking place simultaneously in Dublin in the last quarter of the 19th century was a change in the meaning of national theatre itself. Whereas in 1870, for example, Dublin's Royal Theatre was described as 'Ireland's national theatre' on the basis that it was then the Dublin theatre most patronized by the British Lord Lieutenant and the officialdom of Dublin Castle, by the 1880s and 1890s the term 'national' had acquired a more democratic nuance, and was increasingly seen as a term appropriate only to institutions whose subject matter or composition were representatively Irish. Thus while Boucicault's Irish plays tend to be derided by subsequent Irish theatre historians and commentators (Friel's 1972 article notes dismissively that "Boucicault capers on the Abbey stage"), these and other nationalist melodramas fulfilled a vitally important cultural function. As Harrington so ably points out, such plays functioned as an important counterweight to the misrepresentation of Irish character on the English stage and thus helped to prepare the way for the possibility of a somewhat more independent Irish theatre.

But if the omission of Irish nationalist melodramas in the late 19th century has at least been acknowledged by some theatre scholars, a far more radical exclusion from the canon of Irish drama is the tradition of mumming and folk drama. Thanks not to theatre commentators but to the work of anthropologists and social historians, we now know that mumming and folk drama was a major feature in the cultural life of the rural working class in Ireland in the 18th and 19th centuries, and that part of the significance of mumming lay in its close imbrication with the fissiparous symbolic and organizational life of agrarian insurgency groups like the Whiteboys. Not only did such groups share with the mummers similar costumes (usually women's clothing or white smocks) and a roughly simultaneous occurrence during the year (May Eve, November Eve, St. Stephen's Day, New Year's Eve), but there were important crossovers in their methods of recruitment and performance.

The administration of Whiteboy oaths of allegiance across a community and performances by the mummers took place by means of surprise nocturnal visits, the power and effect of which was partly determined by the extent to which the mummers/insurgents functioned metonymically for the community as a whole. Since the masked insurgent/mummer requesting political allegiance/ admittance for performance could represent *anyone* within the community, the person addressed by the mummers or Whiteboys was, to this extent, answerable to the community as a whole. In this way also, a key element of mumming performance is fundamentally at odds with the metaphoric tendency and codes of the traditional theatre in which the unmasked actor is *supposed* by the audience to be the character that she/he is portraying. Moreover, mumming performances were initiated not by the purchase of a ticket — as in the capitalist orientation of the institutional theatre — but rather by the audience's invitation to begin, while the content of mumming was regularly adjusted according to the time, locality and circumstances of performance.

The institutional or traditional theatre, of course, works quite differently: here, the excellence of a given performance depends on its iterability and there is at all times an essential *disregard* for the contingencies of time and space. An audience's experience of a particular production, that is, will or should be exactly the same whether the production takes place in Derry, Rathmines, or Skibbereen. In short, the institutional theatre works according to a symbolic logic that harmonizes with a nationalism predicated in terms of the state and centralized in orientation. Nationalism and the institutional theatre, that is, both seek to evoke in the citizen/spectator an ideal and unifying response that is independent of time and locality whereas mumming may be described as operating according to a symbolic logic that is primarily concerned with the renewal of local solidarities. The extent to which mumming and the institutional theatre are fundamentally at variance with each other in terms of symbolic and cultural logic helps to explain the extent to which the former has been so rigorously excluded from the Irish theatre canon. Regarded as incompatible with nationalist development and cultural modernization, mumming and folk drama is seen as belonging to Ireland's pre-literate oral culture and, therefore, as not properly "theatre".

One reason why Irish theatre is said to begin with the Irish Literary Theatre in 1899 is because the theatre that existed in Ireland prior to that date is thought to have been so compromised by Anglicisation as to be incapable of being described as indigenous. The Irish Literary Theatre is considered as a cultural watershed because this was the first time in Irish history that there existed a self-consciously Irish theatre institution dealing with Irish subjects for Irish audiences. Previous theatre in Ireland, it is argued, was so closely linked to Ireland's colonial administrative apparatus and to a provincial touring network of which London was the metropolitan centre that, insofar as such theatre bothered to represent Ireland at all, it did so in terms of stereotype and caricature. Against this background, Yeats and Gregory successfully construed the Irish Literary Theatre as an act of heroic anti-colonial defiance — a cultural project that bravely contrasted with what Yeats in particular portrayed as the stodgy, unionist recalcitrance of Dublin's Trinity College.

Despite the tenaciousness of this scenario in Irish cultural history and its acceptance by commentators as diverse as Augustine Birrell and Eamonn de Valera, the actual situation is more complicated. True, the Irish Literary Theatre represented a nationalist initiative not only in the anti-colonial bravura of its stated ambition to "show that Ireland is not the home of buffoonery and easy sentiment as it has been represented, but the home of an ancient idealism", but in its declared emphasis on plays dealing with Irish legends (e.g., Yeats' *The Countess Cathleen*, Alice Milligan's *The Last Feast of the Fianna* and *Maeve*) and with contemporary social issues (e.g., Martyn's *The Heather Field* and Moore and Martyn's *The Bending of the Bough*). But in many other respects the nationalism of the Irish Literary Theatre was itself severely compromised. Not only were its opening productions performed by a visiting English theatre company (Frank Benson's acting troupe), but the première of Yeats' inaugural play, *The Countess Cathleen*, had been pre-empted a few months earlier when it was presented as a series of fashionable *tableaux vivants* at the Dublin home of the British Lord Lieutenant. In addition, the critical successes of the Irish Literary Theatre and the Abbey Theatre were to some extent determined by their reception at performances that took place in England. And while the cultural project of the Irish Literary Theatre was determinedly Irish, it also owed its existence to the support, patronage and leisure time of Ireland's ascendancy. Indeed, the principal initiators of the theatre were either prominent West of Ireland landowners like Lady Gregory, George Moore, and Edward Martyn or, as in the case of W.B. Yeats, belonged to a Protestant middle class who supported the idea of an ascendancy elite. The pronoun in the title of Gregory's famous account of the national theatre project, her book *Our Irish Theatre* (1913), is, to this extent, weighted with irony: the national theatre project is "Ours" in the sense that it belongs to everybody in the nation, but it is also "Ours" in the sense that it was initiated, owned, and operated by Ireland's traditional ruling elite.

To insist that Irish theatre begins in 1899, then, ignores the considerable extent to which the national theatre movement was concerned with preserving — by means of ideological renovation — the continuity of Ireland's leadership minority. That the enabling legislation for the Irish Literary Theatre — the 1898 Local Government Act — was also the legislation that abolished the Grand Jury system of local administration in Ireland and replaced it with locally elected county councilors is not, therefore, a coincidence. "Confident of the support of all Irish people, who are weary of misrepresentation, in carrying out a work that is outside all the political questions that divide us", the Irish Literary Theatre functioned as a means by which the social and political leadership role of a section of the southern Irish landlord class could find expression as champions of modernization rather than stand out as colonial anachronisms and remain vulnerable to the now much expanded, increasingly confident, and predominantly Roman Catholic, Irish electorate. In these respects, therefore, the national theatre project should be seen not exclusively as a *nationalist* cultural measure but also as a southern *unionist* one: a conciliatory or assimilative cultural project designed to affirm a leadership role for a minority elite in Irish society and culture at a time when the political and economic supports for this role were fast disappearing. Like earlier conciliatory initiatives by intellectuals and politicians associated with southern unionism in the 1890s — initiatives like Sir Horace Plunkett's Recess Committee and his cross-party campaign on taxation — the Irish Literary Theatre received extensive nationalist support.

Notwithstanding the controversial anti-Catholicism of Yeats' *The Countess Cathleen* — one scene in the play has a character crush underfoot a Catholic religious icon — constitutional nationalists expressed initial enthusiastic endorsement. For Arthur Griffith's *United Irishman* as well as Parnellite organs such as the *New Ireland Review* and the weekly *Independent*, a national theatre institution was an important indication of Ireland's cultural modernization. It demonstrated that Dublin's metropolitan prestige was on a par with other European capitals and thus underlined the necessity for some form of political independence or devolution. A national theatre, modeled according to the audience decorums of European art theatres like the Théâtre Libre in Paris or the Moscow Art Theatre, served as a microcosm for the longed-for nation state in which the citizen would delegate political power to his/her parliamentary representatives. In short, the ideological success of the Irish Literary Theatre was that it lent legitimacy to a modernizing scion of Ireland's landlord class *as well as* fulfilling the requirements of an increasingly self-confident constitutional nationalism. For both groupings the theatre was thought of as an ideal form, dissolving political conflict in the context of an overarching national ideal and reinforcing traditional structures of authority. In the theatre — or so it was hoped — spectators would behave not like a crowd, but like individual citizens, maturely suspending their personal circumstances and vested interests within the context of a national ideal. Yeats put it succinctly in his famous misquotation from Victor Hugo: "In the theatre, the mob becomes a people".

In terms of narrative preoccupation, Irish national drama in its early years is concerned with portraying those features of Irish culture that were perceived as recalcitrant to modernity — issues such as agrarian insurgency, the 1798 rebellion, or the folk beliefs, practices and superstitions of the peasantry — so that these appear either as consistent with the nationalist struggle for political independence or as bizarre reminders of atavisms that must be elegized or repudiated. In Gregory's and Yeats' *Cathleen ní Houlihan* (1902), for example, Michael Gillane's conversion to republicanism is rendered not as an education or empowerment but as a sublimation and surrender. Ironically this celebrated nationalist drama shows politicisation as amounting to a loss of individual agency and volition. Here, as in several other plays of the period, social divisions experienced in terms of class or gender inequality seem to disappear in a puff of nationalist transcendence. An ironic twist to this process of national modernization is offered in the plays of J. M. Synge, the majority of which were written at a time when constructive unionist cooperation with constitutional nationalism had collapsed in a welter of sectarian recrimination. While in *Riders to the Sea* (1902) rural life in the West of Ireland is shown as caught in a doomed, atavistic cycle outside of modernity, in *The Playboy of the Western World* (1907) Pegeen Mike's final illumination — "there's a great gap between a gallous story and a dirty deed" — articulates the audience's similar recognition of the disparity between the sordid physical immediacy of violence and its glamourization by the same oral-based peasant culture so valorized by the nationalist movement. In this context, it was entirely unsurprising that contemporary audiences reacted with such outrage to *The Playboy of the Western World*. As the theatre critic for the *Irish Times* remarked in 1907, Synge's play "led our vision through the Abbey street stage into the heart of Connaught, and revealed to us there truly terrible truths, *of our own making*, which we dare not face for the present" (my emphasis). Once the Irish state is established in 1922, the dominant narrative of the drama changes briefly to an even more polemical register: in Sean O'Casey's Dublin trilogy and in Denis Johnston's *The Old Lady Says, 'NO'!* (1929) and *The Moon in the Yellow River* (1931) republican resistance against the state is excoriated by rendering it incompatible with the humanity of the individual. Indeed, this — the statist orientation of Irish drama — might be described as a perennial characteristic. As Nicholas Grene points out in a perceptive 1986 article, the attempt to "de-dramatise" political violence (and most especially republican political violence against the state) amounts in Irish drama to "a distinctive theatrical tradition". In this respect, Grene argues, plays as diverse as Sean O'Casey's *The Plough and the Stars*, Denis Johnston's *Moon in the Yellow River*, Brendan Behan's *The Hostage* and Brian Friel's *The Freedom of the City* may each be described as counter-revolutionary.

One reason why a revisionist critique has not been applied to the nationalist assumptions of the Irish national theatre tradition, then, is because revisionism, like the national theatre tradition itself, shares a fundamental belief in the modernizing power of the state. To this extent a revisionist critique of Ireland's national theatre tradition would be tautological. And yet, and as I have tried to argue, continuing to think of the Irish theatre as an exclusively nationalist phenomenon obscures the complexity of its cultural origins and social context, and narrows our idea of what may be considered as theatre as such. Whatever about the political limitations of contemporary Irish revisionism, the time for a radical reassessment of Irish theatre history is long overdue.

> * Part of this essay draws on my earlier "Irish Theater Historiography and Political Resistance" in Jeanne Colleran and Jenny S. Spencer (eds), *Staging Resistance: Essays on Political Theater* (Ann Arbor: University of Michigan Press, 1998) 13-30.

Works Cited:

Friel, Brian, (1972), "Plays Peasant and Unpeasant", *Times Literary Supplement*, 17 March 1972: 305-06

Frazier, Adrian, (1990), *Behind the Scenes: Yeats, Horniman, and the Struggle for the Abbey Theatre* (Berkeley: University of California Press)

Gregory, Augusta, (1913), *Our Irish Theatre* (London: G.P. Putnam's Sons)

Grene, Nicholas, (1986), "Distancing Drama: Sean O'Casey to Brian Friel" in *Irish Writers and the Theatre*, edited by Masaru Sekine (Gerrards Cross, Bucks.: Colin Smythe, 1986) 47-70

Harrington, John P., (1995), " 'Rude Involvement': Boucicault, Dramatic Tradition, and Contemporary Politics", *Éire-Ireland* 30.2, (Summer 1995), 89-103

Herr, Cheryl, (1991), *For the Land they Loved: Irish Political Melodramas, 1890-1925* (Syracuse: Syracuse University Press)

Watt, Stephen, (1991), *Yeats, O'Casey, and the Irish Popular Theater* (Syracuse: Syracuse University Press)

Gender, Authorship and Performance in Selected Plays by Contemporary Irish Women Playwrights: Mary Elizabeth Burke-Kennedy, Marie Jones, Marina Carr, Emma Donoghue.

Anna McMullan

During the twentieth century, the staging of the Irish nation's struggles to define itself was primarily in the hands of male authors from W.B. Yeats to Brian Friel. The absence of women from the national pantheon of playwrights does not necessarily mean that Irish women do not write plays, but that for a variety of reasons, Irish women playwrights in the past have had no place in the selection of playwrights and texts that the culture has endorsed as being of significance and value. These selected texts, often referred to collectively as a "canon", are presented in established venues, and are circulated, published, re-produced, studied and written about. They often refer to each other, drawing on a literary and dramatic heritage which extends back through Western culture to ancient Greece. That heritage is largely shared between men — when women authors have been recorded in Western theatre history it has been as rare exceptions. Until recently, the only woman who figured in the Irish theatrical canon was Lady Augusta Gregory, and then mainly as co-founder of the Abbey Theatre rather than as a playwright.

C.L. Innes suggests that the dominance of the male literary writer in Irish culture is linked to the Modernist emphasis on the role of the individual artist in contesting dominant models of authority. In *Woman and Nation in Irish Literature and Society 1880-1935*, she refers to the focus of most Irish critics on

> Irish modernism, and their interest in the obsessive intertwining by Yeats and Joyce of their own unfolding identities with the creation of an Irish identity.... Male critics and male writers alike have also been absorbed into the 'family romance' which becomes linked to the colonial relationship; their concern is to challenge the authority of the father — the colonial power and the colonial cultural hegemony and tradition. Women writers and critics have often been marginalized in this contestation and struggle for authority (Innes: 1993, 4).

However, the parameters of Irish dramatic authorship are currently being renegotiated. Traditional issues of identity, politics, authority, dispossession, language and history are being redefined through the re-evaluation of the work of earlier women playwrights, including Lady Gregory and Teresa Deevy, and in the work of the current generation of women writers. Women playwrights are reclaiming the theatre as a space where they can explore the relationship between the public and the private, the political and the personal, sexuality and gender on their own terms.

The traditional canon is also being challenged by the increasing diversity of theatre practice in Ireland (See Bort, ed.: 1996). These theatre forms, including Theatre in Education and community theatre, are often geared towards particular, rather than "universal" audiences, and use a variety of modes of theatrical authorship, where members of the company and the community may have an input into the text through improvisation sessions or collaborative creation. Since the origins of the modern Irish theatre movement, women have been involved in collaborative theatre making. Such working practices in theatre or culture tend not to be recognised according to the traditional criteria of authorship. Writing of the decades preceding and following the founding of the nation, C.L. Innes notes that:

> An approach to history and to political change as the work of groups rather than individual personalities, articulated by Anna Parnell, also typifies much literary and cultural activity carried on by women with a commitment to Irish nationalism. Here too, the merging of individual identities, or rather, the lack of concern about personal acclaim, is noteworthy.... Too often critics have taken the self-effacement of such women writers as an excuse for ignoring them (Innes: 1993, 125, 127).

In the contemporary theatre scene, many women are involved in non-traditional theatre forms, including those which are educational or community based. There is an increasing recognition of difference within the nation, and that there are many different audiences, with different needs and expectations. Jill Dolan emphasizes that: "Canons, by implication, exclude not only worthy plays but worthy spectators on the basis of their ideological perspectives.... A useful by-product of the deconstruction of traditional canons will be the dismembering of the generic spectator whom the dramatic canons once addressed" (Dolan: 1993, 40). Many Irish playwrights, male and female, established and emergent, work with communities helping them to explore their experiences, conflicts and traumas through the languages and structures of theatre.

Charabanc, a Belfast based professional theatre group with a strong community base, was founded by five out of work actresses and operated from 1983 — 1995. They brought in the playwright Martin Lynch to help them script their first play, *Lay Up Your Ends,* but he encouraged them to find their own voices (See Harris: 1996). They carried out research on women working in the former Belfast linen mills, where the play was set, and this community research became characteristic of their future work. They foregrounded frequently anarchic humour and the use of non-literary and popular forms in their work, in order to address an audience who would not usually go to the theatre. Through the research and devising processes Marie Jones, one of the founder members, emerged as an author in her own right. In an interview with Luke Clancy, she speaks of her responsibility to her audience: "The people I write for are the people in my plays. They are really just ordinary people who are really are powerless; who really don't have a voice. I've always felt that I have this huge responsibility, because the background I came up in nobody had any power, nobody had any voice" (Jones: *Irish Times*, February 20th, 1996).

While women are involved in a range of theatre practices in Ireland, women remain underrepresented in the profession of playwriting. The reasons for this may include lack of resources, alienation from traditional working practices and forms of authorship in the theatre, and a lack of engagement with women's playwriting in the channels of public discourse. This is beginning to change, and there is a growing interest in the perspectives on identity, sexuality and the legacies of myth and history which Irish women playwrights have presented. The playwrights whose work I shall be looking at in more detail below contest traditional stereotypes of women as a-sexual self-sacrificing mothers, powerless victims, or sexual comforts. Women are centre stage, propelling the action, and forcefully articulating their subjectivity and their sexuality. These playwrights present a range of theatre languages and often exploit the corporeal medium of performance to destabilize traditional concepts of gender.

Mary Elizabeth Burke-Kennedy worked in Focus Theatre, Dublin, as an actress and became resident director from 1976 to 1983, when she founded Storytellers Theatre Company. Several of her plays have been based on the material of Irish folk tales and mythology. *Women in Arms* was shortlisted for the Anglo-American Susan Smith Blackburn Award at the time of its first production by Cork Theatre Company in 1984. This play tells the story of four of the major female figures from the Ulster cycle of stories in Irish mythology: Nessa, Macha, Deirdre, and the proud warrior queen, Maeve. They are variously positioned in relation to authority and handle power differently.

The once gentle Essa, intellectual and writer, is rechristened Nessa, the tough one, after her humiliation at the macho court of King Fergus, and, on her return, she discovers her home in ruins and her beloved twelve tutors murdered. In spite of her father's warning that "there was nothing she — a woman — could do in the circumstances" (unpublished typescript), she becomes a warrior, meets Cathbad the Druid, unbeknownst to her the slayer of her tutors, and has a child by him.

Cathbad is a renowned prophet and guardian of secret knowledges which he passes on to Nessa. Nessa's skill therefore lies not only in physical prowess but in her use of the knowledges she has acquired. Thus armed, she arrives at Fergus' court, seduces him and marries him. Thereupon, she insists that her son, Conchubar, is king for a year, during which time she wields the real power, and does so so successfully, that Fergus is unable to recover his kingship again. Through her young son, she rules Ulster, using her power with her knowledge to maintain her own position and to civilize the land, at once manipulative ruler and benevolent educator:

> **NESSA:** She supervised the building of the three houses of Eamhain Macha. The Red Branch House became famous for civilized entertainment.
> **MAEVE:** No more orgies.
> **NAOISE:** Weapons were kept in the second branch. Drink in the third.
> **DEIRDRE:** Bronze mirrors in Conchobar's apartment; spies in every other.
> **MACHA:** She encouraged the visitations of poets and musicians.
> **DEIRDRE:** She 'invited' the women to take instruction.

In the second story, Macha appears to Cruinniuc, the farmer, and his sons: "She poked up the fire, swept the hearth and laid her hand, companionably, on his thigh". She warns her new family not to speak of her, but, during a festival held in honour of the new king Conchobar, from which she is absent because heavily pregnant, Cruinniuc cannot contain a boast that Macha can run faster than the King's magnificent horses. Reluctantly, Macha runs and wins the race, but, as she gives birth to twins immediately afterwards, she curses the warriors of Ulster. Her curse condemns them to experience the agony of childbirth just as they are preparing to go into battle, transforming the traditional suffering of women into a powerful weapon.

Mary Elizabeth Burke Kennedy's Deirdre is neither tragic heroine nor treacherous seductress — some of the roles she has played in numerous retellings of the myth. Maire Herbert emphasizes that the material of Celtic myth was "protean, reflecting the manner in which the theme was constantly reworked throughout the centuries, to suit the changing circumstances in which it was being re-counted" (Herbert: 1991, 14). This Deirdre is determined and sure of what she wants, trusting her own sexuality and emotional responses. She runs away from the fortress where the King Conchobar is keeping her until he can marry her, because he was beginning to stifle her, and his lust repelled her. Conchobar's, and indeed, other powerful men's desire to possess Deirdre is seen as instrumental in the disaster. When she is a young girl,

Conchobar tells her the countryside she loves will be hers as his bride. Deirdre comments: "That meant nothing to her. Owning it. Older people were always on about ownership. Just be". The economy of patriarchal ownership over land and women is opposed to Deirdre's unselfish and uncalculated responses:

> FERGUS: They loved her without reservation, for that was how she gave her own love.

(This opposition is similar to the French writer, Helene Cixous' opposition between the masculine economy of the Proper (propriety, ownership, calculated measurement of assets) and the feminine economy of the Gift. For a discussion of this see Toril Moi: 1985, 110-13.)

When Naoise and his brothers are killed by Conchobar on their return, despite his promises of forgiveness, Deirdre is again imprisoned by Conchobar. Exasperated by her refusal of him, he orders her to be exchanged between him and the man who killed Naoise. Deirdre kills herself rather than become "a ewe between two rams", thereby taking her destiny into her own hands by the only means available to her.

In the next and final story, we see that women can also become obsessed with ownership and rivalry. Like the other three women, Queen Maeve is comfortable with her active sexuality:

> MAEVE: Maeve was the queen of Connaught; a warm-hearted hospitable woman, as every man who ever stayed at her house could testify, for she went out of her way to fill his plate, his goblet and his bed. And the one man was never enough for her.

She is the equal of her husband, Ailill, in wealth and possessions, and they are "delighted with each other", until it is discovered that Ailill has in his herd a magnificent bull, which Maeve cannot match. She sends an expedition to Ulster to bring back their famous bull, the Dun Bo Cuailnge, and a bloody war ensues.

These figures are all strong influential women who have left their mark on Irish myth and history. They contrast with the highly feminised images which emerged during the nineteenth century, as women became symbols of a national loss of authority under the imperial rule of England. Citing Lorna Reynolds, Lyn Innes refers to the "change from one kind of society to another, in which the powerful and sovereign Mother-goddess figure of Maeve is supplanted by a romantic and tragic heroine in a society where women lose their rights and become chattels" (Innes: 1993, 22, 34). Burke-Kennedy reclaims these powerful women without idealising them.

The play challenges traditional assumptions about gender, power and language — the women are self-assured and articulate with a strong sense of humour. However, when power is involved, it can be both used and abused. While we are presented with a spectrum of attitudes and characters, all four main figures have actively participated in the violent events which have shaped their people's history, for good or ill, thereby restoring women's place in and responsibility for political/historical processes. As Gerardine Meaney insists:

> Women are not... essentially more peaceable, less dogmatic, uninfected by bloodthirsty political ideologies.... Women have supported and carried out violent actions. They have gained and lost from their involvement. If patriarchal history has portrayed us as bystanders to the political process, it has lied (Meaney: 1993, 238).

The form of the play is highly performative, and, while the set is bare apart from isolated boulders, the actors' bodies are used to create landscape. While the story of each woman is told, the other characters act as chorus, and take up other parts as required.

> *There is the sound of wind blowing over a vast empty space. The actors take their places around the boulders, sitting, leaning, curled around them, becoming extensions of the landscape. Each actor speaks as if beginning a particular story. Each story should be allowed to hang in silence for a beat, before the next cue comes in.*

MACHA: One time...
DEIRDRE: Once, there was...
CON: Now in those days...
MAEVE: Upon a time...
NAOISE: Now once...
FERGUS: Now there was once...
NESSA: Then there was the...
They keep repeating their lines, letting their voices mingle. As the voices build to a gentle climax, Naoise cuts through them.
NAOISE: Now once.

In *Women in Arms*, story-telling is an important vehicle for alternative histories. The focus on four different stories and on an ensemble playing team creates a flexible, accessible and rhythmic style which rejects a linear unfolding of narrative, and reclaims an oral tradition of story-telling and performance, anchored in the corporeal presence of the narrator/s. The particular mixture of corporeal enactment, dialogue and oral narrative enables each of the four women to be simultaneously inside and outside her own story, actor and commentator, past and present, each becoming part of the others' stories.

Marie Jones developed as a writer with Charabanc Theatre Company which operated from 1983 until 1995. Since the disbandment of Charabanc, she has achieved broad popular success with several plays, including her one man show, *A Night in November*, which explores sectarian attitudes in Northern Ireland and one man's rejection of them, *Women on the Verge of HRT*, and *Stones in His Pockets*, which explores the effect on a small community of the installation of a film crew working on a Hollywood version of Irish life. Her main characters are not drawn from myth — they are "ordinary" individuals, usually working class, fighting prejudice, discrimination and narrowmindedness in others and sometimes in themselves. However, she often takes her characters into a "mythical" realm of play through theatre, where the usual barriers of communication or perception become flexible, capable of being examined and changed. She draws on popular culture, from football (*A Night in November*) to popular music (*Women on the Verge of HRT*) in order to extend the potential of theatre to question dominant ideologies and attitudes to a wide audience. An important tool in this project is her use of the ironic and deflationary force of humour.

Women on the Verge of HRT is set in a bedroom in the hotel in Donegal owned by the well-known singer, Daniel O'Donnell, where each year he holds a tea party to meet with his fans. The bedroom is occupied by Vera, whose ex-husband Dessie has just had a son with his new wife, twenty-five years younger than him, and Anna, who is trying to hide from others and herself the fact that her marriage to Marty went stale a long time ago. Vera, the more extrovert and questioning character, complains about the double standards applied to male and female sexuality. She feels that if she were to choose a man twenty five years her junior, tongues would wag. She has been dating but no one special:

> I wanted to shop around, there is no harm... the harm is the shop is about to close and I haven't finished my messages... its like... going for your groceries at a quarter past five and then you hear... 'This shop will be closing in five minutes', and you panic and take something you don't want... that's what I'm scared of... panic buying (Jones: 1999, 5).

The two women start up a conversation with the room service waiter, Fergal, who performs conjuring tricks, and has a passing resemblance to Daniel O'Donnell himself (the role was originally played by Dan Gordon). He invites them to come and watch the dawn on the nearby beach. The second act is set on the beach, which turns out to be an "enchanted" realm, haunted by the suppressed voice of the banshee, where the waiter becomes a kind of "shape-shifter" (a traditional Irish spirit which can take any shape), acting out the roles of those most closely connected to Vera and Anna, including Marty, Dessie and his new wife. In this "magical" space of performance, where hidden assumptions and attitudes are brought to the surface and exposed, they are able to confront the sources of their grievances, and evaluate the possibilities of change, in themselves and others. *Women on the Verge of HRT* protests vociferously against dominant attitudes towards women's sexuality and the menopause, celebrating women's refusal to be shut up and rendered sexually invisible after a certain age. The play is punctuated with songs, breaking the traditional narrative framework. The recurrent refrain is a refusal to be thrown on the "sexual scrap heap":

> **Chorus:** I wont go easy I'll go down protestin'
> The rest of my life is too long for restin'
> All I'm askin' is the right to reply
> When I'm told my passion should lie down and die
> (Jones: 1999, 6).

Marina Carr is one of the most prominent of the younger generation of Irish playwrights, in national and international terms. She was born in Dublin and was brought up in the Irish Midlands. Her first play, *Ullaloo*, not the first to be performed, was presented at the Peacock Theatre, Dublin, in 1991. *Low in the Dark* is Marina Carr's second play and was first presented at Project Arts by Crooked Sixpence Theatre Co. in 1989. Carr's plays have spanned a wide range of theatrical genres. Her latest three plays, *The Mai* (1994), *Portia Coughlan* (1995) and *By the Bog of Cats* (1998) combine elements of realism with mythical references, otherworldly visitations and black humour. Set in the Midlands, each play focuses on a central female character struggling to establish her identity which is symbiotically connected with a lost other, whether husband, brother or Mother. Although for each of the protagonists the struggle ends in suicide, their lucid perception of their own alienation, their evocation of mythical forces, and their critique of the lack of accommodation of difference in small town or rural Ireland is powerfully articulated.

Carr's early work discards realism altogether, and is characterised by non-naturalist settings, non-psychologized characters and a non-linear structure. The names of the characters in *Low in the Dark* are abstract and symbolic rather than indicative of social or familial status.

> *BENDER, in her fifties, attractive but ageing.*
> *BINDER, BENDER's daughter, in her mid-twenties, a spoilt brat, whimsical.*
> *BAXTER, in his mid-thirties, CURTAINS' lover.*
> *BONE, in his late twenties, BINDER's lover.*

> *CURTAINS, can be any age as she is covered from head to toe in heavy, brocaded curtains and rail. Not an inch of her face or body is seen throughout the play* (Carr 1999: 5).

The gender divide is literalised as the stage is split between the female area, representing a bathroom (associated with intimate bodily functions), and the male area, a work space, consisting of tyres, rims, blocks and unfinished walls. Curtains opens and closes the play, telling a story of the man from the north and the woman from the south. The dialogue is punctuated by fragments of her tale of their vain attempts to communicate: "Long after it was over, the man and woman realized that not only had they never met north by north east or south by south west, much worse, they had never met. And worse still, they never would, they never could, they never can and they never will" (Carr 1999: 99).

There is no unfolding of story or action, but rather a series of juxtaposed dialogues or role plays, like Estragon and Vladimir's "canters" in *Waiting for Godot*, or the music-hall and variety acts which inspired them. The main focus is on the performance of identity. With the exception of Curtains whose body cannot be gender identified since it is never seen, the women adopt male roles and the men, female roles. Such self-conscious performances of gender identity question any kind of gender essentialism, and comically frame our expectations of gender roles and differences. The lack of communication between the sexes is both recounted in Curtains story and articulated on stage:

> **BONE:** I want a woman who knows how to love. I want lazer beams coming out of her eyes when I enter the room. I want her to knit like one possessed. I want her to cook softly.
> **BINDER:** I want a man who'll wash my underwear, one who'll brush my hair, one who'll talk before, during and after. I want a man who'll make other men look mean (Carr 1999: 48).

Low in the Dark refuses to idealize or essentialize the role of mother in relation to female identity. Maternity is taken to parodic extremes as both male and female characters become pregnant:

> **BENDER:** There's plenty where she came from... as soon as I get my figure back I'll have another and then another, because I am fertile!
> **BINDER:** I had a dream last night your uterus fell out.
> **BENDER:** I dreamt your ovaries exploded!
> **BINDER:** At least I have ovaries and eggs, lots of eggs, much more than you because I'm young. I'm in my prime.

BENDER: I've had my fair share of eggs. Now give her to me.
BINDER: Take her then! *(Throws the baby)* (Carr: 1999, 10-11).

Items of costume such as pink socks become signifiers of gender which can be exchanged between male and female characters. The foregrounding of the body and costume point to the construction of identity through social and gender conditioning inscribed on the body. Role play and performance are used to emphasize the rigidity of traditional gender roles. Curtains' story, however, offers a final note of hope or perhaps a challenge, as the woman from the south confronts the man from the north: "'You' she said, 'if you have courage get off your bicycle and come with me'" (Carr 1999: 99).

Emma Donoghue was born in Dublin in 1969. She has published an academic study of *Passions Between Women: British Lesbian Culture 1668-1801*, as well as works of fiction, including the novels *Stir-Fry* and *Hood*. Her play, *I Know My Own Heart*, subtitled a Lesbian Regency Romance, was first premiered as a lunchtime show by Glasshouse Productions, then given a full production by the same company in October 1993 at Andrew's Lane Theatre. Based on Anne Lister's diaries (1791-1840), this play explores female sexuality and the performance of gender roles from a lesbian perspective. Teresa de Lauretis argues that within the masculine sexual economy "female desire for the self-same, an other female self, cannot be recognised" (De Lauretis: 1990, 18). Lesbian sexuality claims women as both objects and subjects of desire. Jill Dolan writes: "When the locus of desire changes, the demonstration of sexuality and gender roles also changes" (Dolan: 1987, 173).

The main character is a squire's daughter, who has liaisons with three women, one of whom, Tib, is her social equal while the other two — daughters of Farmer Brown — are social inferiors. The play focuses on her negotiations of her desire, on the one hand, and social conventions and distinctions on the other. She tries to resist her infatuation with Marianne Brown, musing: "Think what damage this acquaintance may do to my dignity, my social standing" (Unpublished Manuscript). Marianne returns her passion, emotionally and sexually, and continues the relationship after her marriage, though both are tormented by other liaisons — Anne by Marianne's "connections" with her husband, Marianne's by her husband's infidelities and Anne's liaisons with her friend Tib, and Marianne's sister, Nancy. Again, the central character is not romanticized — we are aware of her class position operating in relation to her socially marginalised sexuality, producing a complex profile of privilege and constraint, confidence and vulnerability. Costume, in particular her cloak, is important in signifying Anne's hybrid gender identity — while enjoying female intimacy her dress code and behaviour appropriate the masculine.

Ladies and Gentlemen also focuses on a historical story — a love story set on the East Coast of the U.S.A. between a late nineteenth century male impersonator, Annie Hindle, and her Irish immigrant dresser Annie Ryan, or Ryanny, who decide to get married. Their happiness is short-lived, however, as Ryanny dies of breast cancer. The first part of the story takes place in the dressing rooms/stage of Tony Pastor's Vaudeville Troupe. The other characters are a female impersonator, Gilbert, and another dresser, Ellie, one time lover of Annie, who graduates to becoming a male impersonator as the play progresses. Costume is foregrounded, as the stage personas of the characters parody gender stereotypes and unsettle gender identities through cross-dressing and songs such as "A Real Man" sung by Annie: "As men go I'm much realer than some" (Donoghue: 1998, 103). The play draws on the musical hall, vaudeville and variety act format to both entertain and foreground issues of performing gender, while the enigma of Ryanny, partly conventional Irish Catholic girl, but married to a woman, provides the emotional centre of the play.

These plays present a range of very different perspectives and identity positions, whose relationship to dominant concepts of cultural identity is complex and contestatory. The work of these and other playwrights challenges conventional representations of women, clearing a space for the representation of female subjectivities, in pain or pleasure. While many of these plays show the rigidity and restrictions of gender roles in Irish culture, they also frequently embrace performative strategies such as cross-dressing to unsettle traditional gender positions, presenting gender not as destiny, but as subversive performance:

> As a corporeal field of cultural play, gender is a basically innovative affair, although it is quite clear that there are strict punishments for contesting the script by performing out of turn or through unwarranted improvisations. Gender is not passively scripted on the body, and neither is it determined by nature, language, the symbolic, or the overwhelming history of patriarchy. Gender is what is put on, invariably, under constraint, daily and incessantly, with anxiety and pleasure, but if this continuous act is mistaken for a natural or linguistic given, power is relinquished to expand the cultural field bodily through subversive performances of various kinds (Butler: 1990, 282).

Works Cited:

Bort, Eberhard, (1996), *The State of Play: Irish Theatre in the 'Nineties* (Trier: Wissenschaftlicher Verlag Trier)

Burke-Kennedy, Mary Elizabeth, *Women in Arms* (All quotations from unpublished manuscript)

Butler, Judith, (1990), 'Performative Acts and Gender Constitution: An essay in Phenomenology and Feminist Theory', in *Performing Feminisms*, ed., Sue-Ellen Case (Baltimore: John Hopkins Press) 270-282

Marina Carr, (1999), *Plays 1* (London: Faber and Faber)

Case, Sue-Ellen, (1990), *Performing Feminisms: Feminist Critical Theory and Theatre* (Baltimore and London: John Hopkins University Press)

De Lauretis, Teresa, (1990), 'Sexual Indifference and Lesbian Representation' in ed., Sue-Ellen Case, *Performing Feminisms: Feminist Critical Theory and Theatre* (Baltimore and London: John Hopkins University Press) 17-39

Dolan, Jill, (1987), 'The Dynamics of Desire: Sexuality and Gender in Pornography and Performance', *Theatre Journal* 39.2, May, 156-174

------ (1993), *The Feminist Spectator as Critic* (Ann Arbor: University of Michigan Press)

Donoghue, Emma, *I Know My Own Heart* (All quotations from unpublished manuscript)

------ (1998), *Ladies and Gentlemen* (Dublin: New Island Books)

Gallagher, S.F., (1983), *Women in Irish Legend, Life and Literature* (Gerrards Cross: Colin Smythe)

Harris, Claudia, (1996), 'Reinventing Women: Charabanc Theatre Company' in ed., Eberhard Bort, *The State of Play: Irish Theatre in the 'Nineties* (Trier: Wissenschaftlicher Verlag Trier), 104-123

Herbert, Maire, (1991), 'Celtic Heroine? The archaeology of the Deirdre Story', in eds., Toni O'Brien Johnson and David Cairns, *Gender in Irish Writing* (Buckingham: Open University Press), 13-22

Innes, C.L., (1993*), Woman and Nation in Irish Literature and Society 1880-1935* (Hemel Hempstead: Harvester Wheatsheaf)

Jones, Marie, (1995), *A Night in November* (London: Nick Hern Books)

------ (1996), 'Speaking for the Powerless', Interview with Luke Clancy, *Irish Times*, February 20

------ (1999), *Women on the Verge of HRT* (London: Samuel French)

Meaney, Gerardine, (1993), 'Sex and Nation: Women in Irish Culture and Politics', in ed., Ailbhe Smyth, *The Irish Women's Studies Reader* (Dublin: Attic Press), 230-244

Moi, Toril, (1985), *Sexual/Textual Politics: Feminist Literary Theory* (London: Methuen)

Johnson, Toni O'Brien and David Cairns, (1991), eds., *Gender in Irish Writing* (Buckingham: Open University Press)

Reynolds, Lorna, (1983), 'Irish Women in Legend, Literature and Life', in ed., S.F. Gallagher, *Women in Irish Legend, Life and Literature* (Gerrards Cross: Colin Smythe), 15

Smyth, Ailbhe, (1993), *The Irish Women's Studies Reader* (Dublin: Attic Press)

Irish Theatre: The State of the Art

Fintan O'Toole

John Millington Synge, writing about Goethe, felt that his weakness was that he had "no national and intellectual mood to interpret. The individual mood is often trivial, perverse, fleeting, [but the] national mood [is] broad, serious, provisionally permanent... the great artist, as Rembrandt or Shakespeare, adds his personal distinction to a great distinction of time and place" (quoted in Shelton: 1971, 60). The relevance of this view to his own work and to that of his co-workers in the creation of the modern Irish theatre is obvious. But, at the same time, it raises a question about contemporary Irish theatre. If the greatness of the artist is dependent on the greatness of the times, if artistic originality is in some sense conditioned by time and place, then what can be said to be distinctive about this particular time and this particular place, and how do those distinctions help to shape the theatre? What national or intellectual mood is there to be interpreted? Is it, indeed, possible to talk at all of either the nation or its moods in the singular?

Synge's view is useful at least as a reminder that contemporary Irish theatre cannot be interpreted as a mere lineal descendent of Synge's. The fact that Synge's theatre, the Abbey, still exists and is still at the core of Irish theatre, lends a superficial appearance of continuity, but like most superficialities in Ireland, it is deceptive. The playwright Denis Johnston, writing in the 1950s, identified four distinct Abbey acting companies, remarking that the "present Irish-speaking Cumann... has no more to do with the past than the Holy Roman Empire had to do with Hadrian". He compared the Abbey to a "knife that having had four new blades and five new handles still insisted that it was the same implement". Synge usefully reminds us that what is true of actors is just as true of writers — that they give shape to and are shaped by their own times and places, and that times and places change.

Yet it strikes me that anyone looking at the theatre in Ireland in the 1990s would find more similarities with the theatre of Synge than they would have done even a decade earlier. Neither Synge's language nor his peasant world remains at the heart of Irish theatre, yet the theatre of the last few years shares much with Synge's. It is strongly marked by a concern with language for its own sake. It is primarily poetic rather than naturalistic. It has an angular rather than direct relationship to Irish society. It works, as the Synge of *The Well of the Saints* works, through evocation rather than dramatisation. What I want to try to do is to suggest, in broad strokes and with a concern for woods rather than trees, why this should be so, keeping in mind at all times, of course, that every generalisation can be contradicted by particulars.

What I want to suggest in essence is that we have been through a particular movement in our theatre and in our society over the last 30 years, and that that movement is now at a close. If we want to trace broad patterns, we can say that we have had in this century in Irish theatre three quite distinct movements. The first is the theatrical revival centering on Synge, Yeats, Lady Gregory and O'Casey. That revival effectively ended at the end of the 1920s, its end marked by the Abbey's failure to produce either Johnston's *The Old Lady Says 'No'!* or O'Casey's *The Silver Tassie*. It was followed by a long period of decline and decadence, the counter-currents to which are too scattered, too marginalized and too isolated to be called a movement.

A second revival, in my own view no less powerful, began in the late 1950s and continued well into the 1980s. It is marked, obviously, by the work of Tom Murphy, Brian Friel, John B. Keane, Thomas Kilroy and Hugh Leonard. And we have now entered into some kind of third phase, a phase that is too new to be fully defined, but whose outlines can be at least tentatively suggested. In some important respects, this third phase has more in common with the first revival than with the second, yet it is important to stress that it includes the later work of two of the most important writers of the second revival, Murphy and Friel.

I realise that these distinctions are crude and schematic, yet I think we have to make them if we are to understand where we are now. This is particularly important because the process of transition from the second phase to the third has been a confusing and difficult one for audiences and critics. We have become used to a theatre of conflict, a theatre of doubleness, and those expectations were met in ever more spectacular ways in the 1960s, 1970s and 1980s. We have had in recent Irish theatre great, highly wrought, intensely dramatic, and in a real sense classical works. What I want to suggest is that we will not get such works in the immediate future, that something has shifted and that criticism needs to come to terms with whatever that something is. The drama which has been present in our society has moved on, and the theatre is moving on with it, moving away from that conflict, that doubleness. If this is true, then we have to find new ways of talking about it, of evaluating it, even of defining what is and is not dramatic.

One of the striking things about the world of John Synge is precisely that it is to him, a world — a unified nexus of time and place. His seeking out of the Aran Islands, of the sharp spatial definition that an island affords, is symbolic. *The Aran Islands* begins by asserting a control over place and time that are impressive in their rigour. The book's first sentence — "I am in Aranmor, sitting over a turf fire, listening to a murmur Gaelic that is rising from a little public-house under my room" — is dense with the specificities of place (Synge: 1964,249). The next sentence — "The steamer which comes to Aran sails according to the tide and it was six o'clock this morning when we left the quay of Galway in a dense shroud of mist" — is alive with the imperatives of time. And these essential fixtures remain in place throughout the book. As Tim Robinson points out, "its exclusion of matters relating to the past and the future of the Aran Islands, except as they arose in thought and conversation during his visits, is... absolute". The frame of the book, as of the plays, is classical in its preservation of unities — time, place and action: each remains essentially singular.

To travel around Ireland with Synge in his prose works is to encounter a society that is certainly not simple — on the contrary, it is full of subtle gradations of class and region, and of the infinite colours of human personality — but it is, broadly speaking a single cultural entity. It is a world whose borders are already leaking as people continue to make their way to the New World, but within those borders, the people are in essence one people. In the theatre of the first revival, there is a substratum of nationalism: Irishness is what defines the cast of characters, "Ireland", a single thing which does not need to be spelt out, is the oil that makes the plot run.

The societies of the great early Irish plays, Synge's included, are patently bounded, close, sharing a common ground that is so clear that it hardly needs to be marked at all. It is not that outsiders do not play an important role in these plays. It is precisely that in order for outsiders to play the role they do, they need to be set against a bounded and closely-knit society. It is essential to *The Playboy*, for instance, that Christy Mahon is so patently an outsider. The play works by setting the closeness of the tribe, manifested in the forthcoming wedding of Pegeen to her cousin Shawn Keogh — against the threat of the outsider. Pegeen, at the start of the play, talks about the loose, uncontrolled, unbounded men who might be abroad and threatening.

Or think of *The Plough and the Stars*. Again, the outsiders are immediately and overwhelmingly obvious as outsiders. The society of the play is so obviously one that it can incorporate the political or personal oddities of a Bessie Burgess or a Young Covey without difficulty. In the discourse of the play, those who are outside the discourse can literally hardly be spoken to. The Woman from Rathmines or the British soldiers who occupy the stage at the end cannot, in a play where conversation is the very stuff of life, be engaged in conversation.

This assumption that society is essentially single, that even its divisions are divisions *within* rather than *between*, reflects the reality of the vestigial Gaelic culture, a peasant culture in which class distinctions tended to be obscured by the general poverty and the common sense of a far greater division between native and foreigner. If you look at one of the more important documents of that culture from this period, Tomas O'Crohan's *An tOileanach*, what is striking is the way in which every action, every word, every person, has meaning only in relation to a whole, a whole that is defined by the timeless truths of custom. The view of reality that we get is never a personal view. At no time is it at variance with the values of the society as a whole. The author boasts that never once in a whole lifetime did he break a custom, and custom is the only acknowledged law of his society. When he mentions people who do break the law of custom, it is with a mixture of pity and contempt. To be out of step with a custom is to be all but sub-human.

John McGahern has pointed out how the strange sense of timelessness that O'Crohan's book has comes from "the day, a single day breaking continually over the scene and the action". Actions that require months or years are so reduced that they seem to take on the rhythm of the day. "All mysterious, far-flung places are brought in and reduced to the island frame. The single day breaks over this world to bring light for the action. This immediate action, its hopes and its stresses, its ebb and flow, fills the one day without regard to what went before or will come after". This, of course, is precisely what Synge sought to immerse himself in on the Aran Islands.

It seems to me to be no accident that that McGahern's description of *An tOileanach* could be applied, without changing a word, to Samuel Beckett's *Waiting for Godot* or *Happy Days*. Nor is it any accident that it could not be applied to the work of any serious Irish playwright *after* Beckett. For, in the great gulf that separates the Irish playwrights who began to write before the late 1950s from those who began to write after the late 1950s, Beckett, the exiled Parisian post-Proustian protestant atheist, is closer to Tomas O'Crohan, the Catholic, Gaelic, peasant seldom off the Blasket Islands in his life than either are to the mental world of a Brian Friel, a Tom Murphy, or a Thomas Kilroy.

The mind set of Beckett and O'Crohan, of Synge and Yeats, is that of a single world: Beckett's endless days and continual present tense, Synge and O'Casey's close-knit, well-defined societies, Yeats' notion of "Unity of Being", a state in which all doubles become single, are, in spite of the vast differences in their styles of theatre, in this respect all of a piece. For the playwrights of the second revival, on the other hand, all vision must be double vision. This, in essence, is what differentiates one period from the other.

If we go back to O'Crohan for a moment, one of the striking things is that although members of his family go to the New World, the USA, that new world can still be perfectly encompassed within the frame of the old America. For him America is *deor allais* the land of sweat. Far from threatening the rule of custom, America serves only to reinforce that rule, for O'Crohan is able to complain that America coarsens manners, that its emphasis on self-seeking endangers custom, and that this obviously makes no sense. In the balance between the old world and the new, the new world is found wanting, is self-evidently less. In the Ireland whose national mood the playwrights of the second revival had to interpret, nothing could be *less* obvious. Their Ireland is shaped by America, a place in which the new world is superimposed on the old, like a colour print that's out of key. It is from this that their characteristic double vision comes.

From the late 1950s onwards, "Ireland" as a single, simple notion which might underlie and give formal coherence to a work of theatre began to seep away. This happened because we were no longer merely going to the New World. The New World was also coming to us, in the form of £6 billion pounds of investment from multinational corporations, £4 and a half billion of it from the USA. Government policy of trying to protect a unified, predominantly rural, Catholic and conservative society collapsed and the floodgates holding back Yeats' filthy modern tide were opened. The society became complex, no longer definable as a single reality. Theatre, too, was no longer able to operate with single realities either. The theatre of naturalism, the theatre in which every effect has a cause, in which every action has a motive and in which every character has a fundamental substratum of coherence, became virtually impossible. The very notion of character, as something given, something singular, as a vessel within which words, ideas and emotions could be contained, became highly problematic.

Old worlds don't just become new worlds, and Ireland didn't just become another state of the union. It became a double world, a slippery state in which the traditional and the modern jostled for the status of reality, in which every truth was equally untrue, in which past, present and future seemed to melt into each other, in which the borders of reality and of personality became permeable. Such a place is both a good ground in which to be a playwright, since the clash of cultures is inherently dramatic, and also a difficult one, since the sense of unity which underlies the work of a Synge or an O'Casey is no longer available. The combination of social opportunity and formal challenge gave us an extraordinary generation of theatrical creators, one which is, amazingly, still restlessly active.

John B. Keane's important plays, the ones written between 1959 and 1966, gave the new sense of doubleness and objective an external — and therefore formally unadventurous — expression. They dramatised the causes, if not the psychic consequences, of the kind of breakdown of the notion of a single, defined, bounded, personality that is found later on. They present us clearly with two opposed moral and psychological environments in which their characters have to live. The people of *Sive*, *Big Maggie*, *The Field*, are drawn between a customary world of rights and duties, of fixed forms of family, sexuality and property, on the one hand, and a world of freedom, sexual, financial and moral, on the other. The world of Keane's central figures, Meena Glavin, Big Maggie, the Bull McCabe, like the world of Tom Murphy's great early play *A Whistle in the Dark*, is essentially a tragic one. Doomed to live by old values in a new world, they can literally do nothing right, for what they perceive to be right is no longer, by the lights of the new world, so. There is a fundamental disjunction between actions and their consequences, as there always is in tragedy. The times are out of joint.

With the emergence of Brian Friel, the doubleness begins to be internalised, to infiltrate the borders of personality itself. In Friel, doubleness is characteristically located in the notion of exile, but equally characteristically, even that very notion of exile itself is double. There is the physical exile of the impulse to leave Ireland, most obviously of Gar O'Donnell in *Philadelphia, Here I Come!*, but also, and more profoundly, of Frank Hardy in *Faith Healer*. There is also, though, the sense of being an exile in one's own country that is rooted in Friel's status as a Northern Irish nationalist. This double doubleness of exile leads to a kind of theatre in which character, personality and language itself become slippery, and constantly threaten to divide, as Gar O'Donell divides between a public and a private self, or as Hugh Leonard's Charlie in *Da*, and the entire cast of characters in *A Life* split into past and present selves. In a slightly different configuration, Tom Murphy, in almost all of his plays, divides the self between two characters, often brothers, sometimes friends or mortal enemies, who appear to be separate but who emerge as two halves of the one whole.

In Friel, too, memory is utterly problematic. The relationship between the past and the present is thrown into such doubt by the speed of change that no version of the past can ever be trusted. There is no stable point in the present from which one may look at the past and say with certainty: this is what happened. Gar O'Donnell's sense of himself and of his father is crucially founded on the memory of a happy day they spent together, but the day may never have happened. In *The Freedom of the City* and *Making History*, official versions of what happened are seen to be invented, to be an exercise in the impossible. In *Faith Healer* we get three versions of the events which the play narrates, but instead of confirming memory as something shared and communal, it merely confirms it as something which has collapsed as a public phenomenon into a private fiction. And if the past is unreliable, then not only does the naturalistic law of cause and effect become unworkable, but also the whole notion of character as the sum of all the things that has happened to it becomes untenable.

Characters become open, permeable, unbounded. Frank Hardy, the faith healer, is literally permeable. He lays on his hands, and sometimes, when he touches someone, something flows out of him and heals. He has no essence, no fixed nature. He is nothing except what he can sometimes, mysteriously, cause to happen in others. And he can neither comprehend nor control this power. The power itself does not even provide a fixed centre: it is either miraculous or ludicrous, either magical or a piece of sheer charlatanism. That other cod magician, Tom Murphy's JPW King in *The Gigli Concert* is also utterly permeable, except in the opposite direction. Instead of things flowing out of him, they flow in, in the form of the dreams, obsessions and impossible desires of the Irishman who comes to seek his help. Likewise, the invented, fictional self of Tom Kilroy's Brendan Bracken in *Double Cross* gives way under extreme pressure to another, dormant self of his past life.

The essential point about all of this is that in this second revival of Irish theatre, we had an extraordinary period in which formal adventurousness and the desire to reflect and reflect on one's immediate society were not contradictory impulses but complementary ones. The doubleness of the society, the co-presence of contradictory worldviews, made it necessary for the theatre to evolve forms in which the collapse of personality, the instability of character, the failure of the naturalistic laws of cause and effect, were not just *avant garde* experiments but also necessary forms of social realism. In essence, realistic theatre in Ireland was, for 30 years, *avant garde* theatre. The society simply could not be encompassed within the singular vision of naturalistic theatre.

It is not, of course, that there was anything unique about Irish theatre's concern with the disintegration of personality, with the essential doubleness of contemporary life, with the notion of a radical discontinuity between past and present. It is that Irish theatre had a particularly direct and concrete route to these universal concerns, and that, because they could deal with these things and at the same time be dealing with a society, they could grapple with fundamental aspects of the human condition in the late 20th century without becoming abstract, without losing contact with the social and the political. This was a position of enormous privilege and one which a number of great theatrical imaginations exploited to the full. If the basis of this broad paradigm is right, and the second phase of Irish theatre from the late

1950s to the late 1980s was driven by the intensely dramatic conflict between tradition and modernity, then it should also be true that the collapse of that conflict should mean the end of that phase and the opening of a new one. This is, I think, broadly what is happening.

There is no dramatic conflict between tradition and modernity in Ireland any more. If we take Daniel Corkery's famous definition of traditional Irishness as being constituted by three things — land, nationality and religion — then it is clear that each of the parts is under immense stress (Corkery: 1966, 19). In relation to land, even rural Ireland now is either more or less industrialised or more or less marginalized. More profoundly, land itself has lost its economic value, since, under the reform of the EU's Common Agricultural Policy, land itself is virtually worthless without a production quota attached. Nationality has become more a question than an answer, more a quest than a point of departure. Religion, far from being a serene guarantor of traditional values, is itself the site of a bitter battlefield. Insofar as it still exists, traditional Ireland is alienated, angular and embattled, as strange, with its moving statues and paranoid visions, as any *avant garde* has ever been. Its image in the theatre is no longer John B. Keane's proud, confident, dangerous Bull McCabe, but Sebastian Barry's odd, sad, comic, encircled characters in *Boss Grady's Boys*, imagining themselves as foot-soldiers in Custer's Last Stand: "We're surrounded. The Indians. You never see them, they shoot from behind boulders.... Is there no sign of them bloody horses"?

Such a vision of traditional Ireland cannot be the source of great, sweeping dramatic confrontations. What we have instead are fragments, isolated pieces of a whole story that no one knows. Ireland is not one story anymore, and we cannot expect single theatrical metaphors for it. Instead of one story and many theatrical images of it, we are moving towards a dramatisation of the fragments rather than the whole thing, the whole society. In the plays of the emerging third phase, there are isolated worlds, closed entities, in which we move away from the doubleness of the second revival and back to the singleness of the first, with two very large differences. In the first place, this new singleness no longer assumes a single country underlying the drama, a single social world to which the action refers. In the second, it retains and builds on the key elements of the second phase — the disintegration of personality, the permeability of character, the discontinuity between cause and effect.

In this latter respect, Friel's *Faith Healer*, which looked at first like a glorious oddity in Irish theatre, with its self-conscious lack of dramatic conflict, now looks like a great exemplar, like a key bridge between the second phase and the third. Its evocation of a suspended time and a purely theatrical space, of a dramatic world that is radically discontinuous with the social world outside the theatre is an essential discovery for the plays of this phase. In the ultimate refusal to inhabit fixed categories, Frank Hardy himself is neither dead nor alive. He is, in the narrative, a dead man, but in the drama, before us on stage, he is alive to tell his tale. This metaphorical withdrawal from the social world, this creation of a theatre of suspended animation, is followed directly by some of the important works of the third phase. The same device is used in Tom Murphy's *Too Late for Logic*, in Dermot Bolger's *The Lament for Arthur Cleary* and *One Last White Horse* in Frank McGuinness' *The Bread Man.*

Perhaps symbolic of the way in which this third phase is both close to and radically unlike the first revival is the use of an island community in Sebastian Barry's *Prayers of Sherkin*. In Synge's *The Aran Islands*, in Michael Collins' vision of Achill Island as the essence of Irish nationality, in the writings of the Blasket Island authors, the uniformity of island life stands as a microcosm of the life of the nation, acting by analogy as an image of an assumed fixity and purity. In *Prayers of Sherkin*, staged in 1990, Irish theatre returns to the island, and it is indeed a remarkably certain, unified culture that is on display. Whereas in the only play of the second revival to use the island metaphor, Friel's *The Gentle Island*, the allusion is bitter and sardonic, the isolated island a site for savage and violent conflict, in *Prayers of Sherkin* conflict is almost entirely absent. It is also, like the great plays of the first revival, essentially poetic, relying on its power to evoke a world through language rather than assert it through action. But, on the other hand, the meaning of the island's community is almost directly opposite to the meaning that Aran or the Blaskets or Achill had for the first, nationalist, revival. The island community is not pure native but angular foreigner, an English sect settled on Sherkin. And the island itself is not proof against time, but unstable and unfixed. Fanny Hawke asks of Sherkin "Do you not feel that this island is moored only lightly to the sea-bed, and might be off for the Americas at any moment?"

This isolated community, this world to itself is repeated in various forms in the plays that mark the move into the third phase. In Tom Murphy's *Too Late for Logic*, it is the self-enclosed underworld of a certain sort of middle-class Dublin, a world into which no light enters from any other source. In Brian Friel's *Dancing at Lughnasa*, it is a single house, a single family, both so single indeed that the entry of a new thing can lead only to the collapse of the entire world of the play. In John McGahern's *The Power of Darkness*, we are given a world so cut-off, so much without a single point of outside reference that as soon as the doubleness of reflection enters at all, the action can only and literally stop, refuse to continue and collapse in on itself. In much of the work of Frank McGuinness, the singleness is a matter of gender, men and women existing in different zones whose borders cannot be crossed.

You can mark the shift I'm talking about simply by noting that when outsiders intrude on the worlds of these plays, they are immediately obvious as outsiders, just as they would be in Synge and O'Casey. We are back with Christy Mahon and the Woman from Rathmines. Patrick Kirwan in *Sherkin*, coming from the mainland, represents almost literally a different world when he comes to woo Fanny Hawke. Father Jack in *Lughnasa* trails a whole continent and a whole different culture behind him when he enters. Paddy in *The Power of Darkness* seems to come from a whole different story, even a completely different play. In each case, the outside represents a different country (the mainland, Africa, the war in the Pacific) and speaks a different kind of language. As with Synge or O'Casey, the coming of the outsider serves to emphasise the singleness, the highly bounded nature of the world into which he comes.

Yet that bounded place is not Ireland. In the plays after the late 1980s, Ireland as a bounded place has ceased to exist. Africa and Spain seep into the Ballybeg of Lughnasa. The ocean that laps against the shores of *The Power of Darkness* is the Pacific. Sebastian Barry's *White Woman Street* is set in the American west, Sligo a distant, angular and elusive memory. Dermot Bolger's *The Lament for Arthur Cleary* and *In High Germany* are dominated by Germany. Schopenhauer's Germany of the early nineteenth century is an important presence in *Too Late for Logic*. The bounded fragments which are the worlds of these plays are fragments not of a coherent whole called Ireland but of a mixed-up jigsaw of the continents.

It is too soon to say what the full shape of this change is, but two particular changes are immediate and obvious. One is that conflict is no longer of the essence. The theatre of the second revival was a theatre of conflict enacted through the clash of large forces. Action — what happens moment by moment on stage — was crucial because it is through action that the conflict moves towards resolution. But this is not the case with the new work. In it, there is little conflict and there is little tension or suspense. It is striking the degree to which we know in all of these plays what is going to happen before it happens. In each of the plays, the question what happens next is not the appropriate one. In *Sherkin*, we know as soon as we know the characters that Fanny will leave the island and that the play is an enactment of that inevitability. Nor is there any choice between good and evil — all the characters are remarkably sweet. The plot is slight and could be summed up in a sentence.

In *Too Late for Logic*, *The Lament for Arthur Cleary*, *The Bread Man* and *One Last White Horse*, we know from the start that the protagonist is dead. The end is at the beginning in a way that deliberately removes the notion of an open-ended conflict. In Murphy's case this is truly remarkable, for he is a writer whose sense of not knowing how a play is going to end, of ending a play being a matter of forcing the impossible to happen, is crucial to his work.

In *Lughnasa*, famously, we are told what is going to happen to the sisters long before the play ends, undercutting the whole sense of drama, of something evolving through action or even through narrative suspense. In Friel's *Wonderful Tennessee* there is virtually no plot at all, just a group of characters waiting for something that we know is not going to happen. In *The Power of Darkness*, a narrative of suspense and action is set up only to collapse completely. The story and the action — an exaggerated story and melodramatic action — stop in their tracks, and the whole second half of the play is about the impossibility of the play going on. In Vincent Woods' *At the Black Pig's Dyke*, plot and action are replaced through the medium of mumming by a ritual invocation of an inevitable death.

Related to this loss of tension and suspense is the second obvious change, the re-emergence of poetry in the theatre. If drama cannot be created out of conflict, then it must be evoked through language, though by no means only through verbal language. Again, *Faith Healer* is the obvious forerunner, but it is still striking that the reinvention of a dense theatrical language has involved a virtual obliteration of the fixed distinctions between narrative fiction, poetry and dialogue. The emergence of broken narrative forms in a play like Murphy's *Bailegangaire*, Murphy's own turning to the novel, the fact that key plays like *Prayers of Sherkin* and *The Lament for Arthur Cleary* actually began life as poems, the surge of interest in writing for the theatre by poets like Seamus Heaney and Brendan Kennelly, and novelists like John McGahern and John Banville — all of these are evidence that there is a third phase of Irish theatre in which the specificity of theatre itself — expressed in concepts like conflict, drama, action, character — is on the wane. These plays are all extraordinarily linguistic creations, concerned to evoke or conjure up a world rather than to create one. They have to do so because the worlds they are concerned with are so particular, so angular, that an audience cannot share in them through naturalistic convention.

Because we no longer have one shared place, one Ireland, we can no longer have a naturalistic theatre of recognition in which a world is signalled to us through objects and we tacitly agree to recognise it is as our own. We must instead have a theatre of evocation in which strange worlds, not our own, are in Yeats' phrase "called to the eye of the mind". Our theatre now is about the business of calling up rather than recreating, and this will demand of us new ways of seeing and new categories of criticism. This is hard, but then so is life, and it is because it is still living that the Irish theatre is making itself in new ways.

Works Cited:

Corkery, Daniel, (1966), *Synge and Anglo-Irish Literature* (Cork: The Mercier Press)

Shelton, Robin, (1971), *J. M. Synge and his World* (London: Thames & Hudson)

Synge, J. M., (1964), *Plays, Poems and Prose* (London: Dent)

The State of Irish Theatre

Bruce Arnold

I

Nationalism is a central pillar in the edifice we call Irish Theatre. The rise of nationalism, in the late nineteenth century, gave birth to what was represented as "a tradition", but which was, in reality, an artificial, manufactured device, designed by those who backed it to represent an independent, Irish artistic manifestation of race and identity through theatre. It happened in other art forms, both those connected with the written word, such as poetry and fiction, and in the visual and musical art forms. But theatre had a special attraction. As an art form it offered an easier and more direct means of access to the people than any other. In its day, theatre was television, film and radio entertainment rolled into one. And its "day" was an exceedingly long one, embracing several centuries, and having a popular climax in the Victorian period, when urban society expanded dramatically, and theatres were built in towns and cities throughout these islands.

Every sort of entertainment was offered, and anyone seeking to influence public opinion, or to alter social understanding and progress, saw theatre as having unique powers. It is therefore not surprising that William Butler Yeats, Augusta Gregory, Edward Martin, George Moore, later John Synge, and later still Sean O'Casey, should have subscribed to the idea and practice of theatre. Their involvement in it as an art form was only part of the story. They were also determined that they would influence the feelings, the emotional responses, the politics, and the yearnings of the public, and that they would do so in a way that other art forms they were interested in could not do.

Unlike theatre elsewhere, they were persuaded of the nationalist rather than the socialist purpose in what they did. In the hands of Ibsen in Norway, and later throughout Europe, or in the plays of George Bernard Shaw in London, there were social and moral objectives to be achieved on the stage. But in Ireland the essential purposes were directed at the framing of a programme designed to create and define the national spirit. Within this broad objective lay both the glories and the banalities of Irish theatre. What began as a brave experiment in adapting the most ancient and arguably the greatest art form to overtly political purposes ran into trouble quickly enough as the talent ran out.

This is not the place to write a history of Irish theatre in the twentieth century. Yet a sense of history pervades our theatre to this day, and the relevance of what was done in the early years of the century, which broadly dictated the later development of play writing and directing, hangs still like a cloud over the art and discipline of Irish theatre.

It matters less and less with the passage of time. Theatre is increasingly seen now as a marginal art form. It has lost its political power. It no longer provokes much argument or debate. There is nothing equivalent to the "Playboy Riots" of 1907. Audiences do not go to the theatre in order to develop their understanding of nationalism, their grasp on social change, or to listen to debate about issues affecting the country's future. Nevertheless, the power of theatre as an art form is still potent, the contribution made by writers remains considerable, and theatres flourish. Not all of them, of course. The compulsion of the stage attracts young and idealistic performers, playwrights, designers, artists, who work for less than a living wage. And their admirable sacrifice is augmented by the Arts Council and other agencies, including private business.

This makes of theatre an increasingly artificial art form, and a minority one as well. From a personal point of view I regard it as the greatest of all art forms, greater even than music. But I am increasingly conscious that this is an eccentric view, and that theatre itself has undermined its own relevance, hanging on to the burden of its past and relying on that past to give it relevance and attract audiences.

II

For the past three years, as Chief Critic of the *Irish Independent*, and its main theatre reviewer, I have looked at theatre, mainly in Dublin, from a professional point of view, making judgements with the entirely practical and short-term purpose of informing readers of the newspaper. I want them to know what I have seen, to be aware of the purpose behind a play, the intent of the playwright, the attitude of the director, the level of understanding and performance brought to each production by the actors, actresses, designers, and so on. I have looked at theatre for its subject, intent and quality. I have passed judgement on playwrights, actors, directors and designers. I have done this in the old-fashioned way of reviewing, which is to attend so-called "First Nights", and to write reviews immediately after performances, which then appeared in the newspaper the following morning. It is an exacting professional act, not without stresses and strains. But the convention is of value to the theatres and the performers, just as it is for the public, in making their judgements about whether to patronise individual plays. While it may seem obvious, explaining this, it has to be said that the practice is changing. In part this is as a result of extended theatre previews, in part the difficulties for newspapers of taking review material late at night for publication the following morning. While other newspapers have altered the practice, my own maintains it, and long may this continue. It recognises that theatre is news. Theatre itself does not always recognise the same thing.

One of the advantages of the critical judgement made in this way is that the overall event and its impact, critically speaking, transcends the baggage which is now attached to most of what happens in all of the arts, all of the time. Theatre is no exception to the presentation of artistic events in news and feature terms which have nothing whatever to do with the critical impact. A new play, more often than not, is the subject of newspaper profile for the playwright, analysis of previous writing, an account of subject-matter, possibly a listing of sources, all of which is accompanied by photographs.

If a famous director visits Dublin, as Jonathan Miller did recently to direct Shakespeare's *As You Like It* at the Gate Theatre, a similar parade of profile and other material is delivered by a helpful and largely uncritical press. Both before and after the production, the celebration of its architect, or in the case of a new play, the playwright, represents an end in itself. There is even the possibility of conflicting views being aired by the same newspaper, representing a debate of sorts. The critic's position, in all of this, in more sense of the word than the obvious one, is critical.

In the case of the Shakespeare production, for example, my own critique was broadly negative. I thought the whole production a bit limp. It is a notoriously difficult play; Shakespeare's tongue-in-cheek approach to Arcadia is countered by a real presentation of love in several guises. Neither worked all that well. But such is the impact of a famous director on the news value of the production, that no serious consideration was given to the theatrical lapses, the limpness of the action, the poor set or the meaningless modern costume. And some of the acting was simply second-rate. Despite this, the play, innately appealing, was well-received. It catered to the inexhaustible appetite for good theatre with good language and poetry which is exemplified in Shakespeare's output, and which is too little done on the stage in Dublin. There are many reasons for this, but certainly one is the fundamental problem of there being a thing called "Irish Theatre" which has to be presented.

"Irish Theatre" has limped its way through the whole of the twentieth century trying to assert a purpose and a meaning. Essentially, that purpose and meaning has been the nature of Ireland. Who are we, what are we, where do we come from, why do we exist? Early in the century, through allegory, in *The Countess Cathleen*, W.B. Yeats tried to answer that question. He went on trying to answer it in a succession of comparatively indifferent theatrical offerings which are, today, hardly worth putting on.

He was aided in the effort by other acolytes and followers, none of whom really took fire. Then came Synge, and the world was never the same again. Synge was not a nationalist. Quite rightly, he was reviled by nationalists for letting them down, in a portrait of Irish rural life the truth of which was seen as damaging to the objectives of the National Theatre Movement. And he *was* damaging. Firstly, he ensured that nationalism, in the self-conscious and self-seeking way of the period, would be held up to ridicule, which was the case. Secondly, he provided, in his masterpiece, a touchstone towards which, in vain, all later playwrights have lifted their eyes and turned their hands and craft.

No one, since *The Playboy of the Western World*, has matched it for sheer theatrical genius. Few have come even close. But its impact has created a theatre quite at odds with what Synge believed in. He is wrongly seen as being "nationalist", mainly because of the way in which he was recruited in Paris by W.B. Yeats, and encouraged to commit himself to the National Theatre Movement. But succeeding generations, in their travesty of Synge's character, have also expanded the misrepresentation, creating a kind of theatrical monster whom no one has been able to confront. In today's terms, it has left us with a divided, fragmented theatre. The strands of this may be represented in terms of the physical theatres, their directors, their playwrights, and their attitudes to outside work, whether this is concerned with plays and playwrights, or with actors and actresses.

III

Of the principle theatres in Dublin, the most gifted direction comes from Michael Colgan, in the Gate Theatre. He runs a structured, year-long programme of plays, generally put on in sparkling productions, with fine acting and direction, good design and lighting, and a wide, catholic choice of what to give to the public. There is a commercial motivation; filling seats is a priority, but it pays off in the atmosphere, which is lively and positive. Something of the old Gate Theatre is present. It was always "Modernist", from the day it was launched, and it has retained that atmosphere. It is, of course, much less courageous than the Gate Theatre was in the 1930s and 1940s, but the sense of innovative experiment is strong enough to retain the loyalty and support of theatre-goers whose memories go back as much as half a century. Having attended Gate Theatre productions in the second half of the 1950s, I feel at home often enough to welcome this tradition. The Gate is not overly concerned with nationalism, and never was. It recognised that the craft of the stage, and the art of writing for it, was precarious enough, even if it called upon all traditions, world-wide. And this sense of breadth and variety of choice is still central to its planning.

The Abbey Theatre is an entirely different proposition. Not alone is it burdened by the need to be "nationalist" in its theatrical output. It seems to welcome the burden, and add to it in its overall planning. If it does world theatre, it wants to make it "Irish" world theatre, by having classic international plays adapted, "translated", re-written. It subscribes to the dangerous myth that Anton Chekhov can be re-created in an Irish setting. And something similar is present in the treatment of other classic playwrights of the past. Obviously, in fulfilment of this first objective, a second has to be honoured: that the playwrights themselves are "Irish", not just by birth, but by persuasion and commitment to the concept that they can "improve" Chekhov or Molière. The new director of the Abbey Theatre, Ben Barnes, in what he may find is a bit of a millstone around his neck, delivered a lengthy and detaiedl outline of his intentions for the theatre. Intentions expressed in this way are always dangerous. He seemed to have a team of "in-house" performers and to place on them a considerable burden of responsibility. A broad criticism along these lines provoked strong responses, not just from Ben Barnes himself, but also from one of his playwrights, Hugh Leonard. And the immediate impression was that neither of them wanted criticism if it was going to be fuelled by harsh judgements, in advance, of the outcome of a structure based on the small and quite limited theatrical talent which Ireland has working for it on the stage, both here and in Britain, not to mention occasionally on Broadway. The greatest millstone of all around the neck of any director of the Abbey Theatre is the definition of that theatre as "National". If you are the country's "National Theatre", and the specifically national coffers of theatrical talent are becoming empty, and yet you still have to go on fulfilling the definition, then the going gets tough indeed. This has happened with the Abbey. A hundred years of supposedly living Irish theatre, together with two previous centuries of theatrical energy and occasional genius, are still not evident in any lively programme of what could be termed the "Irish Classics". And this means one of two things: either the Abbey is not delivering any cogent presentation of Irish theatre from the past, or it simply is not good enough, or rich enough, to deserve the kind of exploration which the National Theatre in London carries out for British theatre.

The Gaiety is the third large-scale theatrical undertaking in the capital, carrying a different burden from either the Gate or the Abbey, since it has major undertakings which are brought in, and it depends on high profile productions which do not enjoy, at least not to the same extent, either the loyalty which brings audiences to the Gate Theatre, or the benefit of the tourist industry which helps the Abbey. The Gaiety has been through so many changes of direction, and recently embarked on yet another one. It is the nicest theatre in Dublin. Comfortable, old-fashioned, the right size for the city, with a warmth and intimacy which is very positive. The Abbey is cold, filled with the chilly heart of Irish nationalism; the Gate is awkward and angular, appropriate enough for much of what is put on there, but lacking in flexibility. By contrast, the Gaiety is well-suited to everything, from opera to comedy, from spectacle to serious drama. What seems wrong with it is the absence of a coherent and continuous plan of presentations which will develop and strengthen a particular public. Theatre in the modern world needs loyalty. Patrons want to go regularly, and to know that their visits will be rewarded in a consistent way. Without that, the viability is undermined. But recently, the Gaiety has given us improved theatre, stronger individual productions, and a new sense of expectation under the direction of John Costigan.

The Olympia, another of the old traditional theatre buildings the survival of which is astonishing, has moved to a modified theatrical diet involving more music than plays, more spectacle than serious drama. Of the smaller theatres Andrews Lane in the city, and the Civic Theatre in Tallaght, maintain a full run of productions, and many of the others are home to the lively fringe theatre, and the many small companies which provide excellent work and avoid any ideological, preordained interpretation of what, or where, theatre should be.

IV

In a recent profile, the Northern Ireland playwright, Gary Mitchell, was under some pressure to see himself as "Irish". "Does he see himself in the great Irish writing tradition?" was the way the question was put. "Absolutely not, I don't think of myself as Irish in any way. It annoys me when I see my plays in the Irish section in bookshops. I ask why I'm not in the British section. I describe myself as a Protestant writer. I believe in the dignities of Protestantism, in it being a radical force in the world, being truthful, being loyal. It's my way of saying I'm an honest-to-God writer who tells the truth as I see it".

Rejecting the Irish label is an unusual course of action for a writer from Ireland at a time when it is so widely applied in all the art forms as a response to the undoubted sense of national self-confidence. Equally unusual is the deliberate choice of Protestantism as an alternative self-definition. Clearly, Mitchell's work is inspired by an examination of the Protestant creed and how it affects life in Northern Ireland, which is, after all, the subject-matter of his dramatic writing.

When we look at a playwright like Bernard Farrell we find a quite different approach. With him, the fact that the settings of his plays are in Irish suburban or provincial urban life is incidental in terms of the

Irishness, but inescapable in terms of the social structure which derives from the location, and which gives to Farrell the material for making life funny. He would claim, if asked, not a Protestant nor a Catholic, not a Mullingar nor a Greystones location for self-identification, but a human and social situation, possibly with moral overtones, possibly not, but out of which he is able to construct the circumstance of comedy.

On another playwright, Tom Murphy, another theatre critic, and a distinguished one, Fintan O'Toole, recently wrote about Murphy as a "maker" of what he called the counter-culture of the 1960s. The suggestion is there that Murphy, along with his contemporaries, made the culture of their time, finding it in their towns and in themselves. It then became "the cultural air we breathe every day and think about as little as we think about breathing". The rising tide of O'Toole's praise for Murphy evolves into the statement that he "is not merely a great Irish dramatist, but a great European one," which in turn becomes "one of the half-dozen great living dramatists in the English language".

This is dangerous talk. It raises Murphy beyond where he should be, giving him mythical status in theatre, and making normal criticism of individual plays difficult. I have great admiration for his skills as a playwright; I think highly of several works, among them *Bailegangaire*, and *The Gigli Concert*. But the last play I saw, *The Wake*, disintegrated structurally, and I said so in my review. That is what writing theatre criticism involves: facing the reality of good and bad coming from the same. The other kind of writing, which gives to a playwright the huge additional burden of being the architect of our culture, the shaper of our lives, the soothsayer who gives us meaning and direction, is not only flawed, but self-defeating. Our culture, for what it is and for what it means, is the creation of all of us. There is not a throne-room or inner sanctum, where writers and painters are shaping it, and handing it out for inspection and consumption by the rest of us. Too many publicists, theatre directors, cultural historians and commentators, including those engaged in interviews and profile-writing, see the world like this, and it is unhelpful, to put it mildly, to engage in such activity. It is the world of Aosdána, an academy of definition attempting to teach us how to think and act, and to give as tablets of law about our cultural identity and its development.

The critic is and should be concerned more with the success or failure of the individual play. He does his work because he believes in the playwright's ability to deliver good theatre within the compass of what should perhaps be described as the writing identity. And he wanders onto treacherous ground when he begins to seek a value that is added, perhaps self-consciously, to the sum of an "Irish theatrical writing tradition", something which is largely illusory.

I go to the theatre to find writing that is lively and straightforward, and is providing actors and actresses with the opportunity to bring before us a working representation of the life around us. Place and history, nationalism, republicanism, have as much or as little part to play as the comedy that can be produced out of a dysfunctional family — which happens with Farrell — or the tragedy which can be produced from the same source — which was Gary Mitchell's achievement in *A Little World of Our Own*. It is the sustained conviction we have, the effective and unbroken suspension of disbelief, that matters. Long may it continue on the Irish stage.

Theatre of war? Contemporary drama in Northern Ireland

Ashley Taggart

It is a mantra endlessly repeated in schoolrooms and creative writing classes that theatre is about conflict. The flimsiness of this assertion is never more obvious than in a review of Northern Irish drama. For here is a region which has suffered, and continues to suffer, more than its fair share of conflict. So much so, that for many outside the island, the words "Northern Ireland" conjure up little more than television images of rioting and stone-throwing, flak-jackets and petrol-bombs, barricades and sectarian posturing, set to a running score (religious affiliation duly noted) of the dead and wounded.

As I write, with paramilitary cease-fires still (nominally) intact, no visitor could fail to see this as a place riven by ongoing tensions and unforgiven grievances. After the "war that wasn't", we now have the "peace that isn't". Also, quite apart from the obvious signs of sectarianism — murals, marches and counter-marches — it is clear that much of Northern Ireland still exists in a state of what might be called "casualised segregation". Certainly, there are areas where Catholics and Protestants live side-by-side, but the very fact that these are worthy of comment says a lot. In the late twentieth century, Belfast remains a patchwork of well-defined enclaves. To know someone's address is to know, with a fair degree of certainty, "what foot they kick with": whether they are Protestant or Catholic.

Yet such a grim sketch omits one of the key characteristics of Northern Irish life — the mordant humour which informs even the simplest daily transactions, and which pervades the work of all its writers. No matter how bleak the circumstances depicted in their work, they retain a keen sense of the absurd. We may be watching the comedy of desperation, but the glimmer of wit never quite dies. All the dramatists in this brief survey have lived with "The Troubles", have struggled with its divisions, its political sloganeering, its entrenched myths and predictable cruelties. But besides the obvious violence there are more subtle pressures. Here people have to face issues of identity, loyalty, punishment and revenge, which those in a "healthier" society would have the luxury to ignore.

While the rest of Europe has been able to look towards the millennium with relative confidence, Northern Ireland has been unable to wake from the nightmare of its own history. Here, more than elsewhere, the past is never "over and done with", but is always colouring and distorting present perceptions, present realities. For many in this society, upholding tradition can be a life-or-death matter, and the inability to obtain lasting peace, a real amnesty, is very much an inability to create the necessary amnesia. The injunction is always, on the murals, in the songs and stories, to "remember" this atrocity, or that victory, this victim, that martyr. In Northern Ireland, commemoration, celebration and indoctrination are hard to tell apart.

Consequently, in a region where folk memories run to hundreds of years, forgetfulness can be construed as an act of treachery. In the rueful words of the Ulster poet John Hewitt: "I dare not use that loaded word, 'remember'". Little wonder then, that many Northern Irish playwrights take history, or, in Brian Friel's formulation, the questionable act of Making History, as their overt theme.

The extent to which history can be escaped, evaded, shaped or even understood is a major preoccupation in many of the writers currently at work (the "history play" also provides a way of projecting current disputes onto a carefully delimited arena). Friel is undoubtedly the most celebrated contemporary playwright from the six counties, one whose oeuvre has encompassed short stories and radio plays (starting in the 50s and 60s) and, subsequently, a prolific output for the stage. He was born in 1929 near Omagh, Co Tyrone into a Catholic family who later moved to Derry. As one might expect, his plays, especially in the earlier years, reflect a problematic sense of identity and allegiance. This sense of duality pervades his work, undermining any tendency to proffer simple solutions, unambiguous truths, and eating away at the conscience of many of his protagonists. Growing up as he did in a city where the inhabitants could not even agree on its name ("Derry"?/ "Londonderry"?) Friel was sensitised from an early age to the Orwellian doublethink which pervaded the political and social structures of his "homeland".

It was inevitable that while his drama was exclusively centred in the six counties, he would be seen primarily as a "Nationalist playwright", a playwright whose work would be viewed, despite his best efforts, as representative of only one sectarian camp. To escape such branding he had to find new audiences, and, as it were, paint with a broader brush. Yet like many other writers before him, working in the teeth of political struggle, he faced a pointed dilemma: how to remain morally committed in the face of such events as the Bloody Sunday massacre, without finding himself simultaneously forced into an artistic cul-de-sac. And, like many writers before him, he discovered that history, which at one level seemed to pinion the artist and enslave his native land, could also provide a means of liberation.

Of his early plays, *The Francophile* (1960), *The Enemy Within* (1962) and *The Blind Mice* (1963), only the second has been published. In it, we see one use of history to explore contemporary dualities at a third remove, through its portrayal of the conflicting allegiances of St. Columba. Yet the play is generally regarded as less than successful in its use of quasi-allegorical characters and antitheses. Friel had yet to find convincing theatrical expression for the deep divisions (external and internal) with which he was beset.

It is now recognised that the period after *The Enemy Within* saw a maturing of his dramatic method. It is no coincidence that, in the interim, he left Ireland for the U.S.A, a sojourn which he tellingly describes in the terminology of the ex-con as "my first parole from inbred claustrophobic Ireland". In any case, this break resulted in the more experimental *Philadelphia, Here I Come!* (1964) which explored the feelings of a 25 year-old Donegal man on the eve of his emigration to the USA, and used two separate actors to portray rival aspects of his psyche. It received lavish praise on its appearance, not least for this bold embodiment of ambivalence — a feeling easily recognised by many in Northern Ireland — and all those, from North or South, who made up the Irish Diaspora.

Significantly, the play took leave of certain naturalistic conventions which had hampered Friel's development, and opened up new possibilities of exploring psychology by non-verbal means. The attempt to move beyond words, through music, dance and ritual was, from this point forward, an enduring theme. Friel has been extremely prolific in the decades since *Philadelphia, Here I Come!*, writing 14 original plays together with a translation from Chekhov and two adaptations from Turgenev: *Fathers and Sons*, and *A Month In The Country*. His output has ranged from the politically engaged *The Freedom of The City* (1973) which emerged from the events of Bloody Sunday in Derry, when 13 civil rights marchers were shot by British soldiers, *Aristocrats* (1979) which examines the issues of homecoming and belonging, and *Translations* (1980), set in the early 19th century, which looks at the imposition of the English language upon the native population.

In 1980 Friel, alongside the actor Stephen Rea, founded Field Day Theatre Company in Derry, taking *Translations* as their first production. During the 80s Field Day developed into one of the most potent forces in Irish drama, taking original work on tour year after year, while *Translations* went on to acceptance by the National Theatre in London. It was followed by Friel's version of Chekhov's *Three Sisters* in 1981 and *The Communication Cord* a year later. Field Day did not restrict themselves to Friel's work, also producing plays by Athol Fugard, a version of Molière's *Ecole des Maris* by Derek Mahon, and *Antigone (The Riot Act)* by Tom Paulin, in addition to Stewart Parker's ground-breaking *Pentecost* (1987).

Making History (1988) turned out to be Friel's last play for the company. As a work which declares its intent to scrutinise the very possibility of historiography — of any kind of historical objectivity — it displays many of the strengths and weaknesses of this type of engaged theatre. The action begins in the summer of 1591, and centres around Hugh O'Neill, Earl of Tyrone. At this juncture he is faced with a series of fateful decisions, caught as he is between the forces of the English Queen (to whom he has sworn fealty) and the increasingly rebellious Irish clans, led by the Maguires of Fermanagh. O'Neill is well aware that he has reached a crux, and that the coming months will mark either the end of the old Gaelic order or its glorious rebirth. Either way, he is, self-consciously "making history", an act further complicated by his recent marriage to Mabel, one of the new English, and a woman he dearly loves. As Hugh puts it:

> Do I keep faith with my oldest friend and ally, Maguire, and indeed with the Gaelic civilisation that he personifies? Or do I march alongside the forces of Her Majesty?... It really is a nicely-balanced equation. The old dispensation — the new dispensation.... Impulse, instinct, capricious genius, brilliant improvisation — or calculation, good order, common sense, the cold pragmatism of the Renaissance mind (*MH*: 283).

Faced with a choice which he knows means life-or-death, not just for himself but his civilisation, O'Neill feels the oppressive weight of history on his shoulders — he cannot help but see his own decisions in advance retrospective, as they will be judged by future generations. Staring down the wrong end of a telescope as it were, his perception of himself as a player on the stage of history is intensified by the presence of Archbishop Lombard who is, in fact, writing the chronicle of the O'Neills. There are moments when O'Neill, dazzled by the sheer enormity of his actions, falls into Hamlet-like reverie, hoping that history will write him rather than the other way round:

> ... do I grip the hand of the Fermanagh rebel and thereby bear public and imprudent witness to a way of life that my blood comprehends and indeed loves and that is as old as the book of Ruth?...[or that of the English]... which hand do I grasp? Because either way I make an enemy. Either way I interfere with that slow sure tide of history. No, that's unfair, I mustn't embarrass you. Let's put it another way. Which choice would history approve? Or to use the Archbishop's language: if the future historian had a choice of my two alternatives, which would he prefer for his acceptable narrative? Tell me (*MH*: 284).

And back comes the deadening response (from his sister-in-law Mary), "I don't know anything about history, Hugh" (*MH*: 284). Above and beyond all this, we the audience in our historical vantage, aware that we are watching the approach to what has become known as the "flight of the earls", look on with an ironic eye. Among the play's successes is its ability to make us think about not just the veracity of history, but its unvoiced imperatives — to provide a sense of order, succession, above all, to provide an "acceptable narrative". When, exiled and ruined, towards the end of his life, Hugh begs Lombard not to "embalm him in pieties", the historian's rejoinder is simple enough: "People think they want to know the 'facts'; they think they believe in some sort of empirical truth, but what they really want is a story" (*MH*: 334).

Narrative truths are the only ones available to us. Yet the play is unsatisfactory in its portrayal of central relationships, especially that between Hugh and Mabel, which never attains the intensity required of it by Friel's dramatic structure. Despite the emotionally-charged nature of much of the material, it remains head-bound.

Also set within a historical framework is *Dancing at Lughnasa* (1990), arguably Friel's best-known work and one which has since been adapted for cinema. Taking a more personal perspective on historical event, and a more intimate canvas, *Lughnasa* has been described as a "memory play". Its dedication to "those five brave Glenties women" bespeaks its autobiographical origin; moreover the play is "seen" (narrated) through the eyes of Michael, who is aged seven as Friel would have been at the time of the action. The year is 1936 and the drama unfolds in the impoverished farmhouse occupied by Kate, Maggie, Rose, Agnes and Chris (Michael's mother).

If *Making History* is clearly "about" something, and that something is the historical process, the predominant themes in *Dancing at Lughnasa* are more difficult to define. The women fight, laugh together, struggle against hardship and the outside world, undergo the pain of faithless, lost or absent partners, and try to restore their brother (Jack) to health. Jack has been a missionary in Africa for many years, and has been sent home in a state of mental confusion after some unspecified transgression. In some ways he fulfils the role of Shakespearean fool in the piece, subverting the "respectability" the women strive to uphold. Indeed the human cost of keeping the family together and retaining a sense of dignity is one of the strongest impressions conveyed. Where Hugh O'Neill struggled to shoulder the burden of historical responsibility, these characters strive to retain their pride faced with forces beyond their control. If O'Neill is called upon to show vision, they need primarily the virtues of the oppressed: stoicism, hard work, determination not to be cowed.

Their world is assailed from all sides. The stigma of Michael's "illegitimacy" is a blow that is counterbalanced for a while by Jack's status as a missionary priest. Yet on Jack's return, it soon becomes clear that the man the sisters regard as a "hero and a saint" has a tainted history — the suggestion being that he was dismissed for homosexuality. The handsome young man who had left them so many years before is barely recognisable from the shambling wreck they meet on his return. To make things worse, Jack has clearly lost much of his Christian zeal in favour of a dangerously tolerant Pantheism: he has "gone native" on them. Thus this human symbol of self-sacrificial virtue returns as a ghastly self-parody — a "leper priest" in more than one sense.

Other destabilising forces quickly become apparent. Gerry Evans, Michael's father, turns up unannounced, throwing Chris into a state of anguished anticipation. Meanwhile Rose, the sister who is "simple", and of whom the others are consequently protective, insists on pursuing an affair with Danny Bradley, a married man. Also, Rose and Agnes, who earn a little money by knitting from home, have their source of income suddenly terminated with the advent of industrial knitting machines. Over and above all this, Kate, the only wage-earner, finds her teaching job imperilled because of Jack's dismissal. Even the pagan rites of Lughnasa seem to exert a subversive pull upon the household, undermining the firm hold of Catholicism. Kate sees the dissolution of a way of life occurring in front of her eyes:

> You work hard at your job. You try to keep the home together. You perform your duties as best you can — because you believe in responsibilities and obligations and good order. And then suddenly, suddenly you realise that hair cracks are appearing everywhere; that control is slipping away; that the whole thing is so fragile it can't be held together much longer. It's all about to collapse, Maggie (*DL*: 56).

A lament as heartfelt as any in Beckett, perhaps, and sadly prescient. Yet there are moments of release, even of transcendence, in the general downward curve of the family's fortunes. The spontaneous outpouring of emotion during the women's dance is one such. Yet it should be said that this is a complex, even darkly ritualistic event, not the sanitised come-all-ye of the film version, but something closer to Dionysian abandon, or that of the feast of Lughnasa. The stage directions make this clear.

> They meet — they retreat. They form a circle and wheel round and round. But the movements seem caricatured; and the sound is too loud; and the beat is too fast; and the almost recognisable dance is made grotesque because — for example — instead of holding hands, they have their arms tightly around one another's neck, one another's waist.... With this too loud music, this pounding beat, this shouting — calling — singing, this parodic reel, there is a sense of order being subverted, of the women consciously and crudely

caricaturing themselves, indeed of near-hysteria being induced (*DL*: 37).

We watch the destruction of the household with a sense of horrified fascination. *Dancing at Lughnasa* is, primarily, a domestic tragedy, a reminder that history is a constant questioning of what is meaningful, and itself an answer, based upon the detailed scrutiny of "Ordinary" lives.

By fixing on the domestic arena, the small canvas, many other playwrights attempt to, if not evade, at least humanise the ineluctable political slant given to life inside the six counties. In his 1994 study, *Contemporary Irish Drama*, Anthony Roche analyses Christina Reid's *Tea in a China Cup* (1982) as a memory play with some similarities to *Dancing at Lughnasa*. Reid's play is set in Belfast in the early 1970s, but the narrative voice, that of Beth, roves over two world wars. Yet while Beth, like Michael, provides a unifying consciousness, she takes a more active and varied role in the action, sometimes observing from afar, sometimes intervening, and even conjuring up scenes she could not possibly have witnessed. The world she depicts is that of working class Protestant women, and their "take", alternately bitter, plaintive and grimly funny, on the series of causes their men have felt it necessary to fight and die for.

The message is stark: history as a succession of battles lost and won is a perversion not only of fact, but of moral sensibility. What is edited out is the cost, to wives and children of every soldier killed, and the repercussions of that loss, running down the generations. Perhaps too, there is an echo of Gerry's musing in *Lughnasa*, when he asks himself whether he is doing the right thing by signing up for the Republican cause in Spain:

> ... it's somewhere to go — isn't it? Maybe that's the important thing for a man: a named destination — democracy, Ballybeg, heaven. Women's illusions aren't so easily satisfied... (*DL*: 78).

While the men wrap themselves in "the cause", the women look on with clearer eyes, anticipating the pain ahead, and finding solace in rituals of containment so small they make no attempt to hide their ineffectuality — the tea in a china cup.

Christina Reid has written 10 plays since 1982 and her career has embraced periods as writer-in-residence at the Lyric, Belfast and London's Young Vic. Her work is especially notable for its insight into the differences between how men and women experience the passage of time, for its accurate rendition of Belfast humour, and for its ability to incorporate "The Troubles" into the fabric of her plays without letting political conflicts dominate to the exclusion of all else. Like Anne Devlin, she creates a feminist viewpoint which reminds us how far the

Northern Irish conflict is prosecuted, chronicled, and controlled by men, and in doing so, she forces us to challenge the current political agenda. Not so much a case of making history, but of remaking it: the theatre of revisionism.

There are similarities here with Anne Devlin's play, *Ourselves Alone*, first produced in 1985. This is an examination of the nationalist cause in its effects upon three women, Frieda, Josie and Donna. Frieda and Josie are sisters with a very different attitude to "the struggle". While Frieda, who is a singer, dreams of writing the song that will take her out of the backstreets, Josie is having an affair with Cathal O'Donnell, a (married) IRA man. The contrast in outlook is immediately apparent. Here, Frieda speaks of Donna's loyalty to their brother Liam, who is in the Kesh prison:

> **Frieda**:… That's the only loyalty I know or care about. Loyalty to someone you love, regardless! I'd like to think that if I loved someone I'd follow that person to hell! Politics has nothing to do with it!
>
> **Josie**: One day you will understand when you come to the limits of what you can do yourself, that this is not dogma, that there are no personal differences between one person and another that are not political.
>
> **Frieda**: You can't believe that.
>
> **Josie**: I do. I do (*OA*: 23).

The antithesis between the personal and the political is of course an ancient one, but in the context of Northern Ireland, and examined from a female point of view it allows Devlin to subject ideological "sacred cows" to uncomfortable scrutiny. As Frieda, the (un)free spirit puts it:

> … when there's a tricolour over the City Hall, Donna will still be making coffee for Joe Conran, and Josie will still be keeping house for her daddy, because it doesn't matter a damn whether the British are here or not.

To which her sister dryly answers:

> That's just your excuse for not doing anything.
>
> **Frieda**: Aye. But it's a good one (*OA*: 30).

The argument is not just one of principle, but of focus. Do sexual politics matter more than the politics of nationalism and unionism? Or are they part of the same thing? Are the oppressors the occupying forces on the streets, or the husbands, fathers and lovers of these women who require them to make daily sacrifices on their behalf? John McDermot, member of the Worker's Party, puts the ideologue's case against Frieda succinctly: "…. What you lack is a conceptual framework". But Frieda's light-hearted rejoinder is to the point: "One of these days, John McDermot, you'll collapse in a conceptual framework" (*OA*: 38).

Devlin draws our attention to the issue of who is fixing the agenda, whose "conceptual framework" is dominating, and, almost as importantly, what is being excluded from it. A framework can also become a prison. In this sense, the entire play is an exercise in "collapsing" conceptual frameworks — an act of calculated subversion. In the course of the play all three women find themselves compromised by their own dreams — for a united Ireland, for a transcendent love, for some hope of tranquillity. The men around them twist and turn according to the implacable exigencies of the cause, and their momentary needs for sex and shelter — betraying their partners where they deem it necessary. Meanwhile the women, who have to face up to longer-term realities like the bearing of children, are left battered and disaffected. Towards the end, Donna gives vent to this feeling of radical, almost fatalistic, reappraisal:

> .... All my life I felt I had to run fast, seek, look, struggle for things and hold on to things or lose them, but as soon as I felt the child inside me again, the baby quickening, I knew it was coming and there was nothing I could do. I felt for the first time the course of things, the inevitability. And I thought no, I won't struggle any more, I shall just do it. And all that time — longing — was wasted, because life just turns things out as they are. Happiness, sadness has really nothing to do with it (*OA*: 89).

In the stoicism and suffering of the women, the play's title suddenly appears in its full ironic light, as an acerbic comment on the fact that many of the real battlelines (in the sex war) have yet to be recognised. Devlin leaves us in little doubt who the "Ourselves" of the title might be. Later plays, such as *After Easter* (1994) have tended to stretch the limitations of stage naturalism, taking leave of an overtly political arena to open up such issues as sanity, identity and belonging.

In 1983, the Charabanc Theatre Company was set up in Northern Ireland as a collaborative venture, at least in part to provide strong roles for female performers. It went on, like Field Day, to become a significant player on the theatrical scene. Key figures here were Marie Jones, Carol Scanlon Moore and Eleanor Methven. Although the writing too was initially collaborative, Marie Jones was increasingly to dominate this aspect of the production, eventually breaking away with *The Hamster Wheel* in 1990. In this connection too, it is worth mentioning Martin Lynch, who worked for a time with Charabanc as a writer, and has produced consistently strong work such as *Dockers*, *The Interrogation of Ambrose Fogarty*, and, perhaps his greatest success, *Pictures of Tomorrow*

(1993), a play drawing implicit parallels between the Irish experience and the Spanish civil war.

The Charabanc plays tended towards social satire, with a finely developed sense of political injustice and an ear for Ulster wit. Since Charabanc, Jones has continued to be active, writing for radio and television as well as the stage, with more recent work premiered by the Belfast company DubbelJoint.

A Night in November (1995) a monologue about a Protestant "dole clerk" who suddenly grasps that he is living a lie, provided a recent success. The character, Kenneth McCallister comes to the bitter if belated realisation that all the values he has grown up with, are in fact, questionable, if not repellent.

> We are the perfect Prods, we come in kits, we are standard regulation, we come from the one design, like those standard kitchens with the exact spaces for standard cookers and fridges, our dimensions never vary and that's the way we want it, but what happens when the kit is put together and the appliances don't fit the spaces... what happens... chaos, mayhem and we can't cope, we can't cope. From that moment on, I knew I had to stop, stop before it was too late, stop before I destroyed my wife and our un-putupable little life.... I had to train myself not to think, not to see, just keep your head down and get on with it (*NN*: 23).

But of course his attempt to "keep his head down and get on with it" goes awry, the catalyst for his final step into the dark being shame at the treatment he sees meted out to Republic of Ireland supporters in a qualifying game in Belfast for the football world cup.

Once Kenneth starts to pick at the first thread of his values, the world as he had known it unravels before his eyes. He perceives for the first time the pettiness of his aspirations (for example, to be accepted into the golf club before his Catholic colleague) and the stultifying need for respectability which has hitherto governed his life. He even tries to explain all this to his wife, but receives only uncomprehending hostility in response. More terrifying, perhaps, he begins to question his own identity as a British loyalist; discovering in himself a keen awareness of just how limited his horizons really are:

> It's like we're living at the top of a bloody big house and we think that we've got the best room, so we keep ourselves locked in, and we won't even open the door to let in fresh air. The air in the room is stale and we breathe it decade after decade, year after year, day after day and we are safe in our stale air (*NN*: 35).

Kenneth's act of liberation is a secretly planned trip to New York, to watch the Republic play. When Ireland beat Italy he is caught up in a mass delirium which sweeps away any vestige of reserve. He makes a shocking discovery: "I am free of it, I am a free man.... I am a Protestant Man, I'm an Irish Man" (*NN*: 30).

Each of these dramatists has been obliged to find stage metaphors expressive of a bitterly divided society, where individuals are often put under enormous pressure to conform, to stand up and be counted. For many in Northern Ireland, and certainly those without the buffer of money, it is very hard to sit on the fence. The danger for the writer is that he or she may become overwhelmed by the scale of events and fall into naked polemic. Each of the playwrights examined here has side-stepped this temptation in a different way — by challenging the established political agenda, widening the focus of debate, or taking it into another historical arena.

Bill Morrison, in his trilogy *A Love Song For Ulster* (1991) takes another approach. His play had its genesis in a comment by the SDLP leader John Hume to the effect that Catholics and Protestants were forced to live together in the same house. From this, Morrison, whose writing career stretches back to the early seventies, developed an extended allegory based around the idea of a "mixed" marriage — and a marriage of convenience at that. In the first "panel" of the triptych, we follow the fate of John, a Protestant, and his wedding to Kate, a free-spirited Catholic woman, as she finds herself marooned in the North after the 1922 partition of Ireland. A British sergeant outlines the divide in brutally simple terms:

> .... You are all a pain in the arse. We are fed up with you. So. We are going to divide this island. Those of you who are loyal to the Empire and want to stay within it can have the North, and the rest of you who demand independence can have your own country in the South (*LS*: 9).

The couple are forced to make do as well as they can. As John says to Kate — "We only have one choice. To make the best of it". When Kate refuses to consummate the relationship as an act of protest, John rapes her on the kitchen table. Yet despite this initial cruelty, with the passage of time they do forge some kind of bond, watched jealously by Victor, John's brother and a more hard-line representative of loyalism.

As the years pass, Kate finds herself torn between the demands of her Southern family, (embodied by her brother Gabriel, who has taken up arms in the Nationalist cause) and those of her husband, for whom she has developed a genuine love. With an awful sense of inevitability, we see the two forces inching towards collision when John feels duty-bound to become a B Special, and go out on patrol. As with the marriage, all seems predestined, with little room for the exercise of any personal freedom.

> **Kate**: What have you become? What does this make you?
> **John**: I'm a B Special. It's a part-time militia.
> **Kate**: A local army?
> **John**: It's a bit of extra money.
> **Kate**: We don't need it.
> **John**: I have to join. Everybody has joined. There's been attacks over the border. We have to defend our homes and families.
> **Kate**: Why must you join?
> **John**: There's not much choice in it (*LS*: 27).

Individual choice comes a poor second to the political demands of the time, couched in the ancient terms of land, property, religious affiliation. So too, with Gabriel, who, on the other side of the divide, finds that his loyalty to the cause has brought him to the point where to prove his Republican credentials he must kill his brother-in-law; or as he tries to see it, destroy not a man, but a symbol. Nonetheless, John is killed and Victor, as his name suggests, steps in to take over his brother's wife and his inheritance.

So the cycle begins again, this time with distrust and hatred etched deeper into both husband and wife, especially when the birth of a son raises new questions of upbringing and identity. Morrison's trilogy is a meditation on historical process, but also a commentary on the role played by individual personalities. For, interspersed into the allegorical recreation of Northern Irish history is a series of darkly comic dialogues by Mick and Willie, working class figures who appear as ghosts for most of the action and ruminate at length upon such issues as the "sacrifice" of Isaac by Abraham. Their presence acts as a satirical or choric counterbalance to the mass of events around them, and leavens an allegorical structure which threatens at times to collapse under its own weight. In the long view of history, characters like Mick and Willie are spear-carriers, voices off, the powerless and ignored multitude. Willie puts it succinctly:

> **Willie**: I know about history. History always leaves out what people felt about it while it was happening. It always leaves out that most people didn't like it, didn't want it, protested about it and were generally fucked by it.
>
> **Mick**: That's because it never made any difference to the final result (*LS*: 4).

In the nineties, new voices have emerged from the six counties to provide their own distinctive slant on events there. Daragh Carville's

Language Roulette (1996) brought a postmodern playfulness to bear on issues of love and betrayal, whilst Owen McCafferty first came to attention with early monologues such as *I Won't Dance Don't Ask Me* (1993) and *The Waiting List* (1994) and has continued in later works to tap into an Ulster tradition of storytelling, wordplay, and joyously subversive impersonation. McCafferty's later, more developed pieces, like *Shoot the Crow* (1997) show a delight in reproducing the richly-textured language of Belfast streets and bars, where idle philosophising is interwoven with colourful obscenity, and the inconsequential always threatens to erupt centre-stage. Here Petesy and Socrates, two tilers, discuss "the plumber":

> **Petesy:**... what plumber?
> **Socrates:** What plumber, what plumber, the plumber plumber.
> **Petesy:** There's two plumbers.
> **Socrates:** The big fat geezer.
> **Petesy:** They're both big fat geezers.
> **Socrates:** The one that kicked a hole in an Alsatian's throat — that one.
> **Petesy:** A Doberman and the fella ripped it's lugs off.
> **Socrates:** Ripped its lugs off — what for? You talk a lotta balls, y'know that? (SC: 32).

Shoot the Crow is a pacey, tightly plotted piece of theatre, reminiscent, in its tempo and sardonic humour, of David Mamet's work in the eighties. In the course of the play the four tilers find themselves pushed to the limits of their mutual tolerance and beyond. Under pressure, each of them transgresses the unspoken rules which allow them to work together — the first of which is "whatever you say, say nothin'":

> **Ding-Ding:** I'm graftin' away, he's spoutin' some cleavers in my ear about discoverin' somethin' about his Da or somethin' next thing he's gurnin' away like a child — mad man, know what I'm sayin' name of fuck ye can't be at that crack — that's not on, ye can't be at that.
> **Petesy:** A know that, a know that — fuck 'im.
> **Ding-Ding:** All the years I've been graftin' never witnessed the like of that — I've seen men go through some serious shit but I mean it never got outta order — just burst into tears. I don't know what the fuck he was expectin' me t'do — not equipped to handle that gear like am a?
> **Petesy:** Who the fuck is — he should know better like shouldn't he? (SC: 43)

In 1998 McCafferty had a notable success with *Mojo Mickybo*, a tale of two boys growing up in 1970s Belfast who forge a friendship across the divide. The play captures brilliantly the mixture of fantasy, self-aggrandisement, incomprehension and fear that makes up their world, and deftly depicts the forces that tear it apart. And although it is a two-hander, the fevered imagination of the boys allows the playwright to let them step in and out of the characters around them — sometimes at bewildering speed — bringing to life a substantial cast. As with all ten-year-olds, inner and outer reality tends to merge. What is telling is how we see the adults around them, stunted by alcohol and hopelessness, resorting to the same kind of wish-fulfilment.

> **Mickybo**: Butch and Sundance were gonna go to Australia, but then they got shot so they didn't.
> **Mickybo's Da**: Gooday gooday gooday digga — yer Ma has a brother out there, an eejit like, but doin all right for himself — Australia — be better than this fuckin kip — what do ya think son, think we should all go to Australia?
> **Mickybo**: Can Mojo go?
> **Mickybo's Da**: Aye, why not, we'll all fuck off to Australia — gooday gooday gooday digga.
> **Mickybo**: Wanna go to Australia, Mojo?
> **Mojo**: I'll have to ask ma Ma... (*MM*: 25).

Other distinctive voices have begun to emerge from Belfast in the 90s. Gary Mitchell began his writing career in radio, moving to the stage with an adaptation of one of his own radio plays, *Independent Voice*, produced in 1993 by Tinderbox Theatre Company. Since then, he has turned out roughly a play a year, with titles such as *Alternative Future*, *That Driving Ambition* and *Sinking*. *In a Little World of Our Own* opened in 1997 at the Peacock Theatre, Dublin, and, after a successful Irish tour, went on to receive the "best new play" category in the 1997 Irish Theatre Awards. The play is set in Belfast's Protestant heartland, and revolves around the relationship between three brothers, Gordon, Richard and Ray. Whilst Ray is a committed and feared member of the UDA, Gordon, under the influence of his fiancée Deborah, has "found God". The entire action is set in the claustrophobic confines of a council house on the Rathcoole estate, where Gordon and Ray do battle over the soul of Richard, who is "simple". Although it soon emerges that Gordon plans to move his younger brother out to live with him, Ray is determined to retain control — and to keep Richard living in the house.

Intriguingly, when Mitchell discusses the issue of free will and faith, he turns to the same Biblical example (of Abraham and Isaac) as Bill Morrison in *A Love Song For Ulster*. Here, Gordon questions his religious belief:

> **Gordon**: I'm not too good at praying. When I pray God doesn't speak to me or if he does, I don't know what he's saying.

Everybody else seems to be able to understand him, but not me. I just talk and that's it.

Deborah: Do you want me to pray for you?

Gordon: What if God did answer me? What if he told me to do something that I didn't want to do, or I couldn't do, what then?

Deborah: Gordon. He wouldn't do that.

Gordon: What about Abraham?

Deborah: Exactly!

Gordon: See! That's what I mean. God asked him to kill his own son. Know what I mean? I would have just said no.

Deborah: Then God wouldn't ask you to do that. See? It's all to do with faith. You have to believe.

Gordon: But how do you believe?

Deborah: You pray and ask God to help you (*LW*: 20).

In the moral climate of Northern Ireland, which at times seems closer to Old Testament vengeance than New Testament forgiveness, the lines between belief, faith and delusion can seem dangerously blurred. The only constant in the world at large as much as in this "little world" of the house is the certainty of sacrifice.

Even with a playwright so firmly rooted in contemporary reality, the echoes of the past continue to resound through his work. In many ways it is not surprising then that Mitchell, like so many other Northern Irish dramatists, eventually feels the need to address it directly, as he does in his 1998 work, *Tearing The Loom*, set in the 1798 rebellion. This searing piece of theatre, which begins with the garrotting of a young woman, stares with open eyes at what violence does to families who are caught up in forces beyond their control. By concentrating on a Protestant family who are divided in their sympathies for the United Irishmen, Mitchell cleverly evades the sometimes deadening even-handedness which other "Troubles plays" are forced into. From the first moments, we watch the noose closing around this family, with a sense of awful inevitability. Yet, somehow — and this is its great strength — Mitchell's play keeps us emotionally engaged. Against all our better judgement, we make ourselves believe, right until the chilling conclusion, that there is some way these people can escape their fate.

Mitchell's next play *Trust*, which premiered at the Royal Court, returns to contemporary Belfast, and the dilemmas of the current situation. Whilst undoubtedly well-crafted, its emotional line seems almost too neat after the excoriating power of the previous two works, yet it succeeded in bringing this talented writer to a wider audience. As with Friel, and many of the other playwrights I have looked at who turn to historical material, the past is scrutinised not merely because it is a rich source of dramatic incident and character, but because in Northern Irish society, more than many others, it is inescapable. By holding a mirror up to the past, acknowledging its injustices, the hope remains that we can attain, if not a cathartic release from old hatreds, then at least a fresh take on the current impasse. In one sense it could be said that Northern Irish theatre is thriving because its writers do not have to step outside their front door for material which, in all its tragic intensity, begs to be written.

Yet this is to simplify the situation. An ear for conflict is not enough. The dramatist must have an audience prepared to undergo sometimes painful self-examination. He or she must have the confidence to imbue local events with universal significance; and above all, find ways to humanise the inhumane, while resisting the temptations of polemic. Finally they must give voice to the instinctive dark humour which crosses the divide, and which, consciously or otherwise, unites its people.

Works Cited:

Beckett, Samuel, (1986), *The Complete Dramatic Works* (London: Faber and Faber)

Carville, Daragh, (1998), *Language Roulette* in *Far From the Land, Contemporary Irish Plays*, ed., John Fairleigh (London: Methuen)

Devlin, Anne, (1986), *Ourselves Alone* (London: Faber and Faber)

------ (1994), *After Easter* (London: Faber and Faber)

Etherton, Michael, (1989), *Contemporary Irish Dramatists* (London: Macmillan)

Friel, Brian, (1999), *Plays One* and *Plays Two* (London: Faber and Faber)

Heaney, Seamus, (1990) *The Cure at Troy: A Version of Sophocles' "Philoctetes"* (London: Faber and Faber)

Jones, Marie, (1995), *A Night in November* (Dublin: New Island Books)

Lynch, Martin, (1996), *Three plays*, ed., Damian Smyth (Belfast: Lagan Press)

McCafferty, Owen, (1998), *Plays and Monologues* (Belfast: Lagan Press)

------ (1998), *Mojo Mickybo* (Belfast: Lagan Press)

Mitchell, Gary, (1998), *Tearing the Loom* and *In a Little World of Our Own* (London: Nick Hern Books)

------ (1999), *Trust* (London: Nick Hern Books)

Morrison, Bill, (1994), *A Love Song for Ulster* (London: Nick Hern Books)

Reid, Christina, (1987), *Joyriders* and *Tea in a China Cup* (London: Methuen)

McGuinness, Frank, (1986), *Observe the Sons of Ulster Marching Towards The Somme* (London: Faber and Faber)

Maxwell, D.E.S., (1984), *A Critical History of Modern Irish Drama 1891-1980* (Cambridge: Cambridge University Press)

Parker, Stewart, (1989), *Three Plays for Ireland: Northern Star, Heavenly Bodies and Pentecost* (Birmingham: Oberon Books)

Paulin, Tom, (1985), *The Riot Act: A Version of Sophocles' "Antigone"* (London: Faber and Faber)

Roche, Anthony, (1994), *Contemporary Irish Drama: From Beckett to McGuinness* (Dublin: Gill and Macmillan)

Theatre — Act or Place? *

Caoimhe McAvinchey

Over the past few years the world of Irish theatre has broken through the walls of the Abbey, the Lyric, and Druid Theatre to the streets of London, New York and beyond. Young Irish playwrights have been internationally hailed as the saviours of theatre. The 1999 Edinburgh Festival Fringe was stormed by an influx of acclaimed Irish productions. Presently, the theatre seems to have a clean bill of health, at least artistically if not financially.

But does theatre, particularly Irish Theatre, have a future? Or perhaps the more provocative question is: *should* theatre have a future? Why should we expect that audiences will want to go to the theatre in 10, 50 or 100 years time? And why, when the future of theatre is questioned is there a wave of defensiveness that implies that theatre has an implicit right to exist well into the twenty-first century and beyond?

Presumably you, the reader, have an interest if not a livelihood in theatre. But how often do you go? And, more pertinently, how often do you go *reluctantly*? How often do you leave inspired and elated? And how often do you leave having spent the last two and a half hours thinking about all the things you could have done including the things you dread most like tax returns and hand washing?

If there was no such thing as theatre would we, the prospective audience, actually miss it? I'm not trying to be flippant but there are times when I wonder why I am involved with this bizarre world where a group of people get together for four weeks to make something that, if they have a great marketing strategy, some money and a lengthy run, a few hundred or even thousand people may get to see. And of those who do actually see it, maybe half will feel disappointed, bored and cheated of their ten pounds.However, there are other times that I feel that anyone who doesn't work in theatre is leading a half life, that I'm extraordinarily fortunate to see and occasionally participate in an event that changes the way you look at the world. It is asking an awful lot of theatre to do this all of the time but in my experience it doesn't do it often enough.

Theatre is a nebulous term that covers everything from the actual building that houses the event to the action itself; from Kabuki's highly codified performances to Geese Theatre Company's work in prisons; from Niall Tobin's one man show to Théâtre de Complicité's epic ensembles; from regional rep theatre productions of the classics to the Wooster Group's presentation of reworked texts from the canon; from Macnas, who parade their theatre through the streets with the help of a town's local inhabitants to the student drama companies busying away in campuses across the world. Theatre, as a concept, is huge. It has a well documented past, a seemingly healthy present, but again, what of the future? Other media such as TV, the Internet and now DVD, have ensured that audiences expect and demand a high level of visceral stimulation. These media take on board technological developments and swiftly incorporate them. Audiences have and demand a much greater stimulation threshold now than they did 10 let alone 40 years ago.

A 1950s cinema audience would be traumatised by the sensory overload of contemporary classic films like *Jaws*, *Jurassic Park* and *Star Wars*. However, if the same audience were to find themselves in many of the rep theatres today they may be taken aback at the issues addressed but rarely by the structure or style in which these issues are presented.

Why has Irish theatre not changed greatly over the past few decades? Is it because it is happy to just do what it does so comfortably and occasionally so well? Audience figures may not be overwhelmingly high but at least there are audiences to speak of, so surely theatre in its current form is appealing to someone. And if it's not broken why fix it?

There is also the possibility that theatre practitioners are afraid to push the boundaries of it in case it makes audiences uncomfortable and they decide not to come back. This brings me back to my previous point. An audience, however small, is surely better than none. But there is another even more disturbing possibility. Perhaps theatre has gone as far as it can go? We should consider the possibility that unless theatre develops from its safe haven of well made plays with a persistently linear narrative and fetish for naturalism that theatre, as a contemporary cultural medium, might have a limited shelf life.

This may seem desperately depressing but there are, of course, beacons of hope. Theatre directors like Peter Brook, Robert Wilson and Elizabeth le Compte have shattered the mould of audience expectations. Such internationally acclaimed directors are few and far between and their work is rarely seen here as a possible alternative, exciting and successful approach to theatre. This is where it becomes clear that international festivals, like the Dublin, Galway and Belfast International festivals are vital laboratories of the imagination, where ideas can be sparked and fertilised in response to productions which work in a totally different style than an Irish audience can expect to see.

When I think back to the theatre that particularly excites me, that gives me hope in a vibrant future of theatre, it tends to be work that literally breaks the boundaries of theatre buildings by moving around within them or leaving them altogether.

One of the earliest, striking and influential productions I have seen was an Ulster Youth Theatre production of *Stations* directed by Nick Phillipou in 1990. A number of plays by Irish writers written in response to Seamus Heaney's *Station Island* were performed in promenade, linked by the text of the poem. No sooner had the audience settled into a comfortable position to watch the action than we were ushered around the space, our perspectives constantly changing.

More recently, Katie Mitchell's production of some of Samuel Beckett's shorter plays was presented in the Tower Street Theatre in East Belfast as part of the Belfast Festival at Queens in 1997. This large black box studio space was sectioned into different areas, where the audience was guided through the darkness from one space to another. This installation promenade was utterly disorientating and powerful, as you were made so aware of your environment and ultimately the entire theatrical experience through the continual disruption of your relation to it. You would rarely question this sense of self and place in a traditional environment.

Both these events had powerful texts with a strong directorial vision that shattered the theatre/audience status quo and was welcomed by the surprised and ultimately utterly engaged audience. Another notable site-specific piece that literally stopped people in their tracks was *Flight* by the Australian company, Strange Fruit. This free outdoor performance in 1999's Galway Arts Festival was a truly inspiring occasion. The company shimmied up 5 rubber, bendy 12 foot poles and used simple but effective costumes and no words to tell the story of Icarus and Daedalus in a way that arrested and immersed the attention of the passing shoppers. Five creatures hovered and dived through the air on a fairly dull Saturday afternoon. The small crowd that had gathered swelled until there were a few hundred people entranced by what they were seeing. *Flight* lasted about 30 minutes. No one paid to be there. No one felt obliged to stay if they didn't want to. Yet the audience was one of the most attentive I had ever seen.

Audiences are increasingly sophisticated, constantly caught in and negotiating their way through a barrage of advertising images. Their attention is harder to catch let alone maintain — crudely, they are harder to impress. But audiences also have an established set of conventions of both expectation and behaviour that allow them to slip into a particular mode when they enter a space that is recognised and labelled 'theatre'.

Site specific work disrupts audience preconceptions of theatre. During the 1998 Belfast Festival and Fringe, two site specific theatre productions gripped the media and audience's attention — Grid Iron Theatre Company's adaptation of Angela Carter's *The Bloody Chamber* in the weir running under the Lagan River and Tinderbox's co-production of *Northern Star* in the First Presbyterian Church, the spiritual home of the leaders of the United Irish men in 1790s. By taking the audience and the theatre activity out of the theatre building you are automatically playing with the audience's sense of expectation and allowing them to engage in a different way than they would in a more traditional environment.

The audience curiosity and acceptance of site specific work was confirmed by the sell-out success of *The Wedding Community Play* in the 1999 Belfast Festival at Queens. The play, scripted by Martin Lynch, Marie Jones and the participants of community theatre companies in Belfast, invited the audience into the homes of the parents of Nicola Marshall and Damien Kelly. A limited audience of 72 boarded two buses and travelled to both homes to watch the families prepare for this mixed marriage. The audience then went to St Anne's Cathedral for the church ceremony and the Hilton for the reception. This highly extraordinary event captured the imaginations not only of international critics and regular theatre goers, but also those of people who would never normally consider going to a theatre event in a building labelled "theatre".

I recently saw the Abbey's production of Bernard Farrell's *Kevin's Bed*. It was well received by the audience who gave it great applause. A couple at the front of the auditorium stood up and continued to clap wildly. No one else stood up. As I was leaving the theatre I heard the man who gave the standing ovation say to his companion in great frustration at the rest of the audience's lack of appreciation "What the hell do they expect to see on the stage — God"?

This made me think that, if there is such a thing as God and it appeared on the Abbey stage once a week: would the audiences even react with more than a round of applause and, at a push, a standing ovation? Either audiences are impossible to impress or it seems that a traditionally assigned space, whether it's labelled church, theatre, or school, has fairly rigid audience/congregation expectations and behavioural conventions that are hard to shift within the same known environment. Are we so used to anticipating a particular thing to happen in a particular space that we know the accepted behaviour of convention and stick to it?

I've been doing an experiment with the Lyric Drama Studio in Belfast to see if audiences are as hungry for site-specific theatre as I think they are. In June 1999 we did a site specific promenade adaptation of *The Picture of Dorian Gray* in the disused psychology building at Queens. There was an audience capacity of 25 people per night who were brought on a journey through the house and the play. Our next project, "On the Outside, Looking Inside", was a collaboration with the visual artist Rita Duffy at the old Gasworks at the bottom of the Ormeau Road. This "cathedral to the industrial" as Rita refers to it has been lying empty for years and has recently been bought to be developed into offices. Because the building was too dangerous to allow the public into it we had to make something happen within the building that could be seen from outside. Huge shadow bodies worked in the windows as the audience gathered outside listening to a collage of voices on personal stereos. Both experiments worked. The audience in their response to both productions kept coming back to the same point, that because of the location of the event and their fresh relationship with it, they felt more engaged and involved with the entire event.

I'm not advocating site specific work as the be all and end all — as the *only* future for theatre. But what I am saying is that it is *one* way that allows theatre to find a way to reach beyond its current comfortable boundaries, to shake up and re-educate both theatre audiences' and theatre practitioners' expectations of themselves. Theatre has to reach beyond comfort and complacency if audiences are to give theatre a future that spans well into the next century and, if theatre works hard enough, beyond.

*This paper is based on a conference paper given at 'Theatre and the Future: A forum on new directions in theatre practice and study' hosted by Carysfort Press, Drama Studies Centre, UCD and Project Arts Centre, October 1999.

Come Dance With Me in Ireland: Current developments in the independent theatre sector

Joseph Long

Echoing Yeats, President Mary Robinson's invitation, in her inaugural address, to "Come dance with me in Ireland", has been taken up with particular gusto by the young theatre and dance groups which have come into existence in the past decade. New beginnings often have deep roots, and if the Robinson presidency appeared to many as a sudden enlightenment and a dramatic bid for modernity, it was equally the culmination of more than two decades of radical and far-reaching change. Already in 1993, Gemma Hussey, former minister of education and exemplifying in herself the new and significant role of women in Irish public life, noted: "An inward-looking, rural, deeply conservative, nearly 100% Roman Catholic and impoverished country has become urbanized, industrialized, and Europeanized.... And still the hunger for change is there" (Quoted by Murray: 1997, 245).

That change and hunger for change can be seen in the streets, as Dublin has become a cosmopolitan city, attracting young visitors from all over Europe and beyond. It is expressed with increasing coherence and energy in the practice and policies of the many new and emerging performance groups of the nineties. In the early eighties, a group such as *Rough Magic* was exceptional. Founded in 1984, they brought the work of dramatists such as Howard Brenton and Caryl Churchill to Dublin, as well as fostering new writing and offering professional opportunities to young actors and new directors. Today, they are a well-established company and their pioneering function is shared by younger groups too numerous to list. Many of the newcomers are interested in exploring the limits of theatrical expression. *Pan Pan Theatre Company* has delved into Artaud and the Theatre of Cruelty. Their team includes mute actors and the physically impaired. Their unsettling performances push vocal and physical expression to the limits — even beyond the limits, some might think. They want to shift the expectations of the theatre-going public, and they have organized several international seminars with like-minded companies from across Europe, to share ideas and experiences. *Barabbas... the Company* are a remarkable group of mime and clown artists, who have benefited from technical training in the Lecoq School in Paris and elsewhere. The three artists who form the core of the group, Veronica Coburn, Raymond Keane and Mikel Murfi, combine mime and circus techniques with the skills of straight theatre. Their mode is predominantly comic, though not exclusively so, and their tool is derision. *Half Eight Mass of a Tuesday,* co-produced with Project Arts Centre in 1994, was devised by the company, using mime and puppeteering skills to make the ordinary and familiar event of weekday morning Mass — familiar, that is, to an Irish audience — suddenly appear curious, unexpected and critically framed. When they are not devising their own material, they revisit classical or modern texts, which they expose and deconstruct in performances of hilarious virtuosity. Such was their recent production of Lennox Robinson's social satire, *The Whiteheaded Boy*, directed by Gerry Stembridge, which they took on tour to the USA and to Australia. The techniques of comic deconstruction which they used, with each performer playing multiple parts, including cross gendering, brought this early piece of social comedy, written in 1916, straight into the post-modern period.

Different policies are pursued by *Loose Canon,* under the direction of Jason Byrne. With them, the emphasis is on ensemble playing with predominantly young actors. They have given energetic, open-space productions of classic texts which otherwise would rarely be seen, such as Thomas Kyd's *The Spanish Tragedy* or Shakespeare's *Coriolanus.* The modern European repertory is served by *Bedrock Theatre Company*, directed by Jimmy Fay. They have taken risks in staging foreign plays in translation. Their English-language première of *Quay West* by Bernard-Marie Koltès was staged at Project Arts Centre in April 1999, to a mixed reception. Quite different objectives are targeted by *Passion Machine*, founded in the mid-eighties by director and writer Paul Mercier. His *Buddleia* was the hit of the Dublin Theatre Festival in 1995. From the start, he has been concerned to widen the social base of theatre audiences. He writes and produces for a public who would otherwise look on theatre as something remote from their class culture, and he offers that public representations of their own concerns and experiences. In the early years, he worked in association with the novelist and playwright Roddy Doyle. The film versions of Roddy Doyle's novels, *The Commitments* or *The Van*, give a sense both of Roddy Doyle's own dramatic writing and that of Paul Mercier, reflecting Dublin working-class life with energy and humanity.

Irish theatre has always been writer-driven, unlike contemporary French theatre, for example, which has been predominantly driven by the work of directors. Many of the young Irish companies of the nineties have produced writers or have fostered the work of emergent dramatists. *Fishamble Theatre Company*, formerly *Pigsback*, has sustained a commitment to new playwriting since they were founded in 1988, and they have promoted writers such as Gavin Kostick, Michael West, Joe O'Connor and Marina Carr. Their production of Deirdre Hines, *Howling Moons/Silent Suns* won the Stewart Parker Trust Award for the author in 1991 and transferred to the Abbey. To mark the millennium year, Fishamble organized a Y2K Festival of new, one-act plays which they had commissioned from six playwrights, some well known, some relatively new, and which they put on in several Dublin venues: Dermot Bolger, *Consenting Adults*, Deirdre Hines, *Dreamframe*, Jennifer Johnston, *Moonlight and Music*, Nick Kelly, *The Great Jubilee*, Gavin Kostick, *Doom Raider*, Gina Moxley, *Tea Set*.

The Corn Exchange, set up in 1995, have developed a performance style derived from Commedia dell'Arte, which they apply both to new writing and to devised or adapted work. In 1997, they brought Michael West's *A Play on Two Chairs* to New York and to Dublin. In 1999, they staged a new version, again by Michael West, of Chekhov's *The Seagull*. The latter production, situated somewhere between Commedia and Brecht, pushed the interpretation of the play towards self-parody. Audiences were strongly divided in their response, but all were forced to reconsider the cluster of received values which customarily attach to Chekhov.

In Cork city, *Corcadorca* has been performing since 1991. They have a growing list of productions to their credit, including Enda Walsh's *The Ginger Ale Boy*, and the same author's *Disco Pigs*, which they brought to the Dublin Fringe Festival in 1996. That harsh, raw-edged portrayal of teenage youth and the disco scene has been translated and staged in France and Germany, and it has fascinated and disturbed foreign audiences as much as it did audiences at home. Dermot Bolger was a poet and novelist before beginning to write for the theatre in association with director David Byrne, with *The Lament for Arthur Cleary* (1989) and *One Last White Horse* (1991). The recently published volume of *Rough Magic First Plays*, with contributions from Pom Boyd, Declan Hughes, Paula Meehan, Gina Moxley, Dónal O'Kelly and Arthur Riordan, illustrates the contribution that *Rough Magic*, as a company, has made to new Irish writing.

A conspicuous feature of the performance arts in Ireland over the last decade has been the emergence of young professional dance groups. *Cois Céim*, the company directed by choreographer David Bolger, exemplifies the widely-shared concern to attract new audiences for dance and to integrate dance and choreography with other theatrical forms. Their early satirical piece *Reel Luck*, created in association with Project Arts Centre in 1995, examined cultural stereotypes and national identity, and its subversive verve won an enthusiastic welcome. Choreographer Paul Johnson, founder of *Mandance* company, is committed to exploring contemporary male culture through dance. John Scott's *Irish Modern Dance Theatre* places choreographic work in unusual environments, and has toured extensively in Ireland and abroad with a small company of international dancers. Both *Daghda Dance Company*, the Limerick-based company founded by Mary Nunan, and *Dance Theatre of Ireland* with Robert Connor and Loretta Yorick, have been working over many years with a range of international choreographers to produce innovative Irish dance theatre work. Mary Nunan's piece *Territorial Claims* has toured extensively throughout Europe. In a wider perspective, all these groups have contributed to a heightened awareness of the non-verbal elements of theatrical representation, and their work has led to a significant degree of international cooperation with young artists and groups from outside Ireland.

Throughout the eighties and nineties, there has been a visible shift in the relationship between the capital city and the rest of the country. The uncomfortable cultural divide has now, to a large extent, been eroded. The network of vigorous, professional theatre companies which has emerged in the provinces has helped to move that development forward. An early leader was *Druid Theatre Company*, founded by Garry Hynes and others in Galway, in 1975. Garry Hynes was later artistic director of the Abbey Theatre, Dublin (1990-1993), and became the centre of a debate which sought to reappraise the function of a national theatre. *Druid Theatre Company* remains a major catalyst for new writing. In 1996, they inaugurated a new theatre space in Galway, The Town Hall Theatre, with the premier of Martin McDonagh's *The Beauty Queen of Leenane*, in co-production with the Royal Court Theatre, London. No-one could have anticipated at the time the dazzling rise to international fame that Martin McDonagh was to enjoy, with a quick succession of new plays directed by Garry Hynes, and transfers to London and Broadway. The list of provincial companies which have risen to prominence over the past decade must include *Bickerstaffe* in Kilkenny, *Red Kettle* in Waterford, *Galloglass* in Clonmel, both *Corcadorca* and *Meridian* in Cork, *Blue Raincoat* in Sligo, in Drogheda *Upstage* and *Calipo*, and from Northern Ireland *Prime Cut*, *Tinderbox*, *DubbelJoint* and others.

Given the range and diversity of the work these companies present, their willingness to take risks and try the new, it would be easy to let a sense of optimism obscure the precarious existence of most of these organizations. The fact is that they depend upon the commitment of a very small number of people, often upon a strong working relationship between two persons. There is little to support institutional continuity. A measure of encouragement is be found in the recent development plan published by the Arts Council, in particular, in the declaration that the Council is committed to "enhancing the sustainability of theatre organizations". A welcome change of policy, in this regard, is the prospect offered of strategic funding over several years, alleviating the wasteful practice of tardily disbursed annual funding and the destabilizing effect which such practice was having on management and policy in the independent sector. The newly appointed Artistic Director of the National Theatre, Ben Barnes, has announced plans for the Peacock Theatre which are intended to be supportive of the independent theatre sector. The issue, of course, is not only one of funding, but also one of training, development and opportunity. There remains none-the-less, if not a crisis of arts management throughout the country, at least an endemic unease.

A significant lack, over the past decade, has been the absence of a sustained critical voice. Since the demise of *Theatre Ireland* in 1993, there have been only isolated initiatives, such as Fintan O'Toole's feature *Second Opinion* in the *Irish Times*. A promising new start is the small-format quarterly *Irish Theatre Magazine*, founded in 1998. Edited by Karen Fricker and Maura O'Keefe, it provides a critical chronicle of current theatre productions, festivals and events, alongside feature articles. Theatre criticism generally has not engaged with a wider critique of Irish society, and is the poorer for that. In differing ways, the work of Declan Kiberd, Christopher Murray, Anthony Roche and Fintan O'Toole invites re-assessments. These re-assessments are both ideological and historical. They address the relationship of contemporary dramatic writing to the tradition of the Irish Dramatic Movement, that of Yeats, Synge, O'Casey and Beckett. They explore, in differing ways, the role of the imagination in contemporary Irish society.

The purpose of this article has been, very modestly, to give some sense of the changing conditions of work and the evolving theatre practices characteristic of the younger, emerging companies, over the past decade. It is not a comprehensive survey. The new theatre practice has begun to reflect and articulate the new confidence and the new ethos which characterize the younger generation in Ireland. In his recent study *Twentieth-century Irish Drama: Mirror up to Nation,* Christopher Murray comments that, if old ideas of nationhood and national identity survive among Irish expatriates, at home a different mentality and different concerns prevail:

> The present generation of young Irish people, wanting nothing to do with the ideals of Patrick Pearse or Eamonn De Valera, has found its preferred liberty in secularism, tolerance, and a new, very appealing, humanism. Ireland is rapidly becoming European, its culture cosmopolitan; yet there is a new-found passion for the arts as a means of articulating and celebrating home-based experience (Murray: 1997, 246).

The present generation has widened its concept of theatre and is exploring new forms of expression, across the full range of the performing arts. Its horizons are international and its aspirations innovative. It is no longer the case that a transfer to one of the established theatres would be seen as the ultimate accolade for an independent production. There is a freedom of mind which is being translated into action, as new infrastructures are being put in place, new audiences are slowly and precariously being won, new sites and new modes of engagement with the public are sought out and explored. There is a dominant spirit of inventiveness, energy and commitment.

Works Cited:

Bourke, Siobhán, (1999), *Rough Magic First Plays* (London and Dublin: Methuen/New Island Books)

Kiberd, Declan, (1995), *Inventing Ireland: The Literature of the Modern Nation* (London, Jonathan Cape)

Murray, Christopher, (1997), *Twentieth-century Irish Drama: Mirror up to Nation* (Manchester: Manchester University Press)

O'Toole, Fintan, (1994), *The Politics of Magic. The work and times of Tom Murphy* (London: Nick Hern Books)

Roche, Anthony, (1994), *Contemporary Irish Drama from Beckett to McGuinness* (Dublin: Gill & Macmillan)

(Un)Critical Conditions
Jocelyn Clarke

1

Last year, during an informal talk in Trinity College about his experiences working in Irish Theatre, the director and playwright Jim Nolan told the assembled students that his "ideal critic is someone who comes to see a production, wanting it to succeed". The audience, made up of third year and postgraduate students in Drama Studies, burst into spontaneous applause and cheering as Nolan's words struck a collective nerve: theatre critics, after all, were rarely noted for their kindness and generosity.

During the applause, however, some of the students suddenly seemed to catch themselves in mid applause while others looked uncertainly around them. They seemed embarrassed and uncomfortable — some of them even blushed. These students were part of a unique course in theatre criticism, and had just submitted that morning their reviews of Red Kettle's production of Jim Nolan's play *The Salvage Shop* — which they had seen two days previously. While some of them had been perceptive in their analysis of Nolan's play and Red Kettle's production, all of them had failed Nolan's directive of "wanting [a production] to succeed". Instead, they had been dismissive of both the play and the production, and some in particular — the more blushing of the students — had been snide and cruel.

These students were embarrassed because they found themselves for the first time stuck in the uncomfortable divide that exists between the theatre community and its critics — between "the us and them" opposition that pervades most thinking and feeling about the relationship between theatre practice and theatre criticism. As would-be actors, directors and designers, the students had applauded Nolan's words because they had been both inspirational and aspirational, speaking to them as future professionals who would endure and overcome the sling and arrow of invidious criticism; and they were embarrassed because he had been speaking to them as critics in training, who were, in their criticism, no less unkind and unfair than the kind of criticism Nolan had been excoriating. In a single moment the students had accidentally and involuntarily changed camps: they were no longer "us" but now "them", the enemy.

Further compounding their feelings of embarrassment and discomfort was the fact that they had come to like Nolan in the course of his talk. He had spoken candidly and amusingly to them about his experience of working as both a playwright and director, about the joy and sorrow of writing plays — his as much as others — and about the midwifery process of bringing them to life in productions on stage. He had answered their questions and taken on board their criticism about *The Salvage Shop* and Red Kettle's production, explaining the choices he had made as a playwright and the problems he had encountered with his play — even suggesting possible solutions for those problems. By the end of his talk, after listening and talking with Nolan for 90 minutes, the students felt thoroughly embarrassed about what they had written in their reviews: he was a nice man, and they had been "smart arses" at the expense of both his play and Red Kettle's production.

After Nolan had left the room, I asked the students how they now felt about the reviews they had written about his play. "Stupid", "bad" and "embarrassed" were some of the descriptions they used. I told them I had shown their reviews to Nolan before he gave his talk (of course, I had not) and they collectively turned bright red. I asked them if they would now change what they had written, and most of them said that they would, and when I asked them why, they said that some of what they had written was "hurtful" and "unkind". But if they were honest in their analysis of the problems of Nolan's play and Red Kettle's production as they perceived them, surely the problem was not with what they had written but how they had written their reviews — particularly in terms of their style and tone. They agreed that that was what was most troubling for them, not their analysis of the play and production — most thought there were problems with some of Nolan's characterisation and director Ben Barnes' staging — but rather how to describe and analyse those problems in a fair and generous way. Or as one student put it "there was no point in lying because that doesn't help, it's just a question of finding the best way to say it... of being nicer about it".

Over the remaining seven weeks of the course, the students were increasingly attentive and sensitive to issues of tone and style in their reviews. And as their confidence grew from review to review, individually and collectively, the students again and again returned to Nolan's directive of "wanting it to succeed". Their description and analysis, interpretation and evaluation of the productions they saw achieved an astonishing maturity and generosity in a relatively short space of time as they engaged with ethical issues of theatre criticism — what they were doing and how and why they were doing it. In their moment of embarrassment at the end of Nolan's talk, caught in the uncomfortable no man's land between "us" and "them", they had initially learned and subsequently applied their first, and perhaps most important lesson in theatre criticism: the importance of responsibility.

2

There are several widely held notions about critics, and they are both wrong: (1) they are not very nice; (2) they are not very good.... There is one thing that 99% of all critics share with one another: they are failures. I don't mean failures as critics — my God that's understood. I don't mean they are failures as people; I mean something more painful by far. These people are failures in life... (Novelist and screenwriter William Goldman)

William Goldman's book *The Season: A Candid Look at Broadway* is a funny, passionate and bitchy account about the 1967/68 season on Broadway. In *The Season* Goldman writes about the "business" of the Great White Way, from the creative to the commercial, leaving no turn unstoned. Goldman investigates every aspect of Broadway theatre, from opening nights to box office receipts, from ticket scalping to out of town tours, from "critics' darlings" to audience attendance: Goldman reports it all, everything you could possibly ever want to know about Broadway — and much you would rather not.

Goldman's chapter on Broadway critics, The Approvers — from which the above quote is taken — is probably one of the most pulverising personal and professional attacks on Broadway critics ever written — not least of all because, thirty years on, some of it is surprisingly relevant and apposite. Goldman's biggest beef with the Broadway critics is that not only are they profoundly ignorant about the process of making theatre — from what happens in the rehearsal room to the business of putting on a production — but that they also rarely write about "what actually happens" on stage. Instead they substitute opinion for analysis and interpretation, and descriptions of the play for descriptions of the production.

As a practising theatre critic, it is easy for me to agree with Goldman's assessment of Broadway theatre critics, now and then. It is also easy for me to find similar examples in Ireland: Goldman's beef, thirty years on and a continent away, still rings true. Moreover, what makes Goldman's argument so compelling, aside from the copious examples he offers, is its moral urgency: he lashes theatre critics because they continually fail to do what they are supposed to do — their job. And because they are not doing their job, they fail both the people who make theatre and those who see it and read about it.

If you glance through any week's worth of theatre reviews in any newspapers, regional or national, nearly all of them follow a standard model. Of a six or seven paragraph review, the first paragraph informs the reader of what and where the production is and if it's good or bad. The following three paragraphs recount the plot of the play, the penultimate paragraph lists the actors, designers and the director — and whether they were good or bad — and the last paragraph restates the first paragraph — whether the show was good or bad. There is nothing inherently wrong with this model if the writer is writing a review; if however, the writer is writing a piece of theatre criticism, it is woefully inadequate. In many ways, it goes to the heart of the problem of contemporary critical practice — the difference between writing a review and writing a critique.

The review model is similar to the model used by a reporter filing a news story — who? what? where? when? how? and why? — and enables the critic/reporter to write quickly and concisely, especially given the tight deadlines of most daily newspapers. As reportage, the review is strong on facts — the play, the production and the people involved — and is weak on description (except for plot) and analysis and weaker again on interpretation and evaluation. A review rarely says more than that a production happened but not how, why or what happened in it — in Goldman's words, what "happens on stage" between the production, the play and the audience in the course of the performance.

Moreover, a review demands very little of its writer beyond reporting the facts. As reviewers rather than critics, the writers are passively rather than (pro)actively engaged in their writing: the very act of writing a review is one of reportage and not of analysis or interpretation. The review model not only limits a writer's individuality of style and technique but also discourages alternative approaches to their material — perhaps concentrating on production elements or an individual performance instead of describing the plot of the play. But perhaps, worst of all, it discourages the reviewer/reporter from perceiving him or herself as both a writer and a critic.

Indeed, one of the most frequent charges laid at the door of theatre reviewers is that they are either bad writers or can't write at all. In their defence, it must be said that their working conditions are less than favourable: they are poorly paid compared to news reporters and sports writers, and they have very little copy space (on average 300 — 400 words) and very little time in which to write their reviews (one to two hours for daily reviewers). Equally important is the relative value of theatre in a newspaper's coverage — theatre comes after film, television, music and literature and before visual arts — and the widespread bias towards serious (news) journalism: there is something "frivolous" about theatre criticism. Theatre as an industry is less lucrative in marketing and advertising revenue than either the music and film industries or even the book industry. So, not only is theatre criticism frivolous, its also doesn't generate advertising revenue.

Though the newspaper industry has seen in recent years an unprecedented growth in "lifestyle" journalism, and an expansion of arts sections in daily and weekly newspapers, very little space is given to arts criticism in general and theatre criticism in particular — more space is devoted to profiles and gossip. Moreover there are no arts criticism modules or programmes in most journalism courses. In other words there is no professional training for critics. This lack of formal training and professionalism in arts journalism generally, and in theatre criticism particularly, remains a sore point with many in the arts and theatre communities: we train so why can't they?

In general, theatre reviewers are not bad people, some of them are even quite nice, and most of them love theatre. Many started going to the theatre at a young age, and were involved in amateur and student drama societies. Some may even have wanted to have a career in the theatre, and for reasons best known to themselves, they didn't. But nearly all of them became reviewers by accident. They were asked to be reviewers because they went to it regularly, because they knew something about it, and because there was nobody else available. And they wrote as audience members — with a pad and a pen, recording what was said on stage — and filed their reviews like a reporter.

Reviewers are amateurs, in both senses of the word. They are casual rather than skilled lovers of theatre. They are not theatre academics nor are they theatre professionals but enthusiastic "representatives of the audience" who rush to their newspapers or their computer after the curtain has come down, and write about what they have just seen and heard in the theatre. And as they write their reviews, they report on their experience of that night, what they liked or didn't like, what were the salient stories of the plays and who the characters were, and whether it was a good or bad production. They write as audience members, talking about the show in the lobby between acts or telling their friends about it afterwards the following day — with the implicit recommendation of whether they should go and see it or not.

No matter how good or bad a representative of an audience a reviewer thinks he or she may be, they rarely think of themselves as a theatre critic. Not only is the word reviewer less unpleasant than critic, it also implies a commonality with the audience in the theatre — "the man or woman in the street" — while the word critic implies detachment and judgement, somebody who sits at an intellectual and emotional remove from the audience. A reviewer, on the other hand, is somebody who sits in the audience and reports what happens on stage, and whose lack of specialist training brings him or her closer to the audience rather than further away. Moreover, the word criticism is perceived by many to have a negative connotation because nobody likes to be criticised. Who would want to be a critic?

And yet this is precisely the problem with most theatre criticism in this country: the reviewers don't want to be critics. And who could blame them? They're poorly paid, working in less than favourable conditions, dismissed as much by the people they work for as by the people they write about and all they are trying to do is their job...

But what exactly is that job?

3

"The reason we work in theatre is not to say what it is but to ask 'what is it?'" (Director and visual artist Robert Wilson)

Theatre criticism is an act of engagement. At their best, theatre critics should engage fully with a production on stage, from the moment it begins to the moment it ends, and every moment in between. They should engage completely with each element of the production, from the text and the performances to the design and the direction, from what happens on the stage to what happens in the auditorium. They should engage thoroughly with a production as it happens on stage, in a theatre and in a society; their engagement is intellectual and emotional, but also social, cultural and political. In their criticism, they should describe, analyse, interpret, evaluate and ultimately contribute to the collective experience in the theatre.

And as much as theatre critics should engage fully with a production in the moment of its performance, they should recapitulate this engagement in their writing, bringing to bear on their criticism their knowledge and experience of both theatre and of the world as professional critics living and working in a culture and a society. Since theatre at its core is a meeting place of ideas, experiences, traditions and technologies, and demands that its artists and its audiences engage with and participate in the exchanges which occur in this forum, theatre critics are no less exempt from this demand. If anything, not only are theatre critics obliged to engage and participate in this forum, but also they have to contribute to it. Their criticism is both an engagement with and a contribution to the dialogue that takes place between theatre artists and their work, and between their work and their audiences. And this engagement and contribution brings with it its own responsibility, not only to theatre artists and to theatre audiences/readers but also to theatre criticism itself.

The Drama Studies students from Trinity College and the vast majority of theatre reviewers working in this country share one thing in common: they lack critical responsibility. Unlike the vast majority of theatre reviewers, however, the Trinity students quickly developed an understanding of it, and soon began to apply it to their own critical writing. Because, quite simply, they were obliged to. Designed and taught by my colleague Karen Fricker and by me, the practical criticism course in which the students participated was specifically designed to expose the students to all aspects of theatre criticism, from the practical to the theoretical, and to explore through their writing and discussion of the productions they saw the various cultural, political and — not to put too fine a point on it — moral issues surrounding the practice of theatre criticism.

Based on the National Critics Institute's programme at the Eugene O'Neill Theatre Centre in Connecticut which Fricker and I attended as "critic fellows" — and which I later taught as a "critic mentor" — the Trinity course required that the students see and write about a production once a week, read and critique each other's work in class, and attend twice monthly informal talks by theatre practitioners who would speak about their work in Irish theatre. By asking the students to write about the productions they saw, they were exposed first hand to the problems of writing theatre criticism, and by critiquing their own and each other's papers, they gradually became aware of their own dramaturgy, first as writers and then as critics.

They encountered first hand in these critique sessions the difficulties of describing and analysing, interpreting and evaluating what they saw in the theatre — particularly the use of subjective language and opinion. Moreover, they were asked in the course of these sessions to think about the medium of theatre, not only from the points of view of spectators and critics but also as future practitioners (very few of them went to the theatre regularly) and to formulate a personal "philosophy" of theatre (ranging from "what do I understand by the word 'theatre'" to "why is theatre important to me?"). Much as the course concentrated on the practicalities of theatre criticism — from the necessity of research to the need for clarity in analysis and description — it was also designed to challenge the students into thinking critically about theatre — in their writing and discussions — and to encourage them to ask questions which would deepen their awareness and understanding of all aspects of the medium.

Initially the students' papers were full of "I liked this" and "I didn't like that", and "such and such an actor was wooden" and "such and such direction was bad", and featured long summaries of the plot with very little description of the production's scenography and staging. The similarity between what the students wrote and what appears in most theatre reviews in newspapers was remarkable but not surprising: the only model the students had were what they read in the papers.

However, after discussions during the critique sessions about the need for clear descriptions of what happens on the stage rather than just in the play — and encouragement to focus on different scenographic elements in their subsequent papers — and after examining the necessary distinction between a character, an actor and a performance on stage (most reviewers tend not to see one) and discouraging students from using the overly subjective "I" word, their papers showed a marked increase in attention to both what happened on stage as well as why, and to what it might mean.

While no piece of criticism is either wrong or right per se (and many of the students disagreed with one another in the interpretation and evaluation of different productions and performances), criticism can be either accurate or inaccurate in its analysis and description. Over the nine weeks of the course the students in their writing and thinking engaged more and more with what was happening on stage as well as with the larger cultural and socio-political issues raised by an individual production or play. In other words they began to take imaginative risks, drawing material from a broad range of cultural resources — from art history and literary theory to Freudian psychology and pop culture — and incorporating it into their writing. After the initial frustration of having to write about what they saw and heard in a theatre — with the added burden of deadlines and word counts — the students' writing gradually became clearer and more articulate (aided in part by their reading list of think pieces and theatre criticism from different countries and cultures) as they took on board what was said in both the critique sessions and the informal talks. Whereas at the beginning of the course they were writing reviews, by the end of it they were beginning to write — and in some cases, were already writing — thoughtful and engaged criticism. The final critique sessions proved unusually frank and insightful: their critical thinking had grown more incisive and more rigorous and more importantly the students were beginning to enjoy them much more...

While the Trinity course immersed the students in the practice and practicalities of writing theatre criticism — with the hope that maybe one student out of twenty-three would go on to write criticism full time — it also enabled them to develop a critical attitude to why and what they were doing in theatre as actors, directors, and designers of the future: the analytical tools provided by the course could equally be applied in the difficult negotiations that can sometimes exist between actors and directors and between directors and playwrights, namely, the facility to analyse and articulate a problem or issue without resorting to subjective language and fuzzy opinion which muddies much of the dialogue between theatre practitioners. It was in this context — as both future critics and practitioners — that the concept of critical responsibility was first introduced and greeted with polite bafflement by the students until

Jim Nolan spoke about his ideal critic "wanting a production to succeed" during his informal talk. In the first two weeks of the course, it had been stressed to the students that theatre critics do not write in a vacuum: what they write has a consequence, both for the people they write about and the people who read what they write — practitioners and readers. That not only must a critic write well with clarity and with rigour, but that he or she must also write with care — with generosity and understanding. That is not, however, to say that a critic should ignore the problems of a production or a performance, but rather that the critic should describe and analyse these problems with consideration and thought.

If, as Peter Brook roundly declares in his wise-eyed book *The Empty Space*, it is the critic's duty to "hound out ineptitude", it is equally his or her duty to do it with compassion: theatre criticism is not a blood sport. If a critic writes snidely and cruelly about a production or a performance, it diminishes the criticism and reduces it to an exercise in unnecessary humiliation: it is the "negative" value of being criticised. Though ineptitude, unlike virtuosity, is never deliberate, it does nevertheless deserve the same critical attention and consideration as virtuosity. Irrespective of whether it praises or pans, criticism should educate and inform those who read it as well as those about whom it is written; to write otherwise, badly or bitchily, is both useless and unnecessary because nothing is learned, and only humiliation is experienced.

If, on the other hand, the critic explores the problems of a production or a performance, analysing and evaluating them with consideration and generosity, then something positive can be learned — in spite of the discomfort experienced by those who are criticised. Then the dialogue between the theatre critic and the theatre community, between the theatre critic and the theatre audience/reader is increased and enriched rather than diminished and impoverished. It is here that the critic's role is at its most important and necessary. From an encounter in the theatre, the critic should extrapolate a piece of criticism that informs and educates as it engages and entertains — both those who make theatre and those who watch and read about it.

Needless to say this idealistic, though not impossible, view of theatre criticism was treated with a certain scepticism by the students on the Trinity course. "What does it have to do with us?" they wondered, "we're only writing reviews in class, and they don't mean anything…". It was not until they encountered Jim Nolan in the flesh — no longer a name in a theatre programme — that the students recognised the potential consequences, and if they had been published, very real professional and personal consequences of what they wrote in their papers. When Nolan spoke about his ideal critic, they suddenly understood in a very intimate way, that theatre criticism is more than just reporting an opinion: it is a profound act of engagement which brings with it a no less profound responsibility.

After their encounter with Nolan, there was a seismic shift in the students' approach and attitude to both what they saw in the theatre and what they wrote about it. Most of them started researching plays and productions, and using their research in their writing, particularly in their analyses and interpretations. They spent more time and space describing what happened on stage rather than just in the play, and began to develop a vocabulary to describe both individual performances — how the actors moved and talked on stage — and scenographic elements in a given production.

Where once an actor was dismissed as "wooden", the students now described and analysed why a performance may or may not have succeeded: "did the problem lie with the actor or with the director?" Their descriptions of set, costume and lighting design were more detailed and accurate, and were used by the students to access the intentions of a production — from what they did say about the people doing the production to why it was being done. This kind of interrogation — an active process of engagement rather than the reviewer's passive reportage — resulted in at times some extraordinary and insightful writing as the students began to respond to the challenges of writing fully engaged criticism.

And what the students lacked in experience and technique, they more than made up for in the enthusiasm of their critical engagement: they were willing to take risks in their writing and thinking. Perhaps more importantly, they began to see themselves as theatre critics rather than as reviewers, critics who had a responsibility to what they saw and what they wrote about, and who understood, if at times only intuitively, what they were doing and why they were doing it.

4

"I want to create theatre that is full of terror, beauty, love and belief in the innate human potential for change. In dreams begin responsibility", says director and theorist Anne Bogart.

In this article, I have tried to outline what I believe to be the problems of theatre criticism in Ireland and to suggest solutions to these problems — namely the need to encourage theatre reviewers to write criticism. And while many of the issues that need to be addressed will take time and effort on the part of both the theatre community and those who write about them — ranging from the introduction of press nights/shows to

the negotiation of a new relationship between theatre artists and critics —
it essentially boils down to the need for one simple change: the need for
critical responsibility.

It is no longer acceptable that, while Irish theatre is continually striving
for new heights of professionalism and diversity, Irish theatre critics are
failing to match and support the efforts of the theatre community with
an equivalent level of expertise and professionalism. Not only are theatre
critics charged with the responsibility of engaging fully with a work of
theatre in their criticism but they are also responsible for how that
criticism engages with the theatre community and the public who read it
— including audiences and funding bodies — as both a record and an
assessment of Irish theatre, now and in the future.

Theatre criticism is not an idle pastime but a serious endeavour which
needs to be taken seriously as much by those who write it as those who
read it. Theatre critics have an enormous amount of power — particularly
in the public forum of audiences and the funding bodies who vote with
their money — and for which they take little responsibility. Irrespective
of whether a piece of theatre criticism is favourable or unfavourable, it
must both engage with and communicate to the reader not only what
happened on the night but what the work has to say to the culture and
society in which it is sited — and to the canon of theatre to which it
contributes. Theatre critics cannot afford to be either unaware of or
ignorant about what they write and how they write it; instead they must
take responsibility for everything they write and say in the public domain
because everything they write and say has very real consequences for
theatre artists and audiences alike.

In order to tackle the problems of Irish theatre criticism, a new dialogue
will have to take place between the theatre community and its critics.
Admittedly this dialogue will be awkward and difficult at first — too
much bad feeling and spilt blood in the past — but it is a necessary one if
the current situation is to improve. And inherent in that dialogue should
be the assumption that the theatre community and theatre critics are on
the same side rather than on opposite sides — fundamentally both have
in common a passion for theatre — and that as necessary as theatre is to
the life blood of a society so too is criticism to the health and
maintenance of that life blood. This dialogue does not necessarily require
formal meetings — though that would be helpful: all it requires is that a
theatre reviewer would simply begin talking with a theatre practitioner
some night after a show somewhere, and to start asking questions about
what they saw and heard on the stage that night.

And perhaps, out of that conversation, other conversations would arise,
with more and more questions. And perhaps out of these encounters,
the reviewer would attend a rehearsal or two, perhaps start reading plays,

researching productions, catching up with current thinking and practice in other cultures, and incorporating them into their writing. Or perhaps the reviewer might even attend a course in practical theatre criticism — either funded by the Arts Council as part of its new development programme or as part of a journalism or theatre course. And perhaps then the reviewer would start writing theatre criticism, and finally become a professional theatre critic. A responsible theatre critic.

Brian Friel's Dialogue with Euripides: *Living Quarters*
Redmond O'Hanlon

I have always felt that *Living Quarters*, which is haunted by the detail and technique of Chekhov's *Three Sisters*, deserves a much higher place in the Friel canon than is normally assigned to it; but I have always been puzzled by Friel's addition of "after *Hippolytus*" to the title since its relation to Euripides' play seems somewhat oblique. In the Greek play, the young, pure hero, Hippolytus, is a devoted follower of Artemis, Goddess of Chastity and Hunting, but he rejects absolutely the charms of Aphrodite, Goddess of Love and Sexuality, who vows to destroy him for his spurning of her and for his arrogant rigidity. She plants an all-consuming desire for Hippolytus in Phaedra, the young second wife of Theseus, Hippolytus' father. When Hippolytus learns of Phaedra's passion he explodes with rage and launches one of the most brutal anti-woman tirades in Greek theatre. Phaedra decides to save her reputation by hanging herself but she leaves a note for Theseus in which she falsely accuses Hippolytus of raping her. On learning of this, the outraged Theseus calls down on his son the curse of his father, Poseidon (Neptune), God of the Sea, who unleashes from the deep a black bull which terrifies the horses of Hippolytus who normally has absolute control over them. The horses bolt, shattering Hippolytus' chariot and dismembering his body. Theseus recognizes his error, Hippolytus laments the injustice of the Gods, the mystery of their ways and proclaims, like Frank Butler, his absolute innocence. Father and son are reconciled; and Hippolytus is guaranteed immortality in song and legend by Artemis.

It is difficult, then, to discern, on a cursory reading, many significant links between the two plays. In Euripides, Hippolytus and Phaedra are the main protagonists, in Friel, their counterparts are secondary figures; in Euripides, Hippolytus and Phaedra don't sleep together, in Friel, Ben and Anna do, but their relationship is given short shrift, whereas in *Hippolytus* the desire of Phaedra for her stepson is incandescent. In Friel, the Theseus figure, Frank Butler, is the haunting focus of the action; in Euripides, Theseus, though bearing the pain of his double loss, is not the centre of dramatic attention. However, a closer reading suggests that there are certain formal elements in *Living Quarters* which remind us of its Greek antecedent and which seem to allow Friel to move beyond a naturalism, and even melodrama, which could so easily have engulfed his play. And there are also, it seems to me, some more fundamental concerns which bind Friel to the dramatic and philosophic vision of his illustrious predecessor.

Near the end of Act I of *Living Quarters,* a climactic, typically Frielian moment occurs when Ben engages in some savage verbal play against his absent father and then initiates a carefully modulated build-up to the revelation of his primal crime of perfidy against him. Here Friel moves into quasi-stichomythia as a way of both formalizing and spotlighting this potentially catastrophic moment for the entire family:

> **BEN**: What if he did? After all that's been said?
> **HELEN**: Despite all that.
> **BEN**: The day she died I called him a murderer.
> **HELEN**: Six years have passed.
> **BEN**: And he hit me — don't you remember? — he hit me!
> **HELEN**: That's all over.
> **BEN**: Years of hostility.
> **HELEN**: That fades.
> **BEN**: Does it?
> **HELEN**: You know it does.
> **BEN**: You can preserve it...
> **HELEN**: Why would you want to?
> **BEN**: In case you'd forget (*LQ*: 212).

Here, the impulse to speak his passion is threatening to overwhelm the necessity to hide it, as in *Hippolytus.* For Friel and Euripides, the word is heavy with consequence, and is itself dramatic action; but in *Living Quarters,* as in *Philadelphia,* the passion is anger against the father, in Euripides, it is Phaedra's all-consuming desire for her stepson.

And you could argue that there is a rather botched *anagnorisis* at the end of the play when Anna reveals her guilty secret to Frank who learns nothing beyond the facts of the adultery; who learns nothing about himself or about the wider forces and laws governing human behaviour — as he might have done were he a Greek tragic hero. Like Hippolytus, he protests his innocence, but does so in a rather bleating, pathetic tone: a far cry from the great, plangent cries of Job, Phaedra and Hippolytus. And in an extraordinary reversal, Frank, shattered by Ben and Anna's betrayal, looks around desperately for help, that doesn't come, from the drunken Chaplain and suddenly slides into a reverie on his dead wife's suffering; into a self-indulgent apologia for his attempts to understand it. Both in what he remembers and in the way he remembers his wife's pain he makes it clear that he cannot allow himself to feel deeply the wound of betrayal and that he has at his disposal a spontaneous, chillingly efficient defence-system designed to control any capacity to surrender to emotion or desire:

> **FRANK**: What should a man do? (*Tom is asleep again. Frank looks at him. Then very slowly he walks around the room as if he were trying to remember something.*) (*Finally, conversationally*) You know, when I think

about it — my God, how she must have suffered. Not that I was insensitive to it — far from it; I used to try to imagine what it was like. I would close my eyes and attempt to invest my body with pain, willing it into my joints, deliberately desiring the experience. But it's not the same thing — not the same thing at all — how could it be? Because it cannot be assumed like that — it has got to be organic, generated from within. And the statistics are fascinating too — well, no, not fascinating — how could they be fascinating; but interesting, interesting. It starts around forty; it's estimated that five to six per cent of the population is affected; and women are three times more susceptible than men (*LQ*: 239).

Frank resists initiation into the dark language of desire but a brutal initiation has been forced on him by Ben and Anna — an initiation that brings no new light, no new life, no deepening of soul. Hippolytus dies on stage but will later earn his apotheosis as a demi-god and as a star in the heavens. Frank Butler goes out alone, isolated, whimpering, to meet death by his own hand; here we witness the prototypical isolation of the tragic hero when his *hybris* becomes manifest and the ultimate price has to be paid by him. He makes a desperate plea for help to Fr. Tom who is fast asleep in a drunken stupor. Then, after formally protesting his innocence,

> *He stops and looks around at the others — all isolated, all cocooned in their private thoughts. He opens his mouth as if he is about to address them, but they are so remote from him that he decides against it. He turns slowly and begins to walk upstage* (*LQ*: 241).

And, as if to exalt the moment of his suicide exit above the level of the melodrama threatening it, Friel has Frank leave through a door which is set apart from the ordinary, naturalistic doors of the rest of the play by being used on this occasion only, as the stage-directions tell us. Emotion is kept in check here by this simple device and the moment is ritualised.

It might not be too far-fetched, either, to see another botched *anagnorisis* in Fr. Tom's egregious blindness when he says: "There was never any doubt in my mind that it was an unfortunate accident. Never" (*LQ*: 243). Here he shows no awareness of the fact that he is caught in the trap of tragedy; that after the point of no return there is no way out; that action brings responsibility and consequences. He thinks he is in the world of melodrama where the issues are clear and where accident rules supreme.

At the end of the play, we have another move designed to prevent us from identifying too closely with the pain of the family after Frank's suicide which could so easily elicit from us an over-nostalgic response and which Friel explicitly wants to avoid: *The remaining sequence must not be played in a sad, nostalgic mood* (*LQ*: 242). Friel's attempt to keep a tight rein on emotion in these last minutes of the play brings Sir back into his role of aesthetic distancer in a way that is very reminiscent of the Chorus at the end of so many Greek tragedies. Of course this is a role played by him from the beginning of the play but one which he exercises only sporadically. Sir is a fascinating creation, an amalgam of Greek Destiny, Prologue and Chorus as well as of the modern director and stage-manager. In the complexity of his role he takes his place in a great theatrical lineage that goes from the Greeks to Anouilh (*Antigone*), Pirandello (*Six Characters*), Cocteau (*The Infernal Machine*) Wilder (*Our Town*) and Sartre (*In Camera*). He brings us into the great Greek agon between freedom and determinism, but he does it in a specifically modern, self-consciously theatrical way which provokes in the Friel characters a somewhat Pirandellian anguish about being imprisoned forever in a role that leaves little room for freedom and individual creativity. As becomes clear in *Living Quarters*, the characters are free, in their imaginations, to make minor adjustments to the eternally fixed facts of that fateful day, but they are prisoners of the irreversibility of time and of the consequences of what they did and did not do. Sir it is who moves the play beyond naturalism and reminds us and the characters that the die is cast, that they are agents, actors and spectators; that their margin of freedom is tightly circumscribed. This metatheatrical level, which is so crucial to Friel's entire project in *Living Quarters*, was almost completely erased in Jason Byrne's 1999 production at the Abbey where the placing of Sir downstage right, his make-up, the tone of his delivery, indeed almost everything about him, did little to disrupt a predominantly naturalistic mise en scène whose set looked like a slightly seedy Rathmines flat in a kitchen comedy during the bad old days of the Abbey.

The English philosopher Anthony Kenny once said that the only really interesting question in philosophy is the freedom/determinism issue; and Greek Tragedy was undoubtedly the aesthetic forum in which this was the burning question. And it certainly is a burning question that links *Hippolytus* and *Living Quarters*. From the beginning of Euripides' play it is clear that Hippolytus is going to be a mere pawn in the deadly struggle between Artemis and Aphrodite. Given his absolutely rigid devotion to one goddess only, the Goddess of Chastity and the Hunt, Hippolytus now has to pay the price of his monotheism and must be destroyed by the Goddess of Love whom he has so moralistically spurned. So for Hippolytus the die is cast: he has used his freedom to worship Artemis, neglecting all the other deities in the Pantheon, and, in particular, Aphrodite for whom such a rejection is a rejection of Eros, the very principle of life itself, as we see in Hesiod's *Theogony* and in Plato's *Symposium*. All that remains for the spectator is to experience the depth, the power and the texture of Hippolytus' refusal of erotic attachment and to see what wider meanings and context will emerge into his consciousness. Similarly in *Living Quarters*, the spectator is aware from the outset that nothing can be done to alter what was done and not done on that fateful *dies irae* of Frank's suicide; and yet, as Sir tells us, the characters are still haunted by the possibility that they can escape from the deterministic frame in which the action is set:

> **SIR**: .... And in their imagination, out of some deep psychic necessity, they have conceived me — the ultimate arbiter.... And yet no sooner do they conceive me with my authority and my knowledge than they begin flirting with the idea of circumventing me, of foxing me, of outwitting me (*LQ*: 177-8).

But Sir knows, and deep down they know, that at best they have a very slim margin of freedom; they might be able to shuffle the pages a little or, possibly, discover some meaning or significance in the events of the day. And here, too, as in *The Loves of Cass Maguire*, we see Friel flirting with the rather Pirandellian anguish of characters who are trapped in roles and actions from which they cannot escape.

But the freedom/determinism enigma resonates throughout *Living Quarters* not only through Sir but also through most of the other family members who are obsessed by the past and by their various degrees of responsibility for Frank's suicide. Now the notion of responsibility implies some margin of freedom, but within the inner play (in which the family constantly replays the events of the fatal day) very little can be done. Here, there are many striking examples of the magnetic pull of the past which so often threatens to submerge Friel's characters in nostalgia and inertia, condemning them to a permanent repetition of old wounds that have not been dealt with and transformed. Perhaps the most perfect example of this occurs when Sir goes offstage for a while and leaves the family "free" to act as they will. And how do they exercise this freedom? First of all, they disobey the conventions of the set, and, secondly, they rapidly lapse into a prototypical "Do you remember?" game in which so many Friel characters indulge themselves:

> **BEN**: I do. I haven't felt like this since — (*Stops*)
> **ANNA**: When?
> **BEN**: I can tell you exactly — six years ago, October 19th — the day of my mother's funeral. That's when. That afternoon. After we had come back from the cemetery. Shocking, isn't it?
> **ANNA**: Tell me about it.
> **BEN**: Nothing much to tell. We were all in there (*living-room*) — it was pouring with rain — there were some visitors — the girls were crying — everybody was whispering (*LQ*: 217).

This is a splendid example of what I like to call the Frielian pluperfect, where a memory is generated onstage which then spawns an earlier memory within it. As Sir tells us on his return, the family at this point has been taking "a few liberties" and "some of it is the wishful thinking of lonely people in lonely apartments. But they're always being true to themselves" (*LQ*: 225); in other words, true to the family's obsession with the past and its abrogation of freedom.

In Friel, homecomings are fraught events and they are often transmogrified into funerals. Archetypally, homecomings generate the freedom/determinism, change/no change agon. Early on in *Living Quarters*, Miriam says that "the years may have passed but we're still Daddy's little beavers" (*LQ*: 191), whereas Helen declares firmly that the past is behind her:

> SIR: Do you still feel anger?
> HELEN: No, not a bit, I think. Not a bit.
> SIR: And him — how real is he?
> HELEN: Gerry? That's over.
> SIR: Altogether?
> HELEN: I'm wary. I'm controlled. I discipline myself.
> SIR: Then this homecoming was a risk?
> HELEN: In a way.
> SIR: A test? A deliberate test?
> HELEN: Perhaps.
> SIR: And you're surviving it?
> HELEN: I'm surviving it (*LQ*: 183).

But by the end of Act One Helen learns that the past, the loss of her husband, cannot be eliminated by an act of will; that there's mourning-work to be done, as Freud puts it in "Mourning and Melancholia"; that unless we do this painful work we will be condemned to repetition and harnessed forever to our wounds:

> BEN: I'm sorry, Helen.
> HELEN: (*Simply*) Sorry? What's sorry? 'Never underestimate the regret'. Is that what you said? I've lost him. She killed him. He's gone. Do I love Gerry Kelly still? I thought I'd squeezed every drop of him out of me. But now I know I haven't forgotten a second of him (*LQ*: 215).

Now when we look at the state of the family *outside* the framework of the inner play we get the sense that its members are still in a state of fracture, breakdown and disarray; that they are still frozen in the drama of their father's suicide; that in real life, also, they can do no more than shuffle the pages of the Great Ledger as they endlessly rake over "those dead episodes that can't be left at peace" (*LQ*: 177). But there's no future in repetition, and the family never finds in their oft-repeated linear narrative the hoped-for "key to an understanding of *all* that happened" (*LQ*: 177). The only way for the family members to become unstuck is to tell a new, more creative story governed by a new future. Their only freedom consists in assigning new meanings by undertaking new action without absolute values to guide them in their choice: the existentialist leap of will and faith.

Drama, then, lets the family down in the same way as it lets Ben down when he tries to rehearse various scenarios in which he imagines a way of talking to his father and of telling him how he feels. However, when it becomes theatre, as it did when Ben and Anna *performed* their anger and desire, it found its mark with deadly accuracy and changed everyone's world forever. But the family's drama of the mind in which they are permanently imprisoned, to no great effect, can become for us as spectators the generator of meanings and possible motivations; and for us as agents the springboard of action and change, when we are released back into the real world where the die is not yet completely cast, where we can exercise some level of freedom once we have lived through the deeply imagined experience of impotence experienced by the family.

In Act I of *Living Quarters*, Frank Butler says of his young second wife, Anna: "Look *what* I'm bringing to the reception" [my italics]. We are then treated to an extended hymn to the beauty of Anna and to the joy she brings him. It soon becomes clear that Frank's main passion is for himself and his heroic exploits, that the idealization of Anna obliterates her uniqueness and otherness as a desiring woman, and that she is merely an object of consumption for the male gaze. (Idealization in psychoanalysis is always a smoke-screen, implying distance from, and terror of, the Other's desire.) The only way in which Anna can be heard at all is by engaging in a transgressive act with terrible consequences and complex, unclear motivation which dissolves old boundaries and escapes the rigid control of Frank, the military hero. There is a sense in which Sir, too, attempts to control, and even deny the feminine by sticking to a chronological narrative which can never yield meaning or epiphany, no matter how often the family members replay them. And it is perhaps no accident that it is two women, Anna and Helen, the most sexually alive figures in the play, who sense, like Cass Maguire, that there was something else, (*LQ*: 246) "unease... shadows" (*LQ*: 188), which are undreamt of in the repressive, chronological male narrative proposed by Sir — and, indeed, by Frank whose detachment and control of emotion is very similar to Sir's. And it is no accident, either, that the one slip made by Sir concerns Anna, the outsider in the family:

> **SIR:** Incidentally, Anna, we made a mistake, you and I — well me, really.

ANNA: What was that?

SIR: I never introduced you! You're the only person who wasn't introduced. (*Opening ledger.*) So let's rectify that — right?

ANNA: No, please, Sir —

SIR: But I *want* to —

ANNA: Please. It doesn't matter now, not in the least. It's of no importance now.

SIR: I'm sorry. My mistake.

ANNA: It doesn't matter (*LQ*: 243).

The surprising concentration on this detail in the closing moments of the play invites our special attention to Sir's lapsus: slips and amnesia are rarely accidental in the life of the psyche. If we remember the similarities between Frank and Sir we need to read this slip suspiciously. Can it be that Sir is so trapped in a male narrative and in a male repression that we have to read his amnesia as a sort of psychic murder of the feminine? Sir, then, begins to look like an accomplice of Frank and the family who in various ways have kept Anna and her desire at a distance, an alienation which is rendered too scenically poignant in the First Act of *Living Quarters*, when Tom is trying to take a photo of the family, excluding Anna:

SIR: They won't hear you now.

ANNA: They will! They will!

SIR: Anna, believe me —(*She rushes away from him and out to the garden where she stands facing the group. SIR looks on patiently. She is almost hysterical.*)

TOM: Frank.

FRANK: What?

TOM: This way.

FRANK: I'm glaring at you, for God's sake!

TOM: That's what I'm saying. Will you stop it! Now — terrific — Commandant Butler and his beautiful family.

MIRIAM: He really means me.

ANNA: (*Trying to control herself*) Listen to me, all of you. You, too, Chaplain.

MIRIAM: No film in the camera.

TINA: I'm going to laugh.

ANNA: When you were away, all those months I was left alone here —

TOM: Great — don't move — terrific. And another.

ANNA: Listen to me, Frank! (*LQ*: 202)

In Euripides' play, there is a refusal of heterosexual attachment and of female desire which is much more concentrated, unequivocal and virulent than anything we come across in *Living Quarters*. The savagery of

Hippolytus' anti-woman tirade has few equivalents in world theatre but it could be argued that the implicit erasure of the feminine in *Living Quarters* might well have been realized in a far more violent and explicit way if Friel had had easy access to the conventions of Greek Tragedy which would have allowed him to shed the discretion and understatement of quasi-naturalist drama in prose.

Early on in *Hippolytus*, we learn from an attendant that there's a universal human law which forbids "pride and an exclusive attitude". Hippolytus is thus making a great error in refusing to honour the mighty Goddess Aphrodite without whom the propagation of life itself is inconceivable. Hippolytus replies: "Since I lived cleanly, I greet her from a distance.... I do not care for gods men worship in the night" (Euripides: 1958, 81). Deeply embedded in the play is an absolute refusal of desire and female sexuality which is poetically linked to the sea, the bull, the Underworld, darkness and earth; the world of Otherness, of dream and the unconscious. So, the formally declared innocence of both Frank and Hippolytus can be seen as deeply flawed and culpable; as evidence that it is inhuman to be so attached to the light of reason and control — after all, the Sun God, Apollo, gains his depth and power, indeed has his origins in, the dark Underworld; that to be fully human is to be attached, involved with the messy, murky world of desire and the Other; that any spiritual, emotional or intellectual monotheism is fraught with danger; that sanity, absolute control and purity are pernicious fantasies; that the repressed will always return, with cataclysmic consequences; that the Greek Pantheon has twelve Gods who must be duly honoured.

In *Hippolytus*, there are many elements which link the play to formal initiation rites, not least of which is the very presence of Artemis, Goddess of Initiation. Hippolytus' oblique initiation into sexuality is a brutal one that requires a passage through the Underworld. But at the end of it there will be rebirth both as a star and as a heroic demi-god to whom young virgins will sacrifice their hair before yielding to Aphrodite in marriage. It is worth noting here the intimate connection in the early Greek imagination between hair, sexuality, energy and the taming of horses, Hippolytus' speciality until he met his nemesis on the seashore. Frank Butler's initiation into sexuality and desire is primal, if not as brutally spectacular as that of Hippolytus. But Frank's initiation is a botched one, it leads nowhere, it sparks no understanding, nor does it allow him to transcend the oppression of a long history of silent males obsessed with achievement, reputation, power, control of emotion and of the feminine. This is not to suggest, however, that the psychic world of *Living Quarters* is one where conflict and mystery in human relationships might be fixed by a reconstruction of the male psyche. This is a world which is beyond the optimism of post-Enlightenment progress myths: in Friel, as in Greek Tragedy, there is a fundamental mystery at the heart of things which no advances in technology, politics, sociology, theology or psychology can solve. Gabriel Marcel once pointed out that while we might hope to *solve* problems we can only *contemplate* mysteries and deepen our experience of them: remaining in the confusion and darkness of mystery is not an ignoble condition to be in, as Friel reminds us elsewhere. And most of the main characters in *Living Quarters* flounder in the mystery of human anger, longing and desire.

Indeed, Friel is a past-master at monitoring the hairline fissures in the psyche, the ever-shifting sands of emotion. Before Frank goes out to his hero's reception, Sir remarks:

> **SIR**: You're nervous.
> **FRANK**: Yes.
> **SIR**: Of what?
> **FRANK**: I don't know.
> **SIR**: Can it be to do with Anna?
> **FRANK**: Yes. Maybe. I don't know. With myself. I'm jittery for some reason.
> **SIR**: That's understandable.
> **FRANK**: And unhappy. Suddenly unhappy. Profoundly unhappy.
> **SIR**: It's the tension.
> **FRANK**: Yes? (*LQ*: 192)

But shortly afterwards he tells Helen:

> **FRANK**: (*Simply*) What I was going to say is that for the first time in my life I am profoundly happy. (*Pause.*) And now you're thinking there's no fool like an old fool.
>
> **HELEN**: No (*LQ*: 197).

And Ben's first appearance on stage is marked by the declaration of his great love for his mother:

> **SIR:** 'As he looks into the living-room he imagines for a second that the figure at the mantelpiece is his mother'.
>
> **BEN**: She had her back to me. She didn't hear me. And I stood outside in the garden and just watched her. Everything — her hair, her neck, her shoulders, the way she moved her arms — precisely as I remembered. (*Helen is now fingering the glass ornament.*) Not a sound except the tap-tap-tap of her stick as she moved about. And for a second my heart expanded with an immense remembered love for her, and then at once shrank in terror of her. And then suddenly she turned and came towards the open door, and I saw it wasn't — it w-w-w-wasn't – (*Helen had turned and had moved to the open door. She is startled to see a man staring in at her.*)

HELEN: Who -? (*Loud*) Ben! (*He responds as if someone — a stranger — had called him.*)(*LQ*: 205)

Yet, later, remembering her funeral he tells everyone:

> And suddenly I had to rush out of the room because I was afraid I'd burst out singing or cheer or leap into the air. Honestly. Walked across the sand hills for maybe a couple of hours — I don't remember. Anyhow until that madness passed.

ANNA: Was it madness? (*Pause. He looks at her quickly. Then resumes as before.*)

BEN: And then I came back. Guilty as hell and soaked to the skin. (*Smiling*) And assumed the grief again — a greater grief, a guilty grief. All very strange (*LQ*: 217).

At the end of the play, Ben finally manages to articulate his love of the dead Frank, but in a form that is full of hesitation, qualification and ambivalence, as if to suggest that the murky depths of emotion within a family is beyond the scope of verbal language:

BEN: Maybe I had some intimation of a moment being missed for ever — because there was the sudden necessity to blurt out, to plunge some oversimplification into him before it was too late. And what I was going to say to him was that ever since I was a child I always loved him and always hated her — he was always my hero. And even though it wouldn't have been the truth, it wouldn't have been a lie either: no, no, no lie.

SIR: I see.

BEN: But I suppose it was just as well it wasn't said like that because he could never receive that kind of directness, and I suppose I could never had said it. But I just hope — I just hope he was able to sense an expression of some k-k-k-k — of some kind of love for him — even if it was only in my perfidy — (*He goes off slowly.*) (*LQ*: 245).

And when Anna tries to fix in language the motivation for her adulterous affair the mystery and complexity of her feelings become manifest. Explaining her behaviour to Frank, she talks of his "too simple, too passionate letters" and of finding Frank in Ben, echoing Phèdre in Racine, but not Phaedra in Euripides. Yet earlier on she said that she had betrayed Frank "out of loneliness, out of despair, out of hate!" (*LQ*: 202) and, then, a few minutes later she denies any such motivations (*LQ*: 203): the springs of desire issue from dark, troubled, archaic substrata of the soul that defy language and discursive reason.

Brian Friel, then, puts the Irish middle-class family under terrible scrutiny and lacerating investigation but finds there little haven or consolation, even if at times he's tempted to fall into the snare of a nostalgic, late-Victorian representation of it. A harrowing example of this double vision can be seen in Act One when Anna, "almost hysterical", is trying to break into the family's consciousness with the devastating story about her affair with Ben:

> **MIRIAM**: Thanks be to God Charlie isn't watching this caper.
> **ANNA**: An affair, d'you hear — out of loneliness, out of despair, out of hate! And everybody in the camp knows — everybody except the Butlers! (TINA *can control her laughter no longer — she explodes.*)
> **TOM**: Terrific, Tina! Everybody join in! (*The laughter is infectious. They laugh so much we can hardly hear what they are saying.*)
> **MIRIAM**: *Noblesse oblige!* (*LQ*: 202)

This is a delicious, envenomed and savagely ironic sandwich, elegant in its formal structure and darkly ambivalent in its vision: here Friel asks us to hold in the one stage-picture both the joy of family unity and the imminent, brutal exposure of its meretriciousness. The Friel family is a dangerous entity, primal in its passions and yet ultra-discreet, even awkward, in its expression of deep emotion: clearly no place to bring children up in. Little wonder, then, that Ben has to finally explode in such a violently Oedipal way in order to reach his father at all; and little wonder that his most savage verbal eruption occurs when he's alone on stage and that it hits at the fundamental mystery of close blood relations. Speaking of his fellow-student at UCD, Harry Sproule, Ben muses to himself:

> **BEN**: Called his father and mother by their Christian names, spoke of them warmly — as if they were friends of the family. (*Pause.*) Did you ever think what it must have been like for Anna coming into our family? (*He circles around the wicker chair, looking at it.*) (*LQ*: 229)

The action of Ben places him in a classic Oedipal framework, unlike Hippolytus who never takes on his father nor aspires to his sexual maturity. And even though Ben takes decisive action against Frank he does not succeed in escaping from the *image* of his father or mother, nor from the family home. Neither does he accede for very long to sustained adult sexual maturity. So while *Hippolytus* may have flirted with the nightmarish possibility of quasi-incest, *Living Quarters* explores the deed itself, which shatters the family's unity and severs father from son. The stark contrast between this outcome and that of the Greek original couldn't be clearer:

THESEUS: Alas, what are you doing to me, my son?

HIPPOLYTUS: I am dying. I can see the gates of death.

THESEUS: And so you leave me, my hands stained with murder.

HIPPOLYTUS: No, for I free you from all guilt in this.

THESEUS: You will acquit me of blood guiltiness?

HIPPOLYTUS: So help me Artemis of the conquering bow!

THESEUS: Dear son, how noble you have proved to me!

HIPPOLYTUS: Yes, pray to heaven for such legitimate sons.

THESEUS: Woe for your goodness, piety, and virtue.

HIPPOLYTUS: Farewell to you, too, father, a long farewell!

THESEUS: Dear son, bear up. Do not forsake me.

HIPPOLYTUS: This is the end of what I have to bear.
    I'm gone. Cover my face up quickly.

THESEUS: Pallas Athene's famous city,
    What a man you have lost! Alas for me!
    Cypris, how many of your injuries
    I shall remember.

CHORUS: This is a common grief for all the city;
    It came unlooked for. There shall be
    A storm of multitudinous tears for this;
    The lamentable stories of great men
    Prevail more than of those humble folk (Euripides: 1960,
      290-1).

In *Towards a Poor Theatre*, Grotowski addresses the question of how the modern theatre practitioner can meaningfully engage with the classics. He argues for "a collision with the roots", a brutal confrontation between our mythical roots and our current behaviour or stereotypes; a contest between our today and our mythical yesterday insofar as we still pay lip-service to, or confer power on our great classical myths. Now while *Living Quarters* could never be seen as a brutal confrontation with its Greek ancestor it does force us to situate ourselves in terms of the vision, values and theatrical modes of Classical Greek Tragedy.

Euripides' *Hippolytus* proposes to us a moral universe which, though threatened by late 5th Century religious scepticism, does, nevertheless, validate certain absolute values, chastity and the claims of Aphrodite, in terms of which characters can fully realize themselves, even unto death (it's worth recalling here that *theós* meant both "god" and "force"). The universe of *Living Quarters*, by contrast, is one of absolute scepticism and moral relativity where isolation, breakdown, fragmentation and hopelessness characterize the Butlers: a universe of pathos, not tragedy, where there is no assent to absolute values in terms of which characters might act heroically.

In the closing moments of *Hippolytus*, we witness not only the transfiguration and apotheosis of the hero but also, in the cathartic reconciliation of father and son, a validation of the unified patriarchal family which has survived the assault from the notoriously wild sexuality of Cretan women which were so threatening to the Athenian *oikos*, the corner-stone of the Classical Greek *polis*, one of the most patriarchal, misogynistic social structures in Western history. At the end of *Living Quarters*, on the other hand, we witness the collapse of the patriarchal family whose members are left impotent, alone and hopeless, with their "boring reminiscences and bloody awareness and bloody quivering sensibilities" (*LQ*: 229), endlessly "raking over those dead episodes that can't be left at peace" (*LQ*: 177). *Living Quarters* provides no answer to Ben's repeated angry, anguished question: "There must be another way of ordering close relationships, mustn't there? (*Shouts.*) Mustn't there?" (*LQ*: 229); later, in *Dancing at Lughnasa*, however, Friel, through Uncle Jack, plays with the possibility of a form of social life which radically differs from the nuclear European family. In these two works, Friel celebrates the traditional family and chronicles its demise; is both aware of the dangers of a Victorian nostalgia for the family and of the need to keep such nostalgia in check.

In *Living Quarters*, we are reminded that even the best regulated middle-class families are haunted by ghosts and by mysterious, archetypal forces which cannot be adequately represented by melodrama, linear narrative or quasi-naturalistic modes of representation. As Helen and Anna suggest, "something else" is needed, something that takes account of the feminine and of shadows; something that the Greeks understood in their great daimones and archetypes. But it is too late to simply resurrect Greek theatrical figures and forms: we can, however, still dialogue with them, assess their potential for us or engage with them metatheatrically, at one remove, so to speak, through the device of the outer play which allows Friel, through Sir, to transcend the limiting traps of melodrama and naturalism and to draw on the power of the Classical Greek chorus which Sir calls to mind by his detachment and lack of individualization. But in this particular collision with the roots we are reminded, at the same time, of the great gulf between Sir and his 5th Century Greek homologue which not only kept emotion in check through formal elegance but simultaneously intensified it through the power of its poetry and metrical variation, thus playing the gamut of emotional colour at key dramatic moments. As a choric figure, Sir, is, by contrast, a cool customer, detached and emotionally neutral, a first cousin of the Prologue in Anouilh's *Antigone*. Through Sir we can measure the gaps between a 20th Century sensibility without passion, belief or illusions and that of 5th Century Athens where non-naturalistic, non-individualized theatrical figures could passionately incarnate or engage with the great forces that rule the psyche and the universe. In this great threnody on the traditional Irish family Friel conducts a sustained dialogue with Euripides' *Hippolytus* and in so doing not only deepens his exploration of his subject but engages in a self-consciously theatrical interrogation of new ways of representing it on the contemporary stage.

Works Cited:

Friel, Brian, (1984), *Selected Plays* (London: Faber and Faber)
Euripides, (1958), *Hippolytus*, trans. Rex Warner (London: Bodley Head)
Euripides, (1960), *Hippolytus*, trans. David Grene, in *Greek Tragedies*, Vol.I, eds., David Grene and Richmond Lattimore (Chicago: University of Chicago Press)

Politics, Language, Metatheatre: Friel's *The Freedom of the City* and the Formation of an Engaged Audience

Bernice Schrank

I. *The Play is Not About Bloody Sunday*

Brian Friel has always been uncomfortable with the explicitly political. When, for example, he finished *The Mundy Scheme* (1969), he let it be known that he did not intend to write another such overtly political play (Bell: 1993, 106-7). Even the Field Day Theatre Company of the early 80s, which Friel co-founded, with its explicit commitment to exploring the matrix of history, language, culture and nationality, did so, at least in its theatrical practice, by indirection and displacement, leaving the political gloss to the Field Day pamphlets, none of which Friel authored. Nor has Friel shown any interest in an affiliation with the political theatre of O'Casey. Quite the reverse, in fact. In an interview with the drama critic Desmond Rushe, Friel admits that he is "not an O'Casey fan"(quoted in Murray: 1997, 16). It is fair to say that *The Freedom of the City* is unique amongst Friel's dramatic work (O'Brien: 1990, 78). Rooted as it is in the events of Bloody Sunday, January 30, 1972 and their subsequent investigation, the play is a direct engagement with the "Troubles" in Northern Ireland.

Friel's uneasiness with this kind of political involvement must have been exacerbated by his closeness to the events, which were unfolding as he wrote. A little more than a year elapsed between Bloody Sunday and the opening of *Freedom* in Dublin on 20 February 1973; a little less than a year from the release of the report of Widgery Tribunal on 18 April 1972. As Friel wrote the play, the violence of Bloody Sunday was begetting more violence. Following Bloody Sunday, according to Lacy, "the Provisional IRA bombing campaign took off in earnest. Twice in the same week in June 1972 the Guildhall was badly damaged by bombs deposited inside the building" (Lacy: 1990, 268). By the summer of 1972, it was clear that London/Derry was a war zone.

My use of the slash requires explanation. Like so much else, place names in Ireland, as Friel's *Translations* indicates, are sites of contention. For Irish Catholics, North and South, the place retains its older designation as Derry. For Protestant Unionists, Ulster's second city is Londonderry, its very name yoking Irish and English territory. To avoid the implicit sectarianism of choosing one name or the other, during the period under discussion in this paper, the city was frequently referred to as London/Derry (Lacy: 1990, 81-92). I follow that practice.

Friel's uneasiness with what he regarded as his too direct engagement with the problems of Northern Ireland manifests itself in his efforts to distance and redirect the immediacy of the play's political concerns. Friel hit upon two strategies. His first is to set the action in 1970 instead of 1972. This small alteration of time affects almost nothing that a theatre audience experiences. Any theatre audience familiar with the events of Bloody Sunday will assume that they are the basis of Friel's play because Friel includes so many details associated with Bloody Sunday, from the introduction of an unnamed woman early in the play who speaks the words Bernadette Devlin is reported to have said ("Stand your ground", [*FC*: 111]) on that day as the soldiers arrived, to his, at the time, instantly recognizable paraphrase of the findings of the Widgery Tribunal. For readers and audiences unfamiliar with Bloody Sunday, Friel's alteration of the dates will have little or no meaning. As a distancing device, the date change does not do much.

If anything, the change in dates reinforces and intensifies the politics of the here and now. It enables Friel to incorporate into what was, historically, an anti-internment march all the accumulated grievances of the Catholic population in Northern Ireland from discrimination in jobs and housing to disenfranchisement. Those patterns of discrimination against Catholics were particularly egregious in London/Derry, where Catholics were in the majority. As Coogan points out the

> population of Derry was roughly two-thirds Catholic to one-third Protestant, and the Catholic population kept growing. Nevertheless, the population increase did not mean that Catholics could ever overtake the Protestants. Successive gerrymanders repeatedly redrew the electoral boundaries, so that the Unionist one-third were able to control the city. The results were that Catholics could not get municipal jobs or houses (Coogan: 1996, 34).

As Lily, Skinner and Michael rehearse the slogans ("wan man — wan vote"; "no more gerrymandering" [*FC*: 154]) and the issues that, from the inception of the civil rights agitation in 1968, brought thousands of people into the streets across Northern Ireland ("Eleven children in a two-roomed flat. No toilet, no running water" [*FC*: 137]), it is clear that the date change broadens the play's political perspective.

Friel's concern about the play's explicit politics also manifests itself in his comments about the play. His second strategy was to try to talk his way around a too close identification of the play with Bloody Sunday. In an interview with the *Irish Times* several days before the play's world premiere at the Abbey (20 February 1973), Friel attempts to direct attention to the personal. He is reported as saying that the play is, at its deepest level, about "the self-completion of people". The place where this self-completion takes place is Derry, around the time of Bloody Sunday. But the play, Brian Friel insists, is not *about* Bloody Sunday. It is as relevant to any set of people living through crisis and the threat of death as it is to Ireland, South or North (*Irish Times*: 1973, 12).

Friel's efforts at distancing and refocusing were not successful. Indeed, in his review of the play's first production, Seamus Kelly points out that comparisons with Bloody Sunday are inevitable. As if to validate Kelly's view as well as the reasons for Friel's concern about too close an identification between the play and the events of Bloody Sunday, when the play opened in London several days later (27 February 1973, Royal Court), it was harshly criticized by many English theatre critics as nationalist propaganda (Dantanus: 1988, 140). The connection between Bloody Sunday and Friel's play continues to be made. In the most recent New York production of *The Freedom of the City* at the Lincoln Center in the summer of 1999, Michael Farrell devotes two paragraphs at the beginning of the program notes to a description of Bloody Sunday and indicates that the "events of that fateful day form the backdrop to Brian Friel's play" (Farrell: 1999, 24), an opinion shared by *The New York Times* critic, Wilborn Hampton, in his review of the Lincoln Center production.

II. The Play Is About Bloody Sunday

In *The Freedom of the City*, Friel uses Bloody Sunday and the subsequent report of the Widgery Tribunal to dramatise that watershed moment in the Northern Ireland crisis when the consequences of too long an inequitable distribution of power, wealth and status are made manifest.

On January 30, 1972, British soldiers shot and killed thirteen civil rights demonstrators at the end of an anti-internment march in London/Derry. Obviously, no summary of Bloody Sunday is going to be value neutral, but Thomas Hennessey's *A History of Northern Ireland 1920-1996* offers a brief and apparently uninflected view:

> The shooting began at the end of a banned civil rights march attended by nearly ten thousand people, when part of the crowd tried to climb over a street barrier and were forced back by the British army using rubber bullets and spray from a water cannon.... It was never established who fired the first shots. Major-General Robert Ford, Commander of Land Forces in Northern Ireland, later denied that the army had fired first and said, "There is absolutely no doubt that the Parachute Regiment opened up only after they were fired on" (Hennessey: 1997, 206).

There were counter-claims that a loyalist sniper opened fire as Bernadette Devlin was about to speak to the crowd, while nearly twenty years later a television documentary suggested that members of the Official IRA, acting independently, may have fired on the army (See Bew and Gillespie: 1993, 44-5).

What emerges even from such an abbreviated summary is that the shooting on Bloody Sunday, predictably, produced several opposing versions of how the killing started. Hennessey does not attempt to resolve the divergences he records. Like Hennessey, *Freedom* presents these conflicting views; but by dramatising only unarmed civilians and frightened, trigger-happy British soldiers, Friel discredits the official version that the soldiers were fired on first (and by the dead civilians).

Almost immediately after the killings, the Northern Ireland Civil Rights Association and the National Council for Civil Liberties began collecting eyewitness accounts from participants and observers (Mullan: 1997, 7). These accounts indicate that the march, although banned, began peacefully, and the atmosphere was carnivalesque. Pictures taken before the shooting show conservatively dressed men and women walking together (Lily had on her "good coat" [*FC*: 112] and her "[f]ive pounds in Woolworths'" shoes [*FC*: 129]), with scattered placards (McLean: 1997, 96) and a banner on which is written "Civil Rights Association" (Lacy: 1990, 267; Mullan: 1997, interpages between 32-33). Given the possibilities for provocative street theatre and spectacle which were developing as part of the anti-Vietnam protest movement in the United States at that time, this march looks remarkably subdued.

The connection between the civil rights marches in Northern Ireland and the United States is clear from use of the slogan "one man, one vote", which accompanied American civil rights demonstrations in the early 1960s and was later borrowed by Northern Irish civil rights activists. Also, the Northern Ireland civil rights movement used the American civil rights anthem, "We Shall Overcome". That song receives ironic mention when Skinner suggests to Michael, after it has become painfully clear to Skinner that they are to be killed, "[s]houldn't we go out singing 'We shall overcome'" (*FC*: 166)? Clearly, given the availability of more inflammatory models, the organizers of the anti-internment march on 30 January appear to have opted consciously for a disciplined and orderly protest.

Like the cameras, the press was also present, and their reports are consistent with the eyewitness testimony that British soldiers opened fire on unarmed civilian marchers. Unsurprisingly, these reports generated outrage in the Catholic community of Northern Ireland. The response in the Irish Republic was equally ferocious. Crowds in Dublin besieged the British Embassy for several days and, on 2 February 1972, burned it down. In the House of Commons, Bernadette Devlin, MP, denounced the actions of the soldiers, and then rushed across the floor and pulled the hair and struck the face of the Home Secretary, Reginald Maudling. To quiet growing criticism at home and abroad, the British Prime Minister, Edward Heath, set up a tribunal of inquiry into the events of 30 January in London/Derry to be headed by Lord Chief Justice Widgery (Bew and Gillespie: 1993, 44-46; Coogan: 1996, 161).

Released on 18 April 1972, the report of the Widgery Tribunal did nothing to encourage confidence in the ability of Britain to deal fairly, reasonably and justly with the turmoil in Northern Ireland. Its findings present the conflicting allegations regarding the events of 30 January:

> The army case is that each of these shots was an aimed shot fired at a civilian holding or using a bomb or firearm. On the other side it was argued that none of the deceased was using a bomb or firearm and that the soldiers fired without justification... (Quoted in Lacy: 1990, 265).

The findings establish that no civilian marcher was found with any arms:

> [Although] a number of soldiers spoke of actually seeing firearms or bombs in the hands of civilians none was recovered by the Army. None of the many photographs shows a civilian holding an object that can with certainty be identified as a firearm or bomb. No casualties were suffered by the soldiers from firearms or gelignite bombs. In relation to every one of the deceased there were eye witnesses who said that they saw no bomb or firearm in his hands (Quoted in Lacy: 1990, 265).

Astonishingly enough, the Widgery Tribunal concludes, in contradiction to the evidence it adduced, that the soldiers, despite some excesses, conducted themselves appropriately, while the marchers, by taking part in an illegal activity, were largely to blame for the ensuing disorder:

> There would have been no deaths in Londonderry on 30 January if those who organised the illegal march had not thereby created a highly dangerous situation in which a clash between demonstrators and the security forces was almost inevitable.... Each soldier was his own judge of whether he had identified a gunman. Their training made them aggressive and quick on decision and some showed more restraint in opening fire than others (quoted in Bew and Gillespie: 1993, 51).

Friel's version of the Widgery Tribunal conclusions is nearly verbatim (*FC*: 168). So the report and Friel's adaptation blame the victims and therefore find no reason to provide a mechanism for holding accountable those who did the killings and those who gave the orders. Given such offensive and ridiculous conclusions, the Widgery Tribunal was unable to do the political work the Heath government had assigned to it. Instead of defusing the tensions in Northern Ireland, it provoked a new round of retributory killing and bombing.

The resemblances between Friel's play and the events of Bloody Sunday and the Widgery cover-up are unmistakable. It is, to be sure, a political play in the broad sense of examining the dysfunctional and, after Widgery, criminal relationship of power to powerlessness in Northern Ireland; it is not a political play in the narrow agit prop sense of advocating a specific doctrine or party platform. British reviewers who, blinded by their own biases, dismissed the play as blatant political propaganda, failed to notice that, at the same time that Friel criticizes the role of Britain in Ulster, he declines to validate the pieties of Irish Republicanism. Two of the three dead civil rights marchers, Skinner and Lily, are dispossessed and disaffected, barely political at all. Working-class (but unemployed) Michael does not identify himself as an underdog, is discomfited by Skinner's and Lily's disregard of bourgeois etiquette, and longs for status, respectability and, if he's lucky, a job as a petty establishment functionary. As he explains to Skinner and Lily, he is "going to the tech. Four nights a week — you know — to improve myself. I'm doing economics and business administration and computer science" (*FC*: 122). Michael has the soul of a bean counter. His politics are conservative, and he worries that the civil rights marches are becoming a magnet for undesirable elements, by which he means the underclass to which Skinner and Lily belong as well as the radicals.

None of the three resembles the martyred hero stereotype that fuels Republican agitation and propaganda. In the Balladeer's songs, he identifies Lily, Skinner and Michael as romantic nationalists, latter day Tones, Pearces and Connollys (*FC*: 118), who died to end colonial rule in Northern Ireland. This view of Lily, Skinner and Michael lacks all credibility. It is one of the painful ironies of the play that the Balladeer, the voice of Republican militancy, has, in his own way, got things about as wrong as the Judge. The differences between them are the differences of power and status (important matters, to be sure) not precision and accuracy.

So, while *The Freedom of the City* deals with Bloody Sunday, condemning the role of the British in Northern Ireland, it does not use the occasion to endorse radical Republicanism, or indeed the institutional underpinnings of Catholic society, North or South. The same jaundiced eye that creates the drunken Balladeer also creates Father Brosnan, whose easy transformation from a cautious sympathiser with the people to a fierce denouncer of the influences of godless Communism is a form of collaboration. In short, Friel refuses to present the public face of the crisis in Northern Ireland in the Manichean terms of salt-of-the-earth Catholic Nationalists and bad-guy Protestant Unionists. Friel's play is impassioned, but it is not politically naive. Notwithstanding the hostility of the British reviewers at the time of the first London production of *Freedom*, Friel's work is a positive (and, given the circumstances, moderate) cultural intervention, not a rallying cry to people the barricades.

III. High Up or Low Down: London/Derry Divided

Both in subject matter and dramatic technique, *The Freedom of the City* portrays a world divided against itself. The antagonisms are explosive and apparently irreconcilable, at least by the forces represented on stage: power vs. powerlessness, British vs. Irish, Unionist vs. Nationalist, rich vs. poor, Protestant vs. Catholic. These oppositions affect all aspects of Friel's dramatic practice in *Freedom* (as they do all aspects of life in Northern Ireland), and most especially the uses to which he puts language and stage space.

That language is fundamental to Friel's drama has been widely acknowledged since *Translations* appeared and its connections to George Steiner's *After Babel* noted. Helen Lojek, for example, suggests that all of Friel's plays, including *Freedom*, are about translation in Steiner's sense of the word. For Lojek, *The Freedom of the City* demonstrates that vocabularies of political action, whether social reform, radical agitation, military intervention or judicial investigation, require and produce so great a distancing from the subject that, in the end, what is most valuable in the subject, the subject's humanity and individuality, is lost (Lojek: 1994, 83-99).

In his recent and valuable study of Friel, Elmer Andrews argues for a more intimate and even inexorable connection between the play's presentation of a dysfunctional relationship between public and private discourse and the murder of Lily, Skinner and Michael. In Andrews' reading, the play's verbal discontinuities create and embody an unbridgeable separation between the three civil rights marchers, Lily, Skinner and Michael, and those who oppose civil rights for Northern Irish Roman Catholics (Andrews: 1995, 129-138). The discontinuities of language, for Andrews, determine the tragic outcome and simultaneously deny the possibility that any program that addresses the circumstances of Skinner, Lily and Michael can be successfully articulated much less implemented. (For a similar view, for which the present paper is a modification, see Schrank: 1988, 73).

Although Lojek and Andrews have much of interest to say about *The Freedom of the City*, I think they are too pessimistic about the implications of Friel's manipulations of language. I agree with them that, in *Freedom*, Friel creates a montage of voices, speaking in different idioms and accents, some of which are designed to exclude meaningful communication; but I do not think they are, as Lojek argues, all diminutions of individual experience, or that they are, as Andrews argues, a babel of unintelligible tongues (with the exception of the impermanent communion between Lily and Skinner). The characters use a wide range of discourses, which display very different levels of intelligibility.

Even within the main drama in the Guildhall, for example, the moments of complete communion occur only between Lily and Skinner. Nevertheless, Lily does not hear Skinner correct her when she thanks him for the port, and he tells her it is sherry. Communion they may have, but not perfect communication. Michael never achieves their level of sympathetic understanding. Indeed, his is a persistently hectoring voice that sees Skinner's anarchic playfulness as the acts of "a vandal" (*FC*: 138). He goes so far as to suggest that "[c]haracters like that need watching" (*FC*: 132). Whereas Lily is oblivious to Michael's edginess, Skinner delights in exacerbating his anxiety. Without the intervention of a hostile external force and an accidental meeting, Skinner and Michael would never spend a willing minute in each other's company.

The subtle interplay of speech in the Guildhall is only one of the ways Friel shows language functioning under stress. Including the Guildhall, there are, I believe, at least four distinct ways that Friel handles language to indicate the difficulties with, as well as the potential for, communication in the play:

(1) There is, as I have already indicated, the colourful and highly individualized language of Lily, Skinner and Michael in which real understanding and even communion is possible, if not fully achieved.

(2) There is the crude vernacular working-class speech of the anonymous British soldiers and the anonymous voices of the Bogside which, despite its common idiom, cannot transcend the differences of power and nationality.

(3) There are the translations of private experience into other discourses. These fall into two groups. In the first group, there are the educated formulations of public communication, e.g., the academic study, the news story, the sermon. Some of these translations, like Professor Dodds' lectures, facilitate a measure of communication across the divides of class, nationality and religion, with his talk about third world poverty having an immediate relevance to the situations of Lily, Skinner and Michael; others, like the RTE Commentator's coverage and Father Brosnan's second sermon, profoundly distort (by intention and/or by inadvertence) the reality they attempt to represent.

The second group differs from the first in its dependence on popular modes of address, and is represented by the Balladeer, who translates the experience of Lily, Skinner and Michael into one of the most enduring forms of popular Irish Republicanism, the political song. His first is, like "We Shall Overcome", an American import. It is a translation into the Irish Republican context of the American "John Brown's Body", a song which commemorates the rising and execution of John Brown, a pre-Civil War opponent of slavery. It was later transformed by Julia Ward Howe into the rousing anthem for the Northern armies, "The Battle Hymn of the Republic" (*FC*: 118). The transnational convergences of this song measure the adaptability of this kind of popular translation. His second song is an up-dated version of "Kevin Barry" (*FC*: 148). Like most of the other translations, the Balladeer's songs seriously misrepresent Lily, Skinner and Michael.

Although I have established two separate categories of translation for the sake of clarity, it would be a mistake to see the translations in either category as functioning autonomously. So, in the play's war of words, it is possible to understand Father Brosnan's second sermon in which Lily, Michael and Skinner are cast as communist stooges at least in part as a hostile response to the Balladeer's reinvention of the three civil rights marchers as latter day Irish Republican gunmen/heroes.

(4) There is the self-serving discourse of political power, which is intended to cover up the rawest displays of physical force, the military intervention. It does so by declining to take into account the other side of the sectarian, national and class divide. The most accomplished speaker of this language is the Judge, whose apparently neutral findings gain much of their authority from their appropriation of scientific and technical jargon.

These categories are complicated by the fact that dialogue (in the Guildhall between Lily, Skinner and Michael and at the Tribunal between Judge and witnesses) is interspersed with seemingly random shouts and slogans addressed to imagined audiences and monologues addressed to the real audience. The uses to which monologues are put in this play is a topic to which I will turn later in the paper. There I will argue that they function metatheatrically to break down the separation between stage and audience.

At this point, I want to consider the relationship between the uses to which Friel puts language and his deployment of stage space. The stage is sectioned off horizontally with walled battlements above, and street space with Guildhall, seat of municipal government, at stage level, below the walls. These walls are a constant reminder that the play is set in London/Derry,

> the only town in Ireland whose full circuit of ancient walls still survive intact. While the walls have been modified in the course of

the centuries, particularly by the addition of a number of extra gates, they are essentially the same fortifications that protected the small seventeenth-century colonial city (Lacy: 1990, 93).

These walls feature prominently in the Siege of 1688-89 when Protestant Apprentice Boys shut the gates to keep out James II and retain the Protestant ascendancy in Ulster. This determining moment enters the play when Skinner pokes around in the Guildhall parlour and finds an ancient musket labelled, "'Musket used by Williamite garrison besieged by Jacobite army 1691'" (*FC*: 119).

Within the play, the walled battlements are reserved for "higher ups", the Judge (described by Friel in the stage directions as "high up in the battlements" [*FC*: 107]), the witnesses at the Tribunal, the Priest and the RTE Commentator (who starts in the battlements but moves to ground level to cover the funeral). Friel's directions, moreover, specify that the walls are "embattled" (*FC*: 105) suggesting to readers of the text as well as to audiences in the theatre the degree to which the perception of embattlement pervades the entire action, a sense in which both sides of the divide fear invasion and both sides, despite the disparities of power and, in this play, position (higher/lower), see themselves, however unrealistically, as besieged. (For a useful discussion of the operations of the siege mentality in Northern Ireland, see Buckley and Kenney: 1995, 41-56.)

The language associated with those "higher up" is abstract and detached from the reality on ground level. In the case of the Judge, the language, vocabulary and syntax is of calculated remoteness, designed to eliminate all traces of the submerged world it believes challenges its hegemony. With RTE Commentator and Priest, their words from the battlements advance implausible views of the activities in the streets and in the Guildhall in discourses of inadvertent or intentional incomprehension that are easily assimilated into the Judge's discourse of power.

The space below is partitioned, streets divided between soldiers and civilians, outside space set off from the parlour of the Guildhall. Streets and Guildhall co-exist on the same ground, but as mutually exclusive enclaves. The streets are consigned to those at the bottom of the social heap, those who do not count like Lily and Michael, the no-accounts like Skinner, the expendable anonymous British soldiers who do the dirty work for those in the walled world of safety above, and the drunken Balladeer, who, pied piper-like, will soon be mobilizing an armed resistance to those soldiers. Those in and from the street use a demotic speech of particularity and immediacy, different in vocabulary and in syntax from the discourses of power cultivated in the embattled walls above. Professor Dodds, the down-to-earth, somewhat fuddy-duddyish American sociologist, is the exception, essentially an academic tourist from the privileged world come to observe how the natives live, and the language he uses is a kind of linguistic half-way house between the vernacular idioms of the street and the formal and restricted speech of those in the battlements. In the geography of power, those who dwell in the streets are supposed to remain there.

As the play opens, however, the streets have become contested territory, full of CS gas, rubber bullets, disembodied shouts, the scream of ambulances, the spray of water cannons, soldiers armed to the teeth, and soon, if the Balladeer has his way, Republican gunmen. The danger of the street world outside contrasts with the apparent safety of the inside, the stable world of long-standing power and privilege represented by the Guildhall, "[t]he holy of holies itself" (*FC*: 116), the structural marker of Protestant ascendancy in London/Derry, a city two-thirds Catholic. The differences between the street and the Guildhall, like all the other differences in this play, find expression in language. The vernacular of the street is in sharp contrast to the Guildhall's exclusionary language of political and economic control, the labelled portraits of Protestant leaders and labelled military artefacts, reminders of Protestant victories, as well as the ceremonial robes, the running water, the comfortable chairs, the telephone and the well-stocked liquor cabinet that, taken together, help define Unionist power. So when Lily, Skinner and Michael, representatives of the dispossessed world outside, by sheerest accident, take refuge inside the Guildhall, they are not, as they first think, in a sanctuary, but a "no go" zone. Their very presence (as Skinner alone comprehends) will be understood as a threat to the status quo of apartheid, a transgression so great it cannot be allowed. Embattled walls, street and Guildhall: these constitute Friel's symbolic stage geography of a world in which divisions based on differentials of power, class, nationality, history and religion have territorial and linguistic correlation. What follows is a closer scrutiny of these correlations.

IV: The Guildhall and the Battlements: Two Solitudes

The "embattled" tribunal and the "occupied" Guildhall represent antagonistic worlds. Yet these are the sites of the only sustained dialogue in the play, unstructured talk in the Guildhall, structured testimony in the battlements, but in each case talk amongst characters of similar backgrounds, interests and affiliations. That such communication takes place does not moderate the antagonisms or lessen the distance between groups. The characteristics and purposes of these verbal exchanges are so different that they reinforce and sustain the sense of language as an impediment to the formation of a civil society. There is, after all, no dialogue between those in the Guildhall and those in the battlements.

The central action of *The Freedom of the City* takes place in the Guildhall. There the talk is spontaneous, anarchic, often witty, and highly individualized. The speech at the hearings is its mirror image: formal and depersonalised, tightly organized by its question and answer format, apparently uninflected. Despite its appearance of civility, the uncivil intention of that testimony is to silence Lily, Michael and Skinner and cover up their murder.

Although more politically conscious, Lily, Skinner and Michael are Northern relatives of Sean O'Casey's Juno, Boyle and Bentham (*Juno and the Paycock*), both in their class identities and in their use of personal idioms expressive of their lives, their needs, their poverty and their longings. Their talk, desultory at first, becomes a progressive revelation of their characters and the causes for their involvement in the civil rights movement. Their reasons for participating are highly individualized, and are captured both in their direct statements as well as in the inflections of their personal idioms.

Michael's motives are the closest to the surface and the easiest to grasp: he sees the marches as a means of getting ahead. Socially insecure, he seeks safety in a plodding and undistinguished prose. On the one hand, he lacks both the verbal flamboyance of Skinner and the wrenching particularities of Lily; on the other, his speech lacks the assurance and mandarin authority of the class to which he aspires. He retains this slightly pompous speech pattern to the very end, wrongly assuming that he can extrapolate from his boy scout views to those of the English:

> Give them no cheek and they'll give you no trouble. We made a peaceful protest and they know that. They're not interested in people like us. It's the troublemakers they're after (*FC*: 158).

Here and elsewhere in the final moments of the play, he implicitly criticizes Skinner's verbal pyrotechnics by clinging to his colourless phrases which are the perfect vehicle for his naive and inaccurate view of what awaits them when they leave the Guildhall.

Lily's speech is different. It is always specific, colourful and anecdotal, miniature encapsulations of her world, stated without sentimentality or much insight into what is being revealed. Her loosely constructed but minutely visualized description of her place in the crowd before the soldiers attacked is quintessential Lily-speak:

> I was at the back of the crowd, beside wee Johnny Duffy — you know — the window-cleaner — Johnny the Tumbler — and I'm telling him what the speakers is saying 'cos he hears hardly anything now since he fell off the ladder the last time. And I'm just after telling him 'The street is ours and nobody's going to move us' when I turn round and Jesus, Mary and Joseph there's

> this big Saracen right behind me. Of course I took to my heels.
> And when I look back there's Johnny the Tumbler standing there
> with his fists in the air and him shouting, 'The streets is ours and
> nobody's going to move us!' And you could hardly see him below
> the Saracen. Lord, the chairman'll enjoy that (*FC*: 114).

Johnny the Tumbler is, for a moment, a living presence on the stage, and
Lily's lively, amused recounting of his David/Goliath confrontation
resonates far more profoundly than Michael's enervated descriptions of
the march. Lily shares with Juno the capacity to grasp the specific in the
general experience, and this particularizing is their great strength. But it is
also their weakness: a too narrow immediacy leaves out analysis and
understanding, a point Lily makes in her monologue to the audience:
"life had eluded me because never once in my forty-three years had an
experience, an event, even a small unimportant happening been isolated,
and assessed, and articulated" (*FC*: 150). What Lily regrets, at least in
part, is that she does not command a language of logic and analysis.

Skinner's use of language is the most sophisticated of the group and in
the play. A free-spirit, a ne'er-do-well, a gambler, an orphan, a loner and
an outcast, he is quick-witted and whimsical, cynical and self-conscious.
He is a politically astute realist and a rhetorician of considerable skill.
When Michael insists that non-violent political action is a winning
strategy, for example, Skinner demurs.

> Mr. Hegarty is of the belief that if five thousand of us are
> demonstrating peacefully and they come along and shoot us
> down, then automatically we... we... (*To* MICHAEL) Sorry, what's
> the theory again? (*FC*: 141)

Mimicking Michael's formal and slightly pompous rhetoric, Skinner
pretends to a kind of vagueness which is its own rebuke to Michael's
political sentimentality. For Skinner, civil rights is not about votes; it is
not about job opportunities; it is about affirming the human spirit. The
civil rights agitation, Skinner tells Lily,

> has nothing to do with doctors and accountants and teachers and
> dignity and boy scout honour. It's about us — the poor — the
> majority — stirring in our sleep. And if that's not what it's all
> about, then it has nothing to do with us (*FC*: 154).

For all his insight, Skinner's reasoning does not lead anywhere, certainly
not to the kind of collective action that might ameliorate the conditions
to which he objects.

Side by side with Skinner's realism is his dramatic inventiveness. While
Michael worries about proprieties and Lily thinks of her family, Skinner
performs a series of improvisations in which he enacts his disrespect for
the status quo. From the Guildhall he calls his bookie, bets on a horse,

plays the radio, dances and sings with Lily, drinks whiskey, smokes a cigar, stubs out the cigar on the desk, dons the ceremonial robes of the Lord Mayor, bestows on the others the freedom of the city, pushes Lily to call her sister in Australia, fences with an imaginary opponent using the ceremonial sword, stages a mock meeting of City Council, sticks the sword into a picture of one of the city's dignitaries and signs the Distinguished Visitors' Book. This extravagant naughtiness is bright and often very funny; but it is also idiosyncratic and self-indulgent, a gesture against prevailing orthodoxies rather than an effective action.

The strength of the language Lily, Skinner and Michael use is obvious. Their monologues (*FC*: 149-59) implicitly address its limitations. When Lily, Michael and Skinner talk to the audience, they set aside their highly individualized speech for a uniform rhetoric that conforms in diction and syntax to the requirements of standard English. This is what they would have said if they had a certain kind of education, training and discipline. What these monologues lack in entertainment and colour they make up for in insight. They are simultaneously moving and analytical; in Lily's words, they assess and articulate. When characters and audience can be shown to speak (more or less) the same language, the audience is discouraged from viewing the characters solely as exotic representatives of an alien underclass. The monologues of Lily, Skinner and Michael indicate that there is a language capable of expressing with honesty and compassion their social predicament; it may not be much used in the play, but it is an available linguistic resource.

The second action of *The Freedom of the City* is the creation of a cover-up. Disconnected from Michael, Skinner and Lily is the discourse of power that attempts to rewrite the events at the Guildhall to exonerate power and erase blame. So, Judge and expert witnesses effortlessly and "honestly" reformulate all information to suit the political purposes assigned to the tribunal, the maintenance of the status quo.

The Judge, the state's representative, is the most egregious instance in *The Freedom of the City* of false objectivity. As he explains his role, it is clear that he has established the parameters of an investigation that can only blame the victims and exonerate the perpetrators:

> The facts we garner over the coming days may indicate that the deceased were callous terrorists who had planned to seize the Guildhall weeks before the events of February 10th; or the facts may indicate that the misguided scheme occurred to them on that very day while they listened to revolutionary speeches (*FC*: 110).

In a cool, apparently uninflected (although "callous", "misguided" and "revolutionary" are loaded) officialese that purports to be fact-based, the Judge oversimplifies the situation by creating only two categories to explain the behaviour of Michael, Lily and Skinner, both of which presume them to be guilty. He thereby prevents consideration of the possibility that they are innocent of any wrongdoing. This perverse logic, Friel suggests, is one of the ways state power manufactures consent.

The state apparatus is abetted by the experts from the world of science and technology. The spokesperson for the army, the Brigadier, opines that arrest was impossible and shooting was the only viable course. Professor Cuppley, the pathologist, reports on the injuries. When the Judge attempts to specify precisely the number of wounds, all Cuppley will agree to is "that thirty-four was an approximation" (*FC*: 162). Such pointless and fussy attention to detail (what difference can it possibly make if there were thirty-four or forty-four wounds?), distracts from the real question, which is how unarmed civilians came to be shot by the soldiers in the first place. Providing that focus is the responsibility of the Judge, who steadfastly avoids it, allowing Cuppley's numbing details to create a smokescreen behind which the truth is effectively hidden. Dr. Winbourne, the forensic scientist, gives equally useless evidence about powder burns in a scientific jargon that conceals and so defeats knowledge. When the judge puts the question, "does that mean that that person has fired a gun?" (Friel, 142), Winbourne answers both ways:

> He may have, my lord. Or he may have been contaminated by being within thirty feet of someone who has fired in his direction (*FC*: 142).

It is Winbourne's testimony that Michael, Lily and Skinner may have fired guns themselves, or they may not have fired at all, but were shot at. The only possibility Winbourne omits is that they shot themselves. Since it is uncontested fact that they have been shot, and since there is no evidence that they were armed, Winbourne's testimony ought to lead to the inevitable conclusion that they were murdered. But further questioning by the Judge elicits so many complications, qualifications and possibilities, both likely and unlikely, that Winbourne's evidence is neutralized. In the end, Winbourne assures the Judge of what the Judge has convinced Winbourne, that Michael fired a gun.

The tribunal's ability to suppress the truth and rewrite history is facilitated by two kinds of rhetorical evasion. The first involves defamiliarizing the subject. So, in the evidence, familiar forms of address, and with them the individual identities of Michael, Lily and Skinner, are suppressed, replaced by official names, "Hegarty… Michael Joseph", "Doherty, Elizabeth", "Fitzgerald, Adrian Casimir" (*FC*: 116-118), reductive numbers, "the three" (*FC*: 149), negative political categories, "gunmen",(*FC*: 134)/ "terrorists" (*FC*: 109, 134), and physical condition, "the deceased" (*FC*: 149, 161). The second involves suppression of agency. This technique takes two forms. In the first, abstract nouns (or noun phrases) replace names. For example, the Judge says that the "weight of evidence... seems to be directing"(*FC*: 148); or "the answers to these questions point to the conclusion... " (*FC*: 149). In the second, the passive voice undermines individual responsibility, as when the Judge notes that "all three were killed by SLR rifle-fire" (*FC*: 161). If this phrase is put into the active voice, then it would read that rifles (not persons) killed Lily, Michael and Skinner. Even in the active voice, agency is denied. The intention and the effect of these strategies is to deflect attention from the fact that three people were murdered and therefore that there are murderers who ought to be brought to justice.

To conclude: in the fissured world of *Freedom of the City*, Friel divides the stage into a series of isolated enclaves (the most important of which are the Guildhall and the battlements) in which the occupants either perceive themselves to be, or actually are, embattled. These separate stage spaces correspond to the sectarian, national and class divisions of Northern Ireland. The divisions are maintained by force of arms as well as by filtering of words; in short, by the ability of the language of power to voice over and erase dissent from public discourse.

V. On the Ground

In *The Freedom of the City* stage space, as I have already noted, is not only divided horizontally; it is also partitioned vertically between street and Guildhall, and, in the streets, between soldiers and civilians. Whereas the horizontal divisions speak primarily to differences in power and status and their associated languages, the vertical partitioning between soldiers and civilians reveals differences (British vs. Irish), but also unacknowledged commonalities (class, language). It is one of the painful contradictions of this play that those groups who have the most in common are pitted against each other, while those who have a vested interest in perpetuating that divisiveness hover out of harm's way in the battlements above.

The best illustration of how this contradiction works occurs in the first act between anonymous British soldiers and anonymous Irish civilians. Soon after Lily, Skinner and Michael enter the Guildhall, two British soldiers are revealed at opposite ends of the stage, in the streets around the Guildhall, hugging the ground. The anonymous soldiers talk briefly to each other, exchanging positions and describing their situation. A little later another group of anonymous speakers is heard, their shouting voices floating disembodied onto the stage, providing notice that there is an unseen population on the other side of the battlements. They are the majority of London/Derry who have been marginalized by the political practices of those who hold forth in the battlements. They may be invisible for the moment, but they are not now silent. Like the British soldiers, but with much greater legitimacy, they too occupy the ground and, consistently with the sentiments of the anonymous Woman, they intend to "Stand [their] ground! Don't move! Don't panic" (*FC*: 111). It is, after all, as the Woman says, their city.

Whereas Lily, Skinner and Michael are separated by religion, class and language from the Judge and those he represents, the various anonymous voices that are heard in the street are bound together (and to Lily, Skinner and Michael) by commonalities of class and idiom. Indeed, British soldiers and Northern Irish street people use the same angry words against each other. Anonymous British Soldier I, talking to British Soldier 2 at the opposite end of the stage, explains in an idiom remote from the lofty and upper-class rhetoric of the British Judge, that the "fucking yobbos are inside the fucking Guildhall.... What the fuck am I supposed to do" (*FC*: 117)? Several minutes later, anonymous Nationalist voices from behind the battlements are heard, translating Father Brosnan's funeral address into angry slogans that use the same words: "Fuck them anyway! Fuck them! Fuck them! Fuck them" (*FC*: 125). It is no surprise that, although the anonymous working-class Northern Irish Catholic voices and the anonymous working class British soldiers share a common (but limited) vocabulary, they are unable to communicate with each other. By the time of the events of Bloody Sunday, British soldiers were regarded (and in the play they are) an occupying force. They do the groundwork for the Judge who keeps the unpleasantness and danger at a distance.

Obviously, communication across national and sectarian divides requires more than a shared idiom. It requires a protected space and circumstances in which characters who have in common a mutually intelligible speech and commonalities of interest can meet together, speak to each other and be heard. Although on that divided stage such a space does not appear to exist, it is Friel's intention to try to create it in the theatre.

VI. Implicating the Audience: Translating the Monologues

Besides the verbal exchanges between characters, Friel has a number of speeches spoken directly to the audience. (For a somewhat different assessment of Friel's use of monologues, see Birker.) These include the Judge's report on the findings of the tribunal, Professor Dodds' three short lectures on the culture of poverty, and the formal and elegiac addresses of Lily, Skinner and Michael at the beginning of Act Two discussed above. In a play that so insistently dramatizes separations, these monologues break down the barrier between stage and audience, reminding the audience of the theatricality and constructedness of the staged events, and prod the audience to assume a role other than that of spectators.

The monologues are primarily translations of the events in the Guildhall into the language of public discourse by characters who do not appear to participate directly (with the exception, of course, of Lily, Skinner and Michael). The nimbus of neutrality that surrounds these particular monologues allows their speakers to pass from the war zone at ground level to the battlements above with impunity. The monologues represent a fairly comprehensive dramatization of the ways by which information is transmitted and events are represented outside the theatre: media broadcasts, judicial reports, academic lectures, sermons. And while translation inevitably involves loss, the act of translating, if it is into a more generally accessible language, carries with it the possibility of enhanced understanding. In a world as deeply divided as the world dramatized in *Freedom*, translation, at least in theory, has much to offer.

Unfortunately, the quality of the translation varies. Even more unfortunately, although these public discourses appear neutral, some of them surreptitiously aid and abet the cover-up. The claims to objectivity (RTE Commentator) and/or privileged understanding (Priest and Professor) prove either false or of insufficient relevance.

Although the fifth estate has a special and protected role in democratic societies based on the belief that it is necessary to have an informed electorate, O'Kelly, the television newsman, fails to live up to that high purpose. He delivers two monologues to the theatre audience. Each of them provides inadequate coverage of the events in the Guildhall, and the particular spin that O'Kelly gives to his reports encourages the acceptance of official truth. From the battlements of power, microphone in hand, he looks down on the turbulent street, and, in the absence of hard news, he passes on, uncritically, rumours of terrorist occupation of the Guildhall that will validate the cover-up. After the killing, O'Kelly appears at ground level to report on the funeral. Given that the unconfirmed rumours allege large numbers of terrorists, the fact that only three, putatively identified as gunmen, were found ought to prompt some independent investigation, but O'Kelly declines that option. Instead, he focuses on the spectacle of Lily, Skinner and Michael's public funeral and produces a gossipy who's who report on the important mourners. As translations, O'Kelly's monologues fail to account for the events at the Guildhall, and so they allow the official version of events to stand by default.

Father Brosnan is another unreliable translator. Whereas O'Kelly's limitations as a translator are obtuseness and laziness, Father Brosnan's is an inconsistency based on expedience. He translates the same events differently in the light of changing political circumstances. In Act One, using the conventional language of martyrology, he claims that:

> They died for their beliefs. They died for their fellow citizens. They died because they could endure no longer the injuries and injustices and indignities that have been their lot for too many years (*FC*: 125).

By Act Two, in an astonishingly bold and unapologetic about-face, the sacrificial lambs have become communist dupes. The civil rights movement may have been "initially peaceful and dignified" (*FC*: 156), but, unfortunately, says Father Brosnan, "certain evil elements attached themselves to it":

> Who are they, these evil people: I will speak and I will speak plainly. They have many titles... but they have one purpose and one purpose only — to deliver this Christian country into the dark dungeons of Godless communism. I don't suggest for one minute that the three people who died yesterday were part of this conspiracy, were even aware that they were victims of this conspiracy. But victims they were (*FC*: 156).

Father Brosnan speaks from the battlements of power, and power, Friel suggests, is by its very nature conservative. It is easy to imagine the hostility his first sympathetic sermon would have engendered in that world, and his second sermon needs to be understood, at least in part, as an effort to appease that hostility. It may also be, as I argue above, a partial answer to the Balladeer. Whatever their motivation, both sermons are highly inaccurate translations of the events in the Guildhall, but the second is far more damaging than the first because it supports the official cover-up.

Like Liam O'Kelly and Father Brosnan, Professor Dodds, the American sociologist, is a translator. His commentary on the culture of poverty, based on Oscar Lewis' *La Vida* (Pine: 1990, 102), forms a frame for the activities of Lily, Skinner and Michael in the Guildhall. Unlike O'Kelly and Brosnan, he is not engaged in the production of another version of the events of Bloody Sunday; his lectures in effect translate Lily, Michael and Skinner into case studies in his examination of the general condition of world poverty. His lecture style is dry, academic, factual, numerate in this context ("In Latin America one per cent of the population owns seventy-two per cent of the land" [*FC*: 163]), and, occasionally, colloquial ("What solutions are the economists and politicians cooking up?" [*FC*: 163]; "they often have a hell of a lot more fun than we have"[*FC*: 135]).

Appearing always at ground level, Professor Dodds' general description of the culture of poverty appears grounded in and extrapolated from the behaviours and attitudes of Lily, Michael and Skinner in the Guildhall.

Dodds is the only translator who shows any sympathetic understanding for the conditions that drive Lily, Michael and Skinner. Dodds is, moreover, the only translator who attempts to engage the audience directly: "Middle-class people", he says, calling the audience to attention, "with deference, people like you and me" (*FC*: 135). By this rhetorical strategy, Dodds hopes to gain a sympathetic hearing from the audience.

As a translation into theory of local practice, Dodds succeeds only partially. While his emphasis on issues of class usefully broadens the play's political perspective, his exclusive focus on class leaves out important issues of nationality, history and language. Professor Dodds' theories do not, for example, account for the divisions that exist on the stage between working-class British soldiers and working-class Northern Irish civilians.

Moreover, the politics that underpin Dodds' analysis of poverty are the politics of acquiescence. Dodds, after all, is the translator who explicitly acknowledges the existence of an oppressive power elite. Such an acknowledgement might reasonably be expected to lead to a lecture on the need for a more equitable distribution of power and wealth. Dodds, however, avoids drawing such conclusions. Instead, he indicates that the poor live in the present and they have more fun than "we" (*FC*: 135) do; left unstated but clearly implied is that there are important compensations for a life of deprivation. As long as this calm and conservative didacticism dominates the discourse of social concern, the institutions that create and maintain poverty have nothing to worry about. Despite the explanatory power of Dodds' theories of poverty for the central action in the Guildhall, the politics implicit in his translation have the same effect as the translations of Liam O'Kelly and Father Brosnan. One way or another all three collude in maintaining the status quo.

What the staged action illustrates is the need for a forum in which the questions raised by Bloody Sunday and all it encompasses can be addressed. The courts, the churches, the academy and the streets do not, either on stage, or in the world to which the stage refers, provide such a forum. The theatre, by necessity and default, becomes that place. Theatre, John McGrath notes:

> is the place where the life of a society is shown in public to that society, where that society's assumptions are exhibited and tested, its values are scrutinised, its myths are validated and its traumas become emblems of its reality.... It is a public event, and it is about matters of public concern (McGrath: 1981, 83).

It has long been understood that this view of the theatre motivated the formation of the Field Day Theatre Company. It is, I think, a view of the theatre already immanent in *The Freedom of the City*.

In the created world on stage, where murder takes place with impunity, a great deal is said, but little is heard and almost nothing understood. A multiplicity of voices speak, sing, shout, ask and answer questions, and give orders, but, for all the talk, communication amongst the characters is limited to communities of narrow and, in the case of the tribunal, self-justifying interest. Through the repeated use of monologues, Friel implicates the theatre audience in the politics of the play, encouraging them to move from passive spectatorship to active engagement.

The play's concluding tableau is a transformation of encouragement into challenge: if the audience is not part of the solution, then it is part of the problem. Lily, Skinner and Michael emerge from the Guildhall, their hands raised. "*Then the air is filled with a fifteen-second burst of automatic fire. It stops. The three stand as before, staring out, their hands above their heads*" (*FC*: 169). If the cycle of violence is to be broken it will require the active participation of the audience, since none of the forces represented on the stage is capable of positive intervention.

VII. Metatheatrics: A Final Word

Time has not erased the anger in Northern Ireland over Bloody Sunday. To commemorate its twenty-fifth anniversary, several books of eyewitness accounts appeared (McClean: 1997, Mullan; 1997). In the preface to one of them, *The Road to Bloody Sunday*, Raymond McClean, who witnessed the post-mortems on eleven of the dead, writes:

> The wounds inflicted by Bloody Sunday persist and will not heal....
> I have always been concerned that when future historians come to
> examine the history of our particular time, they will visit the
> libraries and consult the various reports concerning this time.... I
> would be appalled to think that the Widgery Report would be
> consulted as the authoritative text in the case of Bloody Sunday. It
> is imperative that several factual descriptions of what really
> happened in Derry will be available to future historians (McClean:
> 1997, 9).

The facts McClean calls for have yet to be ascertained. The British government, responding to twenty-five years of agitation on behalf of the victims of Bloody Sunday, recently established a new inquiry under Lord Saville in an effort to undo the damage of the Widgery Tribunal and uncover the facts that eluded the previous investigation.

In the program notes to the Lincoln Center (N.Y.) Festival's production of *The Freedom of the City* (July 7-25, 1999), Michael Farrell, himself a leading activist in the Northern Irish civil rights movement, comments optimistically about the role the Saville inquiry may play in reconciling differences in Northern Ireland. In doing so, he links *The Freedom of the City* to the project of reconciliation:

> The Saville inquiry cannot bring the dead back to life but, if it tells the truth about what happened in Derry on that Sunday in 1972, it could help to heal some of the wounds that have scarred Northern Ireland for the last 30 years and prevent any more bloody days in the future. In preparation for that inquiry, which is due to open in the autumn [1999], Lord Saville and his team could do worse than visit this production [of *The Freedom of the City*] (Farrell: 1999, 24A).

For many in Northern Ireland, there is a need to set the record straight. Unfortunately, the hope Farrell invests in the Saville inquiry proved illusory. In the local paper, I read that, as of July 21, 1999, the inquiry was stalled because of a protracted legal battle over how the paratroopers involved in Bloody Sunday would give evidence. The inquiry panel wants the soldiers to testify in open court; the soldiers argue that they require anonymity (Telegraph: 1999). The delay of the Saville inquiry gives added importance to *The Freedom of the City* as part of the not yet completed project of truth and reconciliation to which Farrell refers.

Works Cited:

Andrews, Elmer, (1995), *The Art of Brian Friel* (London: Macmillan)

Bell, Sam Hanna, (1972), *The Theatre In Ulster* (Dublin: Gill & Macmillan)

Bew, Paul and Gordon Gillespie, (1993), *Northern Ireland A Chronology of the Troubles 1968-1993* (Dublin: Gill & Macmillan)

Birker, Klaus, (1984), "The Relationship Between the Stage and the Audience in Brian Friel's *The Freedom of the City*", in *The Irish Writer and the City*, ed., Maurice Harmon (Gerrards Cross: Colin Smythe and Totowa: Barnes and Noble) 153-8

Buckley, Anthony D. and Mary Catherine Kenney, (1995), *Negotiating Identity, Rhetoric, Metaphor and Social Drama in Northern Ireland* (Washington and London: Smithsonian Institution Press)

Coogan, Tim Pat, (1996), *The Troubles, Ireland's Ordeal 1966-1996 and the Search for Peace* (London: Arrow Books)

Dantanus, Ulf, (1998), *Brian Friel A Study* (London: Faber and Faber)

Farrell, Michael, (1999), "Notes on the Program", *Stagebill, Lincoln Center Festival 99*, New York: Stagebill, July

Friel, Brian, (1984), "The Freedom of the City", *Selected Plays* (London: Faber & Faber)

Hampton, Wilborn, "They Sought Change and Found Death", *The New York Times*, 10 July 1999, A15, A21

Hennessey, Thomas, (1997), *A History of Northern Ireland 1920-1996* (Houndmills, Bassingstoke: Macmillan Press)

Irish Times, (1973), "Next Week In the Arts", Feb. 17, 12

Lacy, Brian, (1990), *Siege City, The Story of Derry and Londonderry* (Belfast: Blackstaff Press)

Lojek, Helen, (1994), "Brian Friel's Plays and George Steiner's Linguistics: Translating the Irish", *Contemporary Literature*, Vol. 35, No. 1, pp. 83-99

McClean, Raymond, (1997), *The Road to Bloody Sunday Revised Edition* (Derry: Guildhall)

McGrath, John, (1981), *A Good Night Out: Popular Theatre Audience, Class and Form* (London: Methuen)

Mullan, Don and John Scally, eds., (1997), *Eyewitness Bloody Sunday* (Dublin: Wolfhound)

Murray, Christopher, (1999), "Friel and O'Casey Juxtaposed", *Irish University Review*, Vol. 29, No.1, Spring/Summer

O'Brien, George, (1990), *Brian Friel* (Boston: Twayne)

Pine, Richard, (1990), *Brian Friel and Ireland's Drama* (London and New York: Routledge)

Schrank, Bernice, (1988), "Politics and Language in the Plays of Sean O'Casey and Brian Friel", *Anglo-Irish and Irish Literature: Aspects of Language and Culture*, eds., Birgit Bramsback and Martin Croghan (2 vols., Uppsala: University of Uppsala), vol. II

The Telegram, (1999), "Bloody Sunday inquiry delayed", (St. John's, Newfoundland), July 21, 7

Theatre as Opera: *The Gigli Concert*
Declan Kiberd

Ireland is a land of song and Irish art, more than most, aspires to the condition of music. The playwright Synge had always hoped to be a concert violinist and abandoned the aim only because his extreme shyness left him unable to perform in public: but he compensated as best he could by treating his playscripts as musical scores and writing words like "andante" or "allegro" against chosen passages. James Joyce's literary career, glorious though it became, was also embraced as a second-best option. He would have preferred the life of a singer and in his youth had such a fine tenor voice that it took the legendary John McCormack to defeat him at the competition for vocalists at the Feis Cheoil. (Reportedly, Joyce took a savage revenge by remarking to his rival "John, you sing a good song well, and a bad song wonderfully" (Mahon: 1984, 62).)

The conversation in Joyce's great short story "The Dead" is dominated by reminiscences of opera singers whose greatness seems to grow in direct proportion to their distance in the past. Joyce's interest in the techniques, as well as the history, of opera was obsessive. He opened the "Sirens" chapter of *Ulysses* with the verbal equivalent of an overture in music, filling it with brief, exemplary excerpts from the following narrative, in order to put the reader into the right mood. He was convinced that a verbal equivalent could be found for almost any musical device. For the *staccato* effect, he wrote "Will? You? I. Want. You". For the fermata by which a final note is indefinitely held, he wrote "endlessnessnessness". "Sirens" is full of musical quotations, especially from *Don Giovanni*, and with these, in a parody of the Bloom-Boylan-Molly triangle, Joyce creates the irony of inappropriate song. (Joyce: 1992, 328-76).

Throughout *Ulysses* Leopold Bloom uses his experience of opera as a kind of touchstone for measuring the quality of a fully lived life. When an acquaintance in the newspaper office remarks that Red Murray has a face like "our saviour's", the non-Christian Bloom rephrases the idea by saying "Or like 'Mario', the Italian tenor"? (ibid.: 149) Simon Dedalus opines that Italian is the only language to make love in and Bloom notes that "tenors get women by the score". All their fantasies about romantic Italy are brought to earth during the encounter in the cabmen's shelter of 'Eumaeus': there Bloom praises the lyric qualities of the Italian language, only to be curtly informed by Stephen that the Italians at the next table are haggling over money.

Despite such moments of wariness, Joyce never ceased in his attempt to compose the sort of operatic sentence in which the sound might match the sense. In the 'Nausikaa' section of *Ulysses*, Roman candles explode in mid-air as Gerty MacDowell leans back to watch, revealing more and more of her shapely leg and driving Bloom to orgasm:

> And then a rocket sprang and bang shot blind and 0!
> then the Roman candle burst and it was like a sigh of 0!
> and everyone cried 0! 0! in raptures and it gushed out of it
> a stream of rain gold hair threads and they shed and ah!.
> they were all greeny dewy' stars falling with golden, 0!
> so lively! 0 so soft, sweet, soft! (Ibid.: 477).

The deliberate patterning of 0-sounds rises to a *crescendo* as Bloom reaches a climax, but the romance of the moment is cruelly deflated some lines later by the terse account of Blazes Boylan's ejaculation into the vagina of Molly Bloom: "0, he did. Into her. She did. Done. Ah!" (ibid:482) Here the innocent, open sound of the ecstatic Os is replaced by the more knowing, somewhat accusatory ah, a shout of guilty disclosure rather than of rapt passion. Nor is that the end. Some paragraphs after the climax of Os, that sound is itself repeated, just a single anticlimactic time, as if its echo is a follow mockery of Bloom's earlier ecstasies at the sight of Gerty's bared leg. For now he discovers: Tight boots? No. She's lame! 0! (ibid.: 479)

That half-line stops and starts four times, in reenactment of her limping departure. In a moment such as this, Bloom is revealed as an unconscious poet, whose inner acoustic is perfectly tuned to the world around him. If there is a silent music of the mind, then Joyce expertly captured it again and again, which was why that other music-lover, Samuel Beckett, made the comment that his friend's writings were not *about* something but were that something itself, a perfect incarnation of content in pure form (Beckett: 1929, 14). In *Finnegans Wake*, Joyce's last work, the very notion of content surrendered fully to the exigencies of form and style.

Such passages might be read now as relatively early samples of what is known as performance art, for they are based on a notion of art as a structure beyond ideas or opinion, a pure performance. It is that tradition which is taken up and perfected in the dramatic mode by Tom Murphy's *The Gigli Concert*. Here the "self" is not presented as a fixed, unitary entity so much as a provisional complex at a point in time. The nature of that self may best be revealed, and most usefully defined, in performance: literally through its chastening encounter with available forms. Murphy's central character is a successful builder, unnamed as 'An Irish Man', for whom two million pounds are not enough. He won't be able to live at peace with himself until he has sung like Beniamino Gigli.

According to Richard Poirier in his book of that name, *The Performing Self* is the release of energy into measured explorations of human potentialities... so as to probe all those things which the self might be" (Poirier: 1971, xi). He compares it to the way

> ... a sculptor not only is impelled to shape his material but is in turn shaped by it, his impulse to mastery always chastened, sometimes made tender and possibly witty by the recalcitrance of what he is working on. Performance comes to fruition at precisely the point where the potentially destructive impulse to mastery brings forth from the material its most essential, irreducible, clarified and therefore beautiful nature (ibid.: xiv).

Just as the sculptor is educated by the chosen stone, so is a singer shaped and defined by a chosen song. The encounter of mind with available form leads to a release of energy, as at the climax of *The Gigli Concert*, but the fear of such energy may take the form of a "repressive analysis", often disguised as psychotherapy, such as is practiced in the earlier scenes of the play. Yet it is to the final release of energy that Murphy's masterpiece moves: that moment when, not the builder but his quack-analyst finds in himself the strength to sing like Gigli, to validate a self by a sound.

Criticism is notoriously abashed, even disabled, by such a moment, as were the reviewers on the play's opening night in 1983: unable to reduce the work to a summarisable meaning. (A revised and shortened version was published by Methuen, London in 1991: but my reasons for preferring the original are implied later in this commentary, where I argue for the central role of the character Mona.)

That may have been in part because all performance art exists not so much in eternal time as for the duration of its own enactment. Being a process rather than a product, it lacks a definitive, final form. This problem is especially acute in dealing with the work of Tom Murphy, who from his beginnings as a playwright has shown a distrust of the analytic intellect. Born in Tuam, Co Galway in 1935, he shot to fame in the experimental theatre of London during the 1960s and returned to his native country in the 1970s, offering dramas which implied a scathing rebuke to the 'rational' values which seemed to accompany society's modernisation (O'Toole: 1987, 19-29). The procedures of psychoanalysis are enacted in *The Gigli Concert*, but only at the level of grotesque parody, as when the quack JPW King indulges the pretence that past sexual failures are the real key to the builder's problems. Murphy's plays are, however, critiques of pure reason — another is called *Too Late for Logic* —

and they examine those zones of feeling which mere reason can never illuminate.

It is clear from the outset that part of what attracts the builder to King, rather than to a more orthodox therapist, is the fact that his analyst, far from being a measured professional is a man as confused and helpless as himself. He is therefore someone who will not be able to probe too embarrassingly into those areas which his client wishes to remain unseen. An Irish Man, as his premature resignation from the therapy shows at the end of the play, seeks only an investigation of a strictly limited kind, and certainly not one based on notions of rationality, since it is the rationality of the business world which has driven him all but mad.

Hence the importance of music, not just because it has charms to soothe the savage breast, but because it affords a more sensitive, less invasive way of reading and defining a self. Joyce said that if a person wished to understand an obscure passage in *Ulysses*, all that was needed was to read it aloud and the inner music would be revealed. Patrick Mason, director of the first production of *Gigli*, made a similar remark: "Tom Murphy hears sound as character or he expresses character as sound. All his characters make individual sounds — they have individual sound patterns" (Mason: 1987, 105).

In the play an Irish Man says that one doesn't need to understand the words of an opera to know the feeling: "I could always size a man up more from the sound he makes than from what he's saying" (*Gigli*: 13). This may not be as radical or innovative as it seems. The idea that a play might be constructed on the same principles of onomatopoeia which govern a lyric utterance is at least as old as Shakespeare. A major trend of modern criticism has been the swerve away from a Bradleyan study of a play's characters to the understanding that every Shakespeare play is a poem, with its own iterative images, contrapuntal melodies, vocal registers and so on (See Spurgeon: 1934). Character has been redefined, no longer merely revealed by something that Hamlet says but also by the way in which he chooses to say it. Hamlet is a telling example, indeed, since he is obsessed by the relation between character and performance, as he coaches the players, punctures the disguises of false courtiers, or tells his mother to assume virtues which she may not have in the hope of finally living up to them.

The two playwrights who did most to clear the way for this conception of drama as musical performance were Murphy's Irish predecessors, Bernard Shaw and Oscar Wilde. Shaw first came to prominence as a music critic. Ever afterward, he tried in plays to register clashes in character or even in national types by tonal contrasts. In *John Bull's Other Island*, for example, he contrasted the bass of the Englishman Broadbent with the higher-pitched voices of the nervous Irish; and in *Arms and the*

Man he set the terse staccato logic of the bourgeois Bluntschli against the overblown posturing sentences of the aristocratic Petkoffs. He explained:

> In a generation which knew nothing of any sort of acting but drawing-room acting, and which considered a speech of more than twenty words impossibly long, I went back to the classical style and wrote long rhetorical speeches like operatic solos, regarding my plays as musical performances precisely as Shakespeare did (Shaw: 1969: 284).

The danger for Shaw, as later for Murphy, was the fear of being accused of over-rhetorical, over-determined writing. "I was therefore", recalled Shaw, "continually struggling with the conscientious efforts of our players to underdo their parts lest they should be considered stagey" (ibid.: 284).

Patrick Mason solved this problem by encouraging actors in *The Gigli Concert* to overplay rather than underplay their roles, to surrender absolutely to the emotional extremism of opera. So, in the final scene, when King sings an aria, it is from an opera in which a lover mourns the death of his beloved, before he goes out to commit suicide himself. Critics of the play who argue that Mona's revelation of her terminal cancer in the previous scene is a cheap theatrical shot may be forgetting that it is out of just such blatant emotionalism that opera is always made. Taking another instance, An Irish Man's tearful account of his childhood was *his* aria, his moment to dominate the forestage with his gestures and words. Perhaps the most operatic feature of all — as well as the most Shavian — is the constant resort to melodramatic reversals, which leave the unmasking JPW King himself unmasked.

It would not be an exaggeration to describe Murphy's play as a *verbal opera*. The term was first used by W.H. Auden in an essay on Wilde's *Importance of Being Earnest*, which he dubbed the only pure verbal opera in English. By this he meant a play in which every other element was subordinated to the effect of the dialogue. Wilde, he contended, "created a verbal universe in which the characters are determined by the kinds of things they say, and the plot is nothing but a succession of opportunities to say them" (Auden: 1969: 136). Here character is subordinated not just to plot but to the demands of a pure, elegant language: and this in a play which, like *The Gigli Concert*, deals with the Double, a character split into a real and metaphorical self, who seeks, by the sheer intensity with which he lives out his fiction, to make the two into one.

That sort of fusion is sought in Murphy's play by a surrender of the ethical imagination to pure form. As so often in western literature, that relaxation of the moral for the sake of aesthetic beauty is described as a

Faustian pact. King quotes Marlowe's *Doctor Faustus*: "This night I'll conjure". King is, of course, fixated on his own impossible Helen, the woman at the other end of the telephone line: and the voice of Gigli is the diabolical Siren-song, the pure form taken by the devil to win over his soul. Some moments earlier in the play, he had invoked God, but only momentarily, for like Beckett's tramps he feels a grudge against a God with whom he has severed all connection some time ago. Instead, he makes his bargain now with the satanic powers below, like that Hamlet who asserted that, if he could not invoke heaven, then hell would serve as well.

Tom Murphy bears a grudge against God which is quintessentially Irish — what Kenneth Tynan once called "a very Irish grudge against God which the merely godless would never feel" (O'Toole: 1987, 169). For Murphy art is one way of answering the iniquity of the world which God has created. Whereas traditional religion (such as he had known while growing up in Tuam) offered man a sense of continuity and a way of taming the demonic, Murphy like other artists now seizes the initiative lost by religion: and, far from suppressing the daemonic, he explores and exalts it as a source of creativity. He is, in that strict sense, an aesthete who believes that life at its highest can be as intense and value-free as a work of art. Life for him finds its ultimate justification in a chosen form and all living is but a search for that ideal form. Within such a system, experience in all its aspects, sublime or base, becomes a supreme value, and the lived life is a chronicle of extreme sensations, deliberately sought and prolonged. The impact on the self rather than the moral consequences for society becomes the yardstick used to measure any action.

It is to this precise point that an Irish Man has come when the play begins. He is by then in revolt against the world of work, effort and reward, a world which he has mastered only to discover that such triumph is hardly enough. Though not a sociologist, Murphy shows himself to be a keen observer of social and cultural conditions. Throughout the nineteenth century, the Protestant ethic had taught men to save money and to be modest in their accumulation of goods. Once the transcendental tie with God was broken, however, hedonism was given free rein and soon all kinds of sensation could be purchased on the installment plan. Work could no longer be cast under the aegis of divinity: and so it lost much of its traditional value and meaning. This is what the builder means when he complains: "There's too many facts in the world. Them houses were built out of facts: corruption, brutality, backhanding, fronthanding, lump labour and a bit of technology" (*Gigli*: 16).

So now he comes to JPW King in search of his lost sensuality, his lost artistry, his anima — all those aspects which years of graft and moneygrubbing had led him to suppress and deny in himself. It all goes back in his mind to a day when his older brother Danny scorned his offer of flowers and belittled his childlike question as to which, the daisy or buttercup, was "nicest": "And Danny said 'nicest' like a knife. 'Nicest? Are you stupid? What use is nicest?' Of what use is beauty, Mr King?" (*Gigli*: 56).

If An Irish Man has trouble in relating to his own wife, that is first and foremost because he has spent years suppressing the feminine dimension within himself. Only when his wife takes herself and their son away does that dimension erupt into his full consciousness, demanding his attention.

Nor is JPW King much further developed on this score. He has removed his ideal Helen to a remote zone of pseudo-spirituality, at the end of a phone-line, from which distance she can be safely worshipped without any disillusioning first-hand contacts. Such *amour courtois* worship is merely a fancy way of repeating the builder's sin and avoiding a real relationship. If the builder abuses his wife with obscenities, King mistreats his fantasy-women with heavy-breathing phone-calls. The appalling gap between King's utopia of domestic bliss in a clematis-fringed cottage run by an aproned angel and the sordid brutalities of the builder's actual home life is a proof that, for both men, the world of fact and the world of value have moved too far apart. All the facts are now brutal in the same proportion that all dreams are unreal. There is no remaining connection between the *is* and *ought*, between the realities of their lives and their aspirations. *Is* and *Ought* occupy wholly separate zones. The desire to sing like Gigli is nothing other than the desire to reconnect them, to shape a moment when the literal and the metaphorical might coincide.

Though outwardly opposed — the builder being rich, worldly and repressed; the quack being poor, idealistic and impulse-ridden — the two men at a deeper level share many problems. Within a few minutes, each has separately voiced apprehensiveness about surviving the day; and when the builder mentions his Mandrax sleeping pills, King seems to have a remarkable familiarity with their clinical history, even down to the fact that they have been recently taken off the market. Throughout the play that ensues the initiative in the relationship between the two men will ebb and flow, until at times it seems as if it is the builder who is healing King rather than being healed by him.

At the most obvious level, this *is* what happens, since at the close the quack, as a consequence of the transference, manages to sing like Gigli and, having done so, seems free at last to leave his claustrophobic room and go back into the world. However, this happens only *after* King has helped the builder to heal himself — as far as he wishes to be healed, which is as far as abandoning his career but not to the extent of singing like Gigli. An Irish Man fears an analysis which might excavate too much; and so, at an advanced stage in the treatment, he resigns from it, leaving King to make the final jump alone.

There are many ways of reading this. At a biographical level, Murphy himself is known to have aborted an analysis with the psychiatrist Ivor Browne on the grounds that a successful conclusion might indeed cure his pain but only at the risk of resolving those very complexes which provided him with his art. An Irish Man may represent, therefore, the canny, controlling aspect of Murphy's own personality: his shrewd sense of limits which must not be transgressed, his eye for the main chance, and above all his intuition that it will not serve an artist to become overly self-analytical. That kind of analysis might sterilise the impulses which it investigates. Murphy is one of those Yeatsian artists who is at his best when probing material only half-understood and when allowing that material to speak through him, resisting all attempts to control or master it.

The builder, of course, is not an artist and does not, therefore, have an artist's excuse for one kind of failure of nerve which is displayed by withdrawal from therapy. He is simply a timid, bourgeois soul, and it is clear from his own testimony that he has been through a process of depression and recovery many times. On this occasion, King has brought him so close to resolution that he is unnerved, scurries into retreat, and then threatens the therapist with exposure to the police, before attempting to buy his silence with wads of cash:

> Look, Mr. King, be warned. I could have you locked up, like that, one telephone call. But why go throwing good money after bad. And it was my own fault. I just can't get over what possessed me to come into a place like this when I can cure myself like I did last time... (*Gigli*: 62).

Having been to the river Styx, the builder turns back each time. He is accordingly terrified by King's account of how he engages in criminal acts like stealing books from Easons to assist his client. These satanic activities do not conform to the self-image of a solid citizen. And so, having flirted briefly with his own anima, he decides once again to repress it back into his subconscious and demonise it accordingly.

The repressed feminine principle is never so easily denied: and invades the room in the shape of Mona, the vulgar trollop and faithless wife, who is to King's world of facts as his idealized Helen is to his world of values. His endless skulking in his room is a symbolic portrayal of his refusal to face the world as it really is. Mona, however comes repeatedly in from that world, bringing news of it, as well as practical help.

The original production of *The Gigli Concert* ran almost to midnight (from eight o'clock), prompting inevitable complaints that the play was too long. Much of the criticism focuses on the character Mona, who was considered superfluous to the play's real drama between King and An Irish Man. Richard Kearney on the other side, argued that Mona was a symbolic necessity to the Anglo-Irish sub-theme, since she came from the North and the occupied an intermediate zone between Irish itinerant-hater and English quack who thinks he can solve intractable problems. In that reading of course, Mona's terminal illness would be part of the point (Kearney: 1988). Murphy had lived for a number of years in England between 1962 and 1970, and he married an Englishwoman. There is much curiosity in his plays as to the meaning and destiny of Anglo-Irish relations. The English quack seems more honest and likable than the Irish builder, and ultimately just as unable to cope: and Kearney sees the Northern Mona as "a sort of neglected go-between: the woman victimised by the male-dominated struggle for power". That interpretation would also explain the builder's parting advice to the English muddler:

> Go home, Jimmy. Forget that — Irish colleen.... You are a remarkable man. I know there's kindness in the world, but they'll kill you over here... Go home (*Gigli*: 73-4).

Nor is that advice nastily intended. Far from it, since the builder has just thanked King for all his help, and King has reciprocated by insisting that it is he who is grateful to his client. It would be only stretching matters a shade further to see in this Anglo-Irish process a disguised version of the relationship between Tom Murphy, Irish image-maker, and his English-born director and dramatic analyst, Patrick Mason, who puts a structure on those wayward instincts latent in the play and reveals its inner harmonies (Mason: 1983).

All these readings are valid up to a point, but they leave out more than they let in. The true justification of the character Mona has little enough to do with politics or Anglo-Irish relations. Rather, it concerns the fact that she represents the return of the repressed feminine principle, the hope of creative possibility in the midst of despair — or what she calls "bouncing back". As a broken housewife-turned-prostitute, as a mother who in her teens lost a son to adoption, and now as a victim of lymphatic cancer, she should by rights be as depressed as the men. Instead, she brings kind help, batteries for King's shaver, and so on — and this despite her pained awareness that King worships not her but the Helen of the phone-line.

Near the end, 'Helen' phones to accuse King of being a dirty dialler at just the moment when Mona arrives with the batteries. For the first time, King realises what real love is and that the builder was right to declare that the romantic kingdom *is* of this world. The next scene, preceded by the music of *Lucia de Lammermoor* reveals the lovers in bed together, a classic conjunction of Love and Death, as she breaks the news of her illness and he asserts the importance of seizing every possibility in the here-and-now. Kearney has pointed in this context to the Greek word for 'possibility' *dunamis* as the basis of King's philosophy of *dynamitology* (Kearney: 1988, 76).

This would certainly account for King's obsession with the mis-translation of the message of the Old Testament God as "I Am Who Am" instead of "I Am Who May Be", that principle of pure possibility which, according to philosophers, is glimpsed only on the other side of despair. According to this principle, only when King has known the utter negation of rejection by 'Helen' and then the strange joy of love for a woman who will soon die, is he ready for his own journey to the abyss at which he may sing like Gigli, transmuting all that pain into the balm of art.

It is fascinating that all of this should, in a sense, stem from a retranslation of a key phrase of the Bible. The philosopher who did most in this century to give meaning to that retranslation was Ernst Bloch, a German predecessor of liberation theology, who used Karl Marx's description in a letter to Ruge in 1843 of a revolution which derives from the poetry of the future rather than the nightmare of the past to reinterpret the Bible as a truly utopian document. Bloch's philosophy of the "not-yet" saw the world as an open process rather than a concluded system. He sought to identify and analyse the 'unconscious' dimension of the future which slumbers in the present, in the belief that the arts, more than any other facet of life, contain below the level of consciousness a dream of all that is to come. He shared with Walter Benjamin the conviction that every age not only dreams the next but, while dreaming, impels it to wakefulness. Popular art, in particular, Bloch saw as both reflective of social realities and as projective of human betterment. He was in fact the original dynamitologist: and his greatest book, *The Principle of Hope*, is a three-volume demonstration, written under the shadow of Fascism, of how the principle of hope may be discerned in documents which might superficially prompt only the darkest despair. Bloch was, with Yeats, one of the very few thinkers of the twentieth century who formed a clear idea of the shape of the future, to which he looked with a degree of confidence. That confidence derived, however, not from analytic thought so much as from a sense of the redemptive strangeness of art and from a conviction that in the achievable human community every man and woman would be an artist.

In his essay 'Art and Society', Bloch actually resorts to the image of a dynamite explosion to explain the underlying idea:

> I am talking about an anticipatory illumination that could never be realised in an ideology of the status quo but, rather, has been connected to it like an explosive, as though it could always engender the most stimulating surplus beyond the ideology (Bloch: 1988, 41).

This is what, elsewhere in the essay, he terms "the ideological surplus of genius", something that is not ideology at all because it surpasses the particular epoch in a utopian way by a mode of transformation commonly called *genius*. According to Bloch: "The ideology in a great work reflects and justifies its times, but the utopia in it rips open the times, brings them to an end, brings them to that end where there would no longer be a mere past and its ideology, but rather where it would be shown *tua propria vera res agitur*" (ibid.: 39). In other words, a future could be demonstrated to be opening up. At the centre of his essay, Bloch concedes that all of this is but a reformulation of an idea of Marx, who said:

> ... the reformation of consciousness only consists in letting the world enter one's consciousness, in waking up the world from the dream about itself.... Then it can be shown that it does not concern a large hyphen between past and future, but the completion of the idea of the past (cited by Bloch, ibid.: 41).

In short, there is no contradiction between tradition and utopia, the Bible and the revolutionary community, the imagined past and the actual future. The phrase about letting the world enter one's consciousness while waking that world from a dream about itself is a perfect description of the final scene in Murphy's play. There JPW King arises from the floor, prays to his dead mother not to leave him in the dark, and pinches himself awake by letting up his window-blind, before re-entering the actual world which he had scorned for so long. "It's pretty bad out there, isn't it?" he had said to the builder only moments before, to be told "Oh now". (*Gigli*: 72)

The use of light to welcome the new morning is clear. Light and dark images are employed at every major phase of the play, most obviously in the fact that An Irish Man appears repeatedly in the doorway as a shadow or silhouette, complete with Italian hat and overcoat in the gangster mode (Murphy in another play has equated Irish businessmen with Chicago criminals of the 1930s). The silhouette is of one with no name, known only as An Irish Man: and it may be appropriate in that context to interpret it as a version of the doppelganger in literature. That reading is validated by the many phrases and experiences which the two men, for all their superficial differences, share. The builder cannot be named, perhaps because he is simply a projection of King's imagination. Hence, when King claims to have stolen books from Eason's, he can blithely argue that he did this for the man, and so heap onto his double any guilt-feelings which may ensue.

This is the classic psychological manoeuvre which gives rise to the *double*. In the account of Erich Stern the process "causes man to transfer responsibility for certain deeds of the self to another self, the double; since his tremendous fear of death and damnation leads to a transference to the double" (Stern: 1926-7, 555). In folklore, men are seized by conflicting impulses when confronted by their shadows. On the one hand, if the shadow is seen as representing a hideous past self which clings, it can produce an urge to rid oneself of it, as at various moments King tries to dismiss An Irish Man. Such attempts to deny a darker aspect of one's self are often prevented, as here, by a recognition that the life of the shadow and that of the person are too intimately linked for this sort of facile dismissal. The shadow of course, may also portend death: the folk belief that if a double sights a shadow, the person will die within a year, and forth. There are playgoers who believe that King does indeed die at the end of *The Gigli Concert* and is resurrected on the far side of death — that, in effect, his song is a swansong.

However, beliefs about shadows are often contradictory, since in many cultures it is held that a man who casts *no* shadow will soon die. (That is why sick people are frequently carried into sunlight). This seems ultimately a more useful approach to the closing scene, in which King lets in the sunlight and so for the first time casts his own shadow, instead of seeing his shadow living at one remove in the person of An Irish Man. Now, at the latest possible moment, he has reintegrated himself and can therefore dismiss that shadow. While acknowledging his indebtedness to it, he can now proceed on his own.

In some European folk-tales, men who see their shadows wish to rejoin them — perhaps in a death-wish — but are not allowed since the shadow must always come forward to meet them, as in *The Gigli Concert* (Rank: 1971, 50ff). Men are often described as being afraid of their own shadows, afraid of the dark, repressed, hidden aspects of self which erupt threateningly from time to time. One temptation, at the moment of such eruption, is for the haunted person to identify totally with the shadow side and to engage in persistent assertions of unworthiness: and another, as indicated, is to offload responsibility for everything onto the shadow, as King seems at times to do. All of these ambiguities are reflected in the constant accusations and recriminations through the play, as each man accuses his doppelganger of being "the one to falter" (*Gigli*: 48-50, 64-5).

The Shadow, like the *double*, can also epitomise the soul: and in *The Gigli Concert* there is much talk of the soul which, like that of Marlowe's Doctor Faustus, seems to escape into the firmament. Otto Rank in his book on *The Double* argued that it was man's need for immortality which led to the primitive concept of the soul as a duality, person-and-shadow, one aspect of which betokens immortality (King) and the other death (An Irish Man). The artist, in this scheme of things, is a version of the hero, since he wins immortality through art: and, unlike the neurotic, the artist manages to present the double in an acceptable form, "justifying the survival of the irrational in our over-rationalised civilisation" (cited by Trucker: 1971, xvi). This, again, might be taken as a perfect account of Murphy's achievement.

Within the structure of the play, there are some modifications to this scheme. An Irish Man could have been created as the outcome of JPW King's pathological self-absorption. In that sense, King's shadow is indeed his vanity and a force which, in Rank's terms, "epitomises that morbid self-love which prevents the formation of a happily-balanced personality" (Rank: 1971,48). This is indeed the crisis-state in which King lives: self-enclosure which leads to an inability to reach out to others or recognise love when it is offered to him. As Rank elaborated on the syndrome:

> The pathological disposition towards psychological disturbances is conditioned to a large degree by the splitting of personality, with special emphasis upon the ego-complex, to which corresponds an abnormally strong interest in one's own person, his psychic states, his destinies. This point of view leads to the characteristic relationship to the world, to life and particularly to the love-object, with which no harmonious relationship is found. Either the direct inability to love or — leading to the same effect — an exorbitantly strained longing for love characterise the two poles of this over-exaggerated attitude towards one's own ego (Rank: 1971, 48).

King's exorbitant strain for love focuses on 'Helen', even as his inability to love is perceived by Mona who, at the start, counts it a triumph when he manages to use her name. By the end, however, she has cured him by her offer of a love without conditions. She penetrates his self-absorbed exterior and, at that moment, it is possible for the Shadow, An Irish Man, to disappear for good. This was the Shadow whose sense of hurt went all the way back to that moment in adolescence when he was not allowed to sing the part of a girl-soprano and who has lived ever since in a world of macho achievers. The Shadow can now disappear because of the restoration of the feminine principle.

This was an important moment in the evolution of Tom Murphy's career, for until its arrival he had been accused with some justice of writing largely masculine plays about the repressed hurts endured by males and of writing no strong parts for women. It can hardly be a coincidence that not long after writing *The Gigli Concert* he produced in *Bailegangaire* one of the major female roles in contemporary writing.

Works Cited:

Auden, W.H., (1969), 'An Improbable Life' in *Oscar Wilde: Twentieth Century Views*, ed., Richard Ellmann (New Jersey: Prentice-Hall)

Beckett, Samuel et al., (1929) *Our Exagmination round his Factification for Incamination of Work in Progress* (London: Faber and Faber)

Bloch, Ernst, (1988), *The Utopian Function of Art and Literature* translated by Jack Zipes and Frank Mecklenberg (Cambridge, Massachusetts: M.I.T. Press)

Joyce, James, (1992), *Ulysses: Annotated Student's Edition*, with notes and introduction by Declan Kiberd (London)

Kearney, Richard, (1988), *Transitions: Narratives in Modern Irish Culture* (Dublin: Wolfhound)

McMahon, Sean, (1984), ed., *Rich and Rare* (Dublin)

Mason, Patrick, (1983), interview with Declan Kiberd, "Exhibit A", RTE television, 27 September

-----(1987), interview with Christopher Murray, *Irish University Review: Tom Murphy Special Issue*, Vol. 17, No.1, Spring

Murphy, Tom, (1984), *The Gigli Concert* (Ashbourne: Gallery Press)

O'Toole, Fintan, (1987), *The Politics of Magic: The Work and Times of Tom Murphy* (Dublin: Raven Arts Press)

Poirier, Richard, (1971), *The Performing Self: Compositions and Decompositions in the Languages of Contemporary Life* (New York: Oxford University Press)

Rank, Otto, (1971), *The Double: A Psychoanalytical Study*, translated and edited by Harry Tucker Jr. (Chapel Hill: Beacon Press)

Shaw, G. B., (1969), *An Autobiography 1856-98*, selected from his writing by Stanley Weintraub (London: Max Reinhardt)

Spurgeon, Caroline, (1934), *Shakespeare's Imagery and What it Tells Us* (Cambridge: Cambridge University Press)

Stern, Erich, (1926-7), 'Review of Otto Rank, *The Double'* in *Die Literatur*, xxix, Vienna

Tucker, Harry, Jr., (1971), 'Introduction' to *The Double* (Chapel Hill: Beacon Press)

Bodies and Spirits in Tom Murphy's Theatre

Anne F. Kelly

The theatre of Tom Murphy over the past thirty-eight years has been spoken of as a holy theatre, a search for soul in a soulless world, a theatre of the possible, a theatre of the spirit. His language is a search for images, symbols and myths that will enable us to tell the story of who we are. His dramas in many ways function like rituals offering audiences sites of transformation and transportation. His plays are not afraid to risk that transcendent leap out of the banal and ordinary into the extraordinary moments of grace, healing, love, forgiveness. But if it is a holy theatre it is also a rough theatre (Murray: 1987, 9-17). His characters are the lost, the dispossessed, the destitute, the little people forgotten in the grand narratives of history. His is a theatre of victims, and involves a translation of their stories, their griefs, into public narratives, enacted in the space of theatre. Falling somewhere between deritualisation and reritualisation he exploits the possibilities of naturalist theatre, aware of influences of Artaud and Brecht, conscious always of the numbing effects of deadly bourgeois theatre.

Murphy's theatre may be understood as reflecting the quest for identity and meaning in the lives of its main protagonists, whether they are the inarticulate brutal Carney family of *A Whistle in the Dark*, John Connor, the people's "King" in *Famine*, the "twins" Michael and Tom in *Conversations on a Homecoming*, the Man and JPW in *The Gigli Concert* or Mommo, Dolly and Mary in *Bailegangaire*. But questions of personal identity and crisis are always mirrors of wider cultural crises and so the quest for meaning in these plays actually participates in the meaning making of a culture. The texts of the plays become sites of cultural meaning, discourses we then can consult to answer the questions of identity and belonging, discourses we can study and examine in relation to how subjectivity is constructed.

The theme of home features hugely in the writings of Tom Murphy whether it is a physical sense of place or a metaphysical one. There is no escaping the rootedness of Murphy's work in the Ireland in which he grew up and came to adulthood. His plays are political in that they counter dominant cultural discourse with the corrective of the outsider. The stifling parochialism of the small town policed and defined by the dominant discourses of Church and State exists side by side with an emerging vision of Ireland which is more urban, more economically vibrant, and open to foreign investment, ideas, money and culture. The fragmentation of identity, and the coming of age in a post-colonial society, are among the subjects of the talking, storytelling and singing that underlie Murphy's theatre. Taking the sacred spaces of Irish history his narratives unfold in a pub (*Conversations*), in a Church (*Sanctuary*

Lamp), in a kitchen (*Bailegangaire*). Old myths must be dispelled before a new myth making can happen.

In this article I propose to explore the ways that meaning is made through Murphy's use of theatre. I will look specifically at the representation of women and their role as bearers rather than makers of meaning. I will question, following Lynda Henderson's (1996) lead, whether men and women have equal access to creating the life of the spirit so characteristic of Murphy's work. In exploring female subjectivity in the plays I will explore questions raised by Cheryl Herr (1990) when she stated that the body is the missing link in Irish identity.

Who would want to be a woman in a Murphy play? Lynda Henderson (1996) claims that men and women are not equal partners in creating the life of the spirit so characteristic of Murphy's plays and that they play highly differentiated roles akin almost to the traditional organisation of construction teams. While the men make meaning and culture women play the supporting roles:

> It is the men who do the heavy jobs of metaphorical building and demolishing; and the women who play the supporting roles of literal catering, managing, conniving (Henderson: 1996, 88).

John Joe in *A Crucial Week* may be attempting to work out a constructive relationship to his home place but his mother "cooks, irons, schemes and keeps his bicycle tyres pumped up — allowing him the space for his hero-journey" (ibid.). Henderson goes on to cite many examples of how the women in Murphy's plays fulfil this support role to the male hero journey. Mona in *The Gigli Concert* supplies food, drink and sex and is almost written out of the play. Peggy in *Conversations* is presented as the peacemaker and healer, the forty year old girlfriend of schoolteacher Tom, who patiently accepts and tolerates his brutal insults to her. The Mother in *Famine* is presented as monstrous because of her pragmatism. Women in Murphy's plays have very little to say if we simply count their lines:

> They certainly have nothing to offer to the metaphysical debate which provides the raison d'être for the central male characters and for the work as a whole. They are excluded from the abstract, spiritual dimension (Henderson: 1996, 90).

Women in Murphy's plays are often colourless drudges, or patient icons. They are necessary rather than vital. They are either tolerated begrudgingly, seen in a fragmented way as sexual objects, or presented as symbols of the repressed in the male unconscious. Henderson cites the comment of The Man in *The Gigli Concert*, "It all boils down to the wife for us all in the end", as a "spiritually mean and reductive rendering of the essential, and suggests the inevitable in a context where an alternative would have been welcome" (ibid.: 93). The blatant misogyny of the conversations in *Conversations* when they talk about Josephine, the bank clerk, is juxtaposed with the joyless, charmless drudge that The Missus has become on one hand and on the other an idealisation of the female in Anne's "gentle hope" or Peggy's song *All in the April Evening*. O'Toole talks positively of Anne and Peggy's passage into "the realm of pure symbol" (O'Toole: 1994, 180) and sees in Peggy's song, offstage and in darkness "a moment of stillness and beauty, of simple and true expressiveness, at the heart of the play" (ibid.). While Grene acknowledges a latent or active misogyny as one component of the social malaise of modern Ireland he feels that in the play "something is struggling and failing, to get talked out" (Grene: 1991b, 213). He sees Peggy's song as deliberately off-centred, as one that is made to express genuine feelings associated with "a nearly silenced femininity" (ibid.: 216) at the edge of the stage, "filled with competing voices of male egos" (ibid.). For Grene, "through song and silence, Peggy and Anne together are made to speak for meanings which the conversations of the men, can never express" (ibid.).

This however is not a satisfactory subject position for women. They are simply there to carry meanings that the male characters cannot reach. They are the necessary complement, the anima to the male animus — not subjects in their own right. Equally Mona's position in *The Gigli Concert* may simply be that of facilitating JPW's descent into the underworld, and his embrace of the dark/other, so often symbolised as female in a patriarchal culture. Women are adjuncts to the hero's journey, or sites they pass through in their pursuit of their true selves. They are brought into the realm of pure symbol and they can be made to symbolise anything that the writer wants. As Ailbhe Smyth puts it in her article on "The Floozie in The Jacuzzi", "Woman" always stands for something else, is an empty signifier, and can be construed to mean whatever "we" want it to mean (Smyth: 1991, 7).

The Sanctuary Lamp, considered irreducibly religious in its content and structure (White: 1987, 78): presents us with three derelicts in a city Church trying to come to terms with their pasts, searching for symbols and myths that will ground them in a post-Christian era. Maudie, the sixteen-year-old orphan haunted by guilt and searching for forgiveness, is portrayed as a frightened vulnerable child whose only achieved level of reconciliation is to fall asleep in the overturned confession box, having shared fish and chips with Harry. Her status as abused child with a tragic life reinforces her position as victim. Her sexuality is confused with her spirituality. She recalls times when she would climb lamp posts, "And sometimes, if I waited up there long enough, everything made — sense" (*SL*: 23). Henderson interprets this as the closest Murphy gets "to granting a woman entry to the metaphysical" (Henderson: 1996, 90). As

Maudie came sliding down the lamp-post she would start doing cartwheels. At other times she would run into her own house and take off her clothes. While Henderson feels that this represents an exultation of spirit that leads to an innocent display of sexuality it is difficult to see how the young woman is seen as other than a sexual object when the bigger boys start whispering her name and calling her back out to them. Her religious experience has been eroticised and taken from her.

In *The Feminization of Famine* Margaret Kelleher makes a very interesting point when she refers to the work of Alice Jardine and Jacqueline Rose. She notes:

> the frequency with which 'the unspeakable' is characterised as female; again and again, images of women are used to figure moments of breakdown or crisis — in the social body, in political authority, or in representation itself... expressing... the 'point of impossibility', of any system (Kelleher: 1997, 6).

She draws attention to how often the unspeakable "covers over the 'unspoken', that which needs to be spoken, to be remembered and retold" (ibid.: 7). If famine is conveyed in images of women unable to feed their children, or images of children suckling dry breasts or despairing mothers with dead children in their arms the tendency is to identify famine with a breakdown in the natural order: "The resulting implication that famine is a natural rather than a political or economic event, is itself a political message, regrettable but also convenient" (ibid.: 229).

If we look at the representation and position of The Mother in *Famine* we can make some interesting connections. While Murphy does not depoliticise famine and does connect it quite directly to economic policy of the time he does present the figure of The Mother as pragmatic provider for her family and "eloquent opponent" of the men's actions:

> Jesus Christ above, what's wrong at all, and all the clever persons in the world? Biteens of bread are needed only. Life blood of my heart: hunger, childre, pain, and disease! — what are we going through it for? (*Famine*: 85)

Kelleher alerts us to a troubling stereotype that underlies such strong pragmatic figures like The Mother or Juno in *Juno and the Paycock*:

> the perspective which they are made to represent is not simply apolitical but forcefully "anti-political"; access to political action or to men's political discourse is thus denied, both to Juno and the famine-mother (Kelleher: 1997, 149).

Hence we have a reproduction of the scenario that Henderson describes where the men only have access to making meaning and a separation emerges where the woman is identified with family and nature and the man with the political and the human. Thus Kelleher adds:

> Murphy's construction of the characters of John and "Mother" risks reinforcing this separation: woman's sphere is "nature", John's that of complex political abstraction (ibid.: 149).

In such a scenario the Mother's experience is deemed "parasitical" and her death can easily appear as "a necessary, if dreadful action" (ibid.: 150). While no critic doubts the harrowing, searing, brutal obscenity of the Mother's death the interpretation usually stresses how her choice of death attains freedom, as she finally sheds the myth of dependency. But, as Kelleher reminds us, the sacrificial death of a female famine victim is one of the most frequent motifs in twentieth century representations. Often her death is deemed necessary for the survival of the community, the figure of the woman becoming the means through which the sorrow is given form, tears are shed and in the words of John Banville from *Birchwood*, "the inexpressible expressed" (Kelleher: 1997, 152-153).

The effects of colonisation are seen in many of Murphy's plays, where the male characters are split and emasculated, torn between cultures, languages, worlds, consigned to eternal childishness or lashing out at the twin narratives of Church and State which have dominated their psyches and paralysed their imaginations. The dangerous memories of suffering are at present seen as correctives to the overarching narratives of the past. Challenges to cultural hegemony are much in evidence and discourse increasingly understood in Foucault's terms as the "power which is to be seized" (Cairns & Richards: 1988, 16).

One of the problems faced by the colonised imagination is that when the persons in a post-colonial culture try to define themselves anew they tend to do so in opposition to and over against the previously dominating discourses:

> Colonial discourse establishes the colonized as the repressed and rejected 'Other' against which the colonizer defines an ordered self and on to which all potentially disruptive psycho-sexual impulses are projected.... The colonized are thereby constrained to assert a dignified self-identity in opposition to a discourse which defines them as, variously, barbarian, pagan, ape, female; but always subordinate and inferior (Cairns & Richards: 1988, 8).

This has particular relevance for Murphy's work in relation to how his characters assert themselves over against the previously dominant discourse of Church, how they define themselves in opposition to certain cultural stereotypes and to the place of woman within such new discourse.

Murphy's critique of religion, his anti-clericalism, his obsession with his characters defining themselves against the inherited mythology and symbolism becomes wearing and certainly dated. Francisco's famous speech in *The Sanctuary Lamp*, JPW's new naming of the God of the Hebrew Scriptures, his embrace of the darkness are nothing new. There is no sense of any kind of theological literacy in Murphy's work. Any liberation theologian or feminist theologian has made equally scathing criticisms of institutionalised religion. Prophetic critique of religion is found within the Hebrew Scriptures themselves — the prophet is the one who grieves in order that a new future may emerge. Mystics of the Christian tradition have always been aware of the inadequacy of all language when talking about God and have stressed the *via negativa*, and the dark night as valid paths into the Divine.

Murphy stated in an interview in 1991 that: "When the disenchantment sets in then the person becomes increasingly dangerous as he/she kicks out in agony, against the loss of all these certainties... or... of a central certainty (Jackson, 1991: 19). This state is characteristic of many of Murphy's characters who struggle Job-like with the adversities and disappointments of life. O'Leary in an article highly critical of Murphy's religious sensibilities suggests that *The Sanctuary Lamp* is a "fragile vessel of a religious vision which is imperfectly focused" (O'Leary: 1992, 43). He identifies a dissatisfaction with the paternal order and a desire to return to the womb. He critiques the play for failing to engage this paternal order critically and politically, and sees it preferring helpless rage to critical action. He sees Francisco's indignation as a "generalized floundering hostility verging on sheer propaganda and hate mongering" (ibid.: 45). For O'Leary, Murphy falls into the:

> classic loop of anti-clericalism; namely that it is a posture which remains stickily tied up with that what it opposes.... His attempt to mint a new religious vision remains stuck in dependence on Modern Christian commonplaces and in reaction against out-of-date ones (ibid.: 47).

The *Gigli Concert* (1983) tells the story of an Englishman JPW King, a washed up dynamatologist, a new age quack healer dealing in philosophical mumbo jumbo who is approached by an Irish Man, a wealthy property developer who is suffering from depression and whose one desire is to sing like Gigli. The whole play takes place in JPW's office. The only other character to appear on stage is Mona, JPW's lover who apparently picked him up in a supermarket.

The consistently positive responses by academics to this play makes it difficult to approach it critically. Undoubtedly the play affirms the patriarchal imagination that is at the heart of the cultural process and this may in part explain its popularity. The trajectory of the male protagonists, even if split and mirroring each other's journeys, is nonetheless a typical realist narrative that moves towards closure at the expense of the women in the play.

As *The Gigli Concert* opens JPW is on the phone to Helen, a disembodied woman whom he idealises and abuses through annoying phone-calls. As he tells the Man his story of his childhood the Mama is associated with "the inner world, and a little poetry" (*Gigli*: 5). The Man has not spoken to his wife in a month and when he does it is only to roar obscenities at her. He cannot say aloud that he loves her and instead repeatedly roars out "Fuck you" (*Gigli*: 13), knowing she is standing at the other side of the door. The mirroring of this scene occurs later for JPW prior to his attempts to sing like Gigli. As Mona leaves he shouts both I love you and fuck you (*Gigli*: 36). This has been interpreted as: "the desire to possess is opposed by the desire to relinquish" (Roche: 1994, 187). It is more likely that it expresses the male ambivalence towards the female. The awesome powers associated with the female as life giver and nurturer are both admired and feared and are expressed either in misogynistic denial and rejection or idealisation. In Ireland with our history of Sheela na Gigs we need not be surprised at such ambivalence. Nuala Ní Dhomhnaill expresses it this way:

> You would not accept me when I came
> a queen, like a tree be-garlanded.
> My womanness overwhelmed you
> as you admitted after to a friend
> over a mutual drink.
> Fear, certainly of castration
> fear of false teeth in my cunt
> fear my jaws would grind you
> like oats in a mill (Ní Dhomnaill: 1986, 68).

It is interesting to ask the question that Henderson asks "What do women know?" (Henderson: 1996, 99) What is it that is feared and wanted? What subliminal fears are triggered? Why are women denied access to the Shaman journey in Murphy's plays. What are women to make of the closure of *The Gigli Concert*? Mona's baby haunts the play. The baby she had when she was sixteen, the god-child she invents and the child she wants to conceive with JPW. Murphy usually sees a child in Jungian terms as symbolising the future and creativity, but also admits to loving to be around pregnant women. The life-force in the woman's natural journey is awe-inspiring. But in this play woman is constantly objectified. The men talk about women as tits and breasts and Murphy gives Mona similar lines to say. The men see sex as performance which they can either achieve or fail to. It usually seems to leave them feeling unsure of their masculinity, whether it is with the older girl Maisie who feeds him sweets as encouragement to have sex (which incidentally Murphy admitted was autobiographical (Jackson: 1991, 19)) or with the woman that JPW talks about.

Does this myth of meaning (Swann: 1991, 152) reinforce a traditional patriarchal structure or does it undermine and question it? Roche interprets Mona's line "I'm a subject" (*Gigli*: 16) as a line that "resonates and declares the extent to which the play is concerned with 'woman' as enabling subject of male-centred discourse" and the "construction of male identity through the vehicle of "woman" as subject" (Roche: 1994, 181). He sees triangular rather than doubled relations at work in the play, with Gigli as the shifting object of identification between the Irishman and the Englishman and another triangular structure as JPW, Mona and the imaginary Helen. JPW must work out his identity, caught between the ideal and the real, the idealised unattainable Helen and the very real presence of Mona whom he can ignore. But Lanters would argue that the crises for JPW and the Man are "defined solely in terms of the mind", that JPW seeks a "way out of mental sterility" into "self-awareness" (Lanters: 1992, 280). Lanters feels that the physical aspect of the play is represented by Mona, and her counterpart Helen (albeit disembodied). Her argument stresses how male experience of the play "is given a female counterpart in parallel terms of sterility and creativity, sickness and healing" (ibid.: 278). That there is no "rebirth" possible for Mona is all too obvious as she leaves to face a life-threatening illness and surgery. (Lanters claims she has been neutralised in the play or denied an existence in her own right.) Where Roche interprets the final primal cry which precedes JPW's singing "Mama! Mama! Don't leave me in the dark!" as an ultimate court of appeal to the female, "a plea that abandons the myth of male sufficiency and creation" (Roche: 1994, 188), Lanters sees it differently. She suggests that the King who emerges still needs completion. Too often the woman is simply the projection of male desires and fantasies. Lanters, following Herr's argument on the erotics of Irishness (Herr:, 1990), identifies the body as the missing link in Irish identity. Lanters argues:

> ... since King's former, false self-image was largely sustained and reinforced by female characters who themselves existed for King only as imagined projections of his own mind, the realisation of a true self that would be capable of healthy relationships entails not only the destruction of the false self but also of woman as myth (Lanters: 1992, 281).

Grene writes about Mona that "she is there to represent the bodily reality of love and relationship which both men in their urge towards transcendence ignore or fail to recognise" (Grene: 1991b, 217). She cannot simply be there like the two male characters, a subject in her own right. She must represent something that they are failing to recognise. The ambivalent attitude towards women is also seen in the many ways that female characters are seen as either too good (The Man about his wife) or promiscuous (Mona). To suggest an equality because Mona uses JPW as much as he uses her is to buy uncritically into the patriarchal symbolic. Depicting women as prostitutes is typical of a patriarchal aesthetic, barely masking the hidden desires about the potential availability of all women. Having women supposedly actively choose these positions is the ultimate validation of the same aesthetic. Women are usually only given sexual choices in these realist plays. The exercise of these choices reinforces the patriarchal ideal and does not propose any kind of alternative vision. Roche claims that the two men find different solutions to the question of identity. The Man returns to "the wife", thus continuing to subscribe to the patriarchal ideal. JPW no longer believes in "woman being exchanged as a somatic token" (Roche: 1994, 187). I would like to believe that this is true, that woman is no longer simply seen as an object of exchange within a patriarchal hegemony. But I believe that this comment misses the point of the play which Lanters has stressed. JPW ignores Mona, hardly notices that she has gone. She has enabled his journey of the mind. He is oblivious to the needs of an embodied subjectivity and spirituality; either his own or Mona's. Reconsidering the final moments of the play in which JPW supposedly possibilises the possible by singing like Gigli one must question how satisfactory this really is, after all he has just consumed a cocktail of mandrax and vodka. However some academics have been very positive. O'Toole sees it as a form of magic, a "theatrical ritualisation of optimism" (O'Toole: 1994, 209), White as a "movement towards the ineffable" (White: 1990, 560) when speech breaks down, and music becomes not just indispensable but inevitable. When Roche states that at the end of the play "the symbolic order readmits the female and a theatre of the impossible" (Roche: 1994, 188) he is certainly not talking the same language as that of écriture feminine even though he uses similar words. For the female is what is sacrificed in the patriarchal symbolic and her reinstatement would demand an embodied particular subjectivity with attention to female *jouissance*, laughter, and play. And the men have already "tried, laughing, and crying and philosophy" (*Gigli*: 37). Perhaps it is time for the women to take the stage and tell a different story that is playful, and centred in laughter and history.

Female critics of Murphy's earlier work told him that he did not understand women, that his plays were about male identity and their tribal rituals of belonging, that modern Irish women would not recognise themselves in his female characters. His answer at one level was to write *Bailegangaire*. In 1961 he had written *A Whistle in the Dark*, a dark bleak tragedy of displaced men, driven to violence, brutal competition, self-

loathing and domination. To answer the male dominated world of the
Carney family, in 1984 he wrote *Bailegangaire*, a play with an all female
cast, Mommo and her two granddaughters Mary and Dolly. Mommo
tells the story of how the town came by its appellation, a story of a
laughing competition that had taken place thirty years earlier.

A people without myths becomes a rootless people, a people without a
home. When the myths on offer are perceived as "borrowed images" or
"neon-shadows" (*Conversations*) or "a whole poxy con" (*The Sanctuary
Lamp*) then something must be done to restore spirits that have become
mean and broken. A new myth making is needed that restores links with
history. It will need to provide release from the unending narratives of
the past, offering healing and forgiveness, and promise of a new future.

A particular story must be told. This is Mommo's task and increasingly
as the play progresses it becomes obvious that it is also vital for Mary
that she finish it. But if it is a particular story of identity and belonging it
is also a story of Irish identity in the broader cultural sense:

> Beyond that is the memory of her frozen marriage, her tyrannical
> treatment of her children which drove them to fight or to
> emigrate, the psychic wasteland of deprivation, horror, and loss
> over which her imagination broods and which her story animates.
> It is a grotesque vision of the whole country which Mommo
> voices in the climactic description of the laughing-contest (Grene:
> 1991b, 222).

There are two narratives at work in the play — Mommo's narrative of the
laughing-competition and the children waiting at home for their
grandparents to return and Mary and Dolly waiting in the present as their
own story unfolds and their past is more fully revealed to them. The final
resolution is only achieved when the story that is told and the story that
it is telling unite (Swann: 1991, 153). The play has an almost hypnotic
effect on the audience. Mommo's story sounds like an "unfinished
symphony" that has been playing for ever. For Grene: "storytelling, thus,
in Bailegangaire takes on the full expressiveness reserved in *The Gigli
Concert* for the operatic aria. Mommo's story, like the singing of Gigli,
plays on insistently, repetitively, hypnotically" (Grene: 1991b, 222).

Kristeva's sense of women's time interrupting and backtracking and
weaving an altogether new story is echoed in Mommo's storytelling. At
the core of the play and of the two stories is laughter. The movement in
the play from the original predominantly male environment of the
laughing-competition and the tragedies that ensued to the three women
sharing Mommo's bed, and laughing at their misfortunes as they plan
together to embrace Dolly's unborn child as a promise of a better future
is striking.

How as feminists can we read this play? Henderson claims that no matter how much the play plumbs the complex realities of life and suffering, some of which are by gender out of the male arena, it does not offer its characters access to the level of the spiritual, mystical or metaphorical (Henderson: 1996, 92). And yet it is not strictly true to say that Mommo in particular does not enter the realm of meaning maker with her eventual reconciliation to the painful truths of her past history. In her attempts to recreate a myth of origins and to link that myth with the reality of her own particular history she performs a very meaningful task. Eavan Boland has written extensively in her poetry and in her autobiography *Object Lessons* on the need for women to move from being objects of history and discourse to being subjects. And in a sense this is what Mommo begins in her story. From being the idealised woman of Irish myth whether Irish Mother or Mother Ireland, imaged and defined in her various representations by men and made to be the carrier of all kinds of meanings not her own, she moves in an approach to her own subjectivity. While the stories she tells are in large measure the result of a patriarchal ordering of history there are tentative steps towards a new type of consciousness where laughter is not part of a dominating competitive, destructive and violent myth but shared by women in solidarity facing a new future.

However the new space that the women try to embrace is really no more an embodied space than that of JPW in *Gigli*. Throughout all Murphy's work one would find it difficult to identify one healthy sexual relationship. Even in *Bailegangaire* Mommo has had a cold, loveless marriage where her husband had not spoken her name in years. (This is very poignantly stressed in *Brigit*, the Television play that is part of the *Bailegangaire* cycle.) Mary has had an affair with Dolly's husband Stephen whom we later discover to be a violent thug. What this does to the relationship between the two sisters is not discussed but presumably it would work like the old tactics of the coloniser to divide and conquer. Dolly throws herself into casual sex in ditches to answer some kind of longing. One interpretation offered is that she is engaged in prostitution for economic reasons (Cave: 1993, 96). A healthy relationship with the body and with one's own sexuality would seem to be a definite missing link in Murphy's work. The sexual relationship between Michael and Betty in *A Whistle in the Dark* is totally threatened and inhibited when the family come over to visit. In a scene between Liam and Maeve in *Famine* the young woman eats an apple that gradually begins to transform her and as the couple kiss and cuddle the moon comes out to reveal a family of corpses (*Famine*: 44-47). As Cheryl Herr has written on the erotics of Irishness: "Ireland has literally eroded, in the sphere of representations that constitute social identity, a comfortable sense of the body" (Lanters: 1992, 279).

The traditional severing of head and body in the ancient Celtic warrior tradition is continued in our representations where the "source of spiritual potency" is represented as male and is dominant while the body — the physical is represented as female and is repressed. Further reconciliation is needed than Mommo's achieved level: the reconciliation between spirit and body for the individual characters themselves and the reconciliation between male and female sexuality and spirituality. Such a movement towards wholeness in Murphy's characters might also disclose the holiness that he craves.

Works Cited:

Boland, Eavan, (1995), *Object Lessons: The Life of the Woman and the Poet in Our Time* (Manchester: Carcanet)

Cairns, David, and Sean Richards, (1988), *Writing Ireland: Colonialism, Nationalism and Culture* (Manchester: Manchester University Press)

Cave, Richard A., (1993), 'Tom Murphy: Acts of Faith in a Godless World', *British and Irish Drama Since 1960*, ed., James Acheson (London: Macmillan), 88-102

Grene, Nicholas, (1991a), 'Murphy's Ireland: *Bailegangaire*' in *Literature and Nationalism*, eds., Vincent Newey and Ann Thompson (Liverpool: Liverpool University Press)

------ (1991b), 'Talking, Singing, Storytelling: Tom Murphy's After Tragedy', *Colby Quarterly*, Vol. XXV11, Number 4, 210-224

Henderson, Lynda, (1996), 'Men, Women and the Life of the Spirit in Tom Murphy's Plays' in *Irish Writers and Their Creative Process*, ed., Jacqueline Genet (Gerards Cross: Colin Smythe)

Herr, Cheryl, (1990), 'The Erotics of Irishness', *Critical Inquiry*, 17.1, Autumn, 1-34

Jackson, Joe, (1991), ' "Making the Words Sing": Interview with Tom Murphy', *Hot Press*, Issue 4, 18-19

Kelleher, Margaret, (1997), *The Feminization of Famine: Expressions of the Inexpressible* (Cork: Cork University Press)

Lanters, Jose, (1992), 'Gender and Identity in Brian Friel's *Faith Healer* and Thomas Murphy's *The Gigli Concert*', *Irish University Review*, Autumn/Winter, 278-290

------ (1993), 'The Theatre of Thomas Murphy and Federico Garcia Lorca', *Modern Drama*, 36, 481-489

Murphy, Thomas, (1984), *Famine* (Dublin: Gallery Books)

------ (1984), *The Sanctuary Lamp* (Dublin: Gallery Books)

------ (1988), *After Tragedy: Three Irish Plays by Thomas Murphy (The Gigli Concert, Bailegangaire, Conversations on a Homecoming)* (London: Methuen)

Murray, Christopher, (1987), 'The Rough and Holy Theatre of Thomas Murphy', *Irish University Review*, 17.1, Spring, p. 9-17

Ní Dhomhnaill, Nuala, (1986), *Selected Poems*, Trans. Michael Hartnett (Dublin: Raven Arts Press)

O'Leary, Joseph, S., (1992), 'Looping the Loop with Tom Murphy: Anticlericalism as Double Bind', *Studies*, Spring, 41-56

O'Toole, Fintan, (1994), *Tom Murphy: The Politics of Magic* (Dublin: New Island Books)

Roche, Anthony, (1987), '*Bailegangaire*: Storytelling into Drama', *Irish University Review*, 17.1, Spring, 114-128

------ (1994), *Contemporary Irish Drama: From Beckett to McGuinness* (Dublin: Gill & Macmillan)

Smyth, Ailbhe, (1991), 'The Floozie in the Jacuzzi', *Feminist Studies* 17.1, 7-28

Swann, Joseph, (1991), 'Language and Act: Thomas Murphy's Non-Interpretative Drama', *Perspectives of Irish Drama and Theatre*, eds., Jacqueline Genet & Richard Allen Cave, Irish Literary Studies 33 (Gerards Cross: Colin Smythe) 145-175

White, Harry, (1987), '*The Sanctuary Lamp*: An Assessment', *Irish University Review*, Vol., 17, No. 1, Spring, 71-81

------ (1990), 'Brian Friel, Thomas Murphy and the Use of Music in Contemporary Irish Drama', *Modern Drama*, 33, 553-563

Unionism and Utopia: Seamus Heaney's *The Cure at Troy*

Terry Eagleton *

One evening in November 1990 the city of Belfast witnessed a mildly ephochal moment of theatrical history. A couple of hundred men and women from Andersonstown, a working-class, strongly republican area of the city, crowded into a parish hall to watch a Sophoclean tragedy. For more than a few of the audience it would have been their first experience of theatre, let alone of classical drama; not many Andersonstown folk are habitués of the Lyric, Belfast's "serious" theatre. What was the connection between audience and play?

The play in question was *The Cure at Troy*, Seamus Heaney's translation of *Philoctetes*. It was presented by Field Day Theatre Company, which each year used to tour a new play to about twenty-five venues both north and south of the border. Irish people came to watch Field Day because they expected a play of relevance to their own concerns, and despite its Chorus and Attic costumes *The Cure at Troy* is no exception. For it isn't hard to read the piece as an oblique allegory of the "Troubles", and Heaney's explicit allusions to hunger strikers and police widows in an appended Epilogue are meant to leave no-one in doubt about the bearing of ancient Athens on contemporary Ulster. Philoctetes, you may remember, was the Greek warrior involved in the siege of Troy who was unceremoniously dumped on the island of Lemnos by his disgusted comrades because he stank to high heaven as the result of a snake bite to his foot. But the Homeric heroes have to lever him off the island again, because without his unerring bow Troy will not fall to them. When the play opens, its ulcerated protagonist has dragged out a lonely decade as a castaway, trailing pus and blood behind him and bellowing with agony at every step; but the wily Odysseus puts in to shore with a typically duplicitous scheme for inveigling his erstwhile comrade back into battle. This isn't going to be easy, given Philoctetes' understandable hatred for his treacherous colleagues; but Odysseus sets on his impressionable junior Neoptolemus to sweet-talk the pathetic old cripple out of his magical weapon.

Sullen, rancorous, inwardly gnawed by hatred and paralysed by memories of past injustice, Philoctetes is Heaney's unlovely image of the sectarian North of Ireland. The dramatic trick is to keep the reality of his sense of hurt, and the sterile pathology of his response to it, in subtle equilibrium; and Des McAlteer, the gaunt, grizzled actor who played the part for Field Day, managed magnificently to combine the pathos of this betrayed warrior with his curmudgeonliness. Philoctetes is at once the very image of suffering humanity and sectarian stereotype; in a strikingly, over determined image, he thus incarnates and transcends the Troubles at a stroke, nurturing historic wrongs while providing the play's touchstone of a common humanity at once more durable and more fundamental than such political divisions.

There's more than a whiff here of the cosmopolitan liberal-humanist Heaney at odds with the Derry nationalist, but it isn't a clear-cut case of the "human" versus the "political". Moved by Philoctetes' plight, the vacillating Neoptolemus casts off the shady political role Odysseus has smooth-talked him into, offering instead to lift Philoctetes off the island. But this is to turn his back on the devious *realpolitik* of his senior colleague, the Charlie Haughey of Lemnos, rather than to abandon the political as such. If the humanity of Philoctetes finds an answerable impulse in himself, it is because he rejects a parochial Greek self-interest for an enlightened universal concept of political justice: "The jurisdiction I am under here/Is justice herself. She isn't only Greek". If there is a justice for Ireland, there is no distinctively Irish justice. The difference at stake is one between good and bad politics, sound principle and squalid pragmatism, not between the political and the personal, which would have been unintelligible to the ancient Greeks. Neoptolemus responds as he does because he is bound by a properly global law of comradeship, not because of some errant lapse into personal sentiment.

Moreover, if Philoctetes symbolises the poor forked creature humanity itself, it is in the shape of a raw, recalcitrant, sheerly biological torment with which nothing in itself, politically speaking, can be done. He can figure, to be sure, as an *object* of pity, an index of the compassion (or lack of it) of others; and in this sense he's a negative sort of utopian figure, the recipient of a justice and fellow-feeling which surpasses Odyssean wheeler-dealing. But this humanity is impotent until he himself has shifted from object to subject, relinquished his self-lacerating misanthropy and re-entered the maelstrom of political history by assuming his position once more as a political agent before the walls of Troy. To do so involved strategic compromise, re-embracing the very Greeks who sold him down the river; and the dramatic problem is to distinguish such essential flexibility from the crafty dodges of an Odysseus, superficially alike as they seem. But if Odysseus' hard-nosed utility stands at one pole of the play, the simple intransigence of an historically fixated "principle" stands at the other: and it's up to Neoptolemus, himself pitched between the two alternatives, to remind the surly Philoctetes that "The danger is you'll break if you don't bend". How, in the North of Ireland context, do you demarcate a resourceful openendedness from shopping all you believe in? Philoctetes has to make the transition from the wound to the bow – from a festering contempt for political humanity to an active role in the resolution of historical conflict. He must do so, moreover, by his own free choice: it's a neat irony that his *decision* to re-enter the military fray is itself part of the gods' predetermined programme.

Humanity is an imperative which must be enacted *now*, as the befuddled Neoptolemus finally appreciates and the pragmatist Odysseus doesn't. For utopia to be conceivable at all it must, in Habermasian terms, be somewhere prefigurable in the flesh-and-blood of the present, in the shape of an instinctive creaturely response to another's needs. But the fullest realisation of this humanity is equally, ineluctably *deferred* to the just city of the future, which only political practice can bring about. For Heaney, this means deferring it not beyond the threshold of history, but (in terms of the myth) to the conquest of Troy and the final transcendence of all the old sectarian strife. It is on this glimpse of utopia that the play's Epilogue boldly, beautifully touches:

> Human beings suffer.
> They torture one another.
> They get hurt and get hard.
> No poem or play or song
> Can fully right a wrong
> Inflicted and endured…
>
> History says: *Don't hope*
> *On this side of the grave.*
> But then, once in a lifetime
> The longed-for tidal wave
> Of justice can rise up,
> And hope and history rhyme.
>
> So hope for a great sea-change
> On the far side of revenge.
> Believe that a further shore
> Is reachable from here.
> Believe in miracles
> And cures and healing wells.

If there's a moving utopian hope here, there's also some notable confusion at the level of allegory. Is it really going to take a *miracle* to dislodge the British from Ireland? That was well enough for the Greeks, who had a magic bow conveniently at their disposal, whereas we just have Seamus Mallon, Sinn Fein and the Secretary of State for Northern Ireland. The myth, in other words, covertly determines its own kind of contemporary political stance, which amounts to an openness, to the utterly inconceivable as nebulous at it is courageous. Resolution, as Heaney's naturalising imagery intimates ("tidal wave", "sea-change"), arrives as miraculous gift rather than as political construct, inarticulable epiphany rather than political strategy.

"No poem or play or song", so the Epilogues avers, can fully right a wrong. But in *The Cure at Troy* one allegory is struggling to get out of another, and this is the figure of Philoctetes as *poète maudit*. The trope of the doomed, marooned, mysteriously emasculated artist has of course a complex Romantic history behind it; and there's no doubt that in mediating on the ironies of principle and pragmatism, obduracy and flexibility, political engagement and utopic prefiguration, Heaney is casting a lateral glance at the fraught status of the North of Ireland poet, unsure whether to speak out or keep silent, take sides or just keep warm in his verse a tenderness and sensuousness which might be read as either political, meta-political or depoliticising. Unlike the resolutely *dégagé* Jocyean finale of *Station Island*, *The Cure at Troy* plumps for political commitment of a kind; if you stay on the island, whether in the Aegean or Loch Derg, you fester and rankle, grow self-involved and self-tormenting. But here the Greek myth serves Heaney less adroitly, granting the artist Philoctetes far too central, salvific a status. If it's possible in Homer for such a man to help end a war with his literal or rhetorical shafts, it's hardly on the cards in the six counties. The ignominy of the wound can't be so glibly reversed into the hubris of the visionary bow. In the play's concluding moments, the resolution of the historical conflict and the healing of Philoctetes himself merge gracefully into a single compelling image; and in a general sense this may be also true of the North of Ireland poet, who will find imaginative peace only when the political wounds of his people have been salved and bound. But that poet won't heal himself by spearheading the troops, which is mere idealist compensation for actual ineffectiveness; and if the myth subtly falsifies here, it does so too in its proleptic celebration of the overthrow of Troy. For on any literal translation into modern terms, this can only suggest that the agonies of Ulster will be soothed when the political enemy is brought to its knees. The play pronounces this truth; but it doesn't, as it were, *mean* to pronounce it, since such a scenario is far removed from the mildly reconciliationist politics of a Heaney. Right at the play's end, then, the allegorical use of myth releases an *unintended meaning*, which is only possible because the conquest of Troy has been distanced and stylised to a sort of metaphor of Philoctetes' own personal regeneration. The play thus "unwittingly" inserts into its reconciliationist (Catholic-Protestant) mode the very confrontationalist (Ireland-Britain) model which a good many Northern writers, including Heaney himself, would rush to disown. Paradoxically, in displacing the focus from the political to the personal, from outward to inward warfare, *The Cure at Troy* breeds a political implication which outruns its author's personal mastery.

* Re-printed from *The Eagleton Reader* (Basil Blackwell, 1998)

The Seven Ages of Harry Joy McCracken: Stewart Parker's *Northern Star* as a History Play of the United Irishmen in 1798

Akiko Satake

Northern Star was first performed in the Lyric Players' Theatre in Nov. 1984 and is the first of three plays Stewart Parker wrote as a unit, or a "triptych" as he liked to call them, because of their relative independence in subject matter. They are, in the playwright's own words, "three self-contained groups of figures, from the eighteenth, nineteenth and twentieth centuries respectively, hinged together in a continuing comedy of terrors" (*NS*: 9). *Northern Star* however, in my view deserves attention in its own right as one of the most innovative and persuasive forms of history plays that dramatists have explored in recent years. Parker succeeds in presenting his view of the events of 1798 as part of the ongoing historical process that continues to this day, and in doing so he compels the audience to become party to this process as it takes shape on the stage. Although Parker was extremely meticulous in the way he pieced together historical details, he makes no pretence that what is being presented is an objective representation of what actually took place. (See Madden, McNeill, Stewart, Flanagan). (Parker even takes care to fill in what he left out of the Seven Ages — which I shall explain later — in the bridge scenes between Mary and Harry so that the play can trace a more or less coherent sequence of events surrounding the United Irishmen in Ulster.) It is his perspectives and critiques on the age that are the focus of the play and are strongly reflected, for example, in the theatrical parodies he employs.

Northern Star is centred around Henry Joy McCracken, a Belfast "mongrel" of Scots-Huguenot stock like the writer himself (*NS*: 9,17), who was, perhaps more than anybody else in the United Irishmen, actively involved in the actual task of bringing rural Catholics into unison with the Protestants in the city. Serving as the presenter of his own history, McCracken urges and leads the audience to listen to the voices of the past, i.e. the ghosts. And the play is so designed that as we listen, not only do we share in the experience of what actually happened then, but we participate in the very formation of history. History, in a sense, is a shape we give to the past as we listen to its voices. The past, in other words, becomes a history when there are people to listen to its story, so it can be handed on. Hence the insistence in Parker's play by McCracken that Mary "listen" (*NS*: 65), listen to the story of his life.

The shape he gives to his life is that of the Seven Ages of Man, each age entitled with a morality-like heading going from the Age of Innocence, through Idealism, Cleverness, Dialectic, Heroism, and Compromise, to the final Age, which he may have intended to call the Age of Shame (this is the only Age without a clearly defined name). Each age, moreover, is set up in the characteristic style of representative Irish dramatists in chronological order (from Farquhar, Boucicault, Wilde, Shaw, Synge, O'Casey to Behan and Beckett), so that overall this kaleidoscopic procession gives rise to an impression like that of a series of medieval pageants, (a word used by the Captain) (*NS*: 47)) linked by the cottage scene in which Henry and Mary speak in the casual language of modern Belfast (See O'Flanagan: 1997, 90). Just as the medieval audience followed the footsteps of Christ by moving from stage to stage, the audience of *Northern Star* are led through the course taken by the United Irishmen with a certain sense of inevitability until they see the idealistic movement end in further deepening the divide they set out to bridge.

The audience, who are thus in a position to hold in view the whole comic progress, are at the same time implicated in the action as "the Citizens of Belfast" (*NS*: 14, 34, 49, 76) to whom McCracken tries to address his final speech in front of the gallows. But the final speech that he is shown to compose or rehearse at the beginning of the play does not materialize. Harry's words after, "so what am I to say to the swarm of faces?/ Citizens of Belfast... " at the end, are drowned out by the beating of the lambeg (the instrument denoting violence and aggression in the play in counterpoint to the bodhran; (*NS*: 19,34,51,65,68,72,76), as he puts the noose round his neck. In fact, I suspect one of the reasons that attracted Parker to Henry Joy might even have been the evidence of this historical omission. It is reported that just as McCracken was about to speak, the horses stamped and created such a noise that he had to give up trying to make his voice heard (See Madden: 1857-60, 190 and O'Flanagan: 1997, 92).

In other words, by Fate's devastatingly comic sleight of hand (or was it a cruel manipulation on the part of the officers standing by?), McCracken missed the opportunity to put the stamp of heroic martyrdom on his life as is done by other famous rebels: William Orr on the scaffold and Emmet in the dock among others. Harry's feeble attempt at imitating their speeches whimsically disintegrates into a sales pitch. (His speech begins with a pastiche of phrases taken from the Test of the Society of United Irishmen and the speeches of Orr and Emmet. William Orr was significant to McCracken, who bequeathed his ring with Orr's name engraved on it to his mother on the eve of his execution (Stewart: 1997, 50)). He is turned into a burlesque hero, a transformation which Parker would not have been able to perform as freely with the men who left behind final words that consecrated the meaning of their lives. As Boucicault says in *Heavenly Bodies*, the next play in Parker's triptych, old-style actors needed grandiloquent lines for their exits. And by spotlighting this moment of ultimate failure at the close of the play,

Parker is insisting that McCracken's life, as those of many others like him, should not be understood as the apotheosis of a heroic martyr "Only to glitter in the effigy of another time" (*NS*: 72), but as the unfinished story of Everyman whose endless trials we inherit in today's divided society.

The mediator of history, moreover, is appropriately a fool figure, whose outsider's view can provide a frame from which to look at what is enacted on history's stage. Harry carefully cultivates his jester's role as he introduces the parodic pageant, the Seven Ages of his Life with the familiar ballad of a rogue. "'Twas the night before Harry was stretched. And the boys they all paid him a visit" (*NS*: 27). The boys duly appear scene by scene: his distinguished cronies Samuel Neilson, Thomas Russell, James Hope, (Neilson was the editor of *Northern Star*, Russell a librarian, Hope a weaver, as they are introduced in the play (*NS*: 26)), Wolfe Tone, Edward Bunting and the rest, though in this case McCracken was the first to die.

McCracken was a good mimic as McNeill describes and as is shown in the play with Harry "pontificating" in Russell's and later Castlereagh's voice. (As for Parker's love of magic, see his Dramatis Personae Lecture.) And the same, needless to say, goes for Parker as his hilarious parodies of Wilde, O'Casey, Behan and others bear witness. He must have sensed a kindred spirit when he read about McCracken, who even shares Parker's experience of early success with conjuring to schoolfriends. In his essay "Dramatis Personae", Parker states his belief that theatre should entertain as well as send a social message. But the joke is obviously not just there to sugarcoat his message. Nor are we simply offered another taste of Parker's macabre humour, which we get, for example, in the very idea of the undertakers' strike, (with all its expected consequences) in *Nightshade*. The joke here constitutes the essential part of what the play seeks to convey about Irish history. "Every joke turning into a nightmare. Every nightmare into a joke. That's an Irish lullaby" (*NS*: 16), Harry says. The story of one of the cartful of corpses that raised his head and answered "I come frae Ballyboley" and then was buried with the rest (*NS*: 28) is historical and the severed heads on pikes that "laughed and laughed and then the laugh turned into a howl" in Harry's dream (*NS*: 27), were a common enough sight at that time, and the end for many rebel leaders, including not only James Dickey and John Storey, as mentioned, but a more prominent figure like Henry Munro (Stewart: 1995, 246-7). The whole history of Northern Ireland, such as it is, in Parker's view is a comedy of terrors, and McCracken plays a "poor fool" (*NS*: 75) in that comedy.

Like the cottage that another local "freethinker" (*NS*: 16) O'Keefe had worked so hard to build but left half-finished by his death, McCracken tried to build this bond between people of different religious persuasions and left behind a country further divided and in ruin. The comic pageants of the Seven Ages trace how the republican ideal of United Ireland conceived in the enthusiasm of youth, through its confrontation with reality, is inevitably dragged into the ancient feud over land between Cain and Abel. (As prologue to the pageants of his life Harry begins with a quick summary of his and Ireland's "mongrel" (*NS*: 17) lineage and the origin of the United Irish ideas, as well as the result — his defeat as Commander-in-Chief).

Even from the beginning in the boisterous tavern atmosphere of the Age of Innocence, the lofty language of the Declaration and Resolution of the Society of United Irishmen of Belfast is deflated by its faltering rendition by the infamous spy Belle Martin, who is forced to stutter out the lines on paper she has purloined. (See Madden: 1960, 11; and O'Flanagan: 1995, 21,73.) However, at this early stage, proclaimed to be on St Patrick's Day in the spring of 1791, the air is still declaredly optimistic, at least in songs and banners if not in action, with their faith resting on non-violent means (Madden: 101).

Then in the second Age of Idealism, Harry's gallant defence of the Catholic farmers (Madden: 1857-60,14), playing the undisputed hero of the scene, is already darkened by the foreboding that he will eventually have to take sides with the Defenders against the same men that he had previously recruited into the United Irishmen. The Catholicity of the people Harry saves is deliberately stressed by the mumbling of the rosary and the promise to include him "forever in our prayers" (*NS*: 30). It is a black-and-white situation characteristic of popular melodrama, with even its stage directions for the setting imbued with moralistic overtones and its action charged with suspense. Although the gentlemanly Harry manages here to withstand violence, undaunted in the face of the masked assaulters, all his idealistic talk about his loyalty lying equally with all the members in the room is dismissed as "Belfast prating and preaching" (*NS*: 32) by the Orangemen on the one hand, and the scene ends with the Catholic couple, on the other, hurrying off to the call of the lambeg, leaving McCracken to contemplate the rope.

The Age of Cleverness exposes an aspect of superficiality inherent in the United Irishmen's movement, which boasts a harp as its badge although its leading members cannot bear to listen to one. A similar contradiction is provided by the insignia that Harry recalls here, of a crown placed atop the name of a ship *Hibernia* (McNeill: 1960, 76). The episode of the Harp Festival, which is the setting of the third Age, interposes a cynically apolitical or rather anti-political point of view into their history in the mouth of a man noted for his "biting tongue", Edward Bunting (McNeill: 1960, 58). "Music is only above politics in the way that stars shine above a bog. You would do better, sir, to compare like with like, and say that usury is above politics. Or sodomy perhaps. Or anything else you care to name. For what in the world could be below politics? You will forgive me now, gentlemen, if I return to a better place". To which Tone, in a perfect Wildean response, says, "What a disagreeable fellow, I do hope we shall see more of him. He has quite distracted me from my headache" (*NS*: 41). In fact almost every single line uttered, regardless of by whom, in the sparkling repartee of this Age is a tribute to that master of epigrammatic paradoxes.

The emphasis on the superficiality of symbols and the move away from the political line of action have actually been prefigured in the scene that took place just before it, during which Harry's sister Mary-Ann visited the cottage (O'Flanagan: 1997, 90). One of the insistent motifs in their conversation was Harry's disgust at being cast into roles, with some reference made to Joan of Arc of Ballynahinch (Stewart: 1995, 227) as a recent addition to the long list of "Trophies and symbols. The Shan Van Vocht and Roisin Dubh" (*NS*: 38). Harry is anxious to change the topic to news of his family, which thus occasions Atty's entrance on the stage.

The movement that bravely resisted violence in favour of legal measures in the preceding Age is now called "amateur warmongering" (*NS*: 39) by Bunting, and with the mention of the killing of John O'Neill as a signal, Act I ends with a scene of violence witnessed on stage (McNeill: 1960, 19-20). But it is violence to which the United Irishmen as a political movement are still not committed, and their time is frittered away in "procrastination" — to use the word in the popular phrase of Young's *Night Thoughts*, a copy of which has been handed to Harry by his mother (ibid.: 178).

The Age of Dialectic straddles time to intrude into the present cottage scene in the figure of the Captain who has come to search the house. He proves himself a worthy opponent in the suave Shavian discussion on the validity of the cause of the United Irishmen. Highly intelligent and articulate as Shaw's satirists all are, using overtly refined speech even when expressing simple matters, the Captain contends that Ireland was never a united nation until the British crown accomplished it, and the soldiers they fight are all Catholic peasants. The Society itself is riddled with informers, and moreover, the French to whom they so much look up "were profoundly embarrassed by it all, and greatly relieved that they never did succeed in the attempted invasion" (*NS*: 47).

The dialectic, such as they engage in, is violently resolved by the Captain's death cry offstage as he goes out to meet the Phantom Bride. It is, therefore, left to the Phantom Bride and not the Captain to capture Harry in her deadly embrace. The implication is clear as it has been consistently from the beginning. This is not a play about the glorious fight for freedom against the evil oppressor, it is about the history of a country that destroys a man like McCracken. The cottage (or Ireland) belongs to the Phantom Bride, as Mary well knows, "sure why wouldn't you? Isn't it her house?" (*NS*: 51), and this Phantom can both be a provider of life and death. Moreover, when we realize that it is precisely a "bereaved bride" like Mary, despite her depiction in the play as a sturdy proponent of ordinary life, that becomes transformed by later generations into the ghostly strangler, we may sense a further note of poignancy in this double-faceted nature of the Phantom Bride.

The actual physical threat, that no longer can be kept in check by words and even overrides the double time scheme of the play as I described above, finally drives Harry into taking his oath in the more radically restructured society at the end of Act I. Called the New System, the Society has resolved on the course of using "physical force" as opposed to "moral force", following the steps the Captain has opportunely schematised for us with his 3 Rs: Reform, Repression and Revolution. Thus we enter the phase of the physical force in Act II with Mary singing a song of lament at the end of the first Act.

In a clear indication of the turning point between the two Acts, it is suggested that Harry and Mary's relationship has been physically consummated during the interval (it was not only in the Phantom Bride's arms that Harry was held after all), and Act II opens ominously with Mary's crying on the bed. The conversation becomes increasingly focused on death and the fear of death at this stage, reflecting the imminency of the historical situation. (McCracken's desire not " to die of sickness" as opposed to Hope's attitude (*NS*: 54) and the rebels' preference to die "than be hunted like wild beasts" (*NS*: 64) are probably quoted from Madden (Madden: 1857-60, 104). However, despite the decisive step taken by Harry, that prompts Mary to reprove him, "Why did you allow yourself to resort to the gun?" (*NS*: 53), his supposed company in the campaign do not figure propitiously in this play. All they do is talk about their determination. Ulster's "procrastination" in the rising was fatal. "It was left too late" (*NS*: 56) as Hope says. And the "future ghost", Jimmy Hope, with his significant name, chooses this moment in the play's action to depart from Harry's side ("Moral force" is one of Hope's favourite words. Madden extols Hope as a man of extraordinary fidelity, courage, intellect, and with ideas too advanced for his time (*NS*: 86)).

The Heroic Age, in which Neilson, Russell and Tone proudly declare their intent to fight to the end in the bloated language of a poor Synge imitation, is ironically set between the scenes of short dialogues between Harry and Hope, the only two members of the group who actually did "rise up in the red dawn" to "scatter her scarlet army before us into the foamy tide" (*NS*: 55); Neilson and Russell being in prison at the time and Tone aboard the French fleet. Although Harry was part of the company who went on the famous excursion on top of the Cavehill, an episode which seems to be always described with the grand vista of Belfast spreading underneath as is done in this play (McNeill:1960, 105), Harry's only words here are "An August day. Incandescent. Half a dozen of us up there. High as kites" (*NS*: 55). They are apparently words spoken by Harry from a distance, their tangy succinctness in sharp contrast to the insipid windiness of the language heard at the scene. The group's "fine talking" (*NS*: 56) is inevitably capped by a "sup" of "poteen, cooling in the spring by the fairy stone" to ease their "drouthy" throats (*NS*: 56).

With the Age of Compromise comes the collapse of the United front with Harry becoming sworn in to the Defenders. He betrays no emotion throughout the sequence in which Defenderism, complete with its password "Eliphismastis" and esoteric hand signals, is ridiculed to a hopeless extent in the impeccable replica of a Captain Boyle-and-Joxer pair. A sense of subdued resignation or indifference may already be observed to have stolen into Harry at the way things are turning out, though he does take exception, finally, to the implication of what he calls a "vendetta" against the Orangemen. Gorman, with his imitation legal terminology, the all-purpose word "banjoed" and all the bluff about his exploits as a Defender-on-the-run and the graveness of the business at hand (consigned to him by John Magennis — the leader of the Defenders in Down — as he claims) is true to his prototype; as is McFadden in the sinister ease with which he can go back on his word of fealty expressed not a moment ago. Together, the pair serves to strike a note of falsity and betrayal that will be carried over to the final Age where it will take on an even darker hue. What vexes Harry's mind as he continues to recall the events after the couple had left, for example, is the hollow promise of the number of soldiers pledged to him (Madden: 1857-60, 36).

The final Age at Kilmainham is so fashioned that the hatred between the two sides comes to the fore. We see four prisoners displaying four different reactions to their incarceration. Henry Haslett, depicted as a nervous prowler and ungenerous in spirit (Mary characterises Haslett as "always reckoned a Tyrant" and "so universally disliked" in her reply on 11 Sep. 1797 to her brother's letter in which he tells her that Haslett struck him "on the head with a saucepan of scalding water"), was a Presbyterian shipbroker who had supported the foundation of *Northern Star*, and was arrested together with Russell, Neilson, and Teeling on Castlereagh's September coup in 1796. Young Charles Teeling, a well-to-do Catholic son, had been active in organizing the Defenders with McCracken, and was deceived into accompanying Castlereagh to his house with his father, after which the gate was shut behind him. As the name of the card game he is playing suggests, he is the only character to come out unscathed in the scene as the most patient and rational of the four.

Little is known about James Shanaghan except that he was a lawyer and a member of the United Irishmen who was suspected of being an informer, (See Gilbert: 1893) and the character here could well be largely Parker's creation to add to the grim humour and pathos of the background by representing an innocent mind unhinged under the pressure of prison life. He is beset by forgetfulness about such basic things as whether he has eaten that day or not, and frets over the most irrelevant of people's names. Having retreated into his own world of comic anecdotes, he is adamant in his refusal to take notice of all the venomous bickering that is going on around him. Haslett's abusing of Teeling, who only intervened to shield Shanaghan, as "Don't you come the parish priest with me, you Papish arse-licker!" (*NS*: 72) offers a moment of revelation of what lay hidden of the rift within the Society itself.

Just before we gain sight of how things are in this prison, we hear Harry's declamation about history being a "dungeon" and people "locked in their separate compounds, full of stench and nightmare", "crawling in their own shite and lunacy" (*NS*: 65). The metaphor can be reversed so that the prison scene, in turn, takes on the image of a miniature of the world we live in. It is there that Harry tastes "the tree of knowledge", seeing the world and men for what they are. Once men are stripped of all ideologies in an extreme situation, there comes a point when either they expose the naked emotions that drive their actions or retrogress into a state of bare existence. The obsession with physical needs and the fuzzy confusion about identity that we see in Shanaghan are characteristic of some of Beckett's characters in his existential plays or, for that matter, of the typical clowns' antics that initially inspired Beckett. (The two episodes that Shanahan repeats over and over both involve the disguise of identity by William Putnam (Madden: 1857-60, 115,172) and McCracken (McNeill: 1960, 55) respectively.)

The choice of Behan and Beckett as the basis for the final Age is significant. Parker, having read Huizinga's theory on play, was a firm believer in the instinct of "ludere" to confer freedom and dignity on man in this otherwise deterministic world. He says: "It is the one thing which holds the absolute determinism of the cosmos at bay. Once this capacity for play is lost, however much a burden or torment it may be to them, humanity itself will be extinct" (Parker: 1986, 16). Beckett is a precursor in what Parker renames as the Theatre of the Ludicrous. Both Behan's *The Quare Fellow* and Beckett's *Waiting for Godot* are about "while(ing) away their time" as men wait for an end, just as Parker's prisoners do here. Beckett's characters do this, Parker says, by "playing games, verbal and physical, games of repetition and reminiscence, little ritual games.... And this activity exercises the last remaining faculty which keeps them human. It is irrational but their awareness of this confirms that mind still functions in them"(ibid.: 16).

McCracken and Teeling, at least, start out with macabre jokes about hanging in Behan's style, which is imitated right down to the satiric running commentary on the execution against the beating sound in the background. Meanwhile, with Shanaghan joining in, we can almost hear Beckett's tramps' voices in the exchange of brusque, innocuous questions in between the pauses. The Joker's (*NS*: 67) card Teeling draws at this point throws into relief the condition of these men striving to cope with the nonsensical world in which they find themselves. However, by the end of the scene, the meanness of spirit that Haslett first displayed, when he objected to a salute returned to a thief on his way to the gallows, prevails (Madden: 1857-60). Harry resents the possible release of his inmates and in the vindictive outburst that ensues we see the loss of this spirit of play, or humour, that allows men to accept each other's weaknesses. That is their downfall and their shame.

So they failed, and what remains of the play is a hurried account of its natural consequences. Though Harry does secure a moment for Hamlet-like rumination, outside the prison cell everything begins to converge on Harry to make him take action. The increased tempo of action here is expressed through the liturgical interrogation, that culminates in McCracken's famous dispatch as "Commander-in-Chief of the Army of the North".

The day is about to break in the cottage as well, as we hear the echo of *Romeo and Juliet*. The report of the actual battle given to Mary in his last exchange with her is summarily done with, and Harry stays on to end the play with a kind of prayer in homage to his suffering homeland. This earnest plea for his city with its invocation of familiar placenames and its image of what is now turned into a ghost town, reminds one of Emmet's panegyric to his "strumpet City", which also comes somewhat abruptly at the end of Denis Johnston's satirical play, *The Old Lady Says 'NO'*! In the end, although Harry's final speech never was made, his prayer is left for us to answer: "so what if the English do bequeath us to one another some day? What then? When there's nobody else to blame except ourselves"? (*NS*: 75) It is addressed to us "Citizens" in the full significance of its word, that is to say, in full recognition of our political responsibility.

Harry had no choice but to "act out his small parts" (*NS*: 53) as history ordained him, but in the double time scheme of the play, there is another "night" that he wants to "lift (it) altogether out of time. No future. No past. Just you and me. This night, Mary. Out of time" (*NS*: 19), in which we hear the song of his prayer. Harry, or the "singing-bird" in Mary's lullaby that accompanies the play, sang his song, just as Johnny Patterson, the singing-clown in *Heavenly Bodies*, did — though in a more farcical vein — with his song "Do Your Best For One Another". (Patterson met his death, trying to save the circus equipment from the mob that knocked him down with an iron bar after he sang his song. He held a flag with a picture of a harp in one hand and another with that of a crown in the other hand. Boucicault at first derides Patterson for not knowing how to make his exit, but the play proves Bouciault to be another singing clown and he is happily sent off to the Heavens with much fanfare and mechanical contrivance in the true Boucicaultian style, but amid the cascade of rain that breaks open the roof leaving the heavenly star drenched. *Heavenly Bodies* is a farcical interlude to the subtly ambiguous comedy of *Northern Star*.

To Mary, who warns that "They forget nothing in this country, not ever", Harry counters "It's far worse than that. They misremember everything", and this play was his endeavour for once to make a true account of his own life: "Although whether I'm any different... I've somehow got to get it straight. Tonight. Just this once" (*NS*: 64). And what Parker did was to create a comedy and not a tragedy out of Harry's Seven Ages. In the history of this world we need to retain the spirit of play to keep going, so that we do not turn the past into a dead effigy and still have the ear to hear the living song of prayer for peace.

Works Cited:

Gilbert, John, T. (1893), 'Statements by United Irishmen' in *Documents Relating to Ireland, 1795-1804* (Dublin: Joseph Dollard)

Madden, R.R, (1857-60), *Antrim and Down in '98: The Lives of Henry Joy McCracken, Henry Munro, James Hope, William Putnam McCabe and Rev. James Porter* (London: Burnes Oates and Washbourne)

McNeill, Mary, (1960), *The Life and Times of Mary Ann McCracken: 1770-1866. A Belfast Panorama* (Allen Figgis and Co. 1960; rep. Belfast: Blackstaff Press, 1988)

O'Flanagan, Michael, (1997), *When They Followed Henry Joy* (Dublin: Riposte Books)

Parker, Stewart (1986), 'Dramatis Personae', lecture delivered in memory of John Malone, John Malone Memorial Committee

Parker, Stewart, (1995), *Northern Star* in *Three Plays for Ireland* (London: Oberon Books first publ. in 1989)

Stewart, A.T.Q., (1995), *The Summer Soldiers: The 1798 Rebellion in Antrim and Down* (Belfast: Blackstaff Press)

Tom MacIntyre's Text-ure
Deirdre Mulrooney

"Not all good poets make good playwrights", was an axiom echoed weekly at the Ancient Sun, Modern Light Seminar series on Irish adaptations of the classics at Newman House this Autumn (1999). Tom MacIntyre, I would counter, whose oeuvre has more recourse to Irish mythology than anything Greek, constitutes a glaring exception to this rule. Where does his idiosyncratic work fit in the landscape of Contemporary Irish Drama? What is his nation? Here, he answers:

> My nation is Appalachia, Appalachia,...
> ... busted telly in the bog-hole,
> washing-machine sneezing rust
> on the uninsurable bargain-line.

In that bog-hole there is no grammar that stands on ceremony, no symmetrical sentences, no consumer object beginning middle and end. From inside the bog-hole there is not necessarily "narration" yet. From that bog-hole Tom MacIntyre has learned to speak theatrically in the pre-semiotic. As Roland Barthes asserted, narration only begins once trauma has subsided, and MacIntyre's idiom at its best is characterised by this anarchic, traumatic feel of raw experience, yet un-told.

His theatrical language is incantatory, and three dimensional. It is parole, the spoken word, which lives in the ephemeral moment of performance, as opposed to in the residue of written literature. His is the poetic vision of a true theatre-poet. It's a pity that as a nation we are so hung up on our fine literary theatre, where the residual word reigns supreme. Haven't we learned by now that the residue that's left on the page is just one tenth of it, as Peter Brook would say? Not that MacIntyre the poet doesn't love beautiful words, but they have to be earned theatrically first, and be authentic as the bog-hole they came from. The idiom in which his plays are written is not designed for easy consumption — to be supine, held in your hand, read, digested whole.

As a poet, first and foremost, his idiom is stark and abstract. And in theatre, instead of text alone, he takes responsibility for texture: text-ure. (In the German sense of "Ur" – source. I am aware there is no etymological link here, the connection I am making is purely conceptual.) The tools he employs are colour, movement, sound, pace, rhythm — all translating to his unique theatrical vision. As theatre-poet, his donation to the show extends to casting, rehearsal, devising, and fine-tuning. Collaborating in the creation of theatre images is the third dimension of his full-figured language. Isn't this the true language of theatre?

I am really interested in his work because it does something that only theatre can do. It lives in the moment. Ephemeral medium of the Now. It depends entirely on an intersection of energies to ignite the work. If that doesn't happen, like a pack of damp matches it is, well, frustrating and inadequate. His idiom is daring, naked and exposed.

His exciting theatrical experiment began in the Peacock Theatre in 1972 under the artistic directorship of Pat Laffan, with *Eye Winker, Tom Tinker*. This one was followed by a series of four new plays later in the 70s, starting ith *Jack Be Nimble*, MacIntyre was afforded space to develop his strange new idiom. This idiom appealed directly to feeling, and the subconscious, speaking in a dream-like language, instead of taking the well-worn long-cut through the intellect.

MacIntyre's watershed infusion of charged physicality into the Abbey's literary tradition came about in no small way thanks to his exposure to dance. He devised *Doobally, Back Way*, considered the true precursor to *The Great Hunger*, with Calck Hook Dance Theatre of New York in 1978-'79. An enduring fascination with and admiration for the work of Pina Bausch's Tanztheater Wuppertal informs his neologistic theatrical idiom and his requirements for a much more physical acting style than was common in mid-80s Ireland. A 1997 collaboration with Irish Modern Dance Theatre on *You Must Tell the Bees*, based on his poem *Widda*, continued to trespass boundaries between dance and theatre. Add to this the stringent aesthetics espoused by the likes of Grotowski and Kantor, and you will have some idea of the type of visual poetry in the theatre MacIntyre reaches towards. Though all of the above outside influences were catalysts which stimulated his Irish sensibility, the new theatrical vocabulary he forged is quite unique to his own vision.

Forging this new theatrical vocabulary "affected us all in terms of our general work", says Patrick Mason, the director who brought it into the world. It heightened "our awareness to the power of gesture, to the power of objects on the stage, to the implications of that basic truth of theatre, that every word and act of theatre is both real and metaphorical".

MacIntyre's real achievement according to Mason was of that chimerical "poetic theatre" that Yeats "had been going on about for years and years. And here in his theatre there was this extraordinary development of a genuinely poetic theatre". Unlike Yeats, who paradoxically in his *Four Plays for Dancers* highlighted language alone, to the extent that his actors were required to rehearse in barrels, "MacIntyre as a true poet of the theatre understood the fluidity, the extraordinary magic of that combination of sound and movement and image and gesture and word". Where the physically charged idiom of Conall Morrison's recent popular *Tarry Flynn* was literal and illustrative, MacIntyre's is "poetic, metaphorical. It could be narrative, but at its best it was both narrative and metaphor".

The mid-80s Patrick Mason — Tom Hickey — MacIntyre constellation which fuelled *The Great Hunger, Rise Up Lovely Sweeney, The Bearded Lady, Dance for Your Daddy*, and *Snow White*, in Mason's own words "had its charge, and its day". It was provocative, high-voltage, and unrepeatable. As Mason says: "All creative ventures have a time limit. The energies and talents gather in that time and they may hold for three to five years — rarely longer". MacIntyre's work, by its collaborative nature involves "the kind of naked synergy that really exposes people".

Mason asserts that "it was always misunderstood that he was abandoning narrative". While MacIntyre was "purely preoccupied with the development of the verbal score, equally there was an input into the movement score which came much more my way and into the bodies of the actors". Unusually for a writer, MacIntyre's input was continuous. "We used to talk about the verbal score and the movement score, put them on an equal basis.… I think everybody missed the point that when it came to performance it was something extremely precise, extremely detailed, and extremely well rehearsed".

Despite the high level of collaboration, Mason hastens to emphasise "this extraordinary vision that MacIntyre has — his quite unique sensibility was for us a starting point and a finishing point. It was that vision that led, that instinct for the poetic potential, not the literary poetic, but the deeply poetic potential of theatre language".

As what they were doing, in fact, was setting up new conventions, "very strange and different at the time — less so now", the audience was required to shift its pre-ordained Aristotelian mindset. Mason adds that "the idea of collaboration between writer, performer and audience was very important". Transformation of the audience's Weltanschauung is in essence what MacIntyre's open-ended form of theatre is geared towards.

Striking out at what Nuala Ní Dhomhnaill called "society's funny-bone", in the mid-80s, MacIntyre's disturbing new idiom provoked a hostile reaction indeed. What tended to get lost with people, because of to the overwhelming visual and emotional maelstrom it stirred up when it hit the Peacock stage, was "We were working with a poet, and language was still hugely important as precision of expression". As far as Mason, who directed both is concerned MacIntyre's text "is as nuanced, finely written and precise as *Dancing at Lughnasa*. It's just the form is slightly different". It was "a very complete language of theatre, a very complete exploration of what theatre is, and can be".

Tom MacIntyre does not write in the majority idiom of safe Aristotelian Greek models, but according to an archetypal awareness, as evident in the writings of Jungian depth psychologists James Hillman, and Marie Louise Von Franz. Mason, who has been directorial midwife to all the giants of contemporary Irish theatre considers his collaboration with Tom MacIntyre formative: "In terms of my personal development as a director, it was one of the most significant periods of my life". There is indeed much to be learned from MacIntyre's richly layered opus, "infused with a poet's sensibility as to the presences lurking beneath the surface. The Gods, the Goddesses, the nymphs, the dryads, the forces that would be stirring the earth magic of it". Instead of being propagandist or political, Mason considers the feel of MacIntyre's archetypal theatre to be "haunting… tapping into the cosmos", and thus speaking to our subconscious in the language of our dreams. The dreamscape MacIntyre outlines is one which is in turn "deeply influenced by that Jungian idea of these presences lurking — extraordinary background presences that rise up in our dreams and really inform our being". This interest in myth, symbolism, Jung, and tapping into the subconscious nowhere concedes to the dominant naturalistic tradition of the Abbey theatre: "You're tapping into all kinds of archetypal patterns. Paradoxically they have an archetypal power, but they have a specific almost parochial location. It's that which gives them their force of imagination that opens up the big universal".

This may all seem terribly esoteric, but from the poem *Appalachia* (quoted above), to the 1998 production *The Chirpaun*, MacIntyre never shies away from presenting a "visceral evocation of that reality of Ireland of the devastated rural smalltown Ireland of the late 20th century. The mess is Ireland, and that's his mess". It's our mess too, that he reflects, often unflatteringly, back at us.

As well as joyful abandon, there is something painful inherent in MacIntyre's minority idiom. Painful to watch, painful to be in, painful to direct. It's demanding. It coaxes all of us collaborators (spectator, actor, director) to (at least) the half-way mark. Even if it doesn't always get us there. That's a risky goal these consumerist days. But despite resistance, MacIntyre is not selling out, by allowing his spectator, actor or director to get all cosy and passive.

His exigent vision is dark and deep, looking unflinchingly into the Irish psyche:

> But I'm talking of the hurt mind,
> hurt mind in wait and knowing
> as the hurt mind knows,
> take sweet baby out of the fridge,
> air the house, fumigate the floors —
> (*Appalachia*)

In "airing the house", true to his experience, his perspective is undeniably, and unabashedly "Very male and very Irish". However, not everyone buys MacIntyre's sensibility wholesale. In this respect, MacIntyre's work has met with much resistance. His sexual politics, particularly in productions like *Dance for Your Daddy*, (1987) and *Sheep's Milk on the Boil* (1994), has, unsurprisingly, raised feminist eyebrows.

Mason counters that what MacIntyre is interested in is "archetypal sex" and "archetypal gender", that is: "What it is to be male/female in terms of a male/female presence in the world. The vast inner world, sea of presences". Fascinated with sexuality and sensuality, he is obviously on home turf with *Cuirt an Mhean Oiche*, his latest production. "He is a great poet of the sexual and the sensual. Although he has a huge awareness of and regard for women and the feminine". (The fact that Mason has to qualify this with "although" gives one cause for concern).

MacIntyre's dramaturgical trajectory has taken him into the territory of poems, from (most famously), Kavanagh's "The Great Hunger", to, more recently, the 18th Century Irish language poems, *Caoineadh Airt Uí Laoghaire*, and *Cuirt An Mhean Oiche*. "Drawn to seminal texts", he is looking now for organic dramaturgy coming from the Irish language. His most recent undertaking is to try to dig out the dramaturgy from implicitly theatrical texts in the Irish language and express it in its own idiom. "From Douglas Hyde onwards the trend was to translate English plays into Irish and then perform them. So there was no organic dramaturgy coming from the Irish language. It was being imposed from another language. He (MacIntyre) said "maybe I could try going the other way, try and dig out the new expression of some kind"".

MacIntyre undertook a similar endeavour previously with Irish mythology, albeit in the English language, in *Rise Up Lovely Sweeney* using O'Keefe's edition of *Buile Shuibhne* as a spinal tap and source, and Tom Hickey as creator of its protagonist, Sweeney. He has turned to huge personalities, like Jonathan Swift, whose inner turmoil, torn between the Apollonian and the Dionysiac, was dramatised in *The Bearded Lady* (1984), as well as to the legendary historical figure Michael Collins in *Good Evening Mr. Collins*, (1995), preceded by an exploration of Parnell's mistress in *Kitty O'Shea* (1991).

For the most part, his plays "trying to make sense of the unsaid", are, as Dermot Healy describes them, "beyond paraphrasing". "MacIntyre has always been the maverick of the pack", says Mason, recalling the opening of *Find The Lady* at the Peacock in the 70s: "Friel, Kilroy, Murphy were all there. And there was MacIntyre. All of them have gone their own way in the meantime — each has carved out their particular niche, destiny and vision. And MacIntyre has ploughed his furrow — a more lonely and idiosyncratic one".

Though his upcoming 70th birthday will not spark such pan-theatrical celebrations and revivals as did Brian Friel's who speaks in a majority idiom, nonetheless MacIntyre's oeuvre is a crucial watershed in the 20th century landscape of Irish Theatre. Just as Michael Harding, author of *The Misogynist,* and more recently director of *Cuirt an Mhean Oiche* is influenced as a playwright by MacIntyre, "Frank McGuinness would say that *The Great Hunger* and *Rise Up Lovely Sweeney* were experiences that changed his way of looking at theatre", says Mason. But his constantly evolving minority idiom is often denounced as pretentious, indulgent, and obscure, and MacIntyre himself as a "charlatan".

Is MacIntyre, like Gerard Manly Hopkins, mostly a poet's poet? (Or in this case a playwright's playwright?) MacIntyre's restless search for a shape to his nation, as seen here in the play-text for *Rise Up Lovely Sweeney,* in which the mythological protagonist seeks "a safe house in the maelstrom of Irish history, only to be ousted each time" (Dermot Healy) has not yet found its safe house of conclusion:

> My nation is the howl, some say the whinge,
> I say the howl, but not the black howl.

But his work is neither about safe houses, nor conclusions. His search for an alternative, more authentic form than the shape imported and nurtured in the early days of our national theatre, and the embryonic days of our nation, continues now in his Irish language theatrical adaptations of 18th Century Poems "Caoineadh Airt Ui Laoghaire" and "Cuirt an Mhean Oiche". With MacIntyre we have moved on from those baby steps of the well-made nation-narration to strike out our own note. Thus MacIntyre, exploring our beginnings, can be seen to be asking the fundamental questions, not only about where we are coming from, but who we are, and where we are going as we take our first steps into the 21st Century.

Paradoxically, while his collaborative approach cedes the ultimate power to assign meaning to the spectator (in this Barthesian sense, the book/play reads you) MacIntyre's hand is in every aspect of his productions from casting to direction, acting, sound score and stage design. The non-Aristotelian, anarchic texture of his theatrical idiom empowers the viewer, in its validation of the transformative language of the unconscious. Gone is that Aristotelian "primacy of plot".

Insouciant of providing crowd pleasers, and bums on seats, Tom MacIntyre, "one of the last genuine bohemians that I know" as outgoing artistic director of the Abbey theatre Patrick Mason refers to him, "lives for the muse and that's it". No price is too high in pursuit of his muse, and, courageously, in Barthes' sense of the death of the author, and the birth of the spectator, the confident MacIntyre does not wince before his own authorial "death".

That muse is now moving him towards a version of Diarmuid and Grainne, and a play inspired by the true story of an orphanage in the County Monaghan of his childhood which burnt down in the 40s. Consistently, it focuses (he says), on the metaphor of how "sexual repression set it on fire".

From Playground to Battleground: Metatheatricality in the Plays of Frank McGuinness

Eamonn Jordan

Since 1982 Frank McGuinness has written brilliant, disturbing, rigorous, ambitious and formally inventive plays that have challenged directors, designers and cast members, inspired, satisfied and equally infuriated his audiences. Time and again he has confounded his critics, who had occasionally attempted to pigeon-hole him; and finally, he has encouraged in various ways a younger generation of writers. McGuinness' work has been internationally acclaimed and his versions of classic plays, by the likes of Sophocles, Ibsen, Chekhov and Brecht, have been superbly received.

The work of McGuinness is shaped by an alert and critical intelligence and is guided by a fastidious alertness to rhythm and structure, something that his translation work certainly informs, but it is also something which his writing instincts demand to be there as a significant dramaturgical resource. McGuinness is professional in that way, possessing a keen understanding of the craft of writing for the stage. On this front, his two major guiding spirits are Shakespeare and Ibsen and no better tutors could one have.

War, history, families, religion, myth, oppression, sexuality, gender and elemental conflicts are recurring concerns in the plays. The texts are always theatrical in a fundamental sense, but this theatricality is informed by a substantial layering process that affords a director or critic numerous different points of access and deliberation and it also suggests a variety of approaches or comprehensions that demand particular emphasis and attention. That is not to say that his theatre is idea led nor is it to say that he writes with one eye on an academic audience. McGuinness is a predominantly instinctive writer, in the same way that Tom Murphy is and Brian Friel and Tom Kilroy are less so. McGuinness' writing style heightens and complicates emotional and intellectual responses of the spectator.

To make my argument in this short article, I confine myself mainly to three of McGuinness' best known plays, *Observe the Sons of Ulster Marching Towards the Somme* (1985) which is a dramatisation of soldiers from a loyalist regiment, the 36th Division, who fought at the Battle of the Somme during the First World War; *Carthaginians* (1988) which tells the story of a group of people who have been marked by the deaths of Bloody Sunday (30 January 1972) and who years on still have to come to terms with the incident; and finally *Someone Who'll Watch Over Me* (1992) which is an account of three hostages held in a cell in Beirut and how they deal with their situation and how they cope with the terror of the unknown. Formally, even thematically, these are three substantially different plays that capture the range and dynamic of McGuinness' writing practice, even if the first two are companion pieces.

Confinement is McGuinness' greatest theme; whether it is to be trapped by one's tribal imperatives as in *The Sons of Ulster*, to be imprisoned against one's wishes in a cycle of grief as in *Carthaginians* or to be incarcerated in a cell in Lebanon as in *Someone Who'll Watch Over Me*. If entrapment is the condition, then the obligation placed before all of the characters is to overcome their psychological immobility, to befriend the horror and to go some way towards making sense of their terror. In order to do so, fear must be undermined, cowardice downgraded and anxiety downplayed. The characters must negotiate with their pain, before any release is possible. The driving force behind much of this negotiation is the energy of artifice or play, which runs the whole gamut from self-conscious performativity to impersonation, from trickery, contrivance or the confidence trick to misrule, from the generation of co-operative narratives to masquerade, parody and burlesque, from mimicry to multiplicity, from drag to re-enactment and from storytelling to play-within-a-play, features that have been loosely labelled metatheatricality. Of itself, there is nothing novel in the inclusion of metatheatricality in the plays of McGuinness, but it is worthwhile to identify the persistently successful and recurring usage of the device and secondly the changing significance and purpose of the tactic across a range of the playwright's work.

In *Someone Who'll Watch Over Me*, the characters are terrorised by their hostage experience. They are governed by pre-occupations that have a lot to do with national stereotypes and their responses and perceptions about those responses to events seem to be in part stereotypically motivated. Into the dread of their surroundings they bring with them, like all of the characters in the other two plays under discussion, texts, memories, poems, songs, prayers, quizzes and games that help all of the characters to articulate, with the comfort of both distance and irony, their circumstances and to make more sense of their predicament. For the hostages, fiction is the promise just as fiction is the force, which shapes in part their consciousness or their ways of thinking. Stereotypes may be ingrained, may be superimposed by exterior forces and may be a source of personal consolation, but ultimately the interchange between one's sense of self, one's self-belief and one's public mask is fundamental to an understanding of McGuinness' work.

As is often the case, metatheatricality takes centre stage for considerable periods in his dramas. It is not a singular short play-within-a-play, which is then left at that. The consciousness of metatheatricality is ever present, whether through the recognition of the consistent relationship between identity (the post-colonial self?) and performance or through the idea that performance is an inevitable part of social interaction. This acknowledgement is not intended to down-grade truth, but to impose or suggest a provisionality that can be liberating and challenging.

Play makes room for individual and collective change. All three plays to be discussed look at the notions of the individual self, which is coerced by outside communal forces, and at perspectives of the tribal collective, whether sectarian, national or gender coded. For McGuinness, the individual self is often driven by how others perceive one to be and pressured by demands and imperatives that resist a singularly individual formulation. With role playing, it is easier to distinguish between accepted, imposed, rejected, misunderstood, residual and emergent versions of self. Role-playing ensures that identity is not perceived to be fixed or essentially unchanging, but something that is in process, as it absorbs the impulse and impact of play.

In one of McGuinness' early plays *The Factory Girls* (1982) the women characters work in a shirt factory. As an act of protest against poor work conditions, new work practices and looming redundancies, the women lock themselves into their place of work. Not only is this their protest against the conditions of their employment, but also against the roles and imperatives put before them by their society and by their men folk. Protest will not win the day, but defiance is the only affirmative action open to them. In the midst of this traumatic protest, the characters begin to expand the repertoire of their own resources. Fantasy becomes the principal propelling force behind this change. The imagination along with pretence conspires to liberate a consciousness, without ever having a substantial impact on broader social imperatives and structures. This larger change will take more time, but fantasy may be a concrete propelling force in the quest for freedom and justice, but it will not bring about social change and will not safeguard their employment. The harsher facts cannot be opposed, but the imagination can stir opposition and defiance in the face of such circumstances.

Again, in *Innocence* (1986), some of the characters act out the "carnival of the animals". In McGuinness' play *Mutabilitie* (1997) the suffering Irish rulers and their tribe re-enact the Fall of Troy. This collapse serves as evidence of the trauma of their lives as well as being indicative of both their revenge fantasy and their anticipation of the demise of the English presence in Ireland. Again, fantasy and role-play are to the fore. The "what if" that role play demands takes the momentum and rhythm of the play into a different dimension, and furthermore, the spectator tends to be involved in the performance on a number of levels simultaneously, making the experience equally demanding and rewarding.

As such, play engenders alertness to performance variables that fundamentally destabilises or postpones responses. If pleasure of play is in its possibilities, then the terror of play must be the threat of becoming locked into a role, imprisoned in a stereotype or turned into stone, as Pyper perceives himself to be in *The Sons of Ulster*. The malleability of play is turned rigid by grand, dysfunctional imperatives, over which the individual cannot exercise any control. Play gives rise to a liminal consciousness that disturbs as much as it distorts, that provokes as much as it perverts, that re-states dissent as much as it resists secure points of view. The notion of play confronts rigidity, unsettles lazy thinking and mobilises possibility, principally through the way in which role-playing provides distance, opportunism and an access to an alternative temporary reality, that can be safe and simultaneously energising. Tolerance, difference and understanding can emerge. Play may well be about possibility but seldom is it the easy option.

If play corrupts in some way, then play within the carnivalesque frame doubly corrupts, by offsetting excess against absence, desire against repression and abstinence. Moreover, the persistence of play generates dialogical tensions between opposites, destabilises gender, class, tribal, historical or economic hierarchies and ultimately unsettles fixed meanings. This is achieved by deploying temporary inversions and the subversions of hierarchical authority. This gesture is fundamentally political. Yet Pyper is not truth teller and Edward in *Someone Who'll Watch Over Me* distributes mercenary versions of his own Irishness. In contemporary culture and in contemporary writing practices such blatant hierarchies are less tangible and less visible, whereby play's function is substantially altered. (What I see emerging are two things: the internalisation of play and the complete blurring of the distinction between pleasure and pain and ultimately parody and spectacle replacing ritual as the governing principle of drama.)

In *The Sons of Ulster*, there are eight soldiers, fighting against the German army, (who supposedly learn Gaelic out of malicious intent) fighting for their tribe and fighting for the union between Ulster and Britain. As the play progresses, the soldiers begin to understand the devastation of war, the true substance of their actions and the overwhelming fact that theirs is a blood sacrifice that is driven not by loyalty but by a "blood lust" (*Observe*: 100). To see that in one's self and to acknowledge that about one's activities is a huge step for the soldiers to take. All of the soldiers realise that the perspective offered by the apparently half-crazed Pyper at their first meeting together was in fact more or less correct. Regardless, they find solace in the bonds of a smaller community, without cutting their bonds to the larger tribal unit. Their position is more critically astute. What they do discover is that their tribal bond is more problematic and more complicated than initially perceived to be the case.

They had taken ideas and attitudes on board uncritically and had handed away any responsibility for evaluation of situations and circumstances. Such may be the prerogative of younger men and such may be the reality of the uninitiated.

In *The Sons of Ulster* there are numerous incidents of metatheatricality. There are two Pypers and after all they bear little relation to one another. Likewise Pyper is the teller of stories that are unconvincing, surreal and intent on disturbing the minds of the other soldiers. Pyper is artist as performer in the way that Dido is in *Carthaginians*. The central part of the play is the "true" memory of the event, which the Elder Pyper, upon his return from the war, tries to distort. Therefore in this way the drama is a history within a history as much as it is a play-within-a-play, given that the drama takes place effectively within Elder Pyper's mind. Additionally, the character Pyper is self-consciously theatrical throughout the play. During Part Two, he pretends to be an Army Officer, takes on Craig's name, assaults Anderson through the use of guile and pretence and finally histrionically cuts his hand with a knife to call attention to the symbolism of the red hand of Ulster.

The majority of the soldiers initially enact the tribal role expected of them, one that is governed by myth and by definite expectations. The tribal mask is taken as a given by the soldiers and it is superimposed in a way that does not encourage personal self-knowledge. Beneath such a burden of the collective, little individuality is tolerated. Individuality brings with it its own fears and let us not forget that identity is always forged in a combination of personal, private and public spaces. Sometimes the collective utterly overwhelms the subject. Then a problem arises, as is the case with the soldiers. Even Pyper is not to be excluded from the observation.

The tribal mask is one that protects, disguises and distorts and it bluntly relegates scepticism, provisionality and critical thinking. Pyper is the initial opponent of the tribal mask, but by the play's end, he wears it in a way that is too self-conscious. As his colleagues remind him, he is trying too hard to belong. His is a performance that is forced, unnatural and uncomfortable for the others to witness. It is not grounded in that the consciousness is new and somewhat unfamiliar and unrooted, given Pyper's earlier utter rejection of it.

During Pyper's opening monologue in *The Sons of Ulster* there is another perverted, attempted performance by Pyper, who endeavours to address a multiple audience, that of his dead colleagues, God, his tribe, himself and a theatre audience. Out of his confusion and deceptions something else seeps through. The obligation is that the memory must be replayed in all its complication. No collective agreement must be reached as to the reason why the soldiers died by either historian or tribal representative.

Sense cannot be made of their deaths, political purpose must not be sought in their deaths and simplistic reductions and assumptions are deemed implausible. Motivation cannot be assigned to them adequately. Pyper's ghosts oblige him to remember and the memory is re-enacted for the benefit of Pyper and of the spectator.

If re-enactment of memory is central, then the more serious and disturbing re-enactment is that of unquestioned tribal sacrifice, a deep and profound obligation and loyalty that can only be explained not by love or affiliation, but by hate. The soldiers' experience of recruitment and war leads to an increased tolerance amongst themselves and of themselves, but there is little shift in their prejudice towards nationalism, a nationalism which at the time of 1916 shared a similar belief, as they did, in blood sacrifice.

Regardless of their fear and regardless of the urgency of death awaiting them, the soldiers are never allowed to become heroic role models by the playwright, as their courage is well noted, even seen as laudable, but it is not to be applauded. They go to their deaths with some advancement in their knowledge, but no essential truth emerges, life is not validated, and no forgiveness is sought.

Fear does not prompt in them integrity or an abundant generosity, but there is a slight shift in perspective. Ironically, Pyper swaps attitude with the remainder of the soldiers. The positions they once uncritically occupied at the start Pyper begins to over-invest in towards the end of the play. Certainly the soldiers die almost in vain, certainly they unwillingly sacrifice themselves for a cause, but nothing heroic is sourced in their actions and nothing inspiring is to be deduced from their behaviour. Having experienced the very limited and depleted resourcefulness of the soldiers an audience is asked to give of itself and is demanded to ask hard questions of itself. Personal bias must be challenged.

The soldiers are in themselves, on the one hand strong, brave and kind, and on the other, they are immature, blind and brutal men. McGuinness never allows sentiment to enter into the equation; thereby no easy responses to the play are possible. The soldiers establish a community of sorts, a community whose bond is about friendship, connection and support but is also about violence, sadism, threat and corruption.

At the end of the play, despite how hard they attempt to justify their actions and their dying, nothing really comes into being and nothing can be summoned from the dark to truly satisfy their anxieties. Their bond is neither heroic nor simplistic. This is best exemplified in their last great attempt to consolidate the tribal bond through the re-enactment of the Battle of the Boyne or more correctly the Battle of Scarva, which is a traditional loyalist re-enactment of the Boyne, done on a scale and in a way that is less solemn and less reverential than other celebrations of the Boyne victory. Roles are doled out, an accompanying commentary initiated and the mock battle of Scarva begins.

During the mock battle Anderson's commentary on the action is biblically inspired, playful and ironic, while being initially prompted by certainty. What stands out is that Anderson's usage of a rhetorical language is no longer appropriate to a contemporary consciousness. Along these lines an audience may begin to see how language is a problem in Northern Irish Politics as much as anything else. One can be imprisoned in a mode of expression that is not appropriate and not contemporary. All effort is placed on continuity and not on change. Anderson warns before the horseplay begins: "... you know the result, keep to the result" (*Observe*: 182). History as perpetual re-play is challenged. What Anderson attempts to offer is a sort of strange postmodern bind, without irony. When the wrong result is reached Millen reads it as "Not the best of signs" and no more than that (*Observe*: 71). Nothing can prepare them for the "real thing" (*Observe*: 184). Through it, history is disturbed, discontinuities are accessed and old complacencies are rattled.

The soldiers re-enact the Battle of the Boyne in order to calm them prior to battle and to position their sacrifice within a religious and historical context. With the fall of the half-catholic Crawford, playing William of Orange, the alternative result that is achieved overwhelms and destabilises all certainties. If they cannot get it right during a bit of conscious and pre-meditated play, how can they hope to in the battle before them? History over-heats and is over-rehearsed. There is no calm and no luxury of success hanging over them. Nobody watches over them.

Instead of comfort and assurance, they are left with a profound uncertainty. Nothing could really comfort them, knowing that they face death, but what is remarkable is how little resistance they display to the wrong result, when James emerges victorious. Only Anderson castigates Pyper for the fall. Pyper is not the conscious perpetuator of the fall. Solemnity towards history has no place. Earlier Pyper had offered a critique of war, without a critical distance. It is only when the soldiers re-enact the Battle of the Boyne that things really begin to fall disturbingly into place. It is through the endeavour of play that they become more conscious and that they can consolidate a bond of more considerable depth. But this is a bond that is futile in the face of death. You have lowly army privates playing kings and their horses, without ever displaying delusions of grandeur.

Towards the end of the play both Pypers, Elder and Younger, embrace as if to announce the end of a cycle, as if they can now agree on the details of the event, as if the tension between fact and fiction has been resolved. And as if at last the old man can accept the truth of his memory, which has incessantly haunted him, because he had refuted its essential truth and because he has, as he had accused others of so doing, embellished their truth, distorted the reality of their experiences and distributed a version of events that prolonged the myth of sacrifice, a deed which sent other generations out to kill and die in the name of something which should never have either the benefit or the validation of history. Military historians are guilty of distortion, so is Pyper, and so is the collective myth of blood sacrifice shared by many in the loyalist and nationalist communities.

Only one of the eight soldiers survives. There is no sentimentality to the ending, other than the comfort that can be realised from the embrace between the Elder and Younger Pyper. The victory of the Protestant William of Orange at the Battle of the Boyne over the Catholic King James was the precedent and the religious justification for all that followed in an Ulster loyalist consciousness. This is a myth of destiny and the mock battle suggests that some provisionality, some uncertainty must also be included in the way we view, receive, propagate and perpetuate history.

As history and fact close in around the soldiers, the spectator must above all else recognise that the soldiers are about to take part in a battle that cost close to half a million lives. Nothing can escape that fact. Indeed the pained playfulness of their diversionary game exacerbates it. Pyper will not be left alone until he can accept one truth and re-negotiate with the facts of the past. The spectator, like Pyper, must be capable of differentiating and embracing the distinction between perception and fact and distinguish between the need to give coherence and shape to a painful experience or point of view, which happens to be a loyalist one and the downright lies of those who put the heroic actions of many to ill use, especially those who uncritically attempt to perpetuate a cycle of sacrifice, based on a battle long fought and set in a world and system of values that has no longer any basis in actuality. Continuity must not be the stuff of myth and history; instead discontinuity, provisionality and rupture are the necessary prerequisites.

In *Carthaginians*, almost all of the characters are so pained by the events of Bloody Sunday that they are acting out the fantasy of the dead rising. Sixteen years on (dated by the first performance of the play), theirs is a conspiracy of impossibility, which is perhaps fundamental to the notion of play. The killing of thirteen civil rights protesters on the streets of Derry by British soldiers has done inordinate damage to the characters but also on a broader sphere to friends and relatives of those who died. The impact on the Catholic community of Derry was one of utter devastation. All the characters' behaviour, which followed the event, appears as if the hurt, rage, guilt and incomprehension drove it, engendered by that incident. The severity of the trauma has led to the characters hanging around a graveyard hoping to witness the dead rise.

Their grief, because it overwhelmed so much, has ensured that the characters have become frozen in time. Because the characters have no access to the depths of their pain, their individual life forces are stalled and they are functioning on a destructive automatic mode of being. This shutting down, understandable as it is, becomes a malfunctioned and debilitating performance in its own right. In addition they suffer the guilt, shaped by survivors of devastating incidents. They punish themselves by self-negligence and self-damage, by taking too many risks and by living curiously at extremes. The destructive pattern must be emphasised. Their trauma is over-familiarised by media coverage, sensationalised by political propaganda, yet curiously the characters have no access to it other than by living a life lie, the "pipe dream" of the dead rising. This is non-acceptance at an extreme, yet within the frame of play it is an expression of perverse and macabre possibility.

Carthaginians is a response to the shutting down of pain. What do you do with pain of the scale of the characters, which is a response to the killing of innocent people but also an event with more complex symbolic significance that suggests for the characters the false optimism and naiveté perhaps of peaceful protest. What sense can you make of pain? How does one cope with its presence and its persistence and how does it impact on all that follows? Is it a fact, as the dedication to the published text by Czeslaw Milosz queries that "It is possible that there is no other memory than the memory of wounds"? The play's emphasis on humour and the writers desire to celebrate the dead encourages one to ask how and where does pleasure enter the equation and if it does, what is its relevance? Certain experiences leave pain such that in a way it cannot be resolved, but one can accommodate oneself to it. This has nothing to do with forgiveness, admission, understanding, but with accepting that it is one of the many, not singular, membranes through which one may view the world. The difficulty emerges when the pain or even the perception of pain is so intolerable that one becomes dysfunctional, immobile and damned by the experience or when all things are filtered through the singular event so that it dominates all else. In the instance of the characters the event is Bloody Sunday.

The ritual of mourning over the dead bird, at the opening of the play, is a displacement or transference of their own trauma onto the incidental death of the bird. They over-invest in their concern. It is too earnest, almost provocatively false, yet it allows into play a restrained consciousness of death, whereby a playful, casual everyday use of words associated with death and dying are permissible in their conversations. The unconscious or unwritten agreement is as follows: let us talk about death and grief by talking about something else. My emphasis on performativity is in no way to depreciate the pain of the characters.

On another level, Bloody Sunday, because it is not accessible, becomes a curious symbol in its own right, where fact and fiction, politics and expediency, propaganda and media sensation meet. Justice does not win out. The facts are so incomprehensible and reprehensible that it is only through fictive constructions that it is accessible. Bloody Sunday serves as a symbol for a Nationalist community in the same way that the Battle of the Boyne had in *The Sons of Ulster* for the Loyalist community. In *Carthaginians* the grief of the characters has obliged a certain type of re-enactment of the tragedy of Bloody Sunday and the personal incidents in their lives have bonded to that event.

Each character has constructed a fiction of their own lives, lives that went badly astray or off-track after Bloody Sunday. The narratives that they present are in many ways self-consciously theatrical, driven by the need to fabricate a synchronous, chronological account, shaped by the desire to admit their pain, but also moulded by a coherence that is uncannily distant and disturbing. If one can give such coherence to pain, its unnaturalness is the representation feature that stands out most. Finally, Dido's playlet *The Burning Balaclava* written under pseudonym *Fionnula McGonigle* (who shares the same initials as the writer), with an added French pronunciation for effect, is the best possible example of what I am talking about in terms of metatheatricality, where fact and fiction conspire. Play is the ingredient that helps the characters shift consciousness.

Play likewise is central to the popular-cultural imagination that McGuinness' work thrives on. *The Burning Balaclava* is a *Pulp Fiction* of sorts. Of itself the Burning Balaclava is a cliché-ridden piece. But if we note how the playlet dialogues with other aspects of the play then we begin to realise its strength. The Catholic mother, played by Hark, states towards the end of *The Burning Balaclava* that: "Violence is terrible but it pays well" (*Carthaginians*: 344). The substantial cross-gender casting that Dido encourages creates distance. Throughout the play it might be argued that Dido functions as the carnivalesque misruling mock queen. Through laughter, parody, incongruity and through the ridiculous the momentum to overcome the trauma can be found. Play is the propelling positive energy that enables.

The first obligation facing them is to play with the grief. Dido's script affords them that opportunity. The time for instigating the purgation process is brought about not by a shattering wailing or howling but by the perverse laughter of play and by their resistance towards the inappropriateness of Dido's bizarre text, something that is useless and distasteful in one way, but in another, a text that fundamentally challenges preconceived and incongruous battle lines, where the perversity of disturbing perspectives is confronted by the very blatancy of the writing. "Torment" is the clichéd but not exaggerated response of the characters in Dido's script. Love and passion find no mode of expression except through destruction. Love must lead to murder, as duty demands of it.

In *Carthaginians*, it is not just the notion of the metatheatrical or the carnivalesque that are called upon to open up the play. Intertextuality, popular music and poetry are additional aids and likewise O'Casey's *Juno and the Paycock*, Lorca's *Yerma* and Ibsen's *Rosmersholm* play substantial roles. Secondly, the stage directions to the first published version of the text suggest some representation of a pyramid, "grave chambers found at Knowth", "three plastic benders" to mark the Greenham Common anti-nuclear protests by women. (These do not appear in the more recent published version.) In addition the play includes references to Purcell's Opera *Dido and Aeneas*, the fall of Carthage at the hands of Imperial Rome and ultimately the connection between Derry and Carthage. But for the characters, unlike Carthage, Derry will survive. Towards the end of the play the characters name the dead and rest. The bird which dies at the opening of the play is replaced by a new morning and "birdsong". The dead have not risen but the living can return from the living-dead, the purgatorial consciousness in which they found themselves after Blood Sunday. Their belief in the dead rising is the ultimate expression of their pain, guilt, confusion and horror. The obligation is to play with the memory, play with the pain and hopefully release will be found through imaginative negotiation. Excess, exaggeration and inflation are always central to play. In addition, across a range of McGuinness' work, sexual excess is a transgressive force that queries what constitutes a perception of unnaturalness or deviance. Dido is the transgressive figure that shows the way forward.

In *The Sons of Ulster* irreverence is brought to bear on the solemnity of history. *Carthaginians* theatricalises the structures of memory, where pain is to be acknowledged, re-visited and grieved in a circular, not linear fashion. Memory must be validated and violated, it must be approached with urgency and resistance. In *Carthaginians*, the sacred heart is "riddled with bullets", while in *The Sons of Ulster*, the certainty of history is riddled with illusion. Neither history nor memory can be idolised or immovable. Change and motion are always necessarily relative. In *The Sons of Ulster*, war is on one level a grievous game, where men as bit players were ordered out to die, with little value placed on their lives by those in charge. During the mock battle of Scarva the war game breaks down. The Burning Balaclava furthers the connection between imperialism, violence, wealth and sentiment. The proliferation and variation on the name "Doherty" (Doherty/ O'Dochartaigh, Dogherty, Docherty) suggests interconnection and subtlety that the stage setting, the intertextual appropriations and the action of the play also confirm. Pyper and Dido are trickster or misrule figures that insist that a way must be found out of the underworld, whether it be the hell of battle, the hell that Paul fears that Derry has become or the confined cell which three hostages find themselves in.

In *Someone Who'll Watch Over Me* three men are taken hostage and chained to a wall in a cell in Beirut, Lebanon. Inspired by the experiences of Brian Keenan, John McCarthy and Terry Waite, amongst others, the play is not a factual or composite representation of these men's experiences, instead it is an imaginative account of the pressures and strains of a hostage taking experience. The play starts out exploiting the scenario of a joke. The drama is also a kind of grotesque laboratory experiment, where other types of confinement, in terms of history, culture and stereotype are put under the microscope. Ultimately the play is about surrendering moral high ground, about re-evaluating the Irish/English relationship, about short-circuiting instinctive and unconscious national responses and about undermining expectations. This again is achieved primarily through the notion of play. The captives imagine movies, re-tell famous sporting and personal events in their lives, prejudicially distort the fundamental facts of history, subversively let go of prejudice and cling on to the things which are viewed carelessly as national weaknesses. Edward is Irish and his hostility towards the English is blatant in the litany of clichéd accusations made against Michael (Mick). "Edward:.... Tell us all about the war" (*Someone*: 16). Michael's father suffered greatly as a Prisoner of War during the Second World War and Michael can source some of his own resilience in his father's suffering. When the Irishman plays the role of the Queen of England in Michael's account of Virginia Wade's Wimbledon success, gender and national stereotypes are put to the test.

As the captives begin to suffer more and more in this drama, it is memory and text which come to dominate at the expense of hard fact. The captives do not wish to face down the terror of their precarious existences. Their captors can take them out and shoot them at any time. Does choice mean much under these circumstances?

During the second last scene, Edward is close to breaking point. Michael and Edward conspire to imaginatively escape in a flying car, prompted by the children's film *Chitty Chitty Bang Bang*, a moment which contrasts substantially with the invented movies celebrated during the Third Scene of the play, texts that are critically and confrontationally astute. Here in the penultimate moment desperation is to the fore and intellectual dexterity and resources are noticeable by their absence. To witness in performance two adults indulge in such a fantasy was to sense most certainly their pain and despair. Play afforded them the opportunity to reveal so much, while the imagination is still key to their defiance. Finally, Edward does break down and attempts to communicate with the ghost of his dead father, pleading with his father to "tell" him a "story" (*Someone*: 55). In fact all of the captives had been telling each other stories all the time in order to side-line their pain, to downgrade or downplay the tedium, boredom and the terror of their situation. Likewise, Dido's *The Burning Balaclava* is a similar type of thing, the telling of a story that can be only told within the frame of a disruptive, disrespectful spectacle. Additionally, the mock battle of the Boyne, utilising the subversive elements of the loyalist's Battle of Scarva tradition, is the telling of a story which must be disconcerted and unnerved. The wound is raw, but play is the force which allows the playwright to come close to it without the discomfort of cold water on the exposed nerve.

The great love story in *The Burning Balaclava* between Mercy (Protestant) and Padraig (Catholic) across the northern political divide cannot take place. In *Making History* (1988) Friel indicates through the symbol of seeds that cross-fertilisation cannot take place, that marital union between Mabel Bagenal and Hugh O'Neill can have no future. Mabel's death and that of the child that she bore cement that point of view. Likewise the willingness of official Irish history to exclude her story confirms this impossibility further. In this Friel play no exchange is possible on sexual, political or economic fronts. A leap of the imagination is not possible. Such a leap is possible after much negotiation and desperation in McGuinness' later play *Someone Who'll Watch Over Me*, where exchange, appropriation, tolerance, dialogue and cross-fertilisation can take place, even if identity is a function of nationality and nationality in its narrowest sense is corrupting. After all, the nation sacrifices the individual for the greater good by not negotiating with hostage takers for its citizens. Such moral high ground may need to be expressed publicly, but international manoeuvring between national governments and between individual governments and terrorists are nothing new. Against these facts the noble sentiment of non-negotiation is the demanded public performance of sorts. In another sense, terrorism stage-manages the media response to hostage taking. Likewise literature stage-manages the cliché of violence and opportunity, such as in love across the divide in the case of Mercy and Padraig or in the innocence of the soldier, functioning without knowledge of a political situation.

At one point in *Someone Who'll Watch Over Me*, Edward pretends to be Sam Peckinpah and feigns to shoot Michael with an imaginary gun, something which corresponds to the cruel experiences of the real Beirut hostages, who often had mock executions performed on them by their captives. In *Carthaginians*, the characters turn on Dido at the end of the performance of his script and they all shoot him and later Paul "hauls the gun to Hark's mouth". Paul invites Hark to chew on the toy gun, which momentarily becomes a sign of Hark's suicidal desire, his unwillingness to go on hunger strike as well as his unwillingness to take part in paramilitary violence. Hark has chosen life by not going on hunger strike and he is still guilty because of his choice. Furthermore he is burdened by the guilt of the survivor, having not died on either Bloody Sunday or on hunger strike. There are numerous other examples of such plasticity of props in the play.

Mock death is to the fore in both plays. Resurrection is just as prominent in the form of the fantasy of the dead rising in *Carthaginians* (the only time the dead rise is at the end of *The Burning Balaclava*) and resurrection in the form of the spirit of Adam, watching over the captives in their cell in Lebanon. After *The Burning Balaclava* the characters can begin to bury the dead of Bloody Sunday. When the characters eventually name the dead in *Carthaginians*, it is done within the context of all that has transpired before the incident. In performance, this is a deeply moving and harrowing moment. Likewise Dido's final word is "play", as if play is the invitation, the obligation and an alternative.

In *The Sons of Ulster*, Pyper denies the soldiers the dignity of death, as he keeps digging them up by using them as examples to perpetuate the line of blood sacrifice, by misrepresenting them. The ghosts haunt him so that their truth, not a tribal one, will win out. They must be laid to rest. McIlwaine states: "To hell with the truth as long as it rhymes" (*Observe*: 176) and in *Carthaginians* Hark urges Greta to "Tell the truth" but her response is to "Tell a joke" (*Carthaginians*: 373). The truth is a joke and the joke is the truth, as fiction and fact meet in a complicated way. Without fiction, truth could not be told; without truth, fiction would have no purpose, and such is McGuinness' distaste for postmodernism where there is an implicit denial of truth in the prioritising of difference over truth. The only truth that the captives can lay claim to in *Someone Who'll Watch Over Me* is that under any set of circumstances, they would not torture and terrorise another human being (*Someone*: 28).

Play is the opportunistic assertion of dysfunction, gaps, absences, omissions and transgressions, being validation and violation, the urgency and the resistance. Play is about make-believe, about release and about the establishment of a space of transition, of working out and of recognition, most of all a protective and insulating strategy. Through play anxieties are worked through, blockages negotiated with and adjustments and change prioritised. Memory, history and myth prove to be both the playground and the battleground. In all three plays, the imagination is the playground, exploiting narrative, memory and recollection to good effect. The notion of play is not simply about the exposure of lies and deceptions or about the evaluation of repression but it is about the interplay between truth and lies, reality and illusion, identity and role. It is about the imagination exceeding the limits of the real, about the improbable, about the impossible.

Works Cited:

McGuinness, Frank, (1996), *The Factory Girls; Observe the Sons of Ulster Marching Towards the Somme; Innocence; and Carthaginians* in *Plays One* (London: Faber and Faber)
------ (1992), *Someone Who'll Watch Over Me* (London: Faber and Faber)
------ (1997), *Mutabilitie* (London: Faber and Faber)

Billy Roche's Wexford Trilogy: Setting, Place, Critique*
Christopher Murray

Billy Roche (b. 1949) came into prominence in the theatre through the success of *A Handful of Stars*, staged at the Bush Theatre, London, in 1988. Having won several awards for this play Roche became writer-in-residence at the Bush Theatre in 1989, for which he wrote two more plays, *Poor Beast in the Rain* (1989) and *Belfry* (1991). Each of these also won special awards and the Royal Shakespeare Company subsequently commissioned Roche to write *Amphibians*, for the Barbican, where it premiered in August 1992. It was later (1998) presented at the Dublin Theatre Festival. In July 1993 *The Cavalcaders* was staged at the Peacock, after which Roche got sidelined into Irish film, e.g. *Trojan Eddie* (1995).

The three plays written before *Amphibians* were denominated *The Wexford Trilogy* and were published under that title by Nick Hern Books in 1992. They were not conceived as a trilogy in the classical sense and there is no continuity of character, narrative, or action between the three plays. It is the small town of Wexford in the south-eastern corner of Ireland which lends unity to the plays. Wexford is also the location of Roche's novel *Tumbling Down*, published in 1986. It is interesting to note, however, that for the first of the plays, *A Handful of Stars*, the precise location is avoided and is given instead as "a small town somewhere in Ireland". A native of Wexford himself, Roche was obviously reluctant at first to identify his home town as a dramatic setting, when his audience was in London, but he obviously came to see its usefulness once the first place proved successful. As he said in interview, "the setting is a metaphor for the world" (Woolgar: 1992, 6).

Roche began his career as a singer and musician in various pubs in Ireland, his father owning a pub in Wexford. In the late 1970s he formed his own rock band and toured Ireland, having failed as a folk-singer in London. Wolfhound Press, the Dublin publisher of *Tumbling Down*, described it on the cover as "By Rock Musician Billy Roche", which is significant. Roche's interest in popular music finds its way from the novel into the plays, rather in the way that the plays of Sam Shepard record his early involvement in rock music. Every Roche play has a juke box and guitar music either on or off stage, and the musical reverberations in the narrative can lead to a central theme, as with a song called "One Way Love" in *Poor Beast in the Rain* or "I Can't Get No Satisfaction" in *Belfry*. Alongside popular music, cinema has left its mark on Roche's plays. "In Wexford we had three cinemas. There was no television at that stage so everyone went to the cinema three or four times a week. That filters into my work quite a little bit. I find the setting first – maybe that's the cinema in me" (Woolgar: 1992, 6). The world of cinema provides images and references for each play in the trilogy. This usage, together with the pervasive popular music, is both sociologically realistic and tentatively postmodernist.

Early in 1993 Roche was given a public welcome home to Wexford following the success of *The Wexford Trilogy* at the Bush. In association with a civic reception in his honour, a seminar on "The Writer and a Sense of Place", and a walking tour of "Roche's Wexford", there was a staging of the Bush production of the trilogy at Wexford's Theatre Royal. The whole event was called "The Billy Roche Weekend" (8, 9, 10 January). A recognition that "Billy Roche has put Wexford on the map" (Woolgar: 1992, 6). Coverage of the celebration by RTE, the national radio, and appearances by Roche on both "The Late Late Show" and "Kenny Live" on RTE television, were succeeded by a week-long presentation of *The Wexford Trilogy* at the Peacock Theatre, the Abbey's sister theatre. Thus Roche was accorded national distinction. Thus too, in a manner which has no precedent in recent theatrical history in Ireland, a new talent has had its apotheosis.

Seamus Heaney, quoting Carson McCullers, says in his essay "The Sense of Place" that "to know who you are, you have to have a place to come from" (Heaney: 1980, 135). Irish writing in general is saturated with a sense of place, a topic which formed the theme of a successful IASAIL conference in Galway, the *Acta* of which were edited by Andrew Carpenter (Carpenter: 1977). The topic has by now probably become something of a cliché. Not only has Hollywood got into the act with such films as *The Field* (1991), based on John B. Keane's play of that name, but virtually every country in Ireland has its anthem celebrating its local landscape in the lyrical hyperbole of the travel brochure. Place has become a marketable commodity.

The interesting thing about Roche in this regard is his theatricalizing of place so that it becomes *lieu* in a double sense. On the one hand there is the actual place in mimesis; on the other hand there is place in the theatrical sense *qua* space, which, as Peter Brook says, is only a "tool" in effecting the transformation of which theatre is capable (Brook: 1988,147). Roche plays variations on the two meanings until they interlock in irony, compassion and defiance, interrogating and celebrating small-town life at the same time. It is highly ironic that Roche should now be fêted by Wexford as if he were copywriter to the local branch of Bord Fáilte, since all three places find fault with the town in which the trilogy is set. In short, Roche proposes social criticism by astute manipulation of synecdoche: the setting within the setting, the part for the whole, the pool hall for the town and the town for the nation. Any small town might have served, as it has served Irish playwrights from Lady Gregory to Frank McGuinness, but Roche is different in choosing to define his locale. The distance required for detachment was supplied by the actual ("real") setting of the plays in London: their popularity in London is bound up with their neutrality there. There, they can be seen as narratives of entrapment, but once that invisible London setting is removed the plays take their place among the long line of expositions and assessments of Irish life which characterizes the Irish tradition.

In what follows I shall examine each of the plays in turn, emphasizing the continuity of theme and place and examining their interdependence. I shall then attempt a brief assessment, necessarily limited in view of Roche's subsequent work, and a contextualizing of the plays in relation to contemporary Irish drama.

In *A Handful of Stars* we are given a portrait of a teenage rebel, Jimmy Brady, who gets into trouble with the police and is destroyed. Placed in a narrow working-class milieu Jimmy is shown to have very little room to manoeuvre. An attempt to get a job at the local factory exposes him to the inauthenticity of his surroundings. A seasoned worker in the factory, Conway, immediately accuses Jimmy of currying favour with the management when Jimmy had merely mistaken his interviewer. Conway tells him that this man is not at all what he seemed and is suspected of theft but protected by the management. Since Conway is himself a despicable character, who knows how to exploit his position at the factory, Jimmy sees that this is what he himself might become. He looks for ways to be free: he steals to impress Linda, a girl who seems to believe in him for a time, but soon his reckless, lawless ways lead to his being barred entry to dance hall, cinemas and pubs. As society puts on the squeeze Linda breaks off their relationship and Jimmy goes off the rails.

Staying within the confines of naturalism, where environment counts for a great deal in locating the roots of tragic action, Roche also makes use of heredity. People in the town say that Jimmy takes after his father, a waster and drunkard who is thrown out of his own home and (in disgrace) lives in a dosshouse. He has Jimmy's sympathy. Jimmy sees his father's fate as prognostic of his own. It is that future he rebels against. He mourns, too, how the conditions of time and circumstance have eroded the love and beauty which once his parents' mutual love manifested; he has memories of them dancing happily around the kitchen. Of course, given the conventionality of the culture, Jimmy is overwhelmed with guilt over his mother's sufferings: "She never says anythin' yeh know. But you can see the torment in her eyes if you look close. She never says a word. She just sort of broods" (*Trilogy*: 65). This was the woman whom old Paddy recalls as radiantly in love with Jimmy's father: "To look at her you'd swear she had just swallowed a handful of stars" (*Trilogy:* 50). Hopelessly, Jimmy tries to bring back those stars again.

Undoubtedly, there is a romantic element to Jimmy's attitude. He is a self-dramatizer. An older man, Stapler, who is himself a non-conformist, points out the excess: "Most of us wage war on the wrong people Jimmy. I do it meself all the time. But you beat the bun altogether... You wage war on everybody" (*Trilogy:* 64). Stapler is able to accommodate to the moral pressures of a narrow-minded society: he rolls with the punches and goes his own way. But Jimmy feels more keenly Stapler's defeat in a local boxing contest: Stapler is ageing and will be ground down like Jimmy's father. Jimmy looks at his young friend Tony, facing a loveless marriage to a girl who is pregnant, and he despairs. Tony's lot, as Jimmy sees it, is to join the living dead. In contrast, Jimmy goes on a rampage with a shotgun, settles a few scores, does one more robbery, and wrecks the pool hall. All of this is gestural. "Yeh see that's the difference between me and Conway. He tiptoes around. I'm screaming'" (*Trilogy:* 60). In his afterword, Roche relates Jimmy to the films he (Roche) saw as a young man and to such icons of rebellion as Marlon Brando, James Dean, Steve McQueen, and all the wild ones "who unknowingly sacrificed themselves so that the rest of us could be set free" (*Trilogy:* 187). The romanticism in the vision is undercut by the word "unknowingly": Marlon Brando and James Dean could hardly have been aware that they were liberating Wexford.

Roche's point of view is given sharper focus when the stage setting is taken into account. He confines the action to a snooker hall or poolroom. This move away from the family as setting is significant. To be sure, Tom Murphy, Brian Friel and Tom Kilroy all at various times have forsaken the familiar Irish setting of kitchen, tenement or drawingroom, but never without transforming the location into a version of the home. It is as if they all agreed with Arthur Miller when he said in "The Family in Modern Drama" that the fundamental question to be tackled by the dramatist is, "How may man make for himself a home in the vastness of strangers and how may he transform that vastness into a home?" (Miller: 1978, 85). The disjunction between home and world is far wider in Roche's work than in any preceeding Irish playwright. To that end he chooses settings which are in their ways anti-family: places of gambling, male preserves, places hostile to domestic values. The unit set for *A Handful of Stars* is to an important degree metaphoric. It is a place of play, a club, a lure for the young and a refuge for the middle-aged. With its slot machine, juke box and pool tables its imagery is obvious. It is significant that when Jimmy brings Linda to the club late at night to do their lovemaking (he breaks in through a window) she soon feels alien: "I'd prefer to be somewhere else that's all" (*Trilogy:* 38). It is not a setting which Roche wants to transform in any way, as Murphy transforms the church into a home in *Sanctuary Lamp* (1975) or McGuinness transforms the factory office into a home in *Factory Girls* (1982). The place remains doggedly a pool hall. To the policeman Swan, whose unsympathetic character is a key to the play's criticism of bourgeois order, the pool hall is a school for scoundrels, a "little den of rogues", an image of a "waste of a lifetime": only a "mental pygmy" would frequent such a place (*Trilogy:* 55). Swan scoffs at the name the hall has acquired locally, The Rio Grande, derived no doubt from a diet of cowboy films; he is blind to the association of the name with a border into Mexico, a safe haven from the law.

The hall is divided in two and the division is important. There is a door upstage leading into a private room to which access is allowed only to members. This is an inner sanctum where, according to the opening stage direction, "the older, privileged members go". Inside there is another, unseen, pool table. Young Tony often leaves the outer pool table when he and Jimmy are in a game, to look longingly through the glass panel of the door leading into this "shrine", as Jimmy mockingly calls it. (*Trilogy:* 56). Paddy the caretaker blocks Jimmy's attempt to enter, as if "it was Fort Knox or somethin'" (*Trilogy:* 24). The area comes to represent society's delusion of progress. It is where the likes of Conway hold sway. Yet, despite his contempt for Conway, Jimmy perceives the inner room as for "the élite" (*Trilogy:* 33). Such is the mimicry of hierarchical levels provided by this working class construction. There is a similar experience in *Tumbling Down*, where the seventeen-year-old hero perceives the entrance to the private area of a pool hall as "the forbidden door" (Roche: 1986, 97). Such doors are shut to Jimmy all over town, even though all there is on the other side is one more pool table.

It is significant that when Jimmy goes berserk, following Linda's rejection of him as a hopeless case, and goes on a rampage around the town with a shotgun, he returns to the pool hall in the middle of the night and wrecks the inner sanctum. In scrawling his name in chalk over the door he tried to find his identity in a society which has branded him an outcast. He always knew that he did not "belong in there" (*Trilogy:* 34), but the fact is he belongs nowhere but in prison. And yet Jimmy tries to show that the inner sanctum is itself a prison. Ireland's a prison. Point made.

As social comment, *A Handful of Stars* could probably be called naïve. Its appeal, however, comes from the youth of the protagonist in conflict with his community over the question of his "place" within it. As a version of the "playboy" figure in Irish drama Jimmy Brady is a tragic loser: if he has style it derives from transgression. To an extent he resembles that other Jimmy, that strident rebel of Osborne's *Look Back in*

Anger (1956), but he is far more vulnerable, less intellectual, and less articulate. Jimmy Brady's isolation is the most terrible thing about him because his lapse into criminality is a form of suicide. Inevitably, his fate proposes a strong attack on Irish social structures.

Thus what may appear at first sight in Roche's drama to be entirely banal and mimetic, by accumulation and focus of images becomes metaphoric and even symbolic. His realism may be seen to be carefully constructed. The second play in the trilogy, *Poor Beast in the Rain*, bears out this claim. Here the setting is a betting shop, once more a metaphor for play, gaming, or chance. Once more the location is a public resort of somewhat dubious relation to domestic norms. As in the earlier play, a unit set is maintained: all the action, even some unlikely scenes on a Sunday night (when such a shop, especially in the days before Sunday horse-racing began in Ireland, would not be open), take place in this environment. The action, further, occurs at a time publicly marked as a sporting occasion, the weekend of the all-Ireland hurling final, in which Wexford is competing. The ritual and carnival elements associated with this annual, nationalistic event are used to highlight certain themes Roche explores here, as he expands his concerns beyond the narrow focus of *A Handful of Stars*: heroism, loyalty and freedom.

The plot centres on the return to Wexford of Danger Doyle after ten years to take away the daughter of the woman with whom he illicitly ran away to London. This daughter, Eileen, works in her father Steven's betting shop where the play is set. Much of the earlier part of the play is occupied with the plans by Steven, Joe and Georgie to travel to Dublin for the big game. On Sunday evening, after the game, Danger comes into the shop amid celebrations over Wexford's victory and has to confront many old friends and enemies. Danger is a hero to those who perceive him as a hero, especially to Joe, a former friend who let him down once and caused Danger to be arrested for petty theft but who now basks in nostalgic and fantastic recreations of the past. Danger Doyle is clearly related to an offstage character, Johnny Doran, close kin in turn to Jimmy in *A Handful of Stars*, "wild" and "different". Doran ran away with a carnival troupe and left a girl pregnant: Danger simply ran away with another man's wife. The plot thus concerns the conflict between a subversive and the community.

Somehow the community projects onto Danger Doyle the need for a hero, a theme in Irish drama ever since Synge's *Playboy* (1907). Roche shows the desperation within the community which lives vicariously through such charismatic figures, who, however, bring destruction of one kind or another with them. Objectively, that is, reified by the needs of the community, Danger is correlated to the much-talked-about Big Red O'Neill, a fictional Wexford champion hurler of mythic proportions, and the two men are spoken of in the same terms as film stars, e.g. Paul Newman, Jack Nicholson, Robert Redford and Montgomery Clift. A song in praise of Big Red O'Neill grants him heroic status; when Georgie displays Red's team jersey its gigantic size is a source of wonder: "You'd want to be Charles Atlas to lift it nearly. He'll [Georgie] be a fine fella when that fits him won't he" (*Trilogy:* 93). Danger tried to assure Georgie that it does not matter if he never grows big enough to fill the jersey, that the important thing is to be true to himself, but Georgie is not ready yet to progress to this self-acceptance. Indeed, he confuses the status of his two heroes and is unable to cope with Doyle's honesty over his past weakness.

After the hurling team's victory, Big Red O'Neill, who remains an off-stage character, is accorded almost god-like status. Joe, Steven and Georgie drunkenly identify with his prowess, as if they themselves had somehow beaten the opposition. But Molly forces the recognition that Big Red's supporters are mere parasites. It is interesting that Roche confers on the woman the voice of outspoken honesty which tears away the falsity of public posturing; in Irish drama, in Murphy's iconoclastic plays for example, this role is resoundingly male. To Roche the delusion of heroism is a male construct; its deconstruction is by women's common sense. When Molly turns to Danger Doyle to square accounts, however, she encounters a man who has already seen through the illusory nature of heroism.

Danger Doyle, in this regard, is a most interesting characterization. He comes ready-made, with his lessons learned. He has discovered that relocation in London had changed nothing; the pain of exile and the memory of wrongs done have forged a necessary humility. He is sure of his own identity but cannot help the disabled. On his return he perceives the folly of his exposure to those who will feed off his strength. He compares himself to Óisin (son of Fionn) in the Ulster cycle of Irish sagas, who left Ireland with Niamh of the Golden Hair to live in the Land of Youth (or Promise) for three hundred years. When he pined to see family and friends again in Ireland Niamh gave him her magic horse but warned Oisin not to dismount or set foot on the soil. Having reached Ireland Oisin found vast changes, the Fianna all dead and the new race of men puny and Christianized. Stooping to assist some men to lift a huge stone Oisin fell from his horse and was changed instantly into a blind and withered old man (See Berresford Ellis: 1987, 188-90). In his afterword to the Wexford Trilogy Roche comments that the whole of *Poor Beast in the Rain* is "held together by an ancient Irish Myth as Danger Doyle returns like Oisin to the place of his birth" (*Trilogy:* 188). The play is therefore a reckoning, a coming to terms with the past and a confrontation with the state of exile. Danger Doyle's return is ambivalent to a town which regards him as wrongdoer as well as hero.

Doyle is able to discount the heroic badge and accept the role of wrongdoer. In that guise he makes no attempt to address moral issues. It is as if confronting established Christianity (as Oisin confronted Saint Patrick) Danger Doyle is wise enough to avoid criteria which in Ireland can only lead to victory for the Establishment. Of course, Oisin was a poet (as Yeats well knew, for example) and therefore opposed to Saint Patrick's one-dimensional masculinity. Thus Danger Doyle is on the same side as Molly and against the world of graven images, hero worship and doctrinal certainty.

Doyle survives because of his self-awareness; he knows the myth of Oisin. He is careful not to touch the ground, although Molly angrily orders him to "climb down off of your high horse there mister" (*Trilogy:* 117). He has come single-mindedly for Eileen, who is needed by her mother, ironically as heartbroken in London as Molly is in Wexford. Molly's sense of desolation, her sense that Doyle forgot about her "like some poor beast that had been left out too long in the rain" (*Trilogy:* 121), is paralleled by the picture of the tearful woman in London (Land of Promise) who is on tranquillizers. Doyle has no cure for the society which produced such casualties. He will not get involved. The most poignant moment in the play occurs when Molly, having moved from expressions of hate to admission of enduring love, puts a final question before exiting, "What am I goin' to do Danger?" (*Trilogy:* 122) Her life stretches before her bleakly. Danger remains silent and Molly leaves. Dramatically, it is a wonderful exchange. Roche seems to echo the line at the end of Brecht's *The Life of Galileo*, "Unhappy the land that is in need of heroes" (Brecht: 1963, 108). In Roche's scenario heroes are but fantasies.

Further, Roche's critique of the community is presented by means of a critique of loyalty. There is an unresolved contradiction here. On the one hand Eileen's mother was justified in running away from Steven, a burnt-out case described among the town's graffiti as a eunuch. Yet Danger Doyle's last words indicate her loyalty to Steven: "She's still terrible fond of you, yeh know Steven. She'd never let anyone say nothin' against yeh now nor nothin'" (*Trilogy:* 123). Likewise, loyalty to the local hurling team is paraded as a form of patriotism, though it is also a form of evasion of responsibility. Joe, the most foolish offender in this regard, utters the slogan, "A man without a hometown is nothin'" (*Trilogy:* 108). Steven agrees and adds that such a man is lost. Earlier, Steven had urged, "Get behind your team. Get behind your town" (*Trilogy:* 86). But by the end of the play, after Molly has nakedly exposed Steven's real disgrace over his wife's leaving him, Steven comments mournfully, "This town'll be the death of me yet" (*Trilogy:* 122). That is closer to the truth. Roche reveals the pride and the folly of local heroism and easy loyalty.

When Molly asks Danger why he returned to Wexford he replies: "I just came back to kiss the cross they hung me on Molly. Or maybe I came back to set you free" (*Trilogy:* 121). Here the question of freedom raises itself. In Roche's analysis, in *A Handful of Stars* and in the plays which follow, there is a determinism governing human affairs which cannot be altered. Jimmy agrees when Tony says towards the end of *A Handful of Stars* that "it's nobody's fault" what happened to Jimmy, "Maybe that's just the way it is" (*Trilogy:* 60). Yet it is, Jimmy insists, both nobody's and everybody's fault: "Everyone's to blame" (*Trilogy:* 60). The same sentiment governs the action of *Poor Beast in the Rain.* To bring Eileen with him Danger Doyle must cause her father Steven more pain; to set Molly free he must let her be. Young Georgie is liberated from his adolescent crush on Eileen but not without disillusion. Freedom is entirely relative, and the oscillation between Wexford and London indicates its nature as a no-man's-land. "Maybe that's just the way it is". To be sure, this jettisons analysis and mystifies suffering. Yet we have to bear in mind that Danger Doyle is free to return to London, and he goes with Eileen in the end. That space for movement is something Jimmy Brady never had. In imagining that space Roche is preserving a balance between Synge and Friel, the playboy's romantic liberation and the Faith Healer's tragic surrender of the urge to intervene.

The third play in the trilogy, *Belfry*, more openly confronts the crisis which Roche accepts as lying at the heart of contemporary Irish life. *Belfry* is set in a church – thereby recalling Murphy's *Sanctuary Lamp* – and uses two spaces within it, vestry and belfry, to interrogate the forms which permit or destroy fulfilment today. The play marks a considerable advance in complexity over its predecessors, as it uses a narrator to address the audience and uses time freely and flexibly. The narrative-hero, Artie, a sacristan, tells the story of his love affair with Angela, a married woman who helps in the church. He tells the story retrospectively, one year after the affair, and thereafter appears within scenes relating to the affair and its consequences while from time to time breaking the illusion to act once again as chorus. Although the technique is far from novel, it is worth recalling that *Belfry* quickly succeeds *Dancing at Lughnasa* (1990) and is considerably more adept technically than that other Irish play set in a belfry, Michael Harding's *Misogynist* (1990). Roche's play, while addressing a sexual theme in a church setting, avoids metaphysics and/or theological neuroses, the very stuff of Irish plays with priests in them, and explores instead man's place in society (if the class question is taken as settled) and, secondly, the question of freedom, in a larger context than Roche had so far established.

The classless society is noteworthy in *Belfry*. Nobody pulls rank; there is no hierarchical register of language: all speech is demotic. Instead of the priest being in the role of moral superior to all around him, or instead of his perceiving himself in that role and thereby assuming social superiority also, Father Pat is acutely aware of something bogus in his position. Yet when he tries to express this sense of alienation his language belies his experience:

> I mean to say Artie nobody talks natural when I'm around in this get up. What am I talkin' about I don't talk normal meself when I'm around. I'm like an auld fella so I am. The things I come out with sometimes I'm not coddin' yeh. Methuselah has nothin' on me I swear. Hello Missus, how are all the care?... No I'm just not cut out for it Artie. It don't suit me at all sure (*Trilogy:* 165).

We never hear Fr. Pat use any other diction than the kind recorded here. It is not the idiom or the vocabulary but the formality and lack of intimacy of which he is aware. Fr. Pat's desire to be closer to the people has nothing fundamentally to do with gaucheness; it is not something a crash course in modern communication could put to rights. Essentially, Fr. Pat has lost what used to be called his vocation. It disturbs him that he has no answers for a dying man so overwhelmed by suffering that "He was like a man with no soul inside of him" (*Trilogy:* 146). He regrets not having a woman and children in his life: "I mean it's a queer auld lonely life boy" (*Trilogy:* 165). These confessions are made to Artie, his own sacristan, *servus servorum*. Change places and, handy dandy, which is the sacristan, which is the priest? Indeed, Fr. Pat puts the question, "Fancy tradin' places with me Artie..., no?" (*Trilogy:* 146) "Places" in this sense is a vocational and not a class concept. Dramatically, Roche does change "places": he de-centres the priest and makes the sacristan the centre of attention in this play. We are asked to see Fr. Pat as trapped in the same way as most of the characters in the play. When he takes to drink in act 2 we are informed that this has happened before, and that it is Artie's role to care for him and bring him through the crisis. Roche makes it clear that the crisis is chronic, signifying a society in transition towards greater secularism. As to the question of freedom, it must be emphasized that Artie's sexual awakening, which forms the plot of the play, exists in an amoral atmosphere. Neither guilt nor reprobation comes into the picture. Artie is not judged. Fr Pat makes no comment on the affair, although it is clear in the last scene that he knows about it. The focus is instead on Artie's Laurentian release in middle age through sex with Angela: this release creates his re-birth, as Artie tells Angela (*Trilogy:* 161). Oddly enough the long-term effects of the affair have to do with Artie's initiation into the life of snooker halls, betting shops and card games. These are, perhaps, macho pursuits and so represent the wimpish Artie's self-realization; more importantly, they are the pursuits for which Artie's mother specifically condemned his absent father: "He was a corner boy of the highest order" (*Trilogy:* 174). By adopting and indeed mastering his father's unapproved life style Artie liberates himself from his mother's influence. The fact that she is kept offstage, a conscious alteration of the first draft of the play, is noteworthy, according to Roche's comment in the *Afterword* (*Trilogy:* 188). She is dying and this, too, is significant. Roche is celebrating the enfeebling of the matriarchal power structure, including that of mother church, in Irish society.

Angela's part in this process is less obvious. She is clearly a modern, liberated woman. It is she who seduces Artie in the belfry. She it is, too, who declares the affair at an end in spite of Artie's protestations. There is a reversal here of conventional characterization (in Irish drama), as the woman is empowered both to initiate and to terminate a sexual relationship. But Angela's motive in ending the affair leaves an open question. Once her husband Donal finds out she puts an end to the romance with Artie. Her reaction is detached and unfeeling: "We got caught Artie and now it's over. I thought you understood that" (*Trilogy:* 161). Since her husband later tells Artie that she has begun another affair, one has to see Angela as promiscuous, and yet Roche will not have her judged. He simply reverses the stereotype of the sex-driven male. Donal's attitude is protective; he sees his role, finally, as ensuring that Angela has "somewhere to come home to" (*Trilogy:* 82). This is certainly a new note in Irish literature (one could compare John B. Keane's *The Change in Mame Fadden* (1971), for a more conventional depiction of reception of women's sexual/familial problems in Irish society). By retaining Angela within the social structure, however precariously, Roche calls for a tolerance and a liberation from traditional mores. But he shows at the same time how Angela is both free and unfree.

It is necessary to clarify here the means by which the secret love affair is disclosed to Donal. Roche candidly makes use of the old-fashioned device of the anonymous letter. He often uses newspapers' reports, letters, photographs and diary records in his plays and they have the effect of installing characters in some kind of historical existence. For example, Jimmy Brady has by heart a newspaper account of one of his adventures with the police in *A Handful of Stars*; he pins up a copy in the pool hall. His identity, the one he tries to create for himself, hangs on that piece of paper. As it happens, the anonymous letter in *Belfry* serves to enable Artie also to create his new identity. When he eventually sees the incriminating letter he recognizes the handwriting as his mother's, and the discovery reinforces his determination to seek out his father. In the attic at home, i.e. off-stage, Artie finds a letter from his father asking his mother to join him in England and to marry him there, which she refused to do. The two letters are brought into alignment as Artie subsequently contacts his father and, after his mother's death, arranges to meet him in England. Likewise, the two spaces, belfry and attic, correspond as sites of secrecy, ambivalently presented as places of storage and of love. When Donal gives Artie the anonymous letter he looks out of the window of the belfry at the world below: "A Town Without Pity! Did yeh ever see that picture Artie? Kirk Douglas. It was good" (*Trilogy*: 181). The audience, too, sees the town without pity yet it also sees the belfry as site of Artie's rebirth.

The politics of *Belfry* are brought more sharply into focus through the character of Dominic, a slightly retarded teenager, who is an eccentric altar boy in the church. His mental state gives him the licence of a jester to speak home truths openly. He has no sense of awe before priest, sacristan or woman. He is the voice of vulnerability within a society which decides to lock him up in a special school. It is interesting that there is a somewhat similar character in Jim Nolan's *Moonshine* (1991), staged by the Red Kettle Company in Waterford. In that play Michael is accorded an innocence at odds with the deception and death all around him, and through his involvement in a production of *A Midsummer Night's Dream* he assumes a voice articulating the darkness. He works, paradoxically, to bring light and hope into the lives of the main characters in *Moonshine*. Where priests fail, such characters supply spiritual illumination in recent Irish drama. In *Belfry*, Dominic dies accidentally and absurdly, killed by a passing car when he runs away from the special school. Yet he, too, is a catalyst. His place in society reflects on Artie. Dominic too, like Artie, is illegitimate; he too is in search of some degree of happiness. It is interesting, recalling Arthur Miller's essay once again, that Dominic tries to make a home in the belfry and that his proudest possession is a massive key to the church. But Artie needs the belfry himself for his love-nest, and Artie unforgivably beats Dominic violently and cruelly in the belfry when he believes it was he who sent the anonymous letter to Angela's husband. So, like Michael in *Moonshine*, Dominic knows the darknesses in the lives and hearts of those who are supposed to care for him.

Dominic loves to go up to the belfry to play the bells (workable properties on stage), which Artie allows him to do. On one occasion, however, Dominic causes trouble when instead of a standard hymn he rings out a Rolling Stones number, "I Can't Get No Satisfaction". It is the one occasion when Fr Pat loses his temper, as if his own position in the community has been undermined. Dominic's choice of tune, however, forms a keynote not just to *Belfry* but indeed for all of the trilogy. The characters can get no "satisfaction", although yearning for it in many forms. Dominic further expands on this need. He describes a trip which the school arranged to a hotel to hear a comedian: "My job here today, says he, is to make you people happy" (*Trilogy*: 177). Dominic decides that when he grows up he too will make people happy, and he describes how:

Easy. I'll get them all in a big room, right. And I'll say to them, 'My job is to make you people happy. What do yez want?' And when they tell me what they want I'll give it to them and I'll say to them, 'Now are yez happy?' And when they say yes I'll give them all what they want again. I'll do that about ten times boy. I'm not coddin' yeh I'll sicken them all so I will. They'll never want to be happy again (*Trilogy:* 177).

If we take Dominic's voice to be, paradoxically, the voice of sanity in the play, we can conclude that Roche is saying that happiness in the popular sense of the word is an illusion. His plays are less soft-centred than may at first appear. One may contrast, of course, the politically concerned playwrights in Britain since the time of Osborne, and by such a standard find Roche lacking in political attack. Howard Brenton, after all, entitled one of his plays *Weapons of Happiness* (1976), and he has made no secret of his belief that drama should indeed be a weapon (See Brenton: 1981, 85-97). Roche, on the other hand, does not regard drama as instrumental for social change, or as a weapon of happiness: "I worry about the vulgarity of political banner waving" (Woolgar: 1992, 9). *Belfry*, like its two predecessors in *The Wexford Trilogy*, makes its points in nonpolitical terms, but it would be foolish to deflect the social and political implications of all three plays.

Indeed, to say that Roche is not overtly a political playwright is to say that he is in tune with contemporary Irish dramatists. Apart from Frank McGuinness, Michael Harding and, more recently, Gary Mitchell, playwrights in Ireland today are cultivating a style of drama which turns away from specific problems, such as Northern Ireland. Young writers in particular, Sebastian Barry, Dermot Bolger, Declan Hughes, Paul Mercier, Marina Carr, Jim Nolan, are mining material which avoids directly topical or political issues. What interests them is the confusion in which they find themselves emotionally and culturally. They shy away from politics as from a pit that has ensnared the past generation of writers. If the young writers address topical questions it is in terms of satire only, as Gerry Stembridge packed out the Project with his sendup of the abortion debate, *Love Child* (1992) and his irreverent hunting of sacred elephants in *The Gay Detective* (1996). Mostly, this current generation of playwrights is bored stiff with Mother Machree, Kathleen Ní Houlihan, her four green fields and all the rest of it. Their appeal is to audiences, equally young and disaffected, who can respond to a search for new ways of regarding experience, far from the religious orthodoxies and political concerns of their parents. In turning inward on their own sense of being lost and betrayed, contemporary dramatists are creating new narratives of Ireland's shifting place in the world.

Although slightly older than the latest crop of successful writers, Roche is part of this new movement in Irish drama. *The Wexford Trilogy* encapsulates new attempts to define a sense of place, to define freedom and identity yet again, in terms divorced from those used by Friel, Murphy, Kilroy and others. Technically, Roche's plays display a rapid development towards masterly control over theme and stage. *Amphibians*, indeed, shows Roche continuing to improve in this regard: the controlling image is of evolution and its pains, the pains of growth towards some kind of maturity. Here and in the trilogy Roche acknowledges that he is dramatizing transition. There is certainly nothing utopian about his depiction of contemporary Ireland. Even though the plays all have a basis in popular sentiments, and revel in the non-intellectual, they focus firmly on existential and spiritual dislocation. Roche recognises and articulates the crisis of spirit Ireland is now undergoing. His interrogation of notions of heroism and freedom in a setting historically associated with the rising of 1798 and "the Boys of Wexford" has reverberations which extend far beyond local significance.

It is ironic, finally, to note Roche's own reaction to his public reception in Wexford in January 1993. "I grew up in spite of this town, not because of it. I received no encouragement in my writing. You love the place you come from, and hate it, because you have a stake in it" (Roche: 1993). In *The Wexford Trilogy* we have thus a quiet revaluation of our much-vaunted sense of place.

> * A version of this essay first appeared in *Etudes Irlandaises* and I would like to thank the editor of this journal, Jacqueline Genet, for the permission to include this article.

Works Cited:

Berresford Ellis, Peter, (1987), *A Dictionary of Irish Mythology* (London: Constable)

Brecht, Bertolt, (1963), *The Life of Galileo*, trans., Desmond I. Vesey (London: Methuen)

Brenton, Howard, (1981), "Petrol Bombs through the Proscenium Arch", in *New Theatre Voices of the Seventies*, ed., Simon Trussler (London and New York: Methuen)

Brook, Peter, (1988), *The Shifting Point: Forty Years of Theatrical Exploration 1946-1987* (London: Methuen)

Carpenter, Andrew, (1977), ed., *Place, Personality and the Irish Writer* (Gerrards Cross: Colin Smythe)

Heaney, Seamus, (1980), *Preoccupations: Selected Prose 1968-1978* (London and Boston: Faber and Faber)

Miller, Arthur, (1978), "The Family in Modern Drama", in *The Theater Essays of Arthur Miller*, ed., Robert A. Martin (New York: Viking/Penguin)

Nolan, Jim, (1991), *Moonshine* (Loughcrew, Oldcastle: Gallery Press)

Roche, Billy, (1986), *Tumbling Down* (Dublin: Wolfhound Press)

------ (1992), *The Wexford Trilogy: A Handful of Stars, Poor Beast in the Rain, Belfry* (London: Nick Hern Books)

------ (1993), Quoted by Paddy Woodworth, "Wexford Celebrates the Work of Local Playwright", *Irish Times*, 11 January

Woolgar, Claudia, (1992), "Tumbling Down to London: Claudia Woolgar talks to Billy Roche about his Plays", *Theatre Ireland*, 29 Autumn, 6-9

The Poetic Theatre of Sebastian Barry

Ger Fitzgibbon

A short time after the very difficult tour of his play *Madam Macadam's Travelling Theatre*, the playwright Tom Kilroy, speaking at a symposium on Irish theatre, talked very movingly about the sense of obligation he felt to mediate to a new Ireland the imaginative reality of the Ireland in which he had grown up, to retrieve the past without violating it. The *pietas* he invoked was nothing to do with nostalgia. For writers of his generation, he argued, it was both a duty and a puzzle, for they had grown up in a country utterly different from the one they now found themselves living in. They were, in a real sense, *émigrés* in their own land.

At first glance, Sebastian Barry's work radiates some of those same impulses to retrieve a lost past, picking out figures who are representative of the more occluded or wayward areas of Irish social and political history, and offering them for contemplation to the young cubs of the Celtic Tiger. But the correspondence with Kilroy's mission is superficial. Barry is about thirty years younger than Kilroy, Murphy or Friel; and his childhood Ireland is a very different place, historically, socially and personally, from theirs. In fact his historical pieces draw their matter not from the Ireland of his own childhood but the Ireland of his grandparents or great-grandparents. *Prayers of Sherkin* (first produced in 1990) is set in 1899-1900; *The Only True History of Lizzie Finn* is in the 1890s; *White Woman Street*, set in Ohio, is given a precise date reference of 1916 but constantly harks back to earlier times — to the Indian Wars and even the Irish Famine; the present time of *Steward of Christendom* is the 1930s, and much of the action reflects the 1920s or much earlier. It is not, however, only the playwright who is looking over his shoulder, but the key characters also. Thomas Dunne, John Hawke, Trooper, Mo, Mick and Josey all characteristically spend their time glancing back, recounting, re-living their own story. That Barry claims that the material for many of his plays is based on a kind of familial archaeology, drawn from his own ancestral connections, does not affect the fact that in the writing he is reincorporating these lost figures and what they represent into Irish history.

While atypical in many respects, Barry's first major play, *Boss Grady's Boys* (produced in 1988) set down a number of markers regarding what were to be his characteristic tone and style of theatre. The setting is contemporary, the central characters two old brothers who live on a hill farm on the Cork-Kerry border. Yet the play carefully avoids the issues and conflicts native to the *genre* of the Abbey Play, and concentrates instead on the slow revelation of the texture of the characters' day-to-day existence, their history and their darkening future. The play was partly prompted by specific contemporary incidents involving attacks on old farmers living in isolation. Yet the isolated and decaying world his characters inhabit, their age and apprehension and their characteristic backward glance seem to suggest that they belong to an earlier period — that they are a kind of historical anomaly. There is another, less melodramatic, though more relentless, threat to the two brothers, however. Josey, the older brother, is a little simple, and Mick is aware that old age is gathering like darkness around them: "With all my red heart I wish he might not survive me alone in the house. And yet I wish I might not survive him. I will not live here with his shadow and our father's shadow (*BG*: 88). The innocence of Josey will not protect him. As Mick, the surrogate parent entering into the cowboy world of Josey's films, ironically observes: "We're surrounded. The Indians. You never see them, they shoot from behind boulders" (*BG*: 120).

Through a language rich in image and elegaic tone and a dramaturgy that moves easily between times past and present, memory and fantasy, Barry generates a form of theatre that has the aimless fluency of dream. Yet it is not a theatre of pathos or nostalgic escape. When Josey confesses to feeling miserable, Mick responds with a Beckettian 'Much the same then' (*BG*: 119). And whatever the present threats to their lives, there is no sentimentalisation of the past, with its threatening shadow of Boss Grady, their father. The very mattress on the bed the brothers share has been shaped by the bodies of their parents, so that when Mick thinks of his father and murmurs "I sleep in his dip" (*BG*: 103) he seems to sum up not just something of the relationship between the two men, but also the power of the unchangeable past as a determinant of their whole existence. Untroubled by the urgency of plot or argument, then, the play offers moment after moment of insight into the lives of these specific characters and into the dimension of a forgotten social history they represent.

The initial impressions created by *Boss Grady's Boys* seemed at first to be confirmed by the reaction to Barry's second play for the Abbey, *Prayers of Sherkin*, which opened in November 1990. The bones of the play are to be found in the title piece of Barry's 1989 collection of poems, *Fanny Hawke Goes to the Mainland Forever*. Fanny Hawke is a young woman living with her family — part of a small and dwindling religious sect — in Amish-like simplicity on Sherkin Island off the West Cork coast. They are gentle, spiritual and hard-working people, wary of the distractions and enticements of the outside world, and variously described by other characters as visionaries, millenarians and Quakers.

> **PATRICK**: Millenarians? Hat-makers?
> **MEG**: No, no, that's milliners, Mr Kirwin (*PS*: 40).

On one level, then the play tells the story of how Fanny, the only young woman in the community, meets with a Catholic man, Patrick Kirwin, and makes the decision to leave her family and go to the mainland to marry him. While this play clearly had a more decisive story-line than the earlier work, the poetic style which evoked the texture and rhythm of the pre-industrial lives of this innocent and gentle group of people gave rise to two critical responses. The first was that the very strength of Barry's lyrical language seemed to extinguish the play's dramatic conflict; the second centred on what significance there might be in this sentimental story of a young woman leaving home.

It would be easy to see *Prayers of Sherkin,* underneath its starched collars and bible reading, as yet another Irish play about growing up and going away: about the enclosing pressure of families, and the opposing force of the individual's struggle to assert his/her emotional, economic and biological drives towards independence and autonomy. Fanny's departure certainly marks a crucial transition for her, even though it is a transition from daughter to wife. Her departure is paradoxically made more difficult by the gentleness and decency of the family she is leaving. They may be implacably committed to their religious vision but they are neither harsh nor dismissive. They accept that, although it is based on "kindness, family and love", theirs is a "bitter creed". To regard this as just another family story, however, would be to miss the point. The Hawkes are part of a group of families who, some generations earlier, had been led by a visionary to await on Sherkin Island the coming of the New Jerusalem. Because of their elected isolation, the community has now dwindled to a single household: a father (John Hawke, a candle maker), two grown children (Fanny and Jesse) and two ageing aunts. As Fanny is fully aware, therefore, her departure is more than just an emotional matter; it means an effective end to the families' hopes, the renunciation of the belief that has guided them. According to the articles of their faith, whoever leaves the island must be "outcast and outlaw, and shunned of the tribe" (*PS*: 55). This consciousness of the irrevocability of his daughter's decision and its implications lends a peculiar weight to John Hawke's words to Fanny: "The four doors of the island are open. Walk away out if you wish or must. Ah, you could not return from such a voyage, but it would be a true voyage and your own" (*PS*: 37).

But because Barry is a poet as well as a dramatist, his meanings lie in the imagery as much as in the argument of the play. John Hawke's candle-making is not mere local colour, it is an image of light in the midst of darkness, of tremulous faith in a stormy universe, Fanny's final journey acquires other similar overtones. As the final stage directions indicate, she is literally carried by boat from the light of John Hawke's lamp on Sherkin Island to Patrick Kirwin's welcoming lamp on Baltimore pier. As the linguistic and theatrical imagery of the play make it clear, therefore, the essence of the matter is neither the usual separation anxiety of the Irish family drama, nor Fanny's rebellion against the religious belief of an older generation; it is the growing affront this absolutism offers to her commonsense and her awareness of the world and her own needs. Fanny's step from island to mainland is a step from one view of the world to another, from the transcendent to the contingent, and is only one stage of a dialectic that shapes and unifies the play.

Through the density and coherence of the imagery he deploys, Barry extends the implications and resonances of the story. Jesse Hawke, the odd son who talks of fossils in the rocks, the age of the earth and the casual resemblance of the skeleton of a pig to that of a man, ushers into the play the shadow of Darwinism, with all its implications for religious fundamentalism. The crisis of conflicting knowledges that had grown through the nineteenth century is now lapping against the shores of Sherkin Island. Jesse's re-reading of the signs of the material world points forward to twentieth century revisions of our understanding of time, human history, religion and the relation of humankind to the universe it inhabits. On the imagistic level, the wonderful figure of Patrick Kirwin the lithographer is even more ambivalent. His account of his former work illustrating newspapers touches the play with a consciousness of a violent, urban world of modern mass communication, a world Patrick wants to leave behind. He talks with wonder of the fossils trapped in his lithographer's stone, yet he inscribes onto it the images of the modern world. The primeval images fossilised in the stone and the diurnal inscription covering them offers a startling image of the relation of human to geological time. One might even suggest that the duality of those images in stone is part of a wider commentary the play offers on the nature of history: history as vision (John Hawke), as progressive revelation and reassessment (Jesse), and as successive layers of inscription (Kirwin). This attention to density and detail gives the play its intellectual complexity and imaginative coherence. By occluding the characters' private feelings and containing them within the austerity and simplicity of a particular code of behaviour, Barry is in danger of smothering the emotional life of the drama. But through his imagery he broadens out the meaning of the play and shifts the focus to different kinds of migration — from one community to another, from one vision to another. Fanny's departure is not merely a capitulation to the charms of her unlikely suitor, it is part of an explicit recognition that her community is trapped by the internal dynamics of its own position, that the members are caught between an imperative of their faith — to preserve their separateness and 'abide' the coming of the Shining City — and the logic of natural process which has led them into a generational cul-de-sac. The lyrical Utopianism of their vision, their chasteness of style and honesty of toil does nothing to assuage that contradiction or avert its consequences. As a community, they therefore face a crisis of extinction or absorption.

As the densely patterned structure of the play makes clear, this is a play about the transition between visions, states of consciousness, views of the world and of human destiny. It is an exploration of what it might mean to try to live within an absolute and self-denying religious vision in the face of the contingencies of the larger, changing secular world, and an exploration of what forces animate and inhibit the transition from one to the other. The posture of the play in relation to this process seems at first to be ambivalent. It lingers over the images of the Sherkin community as an integrated, childlike, unproblematic past where work is pleasure and fulfilment and where lives of frugal comfort, permeated by intimations of immortality, are conducted with calm and wisdom. But for every image of happy integration, there is a flicker of change, frustration, of the inherent contradiction of such a life. When John Hawke is told about the siege of Mafeking (city of stones) he may not know or want to know what it means, but that does not prevent the wheel of history from turning. Ultimately the play suggests that to turn one's back on the changing and contingent nature of the world is a kind of death, but in its serious and sympathetic exploration of the human losses and gains in Fanny Hawke's decision, the play is also intimately connected with larger issues in contemporary Irish social culture, a culture which, on many levels, has been negotiating just such a transition.

At first glance, *White Woman Street* (first produced 1992) is a radically new departure in Barry's work as it is set in Ohio and features an unlikely, multinational gang of outlaws led by an Irishman called Trooper and planning a train robbery. Yet the longing for a spiritual home that animates *Prayers of Sherkin* is transformed in *White Woman Street* to a longing for its emotional equivalent. All the characters share this desire for a point of stillness and security. While the men are outlaws, there is nothing of the Hollywood danger and romance about them. They are homeless drifters who have slid to the outer edges of their society but who yet retain something of the quality of tarnished knights errant. Mo, the gentlest of them, has exiled himself from his own Amish community because he sees himself as too venal and violent; Blakely is a displaced Lincolnshire man; Trooper has distant memories of a hard childhood in Sligo and the army he has now run away from. The focus of their longing, the solution to their problems, becomes the Gold Train which Trooper remembers passing through the town of White Woman Street and which they plan to rob. This will allow them to end their roving days and find contentment, a home of the heart. The play, then, is shaped by their quest to meet this train that thunders towards them, shining, out of the darkness.

For Trooper a particular private journey underlies this quest, his journey back to White Woman Street to confront a past that has haunted him for thirty years:

> I aim to head for home again and rest a local man in Sligo. But I can't go till peace is made, till I stand again in White Woman Street and beg a certain ghost for her good word.... At Easter, here, in Ohio (*WW*: 140).

In its characters and plotting the play draws upon the a-historical qualities of both the Western and its remote antecedent, the Medieval Romance. But Barry qualifies this timelessness by lightly reminding us in various ways of the specific historical forces of which his characters are both a product and a component: the genocidal Indian Wars in which Trooper was engaged; the great colonising cattle drives; the flood of men from Europe, Russia and Asia building canals, railroads, towns; the whole mercantile economy that swept across the land, reducing the Native Americans to the level of pests or consumable goods; the spectacle of hundreds of pathetic and dehumanised men flocking into the shanty towns in search of company, drink, women or 'a hint of home'. These casual references and images alert us to the doomed obsolescence of his characters, men whose labour, hunger and desperation built the society from which they are now excluded. On one level, then, the train is a memory and a myth, a beast they must slay to lay claim to its gold-hoard; on another it represents their last attempt to grapple with the onrushing inevitability of history, the future that will destroy them. The ludicrous, almost Quixotic, attempted train robbery with which the play concludes becomes a moment of cataclysm, a point of collapse of their universe.

The subject matter of *White Woman Street* is therefore less of a change than might at first appear, but the play does register a significant dramaturgical shift for Barry. In it he finds a way of reconciling the poetic and the dramatic. The dialogue of the play is fashioned from a combination of Hiberno-English, American English and fractured, non-native English, an invention that gives Barry licence to generate an idiosyncratic poetry for his characters. Ellipses and collapsed syntax constantly open up areas of music and metaphor within their speech:

> I know how them Irish are where Trooper come from. Savage they living. Han't got shoes. Han't got food most of them. Eating nettles and prayers I'll be bound. Lucky to have bones, Trooper! I seen Irish like that, holed up in the crevices of America just as cockroaches do... (*WW*: 159).

The self-conscious mannerism that is evident throughout *Prayers of Sherkin* is replaced by rough individualities of speech that are specific to each character, heightening the sense of disparate individuals attempting to find the basis for a shared culture, and symbolically echoing tne larger historical dialectic of emergent American identity. On the level of plot as well, Barry shows more theatrical cunning, for the story of Trooper's ghost — the real object of his personal quest — is carefully trailed through the narrative in fragments and glimpses. Attention is directed to the character's darkening sense of guilt and dread as he approaches the town; to the stories of the famous whore of White Woman Street and of her gruesome murder; and finally to his failure of nerve when the gang visit the hotel where she used to ply her trade. All point towards a deed of dreadful note the gentle and haunted Trooper may have committed. By building up the dread of Trooper and the apprehension of Mo, his loyal comrade, Barry builds dramatic tension. But his master-stroke is the moment of final revelation, when Trooper confesses to Mo what really happened:

> I didn't kill her like they said she was done, but I killed her just the same.... She were an Indian girl pretty as the dawn with emerald eyes like a wolf's and I bedded her. And I looks down after and that woman is bleeding the way a first-time woman does, and she not crying in her face but I see the thing worse than tears, that dry and fearful look. A lost look. Then fast as a wolf she dips down to take my cold English blade from my breeches belt, and dragged it flashing like a kingfisher across her throat.... Jesus of the world, I couldn't put her together again, Mo, she had a waterfall coming from her wound.... She just choked and died in front of me (*WW*: 177).

The relief at Trooper's relative innocence is replaced by the horror of the event that so starkly figures the exploitation and humiliation of the young Indian woman, and Trooper's awakened consciousness of a shame far deeper than the personal. It is as if one man has been doomed to see the guilt of a whole century. The play's latent meanings suddenly open out into a much wider historical and political vision. Through its structure, its poetry and its fable, *White Woman Street* becomes a more complete theatrical achievement, a more satisfying marriage of the poetic, the dramatic and the intellectually provocative than any play Barry had written before.

The Only True History of Lizzie Finn (premiered in Dublin, 1995) tells the story of how Robert Gibson, the war-traumatised son of a Protestant Big House family in West Kerry, comes to marry a music-hall singer and dancer, Lizzie Finn, and take her back to Kerry with him. For Gibson's strait-laced mother it is bad enough that he married a theatre performer, worse that Lizzie was the daughter of an itinerant singer, but worst of all is the unbearable discovery that her third son changed sides in the Boer

War, turning against the cause that had pointlessly sacrificed two of his brothers. Typically, the play is full of witty cross-references to the world of *White Woman Street*, but here the American West is seen as a place of escape and fantasy: the hero's reading of *The Only True History of Frank James*, the American outlaw, is referenced in Barry's title; the conquest and plunder of the West has become Buffalo Bill's Wild West Show; and Lizzie Finn shares a stage with an impressionist who imitates the birdcalls of Ohio. But the colonial realities that underlie the myth of the Wild West are more broadly addressed here. Through the diverse worlds of Robert, Lizzie and Lucinda (Robert's mother), Barry draws together into one story several different phases of empire. Robert's crisis of allegiance in the Boer War signals the turning tide of imperialism in Africa. The effect of that change on Lucinda reflects the accelerating disintegration and decline of the Ascendancy class in Ireland. Lizzie's impoverished background and successful return to her birthplace to take possession of the Big House may serve to remind us of the imminent shift in Irish political power, but the discomfort and ambivalence of that repossession also signal its complexity. And this process itself finds echoes in the paradoxes of the Wild West Show, bringing back to Europe the emblems of conquest won by its own outcasts.

Perhaps the strongest linkage with the earlier plays, however, is the restless search for home that drives Robert and Lizzie. It is this search that has led them both back to Corcaguiney after wide travels and adventures. When Lucinda, ostracised by her own community because of Robert's actions, is barred from entering the Church, her "refuge", she no longer has a home: she walks into the sea and drowns. Robert and Lizzie, in the Big House, face a future which will see them "grow old and curmudgeonly and... fill the house with scalded-looking brats and love them hugely" (*LF*: 64). But as Lizzie points out, for her, home is "where Robert is" (*LF*: 64). At the end of the play she and Robert decide to leave Corcaguiney and start again, basing themselves in her world rather than his: they head for the exotic life of Cork with its new music-hall.

Although all of Barry's plays are private — in the sense that they concern individuals and families simply trying to get on with their own lives, satisfy their own emotional needs, — and although his characters are all idiosyncratic and individual, his plays frequently direct our attention towards the historical contexts and political and economic forces that make and unmake his characters' lives. Whether it is the slow attrition of the subsistence farm, the hungry advance of an American state or the gentile collapse of the Anglo-Irish Ascendancy, history, in one form or another, cuts into and through the plays. The presence of public history is, however, most palpable in *Steward of Christendom* (first produced in 1995). Through half-senile hallucinations, dreams and memories we are conducted through a progressive revelation of the life and times of

Thomas Dunne, former Chief Superintendent of the Dublin Metropolitan Police, a Catholic and Loyalist.

The key moment to which the play keeps returning is Dunne's formal handing over of Dublin Castle to the representative of the new power, Michael Collins. But while, in *Boss Grady's Boys*, Mick's recollected encounter with Collins radiates the hopes of a new beginning, for Thomas the meeting signifies capitulation and defeat. Overnight he has become the enemy of the state; the old regime and all its servants are passing and Thomas is left, as mad as Lear, clinging to the rags of his humanity in a County Home. Thus the play explores the brutal simplicities of the time. When Dolly, the young and thoughtless daughter, is confronted by a lady on a tram she finds herself shocked into political consciousness: "... she said we were Jezebels and should have our heads shaved and be whipped for following the Tommies" (*SC:* 97). Thomas' later fantasies of "fellas roaming the countryside seeking out the maiming of this man and the death of that man" carry an uncomfortable ring of a truth not entirely belonging to the remote past.

Historical plays are always about the present as well as the past. By putting his central character in a brutal County Home, Barry consciously touches an area of contemporary social sensitivity regarding the use of institutions to quarantine those who do not fit in to the family or the society. In the social reality of the new Free State with its simple binary divisions — Irish and British, Catholic and Protestant, Nationalist and Unionist — Thomas' position no longer makes sense. He is an anomaly and must be removed from power and from history. Even more painfully, that marginalisation by the state is replicated by his own family: he no longer fits their image of family life and respectability and so is sequestered in a home, locked in with his ghosts. Thus is social and family history written.

Sebastian Barry has often claimed that most of his source material lies in his own extended family history and the playful linkages and family resemblances between one play and another reinforce that claim. The Ohio of *White Woman Street* echoes through *Lizzie Finn*; the music-hall world towards which Fanny Hawke is drawn at the end of *Prayers of Sherkin* is the same one Lizzie Finn abandons and returns to; Thomas Dunne's recollections of boyhood on a small farm reprise aspects of the remembered world of Mick and Josey in *Boss Grady's Boys*. In *Our Lady of Sligo* Barry takes this process several steps further. In his own introduction to the published play he identifies the protagonist as his grandmother, "the darkest person I have ever written about", and also confesses that he had been trying to write the play for over ten years. But he also takes the bold step of writing what is almost a gender-reversed version of *Steward of Christendom*. The protagonist is once again in a hospital bed, drifting towards death and wandering in consciousness between present and past, fact and fantasy. Barry uses the memories, nightmares and deliberations of Mai O'Hara, her husband Jack and their daughter Joannie, an aspiring actress, less to explore the present-time events of the play than to revisit key moments of the characters' earlier lives, played out in the shifting cultural and political landscape of the 1930s. Jack and Mai are a generation later than Thomas Dunne, a generation of comfortable, middle-class, educated Home Rule Catholics, who saw the new political conditions of the Free State as an opportunity to secure for themselves the social position, manners, and aspirations of the displaced Protestant professional classes. As Jack puts it, it was a time with "... the civil war settled more or less, a sense of glamour and possibility, the dances in from America, nothing to stop you, you know, from flourishing" (*LS*: 22). But while her husband Jack goes to the colonies, first as a civilian engineer, then as a soldier, Mai is left to rot at home, where the lure and promise of new freedoms shrivel up and die in the economic and cultural isolationism of the thirties and forties: "the sheer boredom... the sheer provincial death-grip... the mewling, pulling death-grip of de Valera and all his lousy crew" (*LS*: 24).

But, even though its characters touch and are touched by their times, social history is not what *Our Lady of Sligo* is about. At its core it is the story of a wild and turbulent marriage, of partners who had loved each other passionately but have no way of co-existing, of their drinking bouts that begin as camaraderie but become a form of mutually assured destruction. As Mai bleakly recalls: "I became the devil in my own house, and the soul was gone out of me and my child was afraid of me" (*LS*: 34). This is the heart and soul of Barry's play, the recreation of a highly individual, complex and vibrant couple whose slide into anger, betrayal, violence and recrimination acquires an almost classical tragic force — a meeting of hubris and fate, of self-will and malign chance. Many of Barry's characters are victims, characters at the mercy of events rather than controlling them. Mai and Jack are among the most individual and unattractive that he has created, precisely because they have no such defence. They are, in their way, in charge of their lives. What rescues them dramatically is not gentleness, charm or wit but their very lack of decency, their full-blooded capacity to make a mess of their lives, to still feel passionately about the mess they have made and to face heart-breaking truths about themselves. In the main, Mai is the destructive force and Jack the one who vainly tries to hold things together, but when some childrens' graves in Glasnevin remind Jack of his young son's death, he is almost overwhelmed by the realisation of his own role in the story of their lives:

> I was saying to you that it was your fault, that the drinking had killed our boy. As if somehow I was a separate being, a shining

being in your company.... I felt the force of my evil and it was like a savage hand on my heart... (*LS*: 62).

Looking at the graves and thinking about the grief of parents forces him into an even more terrible recognition, of the other life they had lost:

> ... to lose our son was awful enough without having to be the people we were in the aftermath, Jack and Mai in all their dreadful misery.... It was as if I were a just man myself and we were burying Colin there and you by my side and we were good people,... going back eventually to some normal household, where we would talk if we could and see each other right in the matter, if it could be done at all (*LS*: 62).

It is this realisation of the life they might have had that fills the end of the play with an almost Faustian longing for grace or redemption "that when we are both dead and gone, something might be winnowed out of the mess, a last suggestion of love, like the ring in the brack" (*LS*: 63). It is Barry's bleakest, darkest and most powerful play to date.

Sebastian Barry has written other works — poetry and novels — but it is the plays that are his most substantial and coherent literary achievement and it is as an unique voice in Irish theatre that his work is most important. It is clear that his drama is distinguished by considerable craft. As he has demonstrated so clearly, he has an ear for quirky and idiomatic speech which he can combine with a sophisticated capacity for poetic evocation. And the works that follow *Boss Grady's Boys* engage in a long, vigorous negotiation between the narrative and dramatic demands of theatre and the lyrical impulses of the poetic voice. At its simplest, the range of linguistic flavours he employs enrich the surface texture of his plays enormously, developing a progressively more individuated and muscular characterisation. But in many of his works the language itself carries the stamp of the truly accomplished dramatist: the rhythm, syntax, sound and texture of his writing resonates with the particularity of a specific character in a specific moment; it demands, provokes and rewards performance. He has not invented all this himself. He has learned it at the hands of other dramatic craftsmen, from Yeats and Beckett back to Sophocles. Most of all, from Shakespeare, he has found how imagery in speech and action can explore and extend the resonance and richness of the worlds he creates.

But craft is not enough without vision. It is Barry's capacity to find "the ring in the brack" that drives these plays. Time and again, he takes the most unpromising characters and situations and reveals within them the remarkable and the memorable. This is what allows the plays to scatter their meanings far beyond their obvious or superficial import so that they move the mind as well as the heart. Read and re-read, they grow into 'new compositions of thinking and feeling' that engage us imaginatively with the stories of particular characters' lives and intellectually with the symbolic and philosophical shadows that their stories cast. As Mr Moore, the boatman from *Prayers of Sherkin* might say, these are works to be puzzled out "Partly by philosophy. Partly by daydreams" (*PS*: 22).

Works Cited:

Sebastian Barry, (1989), *Fanny Hawke Goes to the Mainland Forever* (Dublin: Raven Arts)
------ (1991), *Prayers of Sherkin* and *Boss Grady's Boys* (London: Methuen)
------ (1995), *The Only True History of Lizzie Finn, The Steward of Christendom* and *White Woman Street* (London: Methuen)
------ (1998), *Our Lady of Sligo* (London: Methuen)

The Imagination of Women's Reality: Christina Reid and Marina Carr

Riana O'Dwyer

In an article published in 1991, Eileen Kearney described the frustrations of investigating the achievements of dramatists who are women. A major problem was the lack of published material, epitomised by the response of staff in a leading Dublin bookshop: "Women do not write plays" (Kearney: 1991, 225). Kearney compiled a list, which she describes as incomplete, of seventy-four twentieth-century Irish women who did write plays, and gave details of twelve of them who were then writing both for stage and television. However a high proportion of the work discussed by Kearney had occurred in the nineteen-eighties, and it required the establishment of companies such as Charabanc (Belfast) and Glasshouse (Dublin), dedicated to the production of work by women, to provide the opportunities. Glasshouse, indeed, produced a showcase production, entitled "There are no Irish Women Playwrights" (1993) to make that very point.

Explanations for this situation are as complex as the explanations suggested for the shortage of women in politics, in top management, in the upper levels of the law and medicine. While the slow pace of change in cultural and role expectations is partly responsible, some aspects of the established theatre may have militated against the acceptance of women's plays. This essay will first consider the position of women in Irish theatre in the nineteen-eighties and will then go on to discuss the representation of women's reality in the work of Christina Reid and Marina Carr.

In the 1970s and 1980s, women's plays in the Republic of Ireland have tended to be produced on the margins of the mainstream theatre, assisted by the work of women directors such as Garry Hynes in Druid (Galway), Lynne Parker in Rough Magic at the Project (Dublin), Mary-Elizabeth Burke-Kennedy in Storyteller's Theatre (Dublin) as well as by the all-woman companies Charabanc and Glasshouse. In Northern Ireland, the pressures of living in an on-going situation of violence brought a rush of dramatic response from women in the 1980s, at approximately the same time that the Field Day Theatre Company, with its all-male directorate, was engaged in exploring the political perspectives. The early plays produced by Field Day were concerned with the creation of an imaginative "Fifth Province" in which the traditional political polarities could be interrogated, often in a symbolic and indirect way. Many of the women's plays, however, used theatrical realism to explore the roles allocated to women within the family and the workplace, exposing the consequences of deep-seated and persistent gender divisions. Charabanc's first play, *Lay Up Your Ends*, dealing with the Belfast linen-mill workers strike of 1911, provoked the response from reviewers that it was strange to see all women on the stage, while Frank McGuinness' play *Observe the Sons of Ulster Marching Towards the Somme*, touring with an all-male cast at about the same time, did not provoke any similar comments (White: 1989, 35). All-male societies, particularly military ones, were not seen as extraordinary, were even considered the norm.

Victoria White, taking stock in an important article in *Theatre Ireland* in 1989, was concerned with the under-representation of women in the theatrical decision-making process, pointing to the paucity of women on the boards of the Arts Councils north and south, and on the boards of the Abbey, Gate and Lyric theatres. Yet, the Dublin theatre festival of 1988 was notable for its "rediscovery of women's stories and women's myths" (White: 1989, 34). White interviewed six of the most dynamic women who were then working in Irish theatre, and made the point that all the women she spoke to had founded their own companies: "these women have found their place in Irish theatre *despite* existing structures: (White: 1989, 34). These women were motivated by the need and desire to work, the opportunity to be involved at a decision-making level in theatre and to become directors. However, while gaining experience in the independent companies had provided opportunities to produce their own choice of plays and develop their own styles, those interviewed looked to a future in which "there will be no more plays by women about women because they are women". As Lynne Parker of Rough Magic said: "It will happen naturally. It's inevitable. The sex of the person will be a minor issue" (White: 1989, 35).

In a special issue of *Theatre Ireland*, Winter 1993, edited by Victoria White, she noted the range of opinion expressed by women themselves about the difficulties faced by them as actors, directors and writers for the theatre: "There is strident demand for change from some, and from others, a concern that focusing on women as a separate case ghettoises them" (White: 1993 Editorial, 2). Several contributors to the special issue addressed the question of difference as an explanation for the marginalisation of plays by women. Kathleen Quinn suggested that "women dramatists do share a common voice, a perspective that focuses on individuals rather than societies, and on ways in which these individuals can connect.... Because their voices differ from those of men, however, their approaches may initially seem odd to those accustomed to male perspectives" (Quinn: 1993, 10). Anthony Roche made a related point in his book *Contemporary Irish Drama from Beckett to McGuinness*: "with the change of Friel, Murphy and others to strong female characters, the question must be asked: is this not a move by Irish male playwrights to appropriate and colonise the concerns of women in a feat of expert ventriloquism, a pre-emptive strike against the increasing number of women writing plays and having them staged"? (Roche: 1994, 286) Christopher Murray, discussing some earlier plays in *Twentieth Century Irish Drama: Mirror up to Nation*, also noted that "women were being represented in more courageous terms. In general, however, the empowerment of women in Irish drama was from a male point of view" (Murray: 1997, 172).

This resulted in the representation of idealised women in plays by men. Victoria White traced this tendency back to the foundation of the Irish Literary Theatre in 1898, but found that it emerged in a new version in plays by Tom Murphy, Frank McGuinness, Michael Harding, Sebastian Barry and Brian Friel: "The breakdown of communication between men and women has become a constant theme in our theatre.... There is implied in many of these works the idea that as a nation we would be whole if the sexes could learn how to be together" (White: 1993, 28). Even though these dramatists have written plays which show the world from a female perspective, "there is an element of the male search for wholeness, as the male playwright submerges his voice in the female voice" (White: 1993, 28). Since the audience and the critic have grown accustomed to the male projection of woman, the representation created by a female playwright was not always experienced as authentic. Caroline Williams, administrator of the Glasshouse Theatre Company, put the matter very forcibly in her contribution to the *Theatre Ireland* special issue: "One of the difficulties in this area is that we are so used to men's images of men, and men's images of women on the stage, that a play written by a woman is regularly criticised or rejected for not complying with these norms" (Williams: 1993, 6-7).

Another potential barrier addressed by Williams was the subject matter chosen by women for their plays, in which 'the issues they evoke are explored through strong central female characters'. Examples of issues included domestic violence, alcoholism, sexual abuse, political violence, disability, and sexuality. Williams gives examples of two reviews of a particular play: one by a man which felt the play was "limited in scope and appeal" and one by a woman who commented on its cathartic effect, and on "the total involvement of the audience in the lives of these women" (Williams: 1993, 7). Williams also commented on the experimental aspects of some of these plays, a potential barrier for theatre audiences and critics, as even established playwrights such as Tom Murphy had found to their cost (Williams: 1993, 8). The combination of harrowing subject matter and experimental production methods may have proved too much of an obstacle, narrowing the theatrical experience to an initiated audience, and excluding many. The chemistry between stage and audience is subtle and some companies choose to please a small discerning audience rather than aim for the mass-market. Most women theatrical practitioners, however, do not wish to operate on such a small and elitist scale.

Garry Hynes, who has been centrally involved in the development of scripts by women both in the Druid Theatre in Galway and during her tenure as Artistic Director in the Abbey Theatre in Dublin, has identified some limitations in the scripts she has read, seeing in them a division between public and private spheres: "I just sometimes long for a woman to write, please, on a broader, more public, more epic scale.... I'm talking about the scale of the work which tends to be small and tends to rely on a kind of easy naturalism. The act of theatre is a very public one and it's one where you have to collaborate very publicly with a very great number of people" (Harris Discussion Document, 1995). Hynes suggests that because theatre is a public, interactive process, women have more difficulty participating in it than in poetry or fiction writing. As there has been a gap in women's participation in the public life of Ireland, since the political activities of nationalism and the suffragette movement in the years before 1922, so, up to recently, there has been a gap in women's participation in the public venue of the theatre since that of Lady Gregory at the foundation of the Abbey and Teresa Deevy in the 1930s. Through the developments which have been outlined above, however, that situation has now begun to change, and some aspects of how women represent their own reality on stage will be explored through the work of Christina Reid and Marina Carr.

Though Christina Reid was born in 1942 and Marina Carr in 1964, making them a generation apart in age, they both began to have plays produced and come to public attention in the mid nineteen-eighties. Christina Reid was born and brought up in Belfast; Marina Carr near Tullamore, County Offaly. Reid got involved in theatre through winning the UTV drama award in 1980 and coming second in The Irish Times Women Playwrights Competition in 1982. Two of her plays were first produced by the Lyric Theatre in Belfast, the others by small independent companies, mostly in London. Marina Carr's early plays had independent productions or rehearsed readings in Dublin from 1989. Her more recent work has premiered at the National Theatre, either in the Peacock or the Abbey and has also been performed in London. The careers of Reid and Carr identify some routes to recognition in Irish theatre north and south, and the gradual opening of access to plays by women. They also offer interesting contrasts in terms of subject matter, attitude to women's roles and expectations, and use of theatrical resources.

Christina Reid is very explicit about exploring the northern Protestant experience in Belfast and its impact on daily life. As David Grant has pointed out: "towards the end of the decade there seemed to be a flowering of 'Troubles Drama' with writers like Graham Reid, Christina Reid and Martin Lynch at last providing perceptive and thoughtful analyses of the political situation from a wider social and cultural perspective" (Grant: 1990, xi). Her characters are working class, whether employed or unemployed, and she includes the experience of Catholic working class people also, as observed from the Protestant house next door. The impact of the Troubles on the close-knit families of the terraced streets of Belfast is one aspect of her theatre, as is also the impact of violence on the structure of family life, undisturbed in its assumptions and its gender divisions for so long. The device of exploring several generations of one family within one play allows the changes wrought by time and the troubles to be explored, as in *Tea in a China Cup* (1983) and *The Belle of the Belfast City* (1989). The special problems of families who have relatives imprisoned for terrorist offences in the Maze Prison is the subject of *Did you hear the one about the Irishman?* (which won the UTV drama award in 1980 and received a full performance in 1987). *Joyriders* (1986) deals with a group of young offenders on a Youth Training Scheme in Belfast, while a sequel, *Clowns* (1996), concerns the same group of people eight years later, on the eve of the IRA cease-fire. Belfast is the scene for all these plays, and the central period covered is from 1972 to 1994, the years of the Troubles.

Women are central to *Tea in a China Cup* (1983), the play which most clearly celebrates and questions the values of traditional female roles within family structures. Reid explores the absolute division of roles in a working class Belfast household over three generations, from 1939 to 1972. Three generations of men have been soldiers in the British Army: in the First World War, the Second World War and now in partitioned Cyprus. Sarah is daughter, sister and mother to these three generations. While the men go to war, win medals and get killed or injured, the women stay at home, keep the family together, and bring up the children. The difference between being poor and being respectable is the possession of a good set of china. Being house proud and having china is what distinguishes the Protestant women from the Catholic women, until these distinctions break down under the pressure of poverty. In the present, 1972, Sarah is dying of cancer, and her daughter Beth is nursing her, and trying to make sense of the values by which Sarah lived, which are represented for both of them by the china tea-set. The solidarity of loyalism and perceived Protestant values helped Sarah through a hard life, and meant that "no matter how poor we are, child, we work hard and keep ourselves and our homes clean and respectable, and we always have a bit of fine bone china and good table linen by us" (*TC*: 14). Sarah is also sustained by the wish to hear the drums on the Twelfth of July one more time. They represent pageantry and safety for her. Fittingly, she dies on the Twelfth, drinking tea from a Belleek tea cup, the finest porcelain made in Ulster. Sarah's death frees her daughter Beth to escape from the political straitjacket of loyalism and the gender straitjacket of her unhappy middle-class marriage. She does take a Belleek cup and saucer with her into her new life, however. The women of several generations sustain the families we see in this play, keeping the home-fires burning as the men engage in war, drinking and gambling. They accept this gender burden without question, as Beth says to her mother: "You, and all the other women like you. No matter what a man does wrong it's always some woman's fault, isn't it"? (*TC:* 21)

Christina Reid has paid tribute to the indomitable aspect of women through her drama, saying that as a child she was "constantly in the company of women and children. It made me realise how ageless women are, they can talk like young girls at any age, and on their own are tremendously uninhibited and bawdy – a side that they would never show to men" (quoted in Roche: 1994, 234). This is the aspect of women which is celebrated in *The Belle of the Belfast City* (1989) through Dolly, a music-hall star and the matriarch of an extended family. The closeness of family loyalty is tested by the combination of racism and sectarianism at a rally to protest against the Anglo-Irish Agreement in 1986. Dolly's daughter Vi places family solidarity above everything else: "family always comes first with Vi" (*BB:* 25), but politics and extremism put this family loyalty, as well as the political bonds of loyalism, to the test. Jack, who is Dolly's nephew and a Loyalist politician, is also rabidly misogynist: "Women! Women! Temptation! Deception! You're the instruments of the devil! The root of all evil"! (*BB:* 23) His sister Janet, trapped in a celibate marriage, says "They say there are no women in Ireland. Only mothers and sisters and wives" (*BB:* 27), and the central dilemma in the play is how women can escape from the limitations of such roles. The stroke which immobilises the lively Dolly, signals the ending of tight family ties. The women, such as Janet, Rose and Belle, who place a high value on personal freedom, will move to England to live. The hard-liners, who cling to traditional political and family values, will remain. The waste represented by such an outcome is expressed by the lines of the ballad with which the play ends:

> It's to hell with the future and live in the past
> May the Lord in his mercy be kind to Belfast (*BB:* 62).

Did you hear the one about the Irishman? (1989) continues to combine the representation of political challenges by means of family complications. Two families, one Protestant, one Catholic, are connected by marriage and divided by religion. Both families have relatives in the Maze Prison, where paramilitary prisoners are confined. The irony of this situation is that the visitors' waiting room at the Maze thus becomes the only location "where the Prods and the Fenians meet on common ground.…. Where else in Northern Ireland can a Provie wife and a UDA wife take a long look at each other and realise that they're both on board the same sinking ship. Common ground. Common enemy. And there's nothing like a common enemy for resolving a family feud" (*DI*: 72-73). In the case of this play, the family feud is not resolved but ends, as did the feud between the Montagues and Capulets, with the death of the young lovers Allison and Brian.

Such an explicit equation of public politics with family politics is central to Reid's exploration of the ironies of the Troubles, even when she does not use a family setting, as in the case of *Joyriders* (1986) and *Clowns* (1996). The idea for this play came to Reid when she was writer-in-residence at the Lyric in 1983-84 and met just such a group of teenagers when they came to see *The Shadow of a Gunman* (Murray: 1997, 191). Christopher Murray has pointed out the influence of the plays of Sean O'Casey on playwrights in the north of Ireland: "what O'Casey's plays actually do is to highlight, through comedy and ironic juxtaposition, the absurdity as well as the horror of war. That viewpoint, together with O'Casey's technical ability to make audiences see behind political posturing, made him an excellent model for Northern dramatists" (Murray: 1997, 191). Christina Reid made excellent use of the insights and devices of O'Casey's plays, most specifically in *Joyriders*, where *The Shadow of a Gunman* is used "as an ironic frame of reference" (Murray: 1997, 191). The most important plot echo employed by Reid is that Maureen, like O'Casey's Minnie Powell, is killed. Maureen does not die to save a lover, however, as Minnie Powell did. Instead Maureen dies trying to save her madcap brother, whose care and protection she has taken on herself, assuming without question the woman's responsibility for the men in the family.

In *Clowns*, a sequel to this play, set on the eve of the IRA cease-fire of 1994, the survivors of the training scheme meet up again in a new shopping mall on the site of a former linen-mill, symbol of the contrast between the old and the new Belfast. There is literally a sense of laying old ghosts to rest, since Sandra, one of the group, has been haunted by the ghost of Maureen and by her memories of Belfast, even though she has gone to live in London. All the action takes place in the public space of the mall; the little terraces seem far away and forgotten. Molly, mother of one of the youngsters, is attending university. Arthur's facial scars have faded, and he no longer limps. Gaudy and brassy as the new arcade appears, with its romantic statue of a female mill worker and child, there is a sense of new beginnings, new opportunities, and an end to the restrictions placed on everybody, but especially on women, not very many years ago.

Christina Reid represents and celebrates a world in which traditional values, roles and expectations still have a place. There is a strong sense of family and of community, which sustained those who were within, and repelled those who were without. The women prided themselves on being strong and on keeping the family together. Under the stress of the Troubles, these sustaining certainties begin to crumble, and both the family bonds and the political allegiances are called into question. Reid's plays contain elements of celebration as well as questioning, however. She is clear on how the rituals of the Twelfth of July gave importance to women as well as men, so that the dying Sarah in *Tea in a China Cup* wants to hear the drums one more time before she goes. Having represented the sustaining aspects of such rituals, political and personal, however, Reid allows her plays to question them from a position of understanding and belonging. There is a sense that the plays speak from within the confines of both patriarchy and of political identification with the loyalist tradition. The strength which can derive from strong identity with community, both political and gender-based, is represented by the songs in *Belle* and by the Orange bands in *Tea in a China Cup*. However a critique also develops as the restrictions which are the price of solidarity are noted. As long as you remain within the tribe, and conform to its expectations, you will be supported, but step outside the invisible boundary and you forfeit the right to be so considered.

Marina Carr is a playwright of great complexity, identified by Christopher Murray as part of the *avant garde* in Irish theatre (Murray: 1997, 235). Her early plays, *Ullaloo* (1989) and *Low in the Dark* (1989), reject realism and are expressionistic and experimental. Anthony Roche identifies this as an influence from Samuel Beckett, and points out verbal echoes as well (Roche: 1994, 287-8). Her recent plays have been more conventional in their staging: houses and kitchens have featured as settings and also as symbolic places of detention. Moreover, Murray suggests that Carr's agenda is not a feminist one (Murray: 1997, 236). She is not concerned with the overthrow of patriarchy in any simplistic way, although she is interested in experimenting with gender boundaries. Thus in *Low in the Dark* the men as well as the women get pregnant, though all the pregnancies take place in a surrealistic world where babies multiply and dreams provide a greater sense of narrative than the "action".

In Carr's three most recent plays, the central conflict being explored is that between the role of mother and the role of lover. In each case motherhood as a female role is deconstructed: by neglect in *The Mai* (1994), by rejection in *Portia Coughlan* (1996) and by tragic transformation in *By the Bog of Cats* (1998). When the traditional mother's role is not performed, the children are neglected and the family falls apart. The events which lead to this catastrophe are traumatic and apparently inevitable in each play, in a manner reminiscent of Greek tragedy. The plays go beyond realism into a symbolic realm, where explanations are not to be found in common sense or psychology, but in mythic reference, poetic language, the presence of ghosts and the telling of stories.

The Mai is the central figure in the play which bears her name. She is principal in a school in the midlands, is married and has several children, one of whom, Millie, functions as a choric commentator throughout the play. The Mai's husband, a composer and cellist, has left home, and has been away for five years. In his absence The Mai has built a beautiful house beside a lake. She is part of an extended family of women: her grandmother, two aunts, two sisters and her daughter. However, when her husband returns, only he matters. The beautiful house is for him, not for her children, but he is a womaniser and heavy drinker and does not care for her. Grandma Fraochlán had also experienced an absorbing love in her life, for her husband the nine-fingered fisherman, and she alone understands the passion which torments The Mai: "There's two types a people in this worlt from whah I can gather, thim as puts their childer first an' thim as puts their lover first", she explains (*Mai*: 69-70). The narratives of Grandma Fraochlán's two elderly daughters, Agnes and Julie, as well as the commentary of The Mai's daughter Millie, make it clear that Grandma and The Mai put their lovers first: "Mebbe parents as is lovers is noh parents ah all, noh enough love left over" (*Mai*: 39).

When Robert leaves home again, The Mai leaves also, by walking into the lake beside her beautiful but desolate house. Before she goes, she says to Millie: "no one will ever understand how completely and utterly Robert is mine and I am his, no one — People think I've no pride, no dignity, to stay in a situation like this, but I can't think of one reason for going on without him" (*Mai*: 72). Robert presents a very negative image of a lover. He appears utterly self-centred, with no redeeming qualities, nothing which would ever have made him desirable. This makes the abnegation of The Mai all the more inexplicable. She is in the grip of an absolute passion, which cannot be assuaged by everyday consolations, and which eventually annihilates her.

A similar passion is evident in *Portia Coughlan*. Portia is thirty, ten years younger than The Mai, married to Raphael Coughlan and with young sons. Her passion however is not for Raphael. He tries to do his best in an ineffectual way by buying Portia a tasteless but expensive birthday present, while making clear his desire that she should shape up, stop drinking and look after his house and children. Portia, however, is indifferent to her husband and does no housework at all. Her passion is for her dead twin, Gabriel, who drowned when he was fifteen, but exists in the play as a ghost. Portia's desperation and sense of entrapment is evident. There is reference in the stage directions to the variable moods of Portia. Even her friend Stacia, the Cyclops of Coolinarney, confides to Aunt Maggie that Portia is not well. No ordinary advice, such as to leave her husband or seek medical treatment, no amount of drink or casual sex will cure her grief at the loss, fifteen years ago, of her twin. The difficulty for the audience is to empathise with a protagonist who is apparently bent on self-destruction. The difficulty for the dramatist is to engage sympathy for one who is apparently obsessed, when the negative consequences of such obsession are evident all around. In particular, Portia is afraid that she may hurt her children: "Ah'm afraid a' thim Raphael! Afraid whah ah may do ta thim! …Ya think ah don't wish ah could be a natural mother mindin' me children, playin' wud thim, doin' all tha things a mother be asposed to do"? (*PC*: 284) Portia does not harm her children, but is found drowned at the opening of Act II. She turned her pain upon herself, and the rest of the play tries to find reasons for her suffering.

Hester Swane, protagonist of *By the Bog of Cats*, does better as a mother than either The Mai or Portia, although she too is possessed by a grand passion, for Carthage Kilbride, her lover for fourteen years and the father of her little girl Josie. Hester and Josie are devoted to each other; they play games and have fun. There is no sense of neglect, as in *The Mai* and *Portia Coughlan*, but of deep love and affection. The grief which moves the play arises from a great wrong: Carthage has left Hester and is about to marry a rich young bride. The wedding feast is interrupted by the arrival of Hester, dressed in a wedding dress, but she is humiliated and leaves without any satisfaction saying: "I've swallyed all me pride over you. You're laving me no choice but a vicious war against ya" (*BC*: 57-8). Her retribution is indeed terrible, as she burns her house and sheds with live cattle in them belonging to Carthage. Finally, she kills her daughter Josie and herself, taking them both into the land of ghosts, which has an actual stage existence through the characters of the Ghost Fancier and the ghost of Hester's brother Joseph.

The dramatic representation of women swayed by uncontrollable emotions has a long history in drama, especially in the classical Greek drama. There, women were seen to be prone to exceptional emotions which could be very destructive, either for themselves or for others. Phaedra's uncontrollable passion for Hippolyte, and Medea's hatred of her children, became the subject for tragedy precisely because they were not amenable to the usual restraints of communal society. Antigone was seized with an obsession which could not be assuaged by an appeal to common sense or any humdrum set of standards. Portia's love for Gabriel has some parallels with Antigone's for Polynices, and her lack of bonding with her children has echoes of Medea, as has Hester's execution of Josie. In classic Greek drama, as observed by Aristotle, pity and terror were aroused because there seemed to be no way to control these emotions and the actions which grew out of them. They were frequently seen as curses sent by the gods. We are no nearer to understanding them today. These three plays by Marina Carr emerge from a colloquy with dark forces which still stir an audience more than rational argument can. For this, as Marina Carr has written, the writer must call on "the wisdom and circumspection needed when dealing with the dead or the past, with memory, knowledge – all necessary tools for the writer.... It's about the courage to sit down and face the ghosts and have a conversation with them. It's about going over to the other side and coming back with something, new, hopefully; gold, possibly" (Carr: 1998,191).

The women's reality imagined by Marina Carr is painful and terrible, but in its emotional force it stands with the most intense expressions of man's violent reality: the explosiveness of Eugene McCabe's *King of the Castle* (1964) or Tom Murphy's *A Whistle in the Dark* (1961). In the early sixties, when McCabe's and Murphy's plays were controversial, Irish drama was about to begin a great leap forward, shining a light on dark and hidden places of Irish male experience. In their different ways, Christina Reid and Marina Carr have continued this process: Reid with her exploration of the experience of women faced with the Troubles in the North of Ireland; Carr with her depiction of women living apparently humdrum lives in rural Ireland. In the work of both playwrights, the moulds of traditional family roles are broken: under the pressure of political events in the case of Reid and of unbearable personal suffering in the case of Carr. As Sue-Ellen Case has observed: "With the deconstruction of the forms of representation, and dialogue and modes of perception characteristic of patriarchal culture, the stage can be prepared for the entrance of the female subject, whose voice, sexuality and image have yet to be dramatised within the dominant culture" (Case: 1988, 132). Is it perhaps the case that the work of these two playwrights, and the other women whose work is also being performed in recent years, may herald a phase of development similar to that of the sixties, in which the female subject will enter and women's reality will at last be fully imagined on the Irish stage?

Works Cited:

Carr, Marina, (1990), *Low in the Dark* in *The Crack in the Emerald: New Irish Plays*. David Grant, ed., (London, Nick Herne Books). (New edition 1994.) (First performed by Crooked Sixpence Theatre Company at the Project Arts Centre, 1989.)

------ (1995), *The Mai* (Oldcastle, Co. Meath: Gallery Press) (First performed at the Peacock Theatre, Dublin in 1994.)

------ (1996), *Portia Coughlan* (London, Faber and Faber) and in *The Dazzling Dark: New Irish Plays.* Frank McGuinness, ed., (London, Faber and Faber, 1996). And revised edition: (Oldcastle, Co. Meath: Gallery Press, 1998). (First performed at Peacock Theatre, Dublin 1996 before transferring to the Royal Court, London.)

------ (1998), *By the Bog of Cats* (Oldcastle, Co. Meath: Gallery Press) (First performed at Abbey Theatre, Dublin in 1998.)

------ (1998), 'Dealing with the Dead' in *Irish University Review* 28,1 (Spring/Summer), 190-196

Case, Sue-Ellen, (1988), *Feminism and Theatre* (New York: Routledge)

Casey, Madeleine, (1996), 'Ghostly Trio' in British Association for Irish Studies Newsletter, 9 (Summer), 25-26 (Review of *Clowns, Portia Coughlan, Sons of Ulster*).

Coyle, Jane and Charabanc Theatre Company, (1989), 'Charabanc Motors On' in *Theatre Ireland* 18 (April-June), 41-42

------ (1993), 'Now we are ten' in *Theatre Ireland* 30 (Winter), 16-18

Delgado, Maria, (1997), 'Introduction' to *Plays I* by Christina Reid (London: Methuen)

Di Cenzo, Maria, (1993), 'Charabanc Theatre Company: Placing Women Center-Stage in Northern Ireland' *Theatre Journal*, 175-184

Etherton, Michael, (1989), *Contempory Irish Dramatists* (London: Macmillan)

Grant, David, 1990, 'Introduction' to *The Crack in the Emerald* (London: Nick Hern Books (New edition 1994))

Harris, Claudia, (1988), 'The martyr-wish in contemporary Irish dramatic literature' in *Cultural Contexts and Literary Idioms in Contemporary Irish Literature*, Michael Kenneally ed., (Gerrards Cross: Colin Smythe)

------ (1995), Moderator. 'Is Ireland a Matriarchy or not? The experience of Women as Theatre Artists'. Discussion document for ACIS-CAIS Belfast Conference.

Kearney, Eileen, (1991), 'Current Women's Voices in the Irish Theatre' in *Colby Quarterly* 27.4 (December), 225-232

Meaney, Helen, (1993), 'The State of Play' in *Theatre Ireland* 30 (Winter), 32-34

Murray, Christopher, (1997), *Twentieth Century Irish Drama: Mirror up to Nation* (Manchester: Manchester University Press)

Quinn, Kathleen, (1993), 'Silent Voices' in *Theatre Ireland* 30 (Winter), 9-11

Reid, Christina. (1997), *Plays I: Tea in a China Cup; Did you hear the One About the Irishman... ?; Joyriders; The Belle of the Belfast City; My Name, Shall I Tell You My Name?; Clowns*, with Introduction by Maria Delgado, (London: Methuen)

Roche, Anthony, (1994), *Contemporary Irish Drama: from Beckett to McGuinness* (Dublin: Gill and Macmillan)

White, Victoria, (1989), 'Towards Post-Feminism' in *Theatre Ireland* 18 (April-June), 33-35

------ (1993), 'Cathleen Ní Houlihan is not a Playwright' in *Theatre Ireland* 30 (Winter), 26-29

------ (1993), 'Editorial' in *Theatre Ireland* 30 (Winter), 2

Williams, Caroline, (1993), 'This is one for the Sisters' in *Theatre Ireland* 30 (Winter), 6-8

Dermot Bolger's Drama

Martine Pelletier

Dermot Bolger has proved an extraordinarily popular and prolific writer. He came to prominence in the late-80s with the novels *Nightshift* and the bestselling *The Journey Home* and now, at barely forty he has behind him an impressive body of work which includes poems, novels and plays. Recognition came in various forms and guises: his fiction is published by Penguin and Flamingo, he edited the *Picador Book of Contemporary Irish Fiction* in 1993, he has won several literary prizes and has a seat on the Arts Council. He is also the man and mind behind the highly successful collaborative novel entitled *Finbar's Hotel* (1997) with contributions by Bolger himself, O'Connor, Roddy Doyle, Hugo Hamilton, Colm Toibin, Anne Enright and Jennifer Johnston; a sequel, *Finbar's Hotel 2*, is due out shortly.

Not only has his own work reaped numerous rewards but the radical publishing house Raven Arts which he founded in 1977 helped and encouraged many new Irish writers. When the house folded in 1992 it had more than 140 titles on its catalogue, including work by Patrick McCabe, Sarah Berkeley and Eoin MacNamee, to name but a few. Since 1992 Bolger has been general editor of New Island Books and has gone on devoting time and energy to new Irish writing; New Island has about 50 titles to its credit, including Bolger's *A Dublin Bloom*, his 1994 adaptation of *Ulysses*, and a volume gathering *April Bright* (1995) and the earlier *Blinded by the Light* (1990), written for the Abbey. They also brought out his *New and Selected Poems* in 1998 while in February 1999 the Peacock premiered *The Passion of Jerome* which Bolger had written in 1997 while he was writer-in-residence at the Abbey. But this time the text came out as the first in a new series, "the Abbey Theatre Playscript series" under the Methuen imprint with a highly complimentary preface by Abbey artistic director, Patrick Mason.

Yet, despite, or perhaps because of his popularity, Bolger's work has received little attention in academic circles. Many scholars either ignore or dismiss him as a member of the new generation of depressing and crude working-class realist writers. Declan Kiberd has regretted the "mawkish sentimentality of [Bolger's] housing-estate realism" and suggested his success in Great Britain was based on some kind of misunderstanding: "The books of Bolger and his colleagues were very much admired in England, where they were read as indicating a new cutting-edge realism in Irish writing; but soon the conservative undertow was all too apparent, as well as the conceptual clichés of a strangely caricatured Dublin landscape of horses in high-rise flats and doomed young things in squalid bed-sits" (Kiberd: 1996, 609). In many ways indeed, Finglas-born Bolger, like Roddy Doyle and Joseph O'Connor, is breaking new ground, giving urban and suburban Dublin a voice which many find unattractive, not sufficiently literary.

However, one play has attracted unanimous praise and much attention, namely Bolger's theatrical debut, *The Lament for Arthur Cleary*, a play which has enjoyed twenty-eight different productions since its première. Indeed Bolger's plays have won him international acclaim and it is of course to the dramatic work that I now want to turn. Bolger had the rare pleasure of seeing five of his original plays performed within two years, between September 1989 and October 1991. The first four (*The Lament for Arthur Cleary*, *In High Germany*, *The Holy Ground* and *One Last White Horse*) can be found in *A Dublin Quartet* published by Penguin in 1992 with a valuable introduction by Fintan O'Toole, while *Blinded by the Light* only came out in written form in 1997 together with *April Bright*.

Indeed, one can argue that *The Lament for Arthur Cleary* , performed at the Dublin Theatre Festival in 1989 remains Bolger's masterpiece so far. The story behind the production is well worth telling. *The Lament* started life as an 82-verse poem in which Bolger was adapting and updating the traditional eighteenth-century Gaelic elegy written by Eileen C'Connell on the death of her husband, Art O'Leary. Director David Byrne noticed the dramatic potential of the piece. Byrne was then working for Wet Paint, a small Dublin-based theatre company aiming at bringing theatre to a young audience in the more disadvantaged areas of Dublin. The meeting between Bolger and Byrne proved crucial and *The Lament* came to life as a play of extraordinary power and relevance capable of appealing to both the general theatre-going public and the theatrically unsophisticated, yet demanding, audiences of *Wet Paint*. Bolger recalls that when the play went to tour community halls, "Often at times the cast faced hostility yet every night, through their intense commitment and talent, one could hear a pin drop by the start of the second act as the cast won" (Bolger: 1992, x).

This first play is indeed emblematic of Bolger's thematic and artistic concerns. Firmly rooted in the bleak and often violent landscape of suburban, drug-ridden modern-day Dublin, the play is also timeless, creating a dream world of its own with symbolic overtones: the frontiers Arthur crosses are not merely those between European countries, they are also those separating life from death. Arthur is a hero of our times; the transposition of the Gaelic elegy is radical yet retains the anger, the painful sense of loss of the original. Both Cleary and his model, Art O'Leary, died because they longed for justice and refused to surrender their dignity; O'Leary had taken on the new English masters; Cleary takes on the drug and crime underworld in the person of Deignan. Both of them wanted a home yet felt they had returned to an Ireland that had become alien to them; Cleary sadly notices the passing away of the working-class solidarity he remembered from his childhood days. Both found and lost love and, in the case of Cleary, lost it for good as we learn that the girl mourned him for a while but now needs to "let him go" in her mind to get on with her life. Ultimately he also has to learn to "let go" of the ties and bonds that are keeping him in limbo, this borderline state, in this train stuck in the middle of nowhere which cannot depart until he has accepted his fate, death, and relinquished his hold on the past.

Through a highly imaginative use of stage space, of lighting, of props, of masks, of sound effects, Bolger succeeds in creating a play in which dream and reality meet in a highly stylised, terrifyingly effective manner. One of the most obvious achievements of the play resides in the language wrought by Bolger: "My lament for you Arthur Cleary/ As you lay down that crooked back lane / Under the stern wall of a factory/ Where moss and crippled flowers cling" (*Quartet:* 11). Here he combines the poetic, the lyrical and the everyday, even coarse language; here the magic works, the various voices interact, echo, mingle successfully keeping the various levels and layers (realism, symbolism, tragedy...) in tension in the audience's eye and mind. The characters, with the exception of Arthur and Kathy, the girl, keep changing roles, suggesting great uncertainty: friend or foe, you can never tell; scenes overlap, creating echoes and gaps, as in the logic of dreams, with an ever-present, underlying threat of violence suggested by some of the props, (sticks), the strange geometry, part abstract, part sensual of the movements, and materialised in the scene of Arthur's execution.

Because so many of Bolger's plays and novels are set in bleak suburban locations — Ballymun in *The Passion of Jerome* for instance — it would be tempting to see him as some kind of social observer; yet he denies that this is the right way to look at his work: "People are often inclined to confuse the locale of my work with the themes". This does not prevent him from lucidly and acidly pointing out that: "although Ballymun is only three miles from Dublin, it might as well be in Siberia — this extraordinary mental thing in terms of geography on the north side, people get hazy after the Gate Theatre" (Bolger: 1999). Bolger's is no bland social realism; his urban and suburban Dublin is more often perceived in visionary, quasi-apocalyptic terms, a place in pain, the city of the dead as is obvious in *The Lament* or again in *One Last White Horse*. In this play we follow the downfall of a young man, Eddie, his lost fight against poverty and the guilt and despair he feels, never having recovered from the death of his mother in a traffic accident when he was a child. He keeps blaming himself for her death and cannot fill what he calls the "hole in his heart", the loss of his mother's love. This craving, together with crushing poverty, will turn him into a drug addict, causing him to lose his wife and child. Heroin and his dead mother become united in the double image of need and the white horse he sees during the last fix, just before dying. Heroin appears as the new plague in several of the plays, the curse of a lost generation.

Many critics have pointed out the absence of tradition, the way Bolger depicts an Ireland that is breaking free from the constraints of the past and the "historical continuity on which national identity depends". Fintan O'Toole sees Bolger as the champion of those "new places,... places without history... where sex and drugs and rock'n'roll are now more important than the old totems of Land, Nationality and Catholicism" (O'Toole: 1992,1). New journeys, more individual than collective have to be mapped out. In this new, post-nationalist and increasingly secular Ireland what does being Irish mean? This is very much the central question raised by Eoin in *In High Germany,* a play in the form of a monologue, performed as a double bill with *The Holy Ground,* another monologue, this time with a female protagonist, in 1991. Like Cleary, Eoin belongs to the new European context: he has emigrated to Germany where he has a job and a girlfriend. Not that emigration is new: his father before him had been in and out of the country, looking for work to support his family, in England or the States. To Eoin, football has become the new rallying cry and religion; supporting the Irish football team is the only way in which he feels he can still connect with his past, with his childhood friends, with his father's dream: "Dreams that I'd grow up under an Irish flag, knowing I belonged somewhere, a free person in a free land. (*Smiles ironically*)" (*Quartet:* 82). They are not, as they were told, the chosen generation; this is an illusion that has to be shed: "I thought of my father's battered travel-light bag, of Molloy [the old schoolmaster] drilling us behind that 1798 pike, the wasters who came after him hammering *Peig* into us, the masked men blowing limbs off passers-by in my name. You know, all my life, it seems, somebody somewhere has always been trying to tell me what Ireland I belonged in. But I only belonged there" (*Quartet:* 107). "There" being the football stadium where he has just seen the Irish team lose their chance of making it to the final... Emigration and violence are still the name of the game, though nationalism is being emptied of any substance, the unfinished business of the North a cruel anachronism, an irrelevance. Eoin may or may not be free from his past; this freedom is born out of loss. "Home" is not Ireland any more, it is the German city where a young pregnant woman is awaiting him. The son she is going to give birth to is his future, the only continuity available to him a personal, not a "national" one...

This continuity and consolation have been denied to Monica, the protagonist of *The Holy Ground.* A widow, she recalls her married years, her growing estrangement from her husband and her despair. After several months of courtship and happiness, Myles, the humble post office clerk and football player, discovered he was sterile. Hurt in his pride, he turned away both from his wife and football; instead, he changed his name from "swifty" Hurley to O'Muirthile, joined the Legion of Mary and the Confraternity. Thus, Bolger associates him with traditional Ireland in various ways, his piety verging on bigotry, his newly-adopted Gaelic name and of course his work in the GPO, in the shadow of the statue of the great Cuchulain. Meanwhile, Monica is left to talk to her imaginary children in a lonely house, quietly going mad. Her bitterness reached such a point that during the divorce referendum, unable to stand her loneliness and the slogans her bigot of a husband kept mouthing, she started poisoning him with rat poison; ironically though it was not the poison that killed him but a blood clot in the brain. At the end of the play she is left to contemplate the utter emptiness of her life: "I tried to pray but nothing would come. You've stolen my youth and left me barren, you've stolen my gaiety and gave me shame, and when I die I will die unmourned.... But I could forgive you, Swifty, everything except that... seated there at the right hand of God, you had stolen my Christ away from me" (*Quartet:* 142).

April Bright again revisits the theme of hopes crushed and reborn. In post-war Ireland, lively, sprightly young April died before she could fulfil her hopes and those of her family. Years later, her sister, a ghost-like caller from the past, pays a visit to the young couple who have just bought the house and are preparing to spend their first night there. Through the elderly woman's eyes we see enacted the joys and tragedies of the Bright family, until the untimely death of April. Back in the present of the play, the girl has already suffered the shock and disappointment of a miscarriage but she is pregnant again and the visitor assures her that everything will be all right this time, that the house is going to see life take over from death. The play ends on an optimistic note, the promise of a precious child to come. Overtly sentimental, *April Bright* is a moving play in which Bolger resorts to a double time frame to link and contrast past and present.

Ghosts are everywhere in Bolger's drama, counterbalancing or even belying the surface realism. Cleary is a kind of ghost in limbo, Eddie is dying, haunted by the figure of the Horse-woman in *One Last White Horse*; the shadow of April Bright hangs over the house, and in *The Passion of Jerome*, a middle-aged man becomes haunted by the ghost of a young boy. Through the presence of ghosts, life and death, past and present become interrelated in ways which can be either tragic or ultimately liberating. Ghosts are also symbols of incompletion, as is, in a sense, the sterility of various characters. In such images we may find a sign of Bolger's overall concern with continuity and rupture, both in a personal and in a cultural sense. Bolger's world, his Ireland, is definitely post-nationalist and secular, yet his imagery and his tone are almost visionary, hence the tension one feels between surface realism and some kind of epic or apocalyptic dimension in his writing.

God is absent from Bolger's plays but the need for some transcendence cannot be avoided. In this respect the progression from *Blinded by the Light* to *The Passion of Jerome* is clear. Religion is openly derided in Bolger's only comedy *Blinded by the Light*, what with the caricatural Mormons and the counter-offensive led by the elderly couple from the Legion of Mary. Poor Mick simply wants to be left alone in his bedsit to get on with his reading and recreational drug-taking. But the whole world seems determined to wreck his budding love affair with Siobhan. Because it is slapstick comedy (the part of Mick was played by the extraordinary Donal O'Kelly in the first production), *Blinded by the Light* revisits many of the elements we find in the darker plays and novels but in a lighter mode. Mick eventually gets rid of all the trouble makers and intruders except for the most unlikely one, the head of Oliver Plunkett which has been stolen in Drogheda Cathedral by some of his mates, in the hope of having some fun and perhaps getting a ransom. Of course it turns out not to be the head of Plunkett at all but that of an unfortunate individual caught up in the turmoil of history. The poor head was feeling so lonely in the cathedral that it begs Mick to keep it. Mick pretends he has put it in the fire, incurring the unexpected wrath of Ollie, the kidnapper, outraged at such an act of blasphemy: "Have you no respect for culture, for the past, no respect for your heritage? If it's one thing I hate it's you city slickers with your pluralist society, kinky sex and rock and roll" (*Quartet:* 203). Safe at last, the head indulges in some philosophising in the best Synge-style: "We're two of a kind, Mick. The little men of history, unimportant, overlooked, just getting on with living as best we can. You've only been hounded for three weeks. I've been hounded for three centuries. But it's a great rest we'll have now, and great sleeping in the long nights after Samhain" (*Quartet:* 204).

Bolger has said he never had an upbringing that led him to rebel against the Catholic Church. In a somewhat provocative spirit he also felt that new dramatists were reluctant to deal with religion, as if it was something outdated in an increasingly secular world. "There is this notion that people are afraid to explore religion because there's a sense that it's a clichéd part of the past" (Bolger: 1999). Hence his latest play which, as Patrick Mason saw it, is "unchic yet radical in that its subject matter is the sacred phenomenon of the stigmata". *The Passion of Jerome* suggests a reappraisal, or at least a different approach to the troubling question of whether or not spirituality can have a place in our secular world. The play, as the *Irish Times* reviewer noted, can be read at different levels — it is the story of a haunting, a metaphor for the rescue of a Catholic soul from some kind of living purgatory as well as an allegory about a dysfunctional, materialistic society — but it is ultimately a meditation upon faith, mixing the real and the surreal, as most Bolger plays do.

Jerome, the central character, works devising jingles for a second-rate advertising agency. He and his Protestant wife have lost a baby girl and their marriage has never recovered from that blow. Jerome has drifted away, unable to face his grief and share it, giving up on his career and embarking on a sexual relationship with Clara, an attractive younger colleague. For the sake of convenience, Jerome has agreed to look after his brother's flat in Ballymun while the latter is away: he can meet his lover there without any danger of running into anyone they know. What he soon finds out, though, is that the flat is haunted by the ghost of a young boy who committed suicide there, one of the many victims of poverty, alcoholism and despair. At first he pays scant attention to the story but after Clara's departure, Jerome goes to sleep only to wake up with his hands pierced by nails: he has been afflicted with the stigmata and as the play unfolds it becomes clear the wounds won't heal until he has freed the boy's soul and confronted his own past.

Faced with such a harrowing and unexpected experience, Jerome also realises no one will believe him. Everyone is looking for a rational explanation: either he has gone mad and has inflicted these wounds upon himself or he has been attacked by thugs; after all, what can you expect when you hang around an area like Ballymun? Even the representative of the Catholic Church, the priest, has no sympathy to offer and refuses point-blank to even envisage that what has happened could be some kind of miracle or a sign from God. He has grown cynical and is at first unimpressed by this "yuppie Matt Talbot": "The last thing I need here are miracles. They're a nuisance, freak show curiosities. I'm sorry, but what I need is a hostel for homeless boys, a stable for stray horses, schools for traveller children.... Personally (if you're talking to God) I'd like to own a small alarm clock radio for more than a week without it being stolen. I need people looking up to demand their rights, not down on their knees before some mutilation" (*Jerome:* 69). But God moves in mysterious ways and, willy nilly, Jerome will help free the boy's soul and, in return, the dead boy will scare away the thugs who have come to beat up Jerome.

Jerome is travelling the same road as the priest but in the opposite direction: from the material to the spiritual; he had silenced his spiritual being after the death of his baby daughter, he had abandoned his childhood ideal of building cathedrals. The strange experience that befalls him forces him to confront his inner self and hopefully start anew; at least that is what the ending of the play suggests.

In his introduction to Bolger's adaptation of *Ulysses, A Dublin Bloom*, Fintan O'Toole even compares Bolger and Joyce; "Bolger shares much with Joyce, a wildly inclusive vision, a great sense of humour, a rich feeling for language, a quest for the mythic in the everyday, and, above all, an attachment to Dublin as a city forever suspended between heaven and hell". Whether posterity will endorse such a comparison is far from obvious; however, it is clear that Bolger has succeeded in dramatising the new Dublin and addressing contemporary issues in ways that appeal and speak to a large and varied audience, while remaining true to an intensely personal vision.

Works Cited:

Bolger, Dermot, (1992), 'Author's Note', *A Dublin Quartet* (London: Penguin)

Bolger, Dermot, (1999), 'Re-opening old wounds', Interview with Bolger, *Irish Times*, Thursday, February 11

Bolger, Dermot, (1999), *The Passion of Jerome* (London: Metheun)

O'Toole, Fintan, (1992), 'On the Frontier', introduction to *A Dublin Quartet* (London: Penguin)

Kiberd, Declan, (1996), *Inventing Ireland* (London: Vintage)

A Cautionary Tale: Marina Carr's *By the Bog of Cats.*

Melissa Sihra

Streams of the sacred rivers flow uphill:
Tradition, order, all things are reversed.
(Medea, Euripides)

Marina Carr's drama *By the Bog of Cats* was first produced for the Abbey
Theatre during the 1998 Dublin Theatre Festival under the direction of
Patrick Mason. It received the award for best new play in the 1999 Irish
Times/ESB Theatre Awards. In the main Theatre Festival competition
the award for best actress was given to Olwen Fouere who played the
role of Hester. The plot is loosely based on Euripides' tragedy *Medea*, the
story of a woman wronged by her treacherous lover Jason. Medea's
vendetta against her common-law husband culminates in savage
vengeance with the killing of their children. The re-working of Greek
tragedies is a common feature of Irish playwriting. Carr's earlier play *The
Mai* is based on Sophocles' *Electra*. In an essay on the creative process
Thomas Kilroy notes that: "The bag of Autolycus is part of a writer's
equipment [as] using the word always involves the writings of others"
(Kilroy: 1998, 58). Repeatedly drawn to the tragic model, Carr asserts the
notion that loss is fundamental to experience and something to be
expected in life. For Carr soul-making is a process "that cannot take
place without an amount of suffering". Carr quotes the lines of Laura
Riding:

> Nor is it written that you may not grieve.
> There is no rule of joy.
> Long may you dwell not smiling
> (Carr, 1998b: 190).

For Carr the family is central to the drama and it is from this microcosm
that implications for culture and nation are cited. It is appropriate to
juxtapose Eamon de Valera's 1943 St. Patrick's day vision of Ireland as
"... a land whose countryside would be bright with cosy homesteads,
whose fields and villages would be joyous with the sounds of industry,
the romping of sturdy children [and] the laughter of comely maidens"
with Carr's antithesis.

A recurring trait of familial representations in Irish theatre is the notion
of absent parents. Hester is an itinerant living on the bog, who at the age
of seven was abandoned by her mother. She is presented as an outsider,
waiting on the fringes, like Beckett's tramps, for someone who will never
show up. Hester has failed to become a fully subjectified individual as
she has never gained a sufficient substitute for the loss of her mother.

Crucial to Carr's work is the symbiotic dynamic of loss and desire: "There's a longing in me that won't quell this while gone" Hester says to the Catwoman in act one (*Cats*: 22). The theatre program for *By the Bog of Cats* features a photograph of a child held in the arms of a blanked-out mother figure. Denoted by a white void, this non-presence, Big Josie Swane, is the protagonist of the play.

The action unfolds as the audience learns that Hester's common-law husband and father of her child, Carthage Kilbride, is about to marry the daughter of the local big farmer, Xavier Cassidy. The locals want Hester, now in her fortieth year, to leave the bog and move into the town with her daughter Josie. Hester wishes to remain on the Bog of Cats as it affords her the only connection with her mother. In a frustrated act of defiance Hester burns down Carthage's house and livestock. Now with a sense of options closing down for her, Hester's tragedy culminates in the act of suicide, following the murder of her child.

The critical necessity for self-definition can be identified in the first modern Irish drama, *The Playboy of the Western World*, which offers an outsider who writes his own identity. Carr re-presents the motherless Christy Mahon's existential concerns in the figure of Hester who ill-fatedly seeks to do the same through collecting stories about her dead mother. Memory and identity are mutually dependent and Carr dramatises how Hester's need to remember is so vital in her effort to construct an identity. Carr notes that "Hester's mother has left her with nothing and she has created a fiction around her mother which everyone contradicts" (Carr 1999a). In act three Hester says to Xavier: "I have memories your cheap talk can never alter", to which he replies, "And what memories are they Swane? I'd like to know if they exist at all" (*Cats*: 70). Hester is not sure how much of her memory is a product of her own imagined narrative. "Tell me about my mother", she asks the Catwoman, for what I remember doesn't add up" (*Cats*: 21). In her search for authenticity Hester implores her brother: "What was she like Joseph? Everyday I forget more and more "till I'm startin' to think I made her up out of the air. If it wasn't for this auld caravan I'd swear I only dreamt her" (*Cats*: 62).

This dramatisation of the subjective nature of memory and of how identity can be destabilised by opposing narratives echoes highpoints in a century of Irish theatre. A poignant scene of mnemonic incongruity is offered in Friel's *Philadelphia, Here I Come!* S.B.'s non-recollection of a "blue boat" on Lough na Cloc Cor shatters the unity of Gar's past, calling into question the actuality of his experience and thus the unity of his identity. Gar remembers the day: "for no reason at all, except that we — that you were happy. D'you remember? D'you remember"? The songs do not even correlate as S. B. does not recall singing *All Round My Hat*

I'll Wear a Green Coloured Ribbono: "It wasn't *The Flower of Sweet Strabane*, was it?" he asks Gar. In *The Playboy of the Western World* Old Mahon's version of Christy as "a dribbling idiot" or "the loony of the Mahon's" deftly unravels the fable of "mister honey".

The anomalous stories surrounding Big Josie display how histories and myths can so easily be perpetuated or dismantled by discordant versions. Of his mother, Joseph states: "she was fierce silent — gentle I suppose in her way". Hester remembers otherwise: "Gentle! She'd a vicious whiskey temper on her and a whiplash tongue and fists that'd land on ya like lightnin'" (*Cats:* 62). As in *Philadelphia, Here I Come!* and *The Playboy of the Western World* it is shown in the Carr play how identity can be created upon myth or illusion, rendering it a conditional, performative or fabricated state. Carr cautions that the opposing stories about Big Josie call into question the possibility of ever accessing the truth about this figure, about narrative in general and consequently, the history of a nation.

In Frank McGuinness' *Observe the Sons of Ulster Marching Towards the Somme* or Brian Friel's *Making History* the question of the narrative structuring of history, who remembers it and who writes it is interrogated. In the former play Pyper asks: "who gave you this version of events?" McIlwaine replies: "Christopher here". To which Roulston asserts: "He invented quite a few details of his own. The best ones". McIlwaine ironically defends his version of history by attributing it to the poetic model: "I can't help that. I'm very imaginative.... To hell with the truth as long as it rhymes". The fallibility of history is dramatised as McGuinness' men re-enact the Battle of Scarva: "And remember, King James, we know the result, you know the result, keep to the result" shouts Anderson as the mock battle begins. Within minutes it falls apart: *Pyper trips. Crawford crashes to the ground* [and there is] *Silence.*

Hester's desire to hear stories about her mother dramatises the need for narrative in relation to the formation of identity. In *By the Bog of Cats* stories act as a source of consolation for Hester's loss. Big Josie is described by the Catwoman as "a great wan for the pausin'" (*Cats:* 22). A Beckettian configuration, Big Josie embodies the notion of perpetually suspended fulfilment. How this relates to loss and desire is addressed when Hester asks: "What was she waitin' for, Catwoman? And did she ever find it?" (*Cats:* 22). In *Waiting for Godot* language offers vital points of reference in the assertion of the existence of the self. Consigned to limbo, Joseph the ghost of Hester's dead brother feels the necessity to hold dialogue, however inane: "[It is] fierce hard to knock the best out of nothin'.... [It is] fierce hard to enjoy darkness the whole time, can't I just stay here and talk to ya a while?" he asks the Catwoman in act three (*Cats:* 45).

The cultural psyche of any nation values music, art and poetry as a vital element of its self-perpetuation and definition. Yet caution is repeatedly made in Irish theatre against investment in songs, stories and narrative. The content of the nationalist ballads bandied about in Friel's *The Freedom of the City* is presented as being as unstable or wobbly as the legs of the inebriated singers. In *By the Bog of Cats* Big Josie was known for the songs that she "stitched" and sang at weddings and wakes. Yet it was noted by the locals that: "sometimes she'd sing somethin' completely different than the song she'd been makin' on the road" (*Cats*: 65). While Hester demands the truth about her mother, in the same breath she chides the Catwoman for "concoctin' stories about others" (*Cats*: 21). Interchangeable, narrative and history become "faithless as an acorn on the high wind" (*Cats*: 66).

The mother-figure in Irish theatre has traditionally been viewed as a personification of the nation. Carr presents the myth of Big Josie Swane as an alternative to the romanticised literary Mother Ireland figure. Big Josie is described by the Catwoman as being "... a harsh auld yoke, [who] came and went like the moon... except when she sang and then I declare ya'd fall in love with her" (*Cats*: 64). This is Yeats' *Cathleen Ní Houlihan* re-imagined. With the legend of Big Josie, Yeats' "Mother Ireland" now metamorphoses into a "rancorous hulk" (*Cats*: 62) with a "brazen walk... and her reekin' of drink" (*Cats*: 40) as opposed to the comely young girl who previously had the "walk of a queen". Illegitimate and unapologetic, like her daughter and grand-daughter, Big Josie is an outlaw spending her nights "Off in the bars of Pullagh and Mucklagh gettin' into fights" (*Cats*: 40). The nation as female is now depicted as an overweight, erotic, foul-mouthed transgressive energy who, according to Xavier Cassidy was "loose and lazy and aisy, a five shillin' hoor", in contrast to Yeats' martyric wanderer (*Cats*: 70).

Yeats' literary configuration of the nation as female is thought by the *dramatis personae* of his 1902 play to have been: "a woman from beyond the world?" [who has led] " many that have been free to walk the hills and the bogs and the rushes [to be] sent to walk hard streets in far countries". Both Cathleen and Big Josie have the power to compel and to seduce those around them. Cathleen states that: "many a man has died for love of me". Hester comments on her mother's Medusian quality: "Who'd believe a look [from her] could destroy ya?" (*Cats*: 64) In Yeats' drama Cathleen's name is remembered by Peter in a song from his boyhood: "I think I heard that name once. Who was it, I wonder? It must have been someone I knew when I was a boy. No, no: I remember, I heard it in a song". Big Josie is also remembered in a song entitled *The Black Swan* (*Cats*: 83), and is described as "the greatest song stitcher ever to have passed through this place" (*Cats*: 22).

Like Cathleen, Big Josie is thought to have been in communion with some otherness. Xavier Cassidy, who was known to have been "in a constant swoon" over the larger than life figure, describes her 'Outside her ould caravan on the bog covered over in stars and her half covered over in an excuse of a dress and her croonin' towards Orion in a language I never heard before or since" (*Cats:* 39). This dead or forgotten language is hermetic to the people that now live on the bog. Big Josie embodies the unattainability of the past and its narratives and the changes that can be imposed on a nation. Her warblings to the moon are reminiscent of the unintelligible ramblings of Doalty imitating the "King's good English" or the "quaint, archaic tongue" heard by Captain Lancey in Friel's *Translations*.

Through the figure of Big Josie, Carr dramatises the notion of otherness and how it is viewed socially and politically. The "settled" locals in *By the Bog of Cats* display suspicion engendered by fear of difference. Both Hester and her mother are accused of dabbling in some "black art thing" because they refuse to conform to the prerequisites of social convention (*Cats:* 66). Similar to the plight of Hester Prynne in Hawthorne's *The Scarlet Letter* the accusations of black magic are based on a distrust of the extra-ordinary. In his inability to understand Hester's mentality Xavier concludes: "You're a dangerous witch Swane!.... You're as mad as your mother and she was a lunatic" (*Cats:* 70). Carr emphasises that "There in no black magic in the play. There is nothing black magic about Hester. It is about how she is perceived" (Carr 1999a).

Repeatedly compelled to the dramatic possibility of the outsider, Carr's depiction of Hester, The Mai in *The Mai* and Portia in *Portia Coughlan*, as women who "will not bow down [and] will not accept things the way they are", completes what can be regarded as a trilogy (Carr 1999a). Amphibiously Hester is both in and out of social convention. The conceptualising of space and property in *By the Bog of Cats* is unstable and indicative of the nature of identity. Hester crosses spatial boundaries more radically than in Carr's previous work (The Mai remains indoors, while Portia flirts with the threshold). Her representation in contrasting spaces such as the indeterminate bog "always shiftin' and changin' and coddin' the eye", a caravan and a fixed house lead to the representation of the self with which they are entwined (*Cats:* 15). "Half-settled", she is neither one thing nor the other (Carr 1999c). Hester displays anomie, itinerancy and exile, all recurring motifs of a century of Irish playwriting.

Viewed as a "savage" by the settled community, Hester's situation is similar to that of Christy Mahon's in *The Playboy of the Western World* (*Cats:* 54). The siting of the savage is inverted in both plays. The locals' desire that Hester should "Go to the next haltin' site" mirrors Christy's enforced exile (*Cats:* 35). Now "a lepping savage" the former playboy is ritualistically scorched on the shins with a lighted sod while Hester is warned: "We'll burn ya out if we have to" (*Cats:* 57). Carr subverts the notion of the outsider in *By the Bog of Cats*. Instead of detachedly observing the excentric figure from within, the audience, through its engagement with Hester also becomes marginalised from the so-called "settled community" in the play. This results in the audience ironically observing themselves (as members of the "settled-community"), a collusion which gives both Hester and the audience "an edge over all of yees... [and]... allows me see yees for the inbred, underbred, bog-brained shower yees are" (*Cats:* 35).

The suffering of the outsider is articulated by Jimmy Jack in *Translations:* "I am a barbarian in this place because I am not understood by anyone". Hester's sense of displacement is furthered by the deliberate ambiguity surrounding her paternity and the mythical quality of her father-land: "I had a father too!... Jack Swane from Bergit's island.... Ya'd swear I was dropped from the sky the way ya go on.... I'm as settled as any of yees-" (*Cats:* 40). Olwen Fouere notes the dialectical tension of Hester's existence: "she sets herself apart from the society she is in, yet she desires to be a part of it" (Fouere: 1999).

Through the figures of Big Josie and Hester, Carr represents the female as outlaw or deviant. Roaming the bog by day and night Hester is both *maenad* and *mater familias*. With her inherited association to the outdoors and nature comes the tendency to excessive behaviour and anarchism. Simon Goldhill writes about fifth-century Athenian drama and "the regular association of women with the inside and the dangers associated with women when they go outside [and how the] requirement to keep women on the inside is so forcefully stated" (Goldhill: 1992, 15). Hester persistently interrogates the rhetoric of authority and demonstrates how the written law possesses no hold over her. Accused by Caroline of breaking a signed and sealed contract, Hester states "Bits of paper, writin', means nothin', can as aisy be unsigned" (*Cats:* 29). Mrs. Kilbride, Carthage's mother, is complicit with existing codes of practice. She is perpetuator *and* cog of the law in all its forms. Hester confronts Mrs. Kilbride: "Have you ever been discarded Elsie Kilbride?" To which she replies: "No, I've never been discarded, Hester Swane! Ya know why? Because I've never overstepped myself. I've always lived by the rules". "Ah rules! What rules are they?" questions Hester (*Cats:* 55).

Carr's drama articulates the dynamics of ownership in relation to personal and political identity. Domineering and manipulative, Mrs. Kilbride is a key figure of the play in her will to overpower and control those around her. Allusions to imperialism are directed at Mrs. Kilbride on two occasions in the play. At the wedding she comments of her shoes that: "The Quane herself wouldn't pay more" (*Cats:* 48). Similarly in scene six of the first act when Josie pretends to be Mrs. Kilbride, she says to Hester: "I had turf stew for me dinner and for dessert I had a snail tart.... Ya wouldn't get better in Buckin'am Palace" (*Cats:* 32).

In scene four of act one Mrs. Kilbride seeks to possess and re-write somebody else's identity. Just as the orthographer in Friel's *Translations* works with the toponymic department in order to ensure the correct spelling of new names of places, Mrs. Kilbride ascribes a different name to Hester's child. Upon asking the child to spell her name aloud, Mrs. Kilbride informs little Josie that she is: "wrong! wrong! wrong!... Ya got some of it right. Ya got the "Josie" part right, but ya got the "Kilbride" part wrong, because you're not a Kilbride. You're a Swane.... You're Hester Swane's little bastard. You're not a Kilbride and never will be" (*Cats:* 25). Mrs. Kilbride continues: "Don't you worry, child, we'll get ya off her yet. Me and your Daddy has plans. We'll batter ya into the semblance of legitimacy yet.... I'll break your spirit yet and then glue ya back the way I want ya" (*Cats:* 26).

The re-named child Josie Kilbride suffers a subsequent crisis of her identity. When her mother addresses her as "Josie Swane" she replies: "Me name is Josie Kilbride.... I'm not a Swane, I'm a Kilbride" (*Cats:* 37). As Hugh asserts in *Translations:* "Confusion is not an ignoble condition". Josie's confusion is born out of having a Grandmother who spoke in a different tongue and whose own name has been changed. The reality intrinsic to re-naming as dramatised by Friel, is articulated by Hester in act three when she states to the locals: "The truth is you want to eradicate me, make out I never existed" (*Cats:* 56).

Clothing and costume are directly relational to the performative nature of identity. Christy Mahon assumes a persona as the *Playboy* upon the acquirement of new clothes. He sees a different image of himself in the looking-glass and conditions his identity according to the reflection: "Didn't I know rightly, I was handsome". Hester's arrival at the marriage celebrations in a wedding dress is similarly a signifier of what she is not. In the scene between Mrs. Kilbride and her granddaughter, it is noted in the text that little Josie's jumper is *"on inside out"* (*Cats:* 24). This is an indication of the deranged state of the child's subjectivity. When Carthage arrives on the scene he tellingly informs his daughter that she must learn to dress herself.

Sense of place is integral to Irish theatre. The repetition of the name "Bog of Cats" throughout the play highlights the link between place, identity and memory. Samuel Beckett is unique in the canon of Irish playwrights in his consistent refusal to localise his drama. Carr's play can be linked with the Beckettian anti-landscape. The bog, a place and a non-place (hovering somewhere between the actual and the imaginary), transcends what Beckett viewed as the aesthetic reductivism of specific geographic allusion. Carr's *mise en scene* has the best of both worlds. While on the one hand it is recognisably Irish, it belongs as much in the domain of Greek tragedy, Gothic horror, Absurdism and Grotesque surrealism. The play possesses the mythic dimension of timelessness. There is a sparseness in the setting of *By the Bog of Cats* that is suggestive of the inescapable limbo of Beckett's *"A country road. A tree. Evening".* Carr offers: *"Dawn.... A bleak white landscape of ice and snow. Music, a lone violin"* (*Cats:* 13).

The genre of the Fantastic, which does not invent other worlds but inverts elements of the *known* world, allows for a distance that affords oblique access to the culture and society in question. By entering spaces outside the frame of the real, Carr replaces familiarity and comfort with estrangement and unease, thus offering the necessary objectivity for self-scrutiny. The rise in materialism and intolerance of otherness currently gripping contemporary Ireland is commented upon in *By the Bog of Cats*. "Why don't yees head off... back to wherever yees came from" declares Mrs. Kilbride to her granddaughter (*Cats:* 25). An upwardly mobile mentality is portrayed in the characters Xavier, Carthage and Mrs. Kilbride. Hester accuses Carthage of being a "jumped-up land hungry mongrel [who is] selling me and Josie down the river for a few lumpy auld acres and notions of respectability" (*Cats:* 34).

The marriage itself is nothing more than an economic contract between Xavier and Carthage. Anthony Roche refers to the play as: "The great bought marriage of modern theatre" (Roche: 1999). In what could be referred to as *Not the Tinker's Wedding* Carr's play echoes the mentality intrinsic to Sara Casey's purchased union in Synge's 1908 Abbey play. At the wedding reception Xavier becomes a parodic hybrid of the Celtic-tiger/lotto-winner as he converses on his mobile phone while the celebrations implode around him. In a hilarious *coup de theatre* Mrs. Kilbride is revealed by Monica Murray as herself having "tinker blood". "My grandfather was a wanderin' tinsmith" defends Mrs. Kilbride, to which Monica replies: "And what's that but a tinker with notions!" (*Cats:* 56)

In *By the Bog of Cats* Carr's allusion to the supernatural and her representation of the dead brings her work deeper into the realm of the fantastic, transgressing as she does, according to Frank McGuinness "... the border always between the living and the dead" (McGuinness: 1998). The play offers contrasting realms and beings "in mortal form or ghostly form" (*Cats:* 18). In act three the ghost Joseph remarks: "Death's a big country" (*Cats:* 60). The presence of the dead weighs heavily on Carr's drama, occasioning six deceased characters. Transactions are attempted as money from the dead is used to buy and bargain, denoting the effect of loss and absence upon the course of the narrative. The Bacchanal mouse-eating Catwoman, inspired by Ratwife from Ibsen's *Little Eyolf*, is the blind "seer" of the play and forges another link between this world and the next through her communion with the dead souls.

As information technology, global systems and genetic manipulation rapidly transform contemporary reality Carr ponders over "... this anti-heroic age... [where]... the all consuming intellectual pursuit seems to be that of de-mystification" (Carr: 1998b, 193). In accordance with Carr's sensibility, Patrick Mason states, "Postmodernism marks for me the death of rationalism.... There is a need to re-animate, to re-enter the imagination" (Mason: 1999). Carr's writing succeeds in re-gaining the paradise lost. Not afraid of rejecting the confines of naturalism her language transgresses the mundane to become poetic, imagistic and sensual by denoting alternative spaces of mythic and spiritual possibility.

Like Big Josie Swane, Carr can be described as a word "stitcher". Her reverence for the word positions her intrinsically in a tradition where orality or that "yearning for the bardic [and] a hunger for stories" is ingrained (Carr: 1995). Carr notes that: "In the theatre there are poets... and there are prose writers" (Carr: 1998b, 196). She regards lyrical or poetic writing as typically Irish: "How we tell a story is so important. It is not the facts we are looking for, it is the details, the embellishments. I think that most Irish people know how to tell a story instinctively and to tell it well" (Carr: 1997, 149).

Carr's use of language reflects a fine ear for a phrase and is "fully flavoured as a nut" (Synge: 1974, xx) making it, as Christopher Murray states of Synge's prose, "exotic" (Murray: 1999). The playwright describes the Offaly dialect, which is dying out now, as "guttural, rough and flat... with a certain beauty all of its own" (Carr: 1999d). Carr remembers overhearing two itinerants arguing on the street: "One of the boys was in a wheelchair and he hit the other one. The younger of the two hit back and called the aggressor a 'piebald knacker'" (Carr: ibid.). Consequently Carr re-wrote act two of *By the Bog of Cats* in order to include the colourful phrase. Synge's theories on language are similar, owning as he did, to acquiring "... more aid than any learning from a chink in the floor of the old Wicklow house... " (Synge: 1974, xix).

An admirer of Synge, Carr describes *The Playboy of the Western World* in sentiments appropriate to *By the Bog of Cats*: "The first thing that grips [me] is the elemental roar off the page. Straightaway you are inhabiting a world of forces, a place of darkness and light, of savagery and infinite goodness" (Carr: 1995). *By the Bog of Cats* can be framed with *The Playboy of the Western World* as more than a contemporaneous re-working of Christy Mahon's anxieties. The animus and anima-like complementarity of Hester's and Christy's existence is underscored by their shared experiences in a grotesque and carnivalesque reality. Hester's nine-mile stretch of the Bog of Cats offers tales of a boy found "strychnined to the eyeballs" with his hands burnt "clean away..., howlin' 'long the bog" with his dead dog in his arms (*Cats*: 69). Such imagery is reminiscent of Jimmy Farrell's dog left hanging "screeching and wriggling three hours at the butt of a string" in Synge's Mayo.

Throughout Carr's drama "hunchbacks", "cut-throats and gargiyles" are referred to with disconcerting nonchalance (*Cats*: 66). Both playwrights depict physical mutilation as a form of sordid fascination. The anecdote relayed in *The Playboy of the Western World* about a voyeur who "... drove ten miles to set... eyes on the man bit the yellow lady's nostril on the northern shore", is re-told in *By the Bog of Cats*. Xavier tells how Big Josie "Wance... bit the nose off a woman who dared to look at her man, bit the nose clean off her face" (*Cats*: 40). The two worlds fetishise and curiously naturalise the symbiotic tendencies of the sado-masochistic through the inhabitants' curiosity and acceptance.

The plays focus upon deviancy and disorder. They can be viewed as carnivalesque in that natural order is momentarily turned on its head or, like Josie's jumper is presented *"inside out"*. The action of the plays takes place within a short time frame, offering concentrated drama, after which the remaining characters must resolve to endure their previous life existences but with a new awareness. They must face the consequences that lie in the wake of the whirlwind.

Carnival deploys parody, irony, mockery and travesty to telling effect with emphasis on transgressive humour. In the first scene of *By the Bog of Cats* temporal unity is inverted as the Ghost Fancier mistakes dusk for dawn. "Is it sunrise or sunset?" he asks before realising that he is "too previous". The crepuscular light affords the confusion, defined by Hester as "... that hour when it could be aither dawn or dusk, the light bein' so similar" (*Cats*: 14). The natural cycle of life becomes warped in *By the Bog of Cats* as a child is present at her parent's wedding and dies prior to that parent. Synge addresses this notion in *Riders To The Sea* as Maurya prepares to bury the last of her sons: "They're all gone now, and there isn't anything more the sea can do to me". At the wedding scene in *By the Bog of Cats* no less than four "brides" are present — one of them a child. Carr has reinscribed Father Jack's account in *Dancing at Lughnasa* of the Ryangan custom of four wives into a local context.

A deviant depiction of Christianity is offered through the figures of Fr. Jack in *Lughnasa* and Fr. Willow in *By the Bog of Cats*. Fr. Willow is hailed by Monica Murray as "having lost the run of himself". He wears his vestments "inside out [with] his pyjamas peepin' out from under his trousers" (*Cats*: 48). His ill-fitting robes indicate the performative nature of his identity as a priest. Like Fr. Jack who cannot remember simple words and phrases, Fr. Willow cannot remember how to say grace.

During his speech at the wedding reception Fr. Willow divulges how he was "almost a groom" himself once but that he and his fiancee "fell out over a duck egg on a walkin' holiday by the Shannon" (*Cats:* 53). The erotic iconography of duck eggs can be identified in *The Playboy of the Western World* when the local girls gather to catch a glimpse of the hero:

> **Sara**: [*Taking the eggs she has brought*].... I've run up with a brace of duck's eggs for your food today.... Hold out your hand and you'll see it's no lie I'm telling you.
>
> **Christy**: [*Coming forward shyly, and holding out his left hand*] They're a great and weighty size (*Playboy:* 1974, 195).

Anthony Roche has noted that "most women's playwriting is a comment on *Dancing at Lughnasa*" (Roche: 1999). A memory play, *Lughnasa* is bathed in the seductive glow of nostalgia. The golden light casts huge shadows over the verity of seven-year-old Michael's narrative and should be viewed as a warning against the romantic tendency of memory. Friel's plays often take place in unusually hot weather in contrast to the "cold white world" portrayed by Carr (*Cats:* 41).

Like the Mundy sisters, Hester does not play by the rules of social convention and faces dejection and ostracisation. Just as it is prophesied that Hester will "bring this place down by nightfall" disaster is imminent for the Mundys as "cracks start appearing" (*Cats:* 20). In both plays the dance can be seen as a ritual of pathos and suffering. In *Lughnasa* the dance has been viewed as a celebration of the body but in its essence it is a lament: a frustrated attempt by the sisters to arrest the inevitable tragedy of their corporeal existences in the face of crises, the ravages of time and the omnipotence of death. The hopeless reality that lies at the core of their frenzy is now revealed in *By the Bog of Cats*. With Hester's last dance her death is realised. The Mundy sisters fail to attain the tragic ecstasy of Hester's final moment. Her death beholds the grace of acquiescence: "Take me away, take me away from here", she cajoles the Ghost Fancier. "Alright, my lovely", he responds and: *They go into a death dance* (*Cats:* 80).

Carr's drama flourishes within the rich legacy of a century of Irish theatre. The works of Synge, Yeats, Beckett, Friel and McGuinness continue to hold dialogue, and Carr adds a new voice to their conversation on the human condition. *By the Bog of Cats* is a play in which discomforting questions are posed. The narrative isolates the notion of fundamental truth and shows it to be an impossibility. The constancy of that which essentially informs who and what we are, memory, is similarly dis-integrated. With the dissolution of memory and truth must come a reappraisal of the ideologies that have informed our existence thus far. As Pozzo asserts in *Waiting For Godot:* "Gentlemen, I don't know what came over me. Forgive me. Forget all I said. I don't remember exactly what it was, but you may be sure there wasn't a word of truth in it".

Works Cited:

Carr, Marina, (1995), Program Note for *The Playboy of the Western World*, Abbey Theatre, November

------ (1997), *Rage and Reason* (London: Methuen)

------ (1998a), *By the Bog of Cats* (Meath: The Gallery Press)

------ (1998b), 'Dealing with the Dead', *Irish University Review*, (Spring/ Summer)

------ (1999a), Unpublished Interview 1 with Melissa Sihra, Dublin, February 8th,

------ (1999b), Unpublished Interview 2 with Melissa Sihra, Trinity College, Dublin, February 17th

------ (1999c), Public Reading, Trinity College, Dublin, June 29th, 1999

------ (1999d), Unpublished Lecture on Playwriting, Trinity College, Dublin, February 12th

Fouere, Olwen, (1999), Unpublished Interview with M. Sihra, Dublin, April 30th

Goldhill, Simon, (1992), *Reading Greek Tragedy* (Cambridge: Cambridge University Press)

Kilroy, Thomas, (1998), 'From Page To Stage', *Irish Writers And Their Creative Process*, eds., Jacqueline Genet and Wynne Hellegouarch'h (Colin Smythe: Gerrards Cross)

McGuinness, Frank, (1988), Program Note for *By the Bog of Cats*, Abbey Theatre, Dublin, October

Mason, Patrick, (1999), *Theatre in a Post-modern World, Symposium*, Royal Irish Academy, April 9th

Murray, Christopher, (1999), 'Theatre as Literature', *Theatre in a Postmodern World, Symposium*, RIA, April 10th

Roche, Anthony, (1999), 'What's New in the Irish Theatre?', Unpublished Lecture: Synge Summer School, July 8th

Synge, J, M, (1974), 'Preface' to *The Playboy of the Western World* (Dublin: Mercier Press)

Barabbas at Play with *The Whiteheaded Boy*

Eric Weitz

Consider the magical spaces of a playground: A group of children throw themselves into a fictional universe, inventively living the gap between reality and desire. Some take charge of the fabrication, spawning a world of make-believe from the raw materials of body and voice. Others adopt a more physically passive part, but are no less involved in the pretending; they join in the adventure by endowing the real, live actions of their playmates with fantastic meanings.

Viewed at such an angle, what is theatre, other than a grown-up form of communal playing not far removed from the fields of childhood? According to the writings of child psychologist D.W. Winnicott, play functions as a self-generated bridge between the "inner psychic reality" of needs and wants, and an external reality, which we discover at an early age to be incapable of willed obedience. Play seeks relief from the tyrannies of "reality" by endowing the here-and-now with alternative significances. On the playground or in the theatre, a wooden platform becomes a bed, a deserted island, a time machine, a sleeping giant, an automobile, and all of these things in rapid succession. The player turns into a star football player, a dragon, a favourite aunt, a feared teacher, a future self, or a wind storm, just by saying so. "When I do this", a child or performer announces, snapping her fingers, "it means I'm invisible".

Through these momentary flights we glimpse the player's inner progress, not only the subjects of preoccupation, but their psychic shadings, how they please, unsettle, entice, or tickle the fancy. In the theatre, practitioners and spectators co-operate in the realisation of fictional worlds, cobbled together from the trappings of real life and animated by society's collective inner currents.

All theatre can be seen to spring from a spirit of play, of pointedly reworking the world under a licensed dispensation from social "realities". Theatre has become a sophisticated rite, acquiring a system of rules or "conventions" to broker absent events from actual presences; at advanced levels it seeks an unabashedly adult refinement, an immediate but practiced play world pinned in the air for each new audience. Given the confluence of history, routine, and co-operative pretending which subtends every performance, it can indeed be tempting to use theatre as the plaything itself — which brings us to Veronica Coburn, Raymond Keane and Mikel Murfi, also known as Barabbas... the Company.

This essay does not intend to revise Barabbas' arrival to a place of prominence on the Irish theatre scene since their inception in 1993, nor to provide a definitive assessment of their rehearsal and performance techniques; and it by no means intends a critique or unravelling of Lennox Robinson's original text for *The Whiteheaded Boy*. It is concerned with an abiding sense of "playing with theatre", always part of the package in a Barabbas venture. It focuses upon aspects of the play spirit inherent in the theatre event, but given a pride of place in Barabbas' production of Robinson's *The Whiteheaded Boy*, which first saw the light of a stage in autumn 1997. It also suggests that such a spirit of theatrical playing, while sharing a private joke with the audience, serves to open otherwise unused windows for the perception of life.

Barabbas have become known for a style of clown-based physical theatre, whose underpinning discipline produces the circumstances for play's best discoveries. A playful quality of behaviour loosens, floats, "frees" its participants from the earthbound embrace of physical laws and social codes, denying worldly obstacles their usual powers. It is by no means new or unusual to approach theatre with a heightened spirit of play toward creative possibility, a "willingness to try, willingness to poke", as paraphrased by Veronica Coburn, presently the company's artistic director. Like other troupes, Barabbas use an array of games and playful techniques in the rehearsal room, very often with an eye toward the physical and mental demands to be met in the work session.

In retrospect, Barabbas and Lennox Robinson's 1916 play, *The Whiteheaded Boy*, would seem destined for one another. Feeling somewhat "devised out" in the middle of 1997, the threesome were inclined to look for something text-based. They were again in cahoots with director Gerry Stembridge, with whom they had worked on Macbeth in 1994 and who chairs their Board of Directors. One might imagine the initial spirit of round-table foolery with which someone tossed out the idea of tackling a chestnut by the exceedingly respectable Robinson. But the play spirit has everything to do with pursuing the unlikely, and Gerry came back with *The Whiteheaded Boy*. He recalls the perfect lateral logic of seeking to mine the company's European-inflected style side by side with their indigenous Irishness:

> I kind of thought if they tackled an old Irish play, it has the advantage of having all the things that theatre audiences like — it has plot and story and yarn and characters that they'll recognise — and so there's the possibility of getting that popular response to it. And then they're allowed into the secret, if you like, of also Barabbas being different to that.

Gerry's accompanying concept for the show sprouted fully formed with his choice of text: "There's a very simple idea behind it which also has to do with Barabbas as a company, how they like to present themselves. We wanted to emphasise, "Look, all this stuff is very easy; it's just about telling a story. It's what kids do, they act out a story".

Barabbas' production of *The Whiteheaded Boy* is literally playful in its premise of three people "making the world" through their own devices. Since the "Original" run in the Project @ the mint, it has toured Ireland, Britain and the U.S. There is, built into the event, an almost unnerving lack of pretence in the way Veronica, Raymond and Mikel welcome theatregoers to the performance as "themselves" (which, in later incarnations has involved going into the auditorium). Their casual behaviour dismantles the formal, even stodgy, barrier we've come to take for granted between performers and audience, which after all are just a bunch of people occupying the same space. "Brechtian" stage worlds are not uncommon, but they are rarely installed with comparably unforced candour. We know very well the show has been previously rehearsed and performed. But the unusually open-handed approach emphasises the sense of co-operation between practitioners and spectators always required for theatre to transpire: it is a genuine invitation to play, which envelops the ensuing ceremony of performance in a heightened air of complicity.

Robinson's play might be described as a light satire on small-town pretension and family machinations, with a whiff of the political allegory claimed by the playwright about Ireland's relationship with Great Britain. It depicts the Geoghegan household upon the return of its favourite son, Denis, who was meant to have been gathering prestige upon the clan at medical school up in Dublin, but whose independent spirit perpetually confounds family plans.

For a dramatic text written under the staid conventions of the well-made play, the production rebuffs traditional analysis, ever unfolding on and between the two levels of Robinson's fiction and Barabbas' enactment. As hosts of the stage world, Veronica, Raymond and Mikel take on all the roles save one, without respect to age and gender. They deliver the text more intact than the playwright could have imagined, taking turns in voicing the original stage directions, surely written out of Robinson's own sense of play. What are usually unadorned instructions to the practitioner or armchair reader, in this case adopt an ostentatiously subjective register, more suitable to a novel's narrator or a storyteller, as if spoken by a character who oversees the proceedings and provides clucking commentary. Here is an extract from the opening stage directions, rather interesting in tone for the one part of the script the audience doesn't usually see or hear:

> William Geoghegan (God rest his soul) was a very genteel man, and when the wife bought him the house and the bit of land instead of getting a tenant for it like a sensible man (and the whole

village knew Clancy, the vet, was mad to take it), nothing would do him but live in it himself and walk down to his business every day like a millionaire. 'Tis too high notions poor William always had...

The stage world builds upon an openly playful approach to characterisation, highlighted by the fact that Veronica, Raymond and Mikel do not pretend to be anyone more than themselves taking on fictional roles, as established by their pre-performance conduct. Dressed for uniform neutrality in trousers, jerseys and waistcoats, they make a point of "putting on" characters which are cut from thicker, broader stylistic cloth than their real-life behaviour. Although crisply staged and well-rehearsed, they allow us to see the fun-loving fraction of their own psyches that spill over the sides of fictional character.

These thumbnail physical signatures and matching voices redolent of Co. Cork, seem to comprise an album of country caricatures known to every Irish theatregoer. But it is as if, under the guiding hand of Lennox Robinson, the performers have stumbled upon an array of comically human archetypes. As one reviewer observed during the production's swing through Wales: "Although the play is set in Ireland, the eccentric characterisations portrayed can be found in any village anywhere". This inkling of the universal is worth a closer look.

Raymond does a memorable Mrs Geoghegan, the widowed nurturer of the family, described in the stage directions as "a hearty woman yet", "not more than sixty-five years of age", having "such a pleasant way with her", and "not what I'd call a clever woman". He inhabits the role by softening his mien, bringing his elbows close to his body, while allowing his hands to float generally upward, one to his collar, the other, bent at the wrist, palm up and fingers gently curled. His head sits slightly back of his shoulders; his facial features knit toward his forehead in a mask of practised concern, a pinched quality carried through in his voice. When under attack his Mrs Geoghegan is stoically defensive, clenched fist to mouth as if squeezing a hanky to choke off the tears.

Raymond enters the role from his default or "neutral" bearing, which throws the palette of fictional character into starker relief. There is no change of costume or make-up: whatever skill is brought to bear in playing the character, the brute features of Raymond's presence remain unhidden. The characterisation is in no way a camp caricature in walk or speech. The expressions of his "womanly" and "maternal" behaviour, though not ridiculed, are accented and clearly emanate from the body of someone who is, to say the least, not the character in the flesh.

All of Barabbas' characterisations in this production gain their sweep by "playing" with choice details of human behaviour, an approach justified by the premise. They receive licence to bypass realistic faithfulness to any given original, and so throw the net wider via more broadly recognisable streaks of personality rendered in boldface. At the same time, the performers do indeed hurl themselves into the fictional situations with childlike abandon; the characters would not resonate as they do if these highlights of human gesture were not infused with the textures of organic feeling whose truths we know in our bones.

It should be noted that "character" does not appear in a vacuum; its attributes emerge through engagement, externally and internally, with specific situations. Robinson's "inner" blueprint, of course, foresees a matrix of potential interpersonal transactions. The "Outer" structure, contributed by Barabbas, means that all three performers may have to keep several onstage characters involved in the action at any given time. The playful spirit, then, needs the support of a theatrical sensibility.

Gerry allocated the roles more or less from the start, according to his assessments of textual logistics and the performers' personalities. During early rehearsals, the company experimented with various incarnations for their respective characters. Sociocultural observation was supplemented by technical considerations, ways of helping the audience to separate characters on sight.

Mikel, for instance, portrays three characters, all of which distinguish themselves physically and otherwise within his personal brand of daft intensity: As George, the eldest of the Geoghegan offspring, described as "always terrible industrious", he adopts a granite-like, forward-leaning carriage; he is apoplectically serious, with a brow-furrowed face, muscle-bound speech, and the obsessive behavioural tic of smoothing his hair across his forehead. His Jane Geoghegan, a "nice quiet girl", contrasts in almost every way, upright and willowy, with a glowing smile, breathy voice and a shyness built in to her movement. And he endows Baby, the youngest of the Geoghegan sisters, with the semblance of a cartoon duck, body lurching awkwardly over pigeon toes, tongue lolling between lips, hands splayed, eyes wide and clueless — she is an unrestrained caricature of the "great lump of a girl" described in the stage directions.

There is ongoing amusement derived from watching the performers try to keep faith with the established "rules of play": All three track their characters through scenes, which becomes especially difficult when the stage gets "crowded"; someone might pop up for a line here, a bit of stage business there, leaping elsewhere again for a third contribution. Everyone has to conduct at least one short scene with themselves. These duologues, usually seen as comic tours de force, challenge the performers' theatrical proficiency in on-the-spot playing. And by expanding the scope from single character to both sides of a conversation, they afford mischief with the nature of interaction itself.

At one point, George and Jane have a sub-scene together. George sits at the table, nearly doubled in consternation about a telegram concerning the latest shame Denis brought upon the family. Jane has previously been placed as standing next to him, profile away. In this case, character qualities conspire with stage positioning to afford optimum contrasts:

JANE: What is it, George?

GEORGE: "Geoghegan's Hope also ran". That's either a race horse, or it's Denis himself.

JANE: I don't understand you.

GEORGE: He's either broken his word to me and is betting on horses again, or else ... he's failed again.

JANE: His examination, you mean?

GEORGE: I do.

JANE: God help us!

The sequence is exhaustively honed and precisely executed so that each character's physical and emotional mark can be hit with minimal "leakage". The three short lines at the end of the exchange bring about a miniature snowballing effect. Mikel bounces up and down between characters like a human jack-in-the-box, the contrast amplified in the antithetical vocal timbres. Filling out the impression is the volley between comically contrasting inner lives, George seized by volcanic, self-righteous passion counterpointed against Jane's retiring naiveté.

These playful conceptions push performance technique to its realisable limit, an impressive accomplishment not lost upon the spectator if Mikel fulfils his obligation to the stage world without faltering. In addition, the silly spectacle of these opposing personas emanating rapidly from a single performer's body moves any satiric stance back a full step to take in the full unit of interpersonal conflict. Mikel's enactment skewers not only the individual types, but the tenor of their transaction, a resonance patently unapproachable by more realistic, less playful, theatrical representation.

Barabbas' rehearsal process includes a fair degree of discussion, complementing the nuts and bolts of practical rehearsals. The mad machine of *The Whiteheaded Boy* underwent an ongoing self-examination as to the fitness of this comic moment or that with reference to the world that was taking shape. In the following sequence, the production "plays with playing" in a manner that stretches the established stage world.

Baby has originally been described as "a great one for music", and opens Act III singing. The piano, in the style of the other onstage furniture, is shaped like the real thing, but a two-dimensional keyboard is pasted where the real one would be. As Baby, Mikel launches into "playing" with an over-the-top delight to a sound cue of someone splashing about on the keys. He flails at the "keyboard", occasionally adding a flourish by reaching one hand over the other, this by way of accompaniment as he drones a remote semblance of "Because God Made you Mine" (the religious song called for in the script) loudly on a single, excruciating note. The opening lines of the scene go as follows:

> **KATE**: That's lovely, Baby. You've a great turn for music.
>
> **BABY**: I have, then. I love them passionate songs. There's some like comics, but give me a song with passion in it. It goes through me like. I suppose I'm queer.
>
> **KATE**: Why wouldn't you like them? Myself, I could never tell one tune from another, but I'd listen to you all day.

The production, which for the most part remains faithful to the fictional reality in its heavily stylistised way, in this case "plays" with its own premise by setting it loose. The characters deliver the above lines without conscious irony. The contrast between their conversation and Baby's rapturously tone-deaf musicality is, of course, seen as highly comic, but occurs as a result of a special liberty taken in the space between fictional strip and phenomenal depiction. The sequence extends the range of play another decimal point, as it were, by stepping wholeheartedly toward the ridiculous.

Similar comic detours are taken periodically. But they would have been mulled over among the group during rehearsals, with an eye toward maintaining an integrity to the stage world and a "truthful core" to the characters, no matter how outrageous. Veronica says: "The job we have is to play with it enough so that it's interesting and good, but not play with it so much that you lose the heart of the play". Ultimately Gerry saw this sequence as involving a character less central to the plot, whose momentary extravagance could well serve to goose the start of the third act: "When you look at the range of some characters, even within the general physical range of the way they're doing some of them, some characters have to be taken better care of and some characters still have the possibility of being let loose". One can indeed discern a sort of sliding scale from the characters central to the plot, like George, Aunt Ellen, Mrs Geoghegan and Duffy, to more peripheral ones like Baby, Peter and Hannah, who are allowed longer leashes in the service of comic effect.

Several aspects of Barabbas' theatrical play spirit can be seen to entwine in the following single sequence. In Act III, John Duffy and Aunt Ellen are left onstage, a widower and dowager upon the brink of a long-delayed romantic connection. Raymond plays Duffy, the sly, small-town entrepreneur, as a chronically humourless rail of a man, his trunk arched slightly forward and eyes steeled, his prune-like lips maintaining parsimonious account of the very words that escape them. Veronica's Aunt Ellen, a woman who long ago chose to bypass romance for business, rests a pair of spectacles low on her nose, turns down the corners of her mouth, and outlines in body and metabolism the toll taken by gravity — physical and spiritual — over the years.

There is a delectable anticipation to the scene, well prepared by Robinson. Duffy has earlier proposed marriage to Aunt Ellen, with whom he was once linked romantically. Her acceptance is his secret demand for the withdrawal of a potentially costly and scandalous civil suit against young Denis, who has reneged on his own engagement to Duffy's daughter. Comic irony abounds as Aunt Ellen, in the company of the three young Geoghegan women, "innocently" expresses interest in a wedding dress pictured in *Vogue* magazine. "Listen to them all laughing", the narrator says of the sisters, who are at all times unaware of the amorous undercurrents. Duffy arrives, asking veiled questions about his proposal, while Aunt Ellen maintains straight-laced indifference.

Finally, the two are left alone, though only in the fictional sense. Mikel has just completed two lines as narrator, clearing the room of the sisters. Duffy stands stiffly, several strides away, left hand behind his back and the right one clenched close to his mouth, apparently unable to break the ice. Mikel prepares to observe the ensuing scene from slightly upstage. The two characters appear locked at some emotional impasse, Duffy struck speechless and Aunt Ellen wilfully lost in her magazine.

The space separating Aunt Ellen and Duffy will be easily recognised as one of those yawning chasms felt between two people, neither of which knows quite how to take the first step towards broaching a monumental issue. Ironic perception is enhanced by the playful style of characterisation, which revels in showing both the hardened shells of these two old coots and the born-again romantic impulses beneath.

After several seconds of silence, Mikel starts to show his growing impatience on behalf of the audience. With a final gesture of exasperation, he proceeds to lift Duffy/Raymond in his frozen pose and transport him right next to Aunt Ellen/Veronica. He then manually pushes Raymond's trunk over slightly so Duffy's head will be close to Aunt Ellen's, thereby jump-starting the scene.

In a flash, the production has pulled the pants down around theatre convention's ankles. It has, in effect, blithely broken the rules, reminding us of the artifice we routinely agree to forget when we settle into the theatre seat. But what gives the moment its huge comic charge is its play with the emotional tension that grounds the real-life situation. Yes, the characters and situation are keyed for amusement. But the moment has no real hook without the spectator's first-hand recognition of this emotional petrifaction. This is precisely one of the places where play and theatre intersect, working through psychic tensions by enacting variations on reality. The solution, so simple as to be invisible, seems dropped from the sky. In an act of communal wish fulfilment, Mikel makes "external reality" obey his will by enacting a level of being usually reserved for gods and fairies. By momentarily overriding the pretence of realistic theatre convention, the production also admits a fleeting perception about the strange hardness of human emotions.

Although occupied with the business of disengaging reality, play nonetheless adopts its own set of rules. It is the production's self-imposed obligation to the dramatic text and the maintenance of a certain continuity which creates the conditions for some of its comic effects. One of the most notable features of the production's theatrical play is its capacity to subvert even itself. By midway through Act I, the stage world has been outlined in terms of three performers from the spectator's own reality, acting and narrating a play they have either rehearsed or collaborate on intuitively. But the entrance of actor Louis Lovett, who plays Denis, asks for the first time that the spectator buy into a theatrical illusion — not an intrusion from the real world, but from the fictional world.

Upon the usual introduction — Veronica as narrator says, "Ah! Here's Denis in the other door. Isn't he lovely? You'd know he was from Dublin by his clothes and his smartness. He's just turned twenty-two" — Mikel has already assumed the role centre stage, epitomising in the production's caricatured style an urbane and confident young fellow, cigar in one hand and brandy snifter in the other. But Louis arrives, apparently "the character himself", embodied in a more old-fashioned theatrical style, with heavily blushed cheeks and bright blond hair, fully costumed in cream suit, scarf and checked vest. His appearance, with an acting style somehow lower-keyed than the rest of the fiction, marks him as made from "Other material" than the rest of the people in the stage world.

Louis is put forth as a (rather Pirandellian) pure inhabitant of the fictional world, and the other three performers behave as if he is an "unexpected" addition to their storytelling. They go through phases of surprise, confusion, amusement and reluctance, as if unsure they should receive his alien presence into their reality. Denis/Louis says, "Hullo, mother"; Raymond suddenly "decides" to continue the play and snaps into Mrs Geoghegan's character. "she" catapults onto Louis' hip, arms around his neck and both legs airborne in double arabesque, for the line, "Denis! My darling boy!"

The production culminates in the act of Louis/Denis earning induction into the bodied status occupied by the other three performers, by receiving one of their costumes and "learning" a bona fide character stance. He is, in effect, trading in his "fictionality" to become "real" — or is it the other way around? The scene unfolds, not as an ultimate comic coup, but as a rather touching ritual of acceptance. A more "realistic" production might seek to distinguish Denis from the others primarily through casting or costume. But herein lies the secret value of theatre's expanded playing field for a company like Barabbas — there are perceptions to be imparted about our dealings with others, about "fitting in", about the notion of reality itself, and rather than the stage world just talking about them, or showing them in the same surface-oriented terms we see every day, the production makes them playfully manifest.

Looking from overhead, it is no exaggeration to suggest that a palpable play spirit presides over Barabbas' production of *The Whiteheaded Boy*. Robinson contributes a vehicle with its own cynical soft spot for various socio-cultural targets; Barabbas suggest themselves as the winking agents of metaphysical cause and effect, at once cheeky and sympathetic toward the world and its goings-on. Their host personalities and inflated characterisations pitch the text more familiarly for a contemporary audience — the fiction, while fully inhabited, is seen through inverted commas. In fact, the concentric worlds created by Barabbas' presence and make-believe serve to collapse the distance between today's audience and the conditions of Robinson's original. Spectators with tastes for the traditional gain access to the time-honoured texture of an early Abbey original; the more theatrically highbrow get a jazzy take on an old play, to which they can apply words like "post-modern" and "deconstruction".

Such is the nature of play for grown-ups offered by Barabbas in this hugely popular production. Under their diligent guidance, people are drawn nightly to contemplate some of the things that still press upon adult psyches 80-odd years after *The Whiteheaded Boy* was born, questions about appearances and truth and humankind's little blemishes. The performers invite collusion in a world tuned risibly to these issues, its building blocks open to the same healthy disrespect, and from the stage they can feel the recognition in our laughter. That, of course, is a factor one can lose sight of amid the admiration for theatre's magical spaces: the ability to view something in a spirit of play also happens to be a defining condition for laughter, and it does tend to make the occasion quite a lot of fun. Now is that the crowning bonus or the most important feature of all?

Works Cited:

Ellis, M.J., (1973), *Why People Play* (New Jersey: Prentice-Hall)

Huizinga, Johan, (1955), *Homo Ludens: A study of the play element in culture* (Boston: Beacon; orig. German pub. 1944)

Lowenfeld, Margaret, (1991), *Play in Childhood* (London: Mac Keith, orig. pub. 1935)

Murray, Christopher, (1997), *Twentieth-Century Irish Drama: Mirror up to Nation* (Manchester: Manchester University)

O'Neill, Michael J., (1964), *Lennox Robinson* (New York: Twayne)

Robinson, Lennox, (1982), *The Whiteheaded Boy* in *Selected Plays: Lennox Robinson*, Introduction by Christopher Murray (Gerrards Cross: Colin Smythe, 63-117)

Wilshire, Bruce, (1982), *Role Playing and Identity: The Limits of Theatre as Metaphor* (Bloomington: Indiana University)

Winnicott, D.W., (1991), *Playing and Reality* (London: Routledge, 1991; orig. pub. 1971)

Personal unpublished interviews: Veronica Coburn, Raymond Keane, and Mikel Murfi (May, 1997); Gerry Stembridge (May, 1998); Veronica Coburn (March, 1999)

Songs of possible worlds: nation, representation and citizenship in the work of Calypso Productions

Victor Merriman

I hate a song that makes you feel like you're no good,
on account of
your poor luck or your hard travellin'...
I'm out to fight those songs to
the last breath of my being...
I want to write songs that make you take
pride in yourself, and in your work...
Woody Guthrie

Calypso Productions (http://homepage.tinet.ie/~calypso) was formed in autumn 1993 by playwrights Dónal O'Kelly and Kenneth Glenaan, with Charlie O'Neill. Unusually, one writer was based in Dublin, and one in Glasgow. Although this arrangement was to prove too difficult to sustain over time, it culminated significantly in O'Kelly and Glenaan's jointly written *The Business of Blood*, which played in both Scotland and Ireland. "Calypso" was attractive to the founders because it evoked the Creole music of the Caribbean islands, where music became the voice of the voiceless. The decision to describe themselves as "Calypso Productions" rather than "Calypso Theatre Company" is a deliberate reflection of their commitment to developing educational programmes, with resource materials, alongside theatre, site specific and street performances. The educational materials are circulated widely, and especially to legislators, to whom they are intended as a challenge.

Calypso's mission statement of 1995 is about as far as you can possibly travel from the blandness of the genre:

> Calypso's mission is simple, practical and humble. We want to change the world... the change we want to effect is small, significant and possible.... By our future world family, we will be remembered in one of two ways. We will either have been caring guardians who nurtured their inheritance — social, political, artistic, environmental and sacred — or we will have been the parasites who depleted some of the hope and possibility from their lives. We are all world citizens. Some of us are lucky enough to have inherited life saving rights, life enhancing social opportunities and life affirming creative possibilities. With those rights and privileges comes a responsibility to defend them for ourselves and for others. (*Information and Action on Arms*, educational resource materials accompanying *The Business of Blood*.)

Calypso Productions is funded by An Chomhairle Ealaíon/The Arts Council, and seeks dedicated funding from other agencies as appropriate to its various projects. For instance *Cell* by Paula Meehan (1999) attracted funding from the Department of Justice, Equality and Law Reform because it addressed the issue of women's experiences of imprisonment. In its focus on partnerships and its dedication to using "theatrical narrative to tell stories and to raise awareness about people whose lives are shaped by dramatic events", Calypso is very much a phenomenon of 1990s theatre and society in the Republic of Ireland. This is borne out by its production history, which includes the following: *Hughie on the Wires* by Dónal O'Kelly (1993), *Trickledown Town* by Dónal O'Kelly (1994), *The Business of Blood* by Dónal O'Kelly and Kenneth Glenaan (1995), *Rosie and Starwars* by Charlie O'Neill (1997), *Féile Fáilte* — a street festival celebrating cultural diversity — directed by Declan Gorman (1997*)*, *Farawayan* by Dónal O'Kelly (1998) and *Cell* by Paula Meehan (1999). *Hughie on the Wires* sites a young Derry man in El Salvador, achieving multiple resonances between the North of Ireland and Central America; *Trickledown Town* is set in the Caribbean, where an Irish-born representative of the World Bank comes face to face with the ironies of his dual identity as citizen of a former colony and agent of neo-imperialism; *Féile Fáilte* is a non-stop carnival featuring a fire-breathing Celtic Tiger, repressive border guards, frightened refugees and a newsman with the slogan "Before you open your mind, poison it — with the Daily Lie". With the exception of *Cell* by Paula Meehan, the other plays will be discussed below.

I have written elsewhere in some detail on *The Business of Blood* by Dónal O'Kelly and Kenneth Glenaan (1995) (See Merriman: 1998), and saw the production in Dublin, and on tour in London. The urgency and the ethical framework of the project are compelling and represent a kind of high point of the O'Kelly/Glenaan vision for Calypso. *The Business of Blood* stages the story of Chris Cole, a Christian pacifist who broke into British Aerospace Stevenage and destroyed components of the nosecones of Hawk jetfighters. He acted in order to draw attention both to their use against civilian populations in East Timor, and to what he saw as the hypocrisy of a British government which publicly announces that it does not sell arms to regimes known to be involved in human rights abuses. The company addresses First World audiences, which have multiple positions on Third World issues. The status of Ireland and Scotland as countries colonised by England is re-affirmed in the visit to London, where the company speaks in solidarity with the struggle of those colonised by Indonesia in East Timor. The reality of the implication of Ireland and Scotland in the oppressions of a colonial past, and of their membership of power blocs of wealthy and belligerent nation-states is raised by performances in Dublin, Glasgow and on tour.

The illustrated booklet, *Information and Action on Arms* which accompanied the play includes the following transcript of a conversation between the journalist John Pilger and Alan Clark MP (Alan Clark, former minister in the Thatcher government was responsible for the sale of the latest batch of Hawk aircraft to Indonesia.):

> **John Pilger:** In East Timor it (Indonesia) has killed more people proportionately than Pol Pot killed in Cambodia. By all credible accounts it [ha]s killed one third of the population. Isn't that ever a consideration for the British government?
>
> **Alan Clark:** It's not something that often enters my... thinking, I must admit.
>
> **John Pilger:** Why is that?
>
> **Alan Clark:** My responsibility is to my own people. I don't really fill my mind much with what one set of foreigners is doing to another.

The link between the arms industry and the fate of subject populations is clearly made. What is also suggested in this carefully selected sequence is that moral blindness and amnesia are now constitutive aspects of governance in the civilised western world, and not a function of ministerial idiosyncrasy. The consequences of such gaps in western consciousness are stark and final for peoples of other worlds. It is Calypso's particular concern to expose the extent to which strategic blindness and amnesia at government level have immediate and long-term consequences within western democratic regimes themselves.

The deliberate, uncompromising selection of incidents which illustrate lethal double standards in high places and in the population at large characterises the episodes dramatised in *The Business of Blood*. Recognisably related to British and American workers' theatre of the 1930s, the play provoked sharp dispute in the columns of the *Irish Times*. It was dismissed in David Nowlan's review as follows:

> ... it has been said, inter alia, that drama is comprised of conflict and change, yet within this work there is no dramatic conflict and there has been no significant change at its conclusion. This is theatre being used to make a point rather than a point being used to create drama (Nowlan: 1995).

The message is clear; this is not dramatic art. Fintan O'Toole responded:

> There is a strong tendency to patronise such writing, to see it as at best a lesser form of art, at worst a corruption of aesthetic purity....
> The question posed by *The Business of Blood* — whether civilisation can be said to exist at all while complicity with mass murder is

treated as a legitimate business — is a question that addresses the very possibility of art itself (O'Toole: 1995).

It is clear that when art begins to address the terrain of geo-politics it opens up the question of its own topography as well. The critical reception of *The Business of Blood* is of considerable interest, and an analysis of its content would yield a rich account of the underpinnings of a range of structuring discourses silently active in popular debates around art, politics and economics. As far as this discussion is concerned, the emphases in the critical debate point to the potential of Calypso's engagement with lives lived on dangerous margins to open up questions of dramatic form and audience positions. Susan Bennett states that:

> with so much theatre activity operating outside recognised cultural institutions, the boundaries of culture are undoubtedly challenged and the feedback of non-traditional audiences has changed, above all else, the product which we recognise as theatre. (Bennett: 1992, 182).

This draws to our attention particular characteristics of Calypso's programme for 1997-1998: *Rosie and Starwars* by Charlie O'Neill, *Féile Fáilte*, directed by Declan Gorman and *Farawayan*, written and directed by Dónal O'Kelly. In O'Neill's case, the broad issues were the implications of cultural representation for social inclusion of marginal groups, and audience composition for theatre events. Both Gorman's production and O'Kelly's play take this up, with *Farawayan* marking a major departure for the company and a signpost toward futures both for the political agency of cultural workers, and for developments in Irish theatre practices in the twenty-first century.

> Too often art and artists travel a journey where the landscapes they move through and the people they encounter become mere observations, ideas to be used. Other artists travel as participants in their landscapes. Their work is about, and comes from their interaction with their fellow world citizens.... Our landscape covers the planet. Our family is global. Our creativity is a critical one (Calypso Productions, *1995 Mission Statement*).

This assertion of artists' implication in, as opposed to detachment from, the world is central to Calypso's cultural project. Calypso consciously addresses the actual/virtual dynamic of late twentieth century globalisation in ways clearly different from John Crowley's *True Lines* (Bickerstaffe Theatre Company, 1993) or *Double Helix* (Bickerstaffe Theatre Company, 1995), for instance. Crowley's work stages young Irish people at large in a shrinking world, engaged with — even embodying — contemporary technology. Formal innovation here foregrounds individual experiences as isolated phenomena elaborated in a global playground. It is of some significance, perhaps, that Calypso's intervention in *The Business of Blood*, along with Dónal O'Kelly's *Asylum! Asylum!* (Peacock Theatre, 1994) addressed a public which had to have issues of race, neo-imperialism and oppression — presented to it as if from afar. Even now — five years on — that Ireland no longer exists. Ireland, newly prosperous under late capitalism, now corresponds to what Ben Agger describes as a 'capitalist, racist and sexist' society, with stark examples of the inequities and exclusions typical of globalised socio-economic orders (Agger: 1992). Since 1995, Calypso Productions has exposed the local elaboration of the new international paradigm in its focus on intranational betrayals: of travelling people, refugees and asylum seekers, and a poor, criminalised "underclass", the latter a most appalling designation, even in "a betrayed republic" (See Michael D. Higgins: 1996, 212).

This stance aligns Calypso with Cornel West's category of "new cultural worker" (West: 1992, 19), whose central task is the demystification of the seemingly bewildering configurations of economic, social, cultural and political coalitions which characterise contemporary living in the western world.

Oppositional texts and their constitutive practices are unlikely to be widely distributed in a culture mediated by, and in the interests of, globalised corporations. Cast in terms which dictate and reflect the norms of bourgeois living, such corporations offer entertainment organised around visual spectacle and narrative closure. The world appears in these texts as a statement of fact, a space which exists to ratify and legitimise existing social relations. It stages the life experiences of marginal persons and groups as departures from the norm. Such departures exist only to facilitate the triumphant return of that norm in the plenitude of narrative closure. Readers are invited to question only to the extent of exercising curiosity about situations which the narrative is structured to disclose. Such situations, and the people within them are structured as events which appear in themselves as puzzling or threatening disturbances of an otherwise stable norm. The world, the people in it and their inter-relationships are known quantities. They are not depicted as subjects for human inquiry, let alone transformative action. Realism the *lingua franca* of dominant cultural production on screen and on stage, is the cultural expression of the social and economic needs of dominant groups.

In the light of this, the transformative potential of any example of cultural production may well depend crucially on the extent to which it structures the world as a question. This task is at the centre of the *Rosie and Starwars* project. As travellers see it, there are two categories of traveller in Ireland: actually existing people with specific life histories and experiences, and a textual fantasy, communicated through mainstream cultural production. Let us call the one, traveller, and the other *Traveller*. As a mediated text, a fiction in which the life experiences to which it claims to refer are often submerged, if not repudiated, *Traveller* is overwhelmingly constructed in pejorative terms. It is an affront to bourgeois social norms in opposition to which it is structured in the first place. The authorship of that text is to be found outside traveller society, in the dominant group. *Traveller* embodies all of the features of stereotype in its quality of being frozen in time, simultaneously childlike and sinister. In a country where many people no longer have day-to-day contact with travellers, familiarity is a function not of lived experience, but of the imperatives of cultural production, notably those of film-making. Film is a fiction, but with formidable power to constitute private and social realities. The classical narrative paradigm at work in *The Field* and *Trojan Eddie* — films popular around the time *Rosie and Starwars* was being written — figures the world — and the people — it depicts as fixed, known and closed to critical questioning. Calypso's intervention in *Rosie and Starwars*, its main project for the European Year Against Racism, might be approached as an attempt to answer the question: "If *Traveller* equals text, and that text fails to map on to experience, how might its injurious impact on travellers' social participation be mitigated or negated"?

Charlie O'Neill's strategy of refiguring an apparently known material world as a problem is achieved principally by means of that great trope of bourgeois entertainment: boy meets girl. The boy is the ludicrous-but-likeable Seánie "Starwars" Whelan. The girl is Rosie Joyce, a settled traveller and single parent. *Rosie and Starwars* is set in Ennis, the capital of County Clare. It is 1995 and Clare is about to win the All Ireland Hurling championship for the first time in over eighty years. In the words of Starwars—a member of the county Under-21 panel — "The whole county was goin' apeshit on skates"! The play derives its narrative force from the confluence of success on the hurling field — with its accompanying protestations of the natural superiority of Clare identity — and a crisis involving the occupants of an unserviced halting site for travellers on the outside of the town. Seánie's father, Tom Whelan, is involved in a consortium that plans to develop land, which includes the halting site. A local reporter, Jim Furlong, becomes involved when another member of the clandestine consortium, Councillor Larry Hartigan, declares at a Council meeting that "Traveller men should be clinically castrated"! Rosie Joyce, who meets and begins a relationship with Seánie, lives in nearby Limerick City where she works at a Travellers' Resource Centre. Rosie was taken from her family on the halting site and placed in care during her childhood. She lost part of her leg in an accident when she was four, the details of which are unresolved between herself and her father in whose company she was at the time.

Rosie's mother, Chrissie Joyce is involved in agitation to have the unofficial site provided with services. The play's narrative reaches a climax on the night the Clare team brings home the Liam McCarthy Cup. Seánie and his pals celebrate wildly on a night that "Ennis was like Rio"! At the same time, Hartigan and a gang of masked thugs attack the traveller families and burn their caravans. Rosie's son, JoJo is trapped in a caravan consumed in flames. In the confusion, Paddy emerges with the child safe and sound. Police and media extol his heroism. In a final twist, Paddy's revelation that it was a masked attacker who retrieved JoJo from the flames and handed the child to him is blurted out in the course of an interview on national radio by Rosie, infuriated at the construction being placed on the events of that night by a man she had trusted, Jim Furlong. The play foregrounds questions of identity, entitlement and power relations. It attempts to contextualise travellers' difference by deliberately situating traveller experience in relation to the assumptions of the sedentary population, both privately held and publicly promulgated by the communications media.

O'Neill's play problematizes the mediation of relationships between travellers and the sedentary population by the text *Traveller*. In setting the action at the time of the Hurling Championship, *Rosie and Starwars* situates sedentary people in discourses of excess, exuberant tribalism and drunkenness — conditions typically associated with stereotypes of *Traveller*. Chrissie Joyce differs from the careworn *Traveller* mothers of the films in her espousal of organised political action as a means of bettering her family's circumstances. Neither childlike nor sinister, the traveller patriarch, Paddy Joyce is a man on whose life the tide has gone out: "Once the skill in me hands was a blessing, now it's a disease". O'Neill's careful depiction of the Joyce family as rounded human beings — grounded in his detailed research into traveller experience, and the warmth of his lively script — entitles them to a legitimate call on audience understanding as they attempt to make their way in the world, and is particularly effective in debunking stereotypical fantasies.

Rosie herself is both protagonist and chorus, actor and observer. She deliberately opts for action in response to a sharp and thoughtful analysis of the needs of her family's situation. It is she who names the racism staged in various episodes. Her stance problematizes the roles, not only of the apparently respectable Tom Whelan, but of the would-be detached Jim Furlong. It is in Rosie's presence also that any escapist impetus to romanticise traveller culture is resisted. *Rosie and Starwars* does more than thematise and stage everyday encounters in which racism becomes visible. In *naming* the perspective which obscures its presence, the play stages the invisible power of racist discourse to structure and marginalize a people. In its explicit interrogation of the reporter Jim

Furlong's mediation of realities apparent to the play's audiences, *Rosie and Starwars* opens up the question of how content comes in these times to be known. The further question as to in whose interests these constructs of factual events circulate and operate is explicit in the action of the play and in Rosie's words. O'Neill's decision to privilege the life experiences of a young traveller woman results in much more than a novel focus for the narrative. It gives rise to a dynamic of action and reflection, of narrative and ethical questioning which situates the play as a potentially transformative text. In this way, the play obliges the audience to engage with the role of culture in the social construction of reality. It raises urgent questions of knowledge, pedagogy and power and their relationship to cultural participation and social agency. In this way, it foregrounds the central issue raised by travellers' life experiences: the effective limits of Irish citizenship.

Rosie and Starwars is a cultural intervention within limitations. While the play is undoubtedly a very different order of cultural production from the films mentioned, left to stand alone it can be marginalized on similar grounds to those advanced as a rationale for travellers' position on the margins of Irish society. It is for this reason that Calypso produced an accompanying portfolio, *Information and Action on Racism*. The company also committed themselves to a programme of exploratory reflection, seminars and discussions during their tour. Both strategies contextualise and problematise the performance text and the range of possible audience positions it may evoke. The point at issue here is not one of access to commodities. The project is specifically and overtly pedagogical. In its commitment to including travellers in audiences for the play, and as participants in workshops and discussions arising from it, Calypso extends its cultural project in important ways. The programme situates audiences in critical sites where difference is textualised as part of, rather than apart from, social and cultural experience. This strategy has significant potential to initiate social development through dialogue. *Rosie and Starwars* marks an important attempt to reposition readers because of choices deliberately made in its (re)construction of the text *Traveller*. This is a highly significant achievement, and one which marks both the radical potential of the project and a real development for Calypso around their understanding of the ways in which traveller experience challenges the credibility of Irish citizenship as a guarantor of fundamental rights and opportunities. If *Rosie and Starwars* obliges audiences to confront the impoverished access to social, cultural and political visibility and participation which characterises travellers' citizenship, *Farawayan*, a performance in eight scenes written and directed by Dónal O'Kelly, extends this focus to the experiences of refugees and asylum seekers in late 1990s Ireland.

Farawayan uses the spectacular potential of theatre form to shift the rigid framing of the texts *Refugee, Immigrant* and *Asylum Seeker* in response to cultural imperatives analogous to those dictated by the pernicious implications of the text *Traveller*. The reader might bear in mind the kinds of editorial perspectives and journalistic tropes which were current in print and broadcast media in the racially-charged atmosphere of 1997/8: a front-page editorial in *The Wexford People* spoke of dubious Romanians who could be found wearing designer clothing and basking on the balconies of brand new apartments while local people went without medical care and adequate housing. Specifically, it alleged that young Romanian men were lurking at the gates of local convent schools for the express purpose of enticing young girls to bear the children which would deliver Irish citizenship to the unscrupulous father. Radio phone-ins and evening paper headlines in Dublin were equally, if not more aggressively committed to demonising the arrivals in terms drawn from the worst excesses of British and American racism. The race card had been played — successfully — in more than one Dublin constituency during the close-run general election of June 1997. In his programme note for the production, Andy Storey names the focus of the project in uncompromising language:

> Despite Ireland's relatively small numbers of asylum seekers, it seems to be beyond the capacity of this state to deal with them in a decent manner.... Immigration is an economic blessing, not a curse. And we should already know this: between 1991 and 1996, there were 177,000 immigrants to this country, people without whom this economy and society could not have functioned... Most of the people now working here are from Western Europe and North America, but there is no reason other than racism not to be equally welcoming to people from elsewhere.... Asylum seekers and immigrants are not burdens to be borne or invaders to be repulsed. They are human beings with life stories and human rights, with abilities and energies, and with a range of contributions to make. They are to be welcomed.

Farawayan was staged at the Olympic Ballroom, off Camden Street, Dublin in autumn 1998. The play's genesis in opposition to the emergence and proliferation of racist discourse in Ireland fits the Calypso profile precisely. So too does the coalition of funders assembled to bring the project to fruition, and the accompanying resource file, *Information and Action on Racism*. My focus is on another aspect of the work's significance to the Calypso project, and to developments in contemporary Irish theatre: its exploration of the languages of theatre itself.

In an article in the inaugural issue of *Irish Theatre Magazine*, Dónal O'Kelly addressed theatre's uniqueness as communal experience, and referred to its capacities to forge connections between people, practices and life histories atomised in an increasingly distanced, privatised and mediated interaction with others. *Farawayan* is above all an audience experience. Queuing outside the Olympic Ballroom, people receive a programme on admission which is a replica of an Irish/EU passport. This document is stamped, and will be demanded throughout the evening by sinister masked figures who control admission to the balcony from where the first two episodes will be viewed, and the ground level – vantage point for episodes 3 to 8. Faraya is discovered by audience members, held in a dimly lit cubicle off the balcony, guarded by the functionaries, Belt and Buckle. The play stages her escape from the hell of Farawaya through a long sea voyage on a makeshift raft, arrival in Ireland, participation in Maud's glittering ball, unmasking as an outsider, bureaucratic assessment, terrified flight and disorientation, physical brutalisation and enforced return from whence she came.

Throughout the experience, *Farawayan* explores the sensual immediacy of live theatre, the suggestive powers of dynamics of light/darkness, sound/silence, music/cacophony, stillness/movement. Crucially — in terms of its formal innovations and adaptations — *Farawayan* addresses the dynamic actual/virtual. It does this on a number of levels, including its embodiment of the horrors of contemporary warfare, exile and wandering: horrors available only through virtual contact to most of the people in the audiences for *Farawayan*. Equally, the traumatic disorientations of enforced exile, which completely defeat and are reduced by theatrical realism, are given form in Faraya's experiences at "Maud's glittering ball" (Episode 4), in "The Forest of Hatches and Flares" (Episode 5) and during "The Assessment" (Episode 6). Episode 6 finds an unmasked Faraya in flight from Maud's dogs, Costas and Airgead, lost and wandering in the forest of hatches and flares. The audience, at ground level, witnesses Faraya's encounter with animate trees, containing hatches which open to reveal terrifying flare explosions. We are in the terrain of folk tale and dreamscape in this episode, where ghastly references to the mutilating power of landmines and the psychic wounds of oppression and enforced migration proliferate. Faraya's youth, innocence and exhaustion are vividly staged in a theatre of spectacle and physicality which implicates the audience in her disorientation.

This search for implication over explication marks a significant deepening of Calypso's application of theatrical imagination to contemporary problems, and characterises a remarkable artistic journey for Dónal O'Kelly personally. In 1994, he wrote *Asylum! Asylum!* for the

National Theatre. It was staged at the Peacock Theatre, in a proscenium format, where the pull of the conventions of theatrical realism diluted its impact as a cautionary statement to a social order beginning to awake to the potential pleasures of flirtations with consumer capitalism. My own production of the play in 1997 attempted to draw on Patrick Murray's in-the-round design in order to open up the theatrical playfulness of the script's African/Irish encounters, and to enable the magic realist ending to emerge more fully. The second production played directly into the kind of society it had anticipated only four years earlier. If the typical comment which greeted *Asylum! Asylum!* in 1994 was "Interesting play… couldn't happen here", the 1997 version evoked similar objections from bourgeois audiences as did *The Business of Blood*: "I don't like being told what to think". Following that second production, the playwright felt that the content, having become more urgently visible in Irish experience needed not so much to be rewritten as rewrought. In what is probably a unique artistic revisitation in a culture dedicated to the idea of the play as completed literary text, he committed himself to a new engagement with theme, space, actors, exiles, musicians and dancers. Reflecting on the centrality of interrogating form to the representation of unprecedented realities, he wrote:

> *Farawayan* is about the feeling of being faraway and unwelcome. In it, I want to use a non-Irish form of theatre. Or to be part by proxy of generating a new Irish form of theatre. We want to celebrate our barely-happening-but-there-nevertheless multi-cultural diversity. So I want to use Farawayan theatre techniques. And even if I didn't have that excuse, I just find naturalistic theatre… well, boring a lot of the time… the form is a bit musty at this stage. It's had its century. Now is the time to shake it off. Maybe. Leave it to the close-up focus-pullers (O'Kelly: 1998, 12).

In 1999, Calypso Productions appointed Bairbre ní Chaoimh as its first artistic director. A collaborator with Dónal O'Kelly and Trevor Knight on O'Kelly's *Catalpa*, Bairbre ní Chaoimh played the cruel, unctuous Maud in *Farawayan*. She sees the company's commitment to formal exploration as equal to its commitment to highlighting issues which go to the heart of the contested terrains of identity, participation and citizenship which are evolving in contemporary Ireland. Bairbre ní Chaoimh sees her task as elaborating the shift in *Farawayan* away from explication of, and toward implication in specific marginal experiences. In terms of its claim on our attention as a constituent part of the broad spectrum of endeavour that is Irish theatre at the beginning of the 21st century, perhaps Calypso's greatest contribution is in its record of drawing attention to the fact that experiences from the edges of the western mindset and social order cannot be represented in forms developed with the representation of lives lived close to the centre in mind.

Works Cited:

Agger, Ben, (1992), *Cultural Studies as Critical Theory* (Falmer Press, London and Washington DC: Falmer Press)

Bennett, Susan, (1992), *Theatre Audiences: a theory of production and reception* (London: Routledge)

Higgins, Michael D., (1996), in an interview in Joe Jackson's *Troubadors and Troublemakers: Ireland now — a culture reclaimed* (Cork: Blackwater Press)

O'Kelly, Dónal, (1994), *Asylum! Asylum* in *New Plays from the Abbey Theatre* eds., Michael Harding, Christopher Fitz-Simon and San Sternlicht (New York: Syracuse University Press)

------- (1998), 'Strangers in a Strange Land' in *Irish Theatre Magazine*, 1.1, Autumn, 12

Merriman, Victor, (1998), 'Cartographic Connections: Problems of representation in Calypso Theatre Company's *The Business of Blood*', *The Irish Review: Special Issue on Contemporary Irish Theatre*, Spring

West, Cornel, (1992), 'The New Cultural Politics of Difference' in Ferguson, R. et al., (eds.), *Out There: Marginalization and Contemporary Cultures* (Cambridge, Massachussetts: The New Museum of Contemporary Art New York, NY/The MIT Press)

Nowlan, David, (1995), *Polemic driven to a foregone conclusion* in *Irish Times*, 15 September

O'Toole, Fintan, (1995), *Second Opinion: A powerful gesture* in *Irish Times*, 26 September

The Gothic Soap of Martin McDonagh

Karen Vandevelde

In January 1996, Martin McDonagh's *The Beauty Queen of Leenane* was staged as the opening performance for the inauguration of a new municipal theatre in Galway. A co-production between Galway's Druid Theatre and the London Royal Court Theatre, this debut by the London-Irish playwright won the hearts of the audience and the critics. Within a year McDonagh was awarded the Evening Standard Award, the George Devine Award and the Writers' Guild Award for Best New Fringe Play of the Year, and four Tony Awards in 1998. *The Beauty Queen* was followed by *The Lonesome West* and *A Skull in Connemara*. This *Leenane Trilogy* procured for Druid Theatre four major prizes at the Irish Times/ESB Irish Theatre Awards.

The critical responses generated by *The Leenane Trilogy* ranged from mildly positive to exuberant praise. Extensive reviews and interviews in popular magazines such as *Hot Press, Elle* and *Rí-Rá*, which generally devote little column space to drama or dramatists, presented Martin McDonagh as an upcoming enigmatic pop-star and the most innovative playwright Ireland or England ever witnessed. "A theatrical star" (*Hot Press*), "a sensation" (*Sunday Telegraph*), "a white-knuckle roller coaster" (*Sunday Tribune*), "punk and disorderly" (*Elle*), "something of a rock star" (*Daily Telegraph — Star Life section*) and "the shocking dark-comic phenomenon" (*Newsday*)… Descriptions such as these are generally attributed to radical contemporary art, pop stars or notorious film directors, and it is quite surprising to meet them in the rhetoric of theatre criticism. The phenomenon of the cult of the new writer which surrounded Martin McDonagh's debut apparently underlines the overall perception of his plays as radical and challenging.

Contrary to the expectations of a new play at the radical cutting edge of the nineties, McDonagh's trilogy does not feature drugs, pop music or trendy lifestyles, but members of a rural community who are victims of loneliness, depression and economic progress. *The Beauty Queen of Leenane* develops the relationship of interdependence between a tyrannical mother and her daughter, Maureen, who misses her one chance of escaping with Pato Dooley from her dreary life. In *A Skull in Connemara*, Mick Dowd has the ungrateful job of digging up old graves to make place for new ones, but the fact that he now has to clear his wife's remains, raises the old suspicions surrounding her death. *The Lonesome West* unravels the story of two hating brothers who are bound together by the secret of their father's murder. McDonagh's radical freshness is definitely not to be found in the plot, language, setting and theme of his drama.

McDonagh's *Leenane Trilogy* is undoubtedly a canonical work with echoes of Synge, Beckett, O'Casey and many more. His plays fit in well with the Irish dramatic canon, so well that it is hard not to suspect that the author is actually *toying* with the stereotypical image of Irish drama. The imitations and echoes of literary precursors are so apparent throughout the trilogy that the playwright's self-reflexivity becomes ironical, if not subversive. As such, this double edge makes it perfectly possible to read the trilogy as either a canonical or a radical text. The radical nature of McDonagh's writing is also manifest in a second feature: his unique style of storytelling, founded on a stylistic fusion of Tarantinoesque gothic horror and melodramatic soap. The Ireland of the 1950s and of the 1990s seem to overlap in one and the same picture. To some spectators this may be simply fine icing on the old cake of Irish drama, but to others it constitutes a very intense, and very funny, tragicomedy.

McDonagh's writing thus finds itself in a very peculiar position: his drama is popular simultaneously because it is canonical and because it is radical. However, others dismiss his drama precisely because it is too canonical, or too radical. Take, for example, Charles Spencer's description of McDonagh as "a sadistic, manipulative writer with an unappealing ruthlessness towards his characters" in the *Daily Telegraph*, or Emer O'Kelly's objection that his writing is "fifth-rate bad Synge" and "stage Irish" in the *Sunday Independent*. It is necessary to cut a way through the packaged persona of the author and the constructions of the meaning of his plays in order to address a more important question: if McDonagh's plays present rural Ireland at the end of the twentieth century in a form that is at once fictional and real, is his "new voice" powerful enough to stage the devastating effects of the modernisation of Irish life?

McDonagh's plays incorporate the setting, language, plot and themes of many of his precursors in the Irish dramatic canon, even if McDonagh denies having read any of these authors before writing his plays. Echoes of Beckett and O'Casey are to be found at various passages in the trilogy, but it is mostly Synge's ghost which is present throughout most of the trilogy. The mother-daughter relationship in *The Beauty Queen of Leenane* captures the same sense of suffocation between Nora and her husband in Synge's *In the Shadow of the Glen*. Maureen, unlike Nora, misses her chance to go off with a tramp (Pato). Instead of discovering a new life in America she ends up driven into bitter revenge. Also the comic treatment of feared, faked and apparent deaths naturally remind the spectator of Christy Mahon and his father in *The Playboy of the Western World*.

The opening scenes of the three plays of the *Leenane Trilogy* are in the style of the traditional Abbey Theatre peasant drama, which developed mainly out of the success of Synge's "peasant plays". Take, for example, the setting for *The Beauty Queen of Leenane:* "The living-room/kitchen of a rural cottage in the west of Ireland. Front door stage left, a long black range along the back wall with a box of turf beside it and a rocking-chair on its right" (*BQ:* 1). The setting for the other two plays is similar, with the exception of a few scenes on "a rocky cemetery" in *A Skull in Connemara* (*SC:* 21) or at "a lakeside jetty at night" in *The Lonesome West* (*LW:* 32). The location in a rural village in the West of Ireland recalls the fascination for the West of the Irish Revivalists and of many a playwright in Ireland. At a time of national and cultural insecurity, they recognised in this wild and rugged part of Ireland a sense of purity in terms of language, culture, landscape and character. This romanticised image of the West became extremely successful both in Ireland and abroad, and still lies at the basis of many Bord Fáilte advertisements for Irish tourism. Drawing on this stereotype image of rural Ireland makes the trilogy sufficiently exotic to fulfil the expectations of English, American and Irish expatriate spectators. At the same time, however, McDonagh distances his setting considerably from this exoticism in order to maintain a high degree of reality and recognisability, and to satirise the romanticised picture of the West: "All you have to do is look out your window to see Ireland. And it's soon bored you'd be. 'There goes a calf'" (*BQ:* 53). Paradoxical as it may seem at first, McDonagh in fact manages to adopt Pato's witty sense of humour for the purpose of simultaneously underlining and undermining this exoticism.

The language spoken by the characters in the three plays is in many ways reminiscent of Synge. McDonagh creates a language which is semi-authentic, semi-artificial and extremely musical, Syngean but highly ironic. The function of the characters' speech is not of the same optimistic nature as Synge's imaginative language and offers no escape from the real world. In McDonagh's trilogy the characters resort to Syngean speech to express hatred, laughter, distress and despair. Their fragmented speech reflects the fragmentation of their lives. As with Synge, the artificiality of such a language comes very close to a new (stereo)type of stage-Irishness, criticised by *Sunday Independent* reviewer Emer O'Kelly as an "'Is it being about to be going from the place you are?' sort of thing". Still, the literary mimicry in the plot, setting and the characters' language is so ironic that it cannot be regarded as a postmodernist game with the reader/spectator. McDonagh's self-reflexivity with regard to the Irish canon suggests rather a conscious questioning and even subversion of their examples. This confrontation with a highly ironic metatext on Irish drama prompts the spectators to question their expectations and definitions of Irish drama.

McDonagh's trilogy refuses to engage directly with particular Irish themes such as emigration, the Anglo-Irish relations, Irish identity and religion, even if they are in one form or another part of the undercurrents of the three plays. *The Beauty Queen of Leenane* is the only play of the trilogy which directly addresses the themes of Irish identity and emigration, but the characters refuse to step too deeply into the matter. Take, for example, this discussion between Maureen and her mother.

> **Maureen:** If it wasn't for the English stealing our language, and our land, and our God-knows-what, wouldn't it be we wouldn't need to go over there begging for jobs and for handouts?
>
> **Mag:** I suppose that's the crux of the matter.
>
> **Maureen:** It *is* the crux of the matter (*BQ*: 5).

The discussion goes on, but ends abruptly with Maureen's accusation: "You're oul and you're stupid and you donut know what you're talking about. Now shut up and eat your oul porridge". The play's characters reduce the major issue of Ireland's relationship with England to small-talk arguing its effect on local life. The dominant theme of Irish literature, emigration, is present in Maureen's past, Pato's life and Ray's hope, but it remains a covert issue, something the play's characters refuse to address. This becomes an interesting feature in the trilogy: whenever characters come too close to major questions of Irish history and identity, they dismiss the topic and change subject. The spectator is left wondering whether this apparent apathy and the fragmentation of identity are typical representations of contemporary Ireland, or whether McDonagh is questioning the magnitude assigned to these issues in Irish drama. Pato's disjointed expression of Irish identity and emigration is another striking example of this: "when it's there I am, it's here I wish I was, of course. Who wouldn't? But when it's here I am... it isn't *there* I want to be, of course not. But I know it isn't here I want to be either" — with a similar dismissal of the subject as in the previous dialogue: "... ah, I don't know". Druid Theatre Company emphasised the significance of these issues and of the emigration theme by the inclusion of Fintan O'Toole's article in the theatre programme for the 1996 English tour. "That gap between place and people, between the search for a fixed national space and the existence of an unfixed, mobile population is the great contradiction of Ireland", claims O'Toole. He recognises the value of McDonagh's writing in the fact that *The Beauty Queen* is a play "that is at once local in its setting and dislocated in its content, that deals truthfully with the way a culture characterised by emigration exists on a continual fault-line between reality and imagination".

As O'Toole suggests, the novelty of McDonagh's writing lies not so much in its dissection of the staple themes of Irish drama, but rather in his unusual writing style which constantly switches between reality and imagination. In a very innovative way his storytelling refreshes and subverts many of the clichés of the Irish literary canon and of Irish rural life. The fusion of a grotesque style, inspired by Tarantino, and a melodramatic mood reminiscent of many contemporary soap operas bring about an unusual juxtaposition of opposite emotions, actions and temperaments: mercilessness and tenderness, love and hatred, dreams and depression. McDonagh's strength lies in the subversion of these dichotomies and blurring of their boundaries, thus transforming the village of Leenane into a place of gothic horror/small town melodrama. Trivial and tragic actions, realistic and eccentric portrayals, nihilism and compassion, they are all part of the imaginary place in the West of Ireland in which the people watch Australian soap, feed the chickens, turn forgiveness into a game, rip off tourists, are depressed, batter skulls, and murder. This passage from the closing scene of *A Skull in Connemara*, for example, illustrates how the trivial and the grotesque go hand in hand in Leenane, to the extent that the spectator begins to doubt where the familiar ends and the extraordinary begins.

> **Mary**: *(pause)* Do you like bumpy slides, Mairtin?
> **Mairtin**: Bumpy slides? Where the hell did bumpy bloody slides come from?
> **Mary**: I won two goes on the bumpy slides at Leisureland if you'd want to go.
> **Mairtin**: You won't catch me going on the bumpy slides with you, missus. I'd look a pure fool.
> **Mary**: No, you could bring somebody else, I'm saying. *(She gives Mairtin the tickets)*.
> **Mairtin**: Oh. Aye. Thank you, Gran. Mayby Mona'd want to go. Heh, this has been a great oul day, this has. Drinking and driving and bumpy slides, and that oul battering them skulls to skitter was the best part of the whole day (*SC*: 63-64).

The oppositions brought about by the grotesque and the soap do not cancel out one another. On the contrary, they are both intensified into an effective hyper-realism: the setting and the characters are not designed to be representative of rural Ireland, but they are still sufficiently recognisable. The particular blending of soap and gothic horror in the trilogy thus becomes more than a stylistic feature. In fact, it is in the *form* of storytelling, rather than in the *contents*, that the novelty of this dark comedy is to be found. The Leenane houses of Martin McDonagh's imagination are still cottage kitchens with an old range and a table. Nonetheless, the significance of the range is far removed from its original function. Rather than for cooking, these particular ranges are used for storing poteen, burning letters, scalding hands and melting fibreglass figurines.

At any given moment when the audience watches the action on stage and thinks, "they can't go that far", the characters in fact do, and sometimes even further than any one would have expected. McDonagh's characters show no mercy for one another. The question whether Maureen had really scalded her mother's hand, remains uncertain until further on in the drama, when the cruel act is repeated on stage in a visually powerful manner (*BQ*: 47-9). The suspense is maintained in the opening of the next scene when Mag sits, as usual, in the rocking chair, until at the very end "she finally topples over and falls heavily to the floor, dead. A red chunk of skull hangs from a string of skin at the side of her head" (*BQ*: 51). Suspense is also pivotal to the plot of *A Skull in Connemara*, where the main issue is whether or not a murder has been committed. This apprehension is repeated on-stage as slapstick when Mairtin appears on stage, showing only "a big bloody crack down the centre of his forehead, dripping onto his shirt" (*SC*: 58). This scene naturally parodies the appearance of Christy Mahon's father at the end of Synge's *Playboy of the Western World*. Also in *The Lonesome West* the expectation of fratricide is deferred until the end, when Coleman decides even more hurt could be done, not by killing his brother, but by blowing his brother's beloved new stove to pieces.

The novelty of McDonagh's horror-soap style is in fact an exaggerated version of the old genre of tragicomedy. The unusual mixture of high emotion and hilarious laughter injects the two traditional genres with new and vibrant life. On a deeper level, however, it is exactly in the fusion of the two genres that Martin McDonagh prompts the audience to think of why it is laughing, and to laugh about its seriousness. Slowly the spectator begins to realise that the three plays of the trilogy are not just a collection of amusing lines and unexpected scenarios, but an uncomfortable realisation that for seven hours they have laughed heartily at victims of the modernisation of Irish life. The plays do not represent the Celtic Tiger, but are dedicated to those who have been left behind in the development of modern, prosperous Ireland.

All of the characters in *The Leenane Trilogy* are tied to their birthplace, but nobody actually feels at home there. Instead, they imagine a better life elsewhere, based on the ideals presented in Australian soaps and American movies. With the exception of Pato, none of them has been able to actually get away from the backward village of Leenane. The romantic image of beautiful rural Ireland is far removed from the play's reality: Leenane offers no consolation, hope or future; religion no longer provides stability; and the characters do not correspond with the global identity of free, enterprising and successful human beings. On the contrary, isolation drives its inhabitants to outrageous acts of violence. This is not the Bord Fáilte image of the West of Ireland, but a dystopia in which loneliness and depression are not the outcome of a rugged landscape, but of the mercilessness of human behaviour.

Tragicomedy operates on a double level, but McDonagh's deliberate overlapping, and even subversion, of the two levels does not make it easy for the audience to distinguish between the gravity and the mockery. On the one hand, the comic element in *The Leenane Trilogy* forces actors and audience to laugh at familiar or deep issues such as emigration, suicide and the Catholic Church. The audience is made to look back on its past, and realise that by laughing it has distanced itself from an atavistic past. On the other hand, as *Irish Times* critic Fintan O'Toole has observed, "the trilogy is a comedy about the need to take some things more seriously". McDonagh's trilogy becomes deeply disturbing as the audience understands, in its laughter, that it should not laugh, because the plays are a painful portrayal of victims of loneliness and repression. Coleman's words "We should not laugh" (*LW*: 50) near the end of *The Lonesome West*, are the very epitome of this complex interplay of the tragic and the comic. They refer not only to the comic potential of Valene and Coleman's revelation of the young priest's name just shortly after the news of his suicide. On another level they also comment on the brothers' absurd passion for ridiculous trivial details such as biscuits, crisps and figurines, and their equally ridiculous trivialisation of serious issues such as murder, brotherhood, love and religion. Finally, they also comment on the spectator's reaction to many of the comic scenes in the trilogy. "We should not laugh" simultaneously denies and confirms the comic potential of the situation, and the audience is torn between amusing itself and realising that on another level the play is no cause for amusement at all.

Marvellously manipulated by McDonagh's dialogues, the audience cannot help but laugh at some of the most intense moments of the plays, but it is an experience which leaves the spectator very uncomfortable. Is the Leenane imagined by McDonagh really so different from the real Leenane? Are the characters simply fictional beings or do they reflect in a grotesque way what rural Ireland means these days? As Garry Hynes, director of *The Leenane Trilogy*, explains in an interview with Martin Doyle, this is in fact what McDonagh's plays are all about. The illusion that former times were better now reveals the cracks in the picture, the cruelty of what goes on behind closed doors:

> That's what Ireland has discovered in the last 10 years about itself… that there wasn't this nice, homogenous, structured, stable, coherent society with slightly funny things on the fringes.

These things were co-existing, the great social events of the last 10 years, the Kerry babies, the X case, the disintegration of the Church; in a way the play could be said to parallel that.

McDonagh's trilogy highlights the two aspects of economic and social progress. Hynes says that the positive side of progress is that a departure from the past makes people look more critically at themselves and at this past. This objective perspective has revealed certain "cracks" in Irish society, but has also put a halt to the ignorance regarding these facts and the blind atavism involved. This is an essential stage in the development of a society. The positive implications of economic progress have, however, also a negative impact. Rapid and sweeping changes in Ireland, such as those caused by the Celtic Tiger, have exerted significant pressures on the traditional fabric of Irish society. In a figurative way, McDonagh's trilogy reflects also the underbelly of progress. He is not depicting these effects directly, but in his unusual dramatic style he compresses a sense of what *may be happening* in rural Ireland. Current statistics in fact reveal a devastating picture of the fragmentation of Irish social life. Suicide rates and the number of people diagnosed with depression reach alarming figures and the rural to urban migration breaks down local communities.

These elements, nevertheless, do not make McDonagh an "engaged" writer, nor is his trilogy solely a social comedy of Irish life. A particular timelessness and powerful universality in the trilogy underlines the idea that these plays are about general human nature rather than economics, that they are, in the words of John Peter of the *Sunday Times*, "universal but could be set nowhere except in Ireland". McDonagh's Leenane is a grotesque modification of what might be a reality in Irish rural life. The fact that this drama can make people laugh about sacred issues and the romantic myths of the West by no means alters the weight of the dramatic action. The absurd is a necessary detour to invite the spectator to look beyond the sacred and the romantic.

The relevance to Irish social life in *The Leenane Trilogy* has prompted a number of foreign critics to find in the trilogy a metaphor for the political situation of Ireland. There are differences between the interpretations of Irish critics and reviewers abroad, brought about by a different knowledge of Ireland and divergent expectations of Irish drama. McDonagh's plays are undeniably receptive to various readings, but more important is the representative status of Irish drama when labelled as "truly Irish" abroad. In Ireland, *The Leenane Trilogy* is an imaginary, exaggerated picture of the West of Ireland, including plenty of elements which simultaneously underline and undermine its authenticity. Abroad, McDonagh's drama is often in danger of becoming the opposite: an authentic, representative picture, made attractive with funny, hilarious incidents.

In such cases, the critic assumes that Martin McDonagh belongs to the canon of Irish drama, in which most plays do in some way refer to the nation's turbulent past, its political situation or its struggle for the Irish language. It then becomes very tempting to read politics or history into the plot and setting, and McDonagh has furnished them with plenty of material to do so. Occasional references to the Irish language, emigration and lawlessness, even if they are not continued through the entire trilogy, make his drama receptive to such readings. In the British *Financial Times*, Alastair Macaulay suggests the following:

> By the end of *The Leenane Trilogy*, it is impossible not to suspect that his banal, boring, backwater village Leenane and its unstoppable, grotesque, blood-guts-subterfuge-and-despair goings-on are an allegory for Ireland itself and "the troubles". The point is that McDonagh wants not to illumine Ireland, or its troubles, but to satirise them.

The "end" of the trilogy alluded to, is the fight between brothers Coleman and Valene in *The Lonesome West*. A cynical Cain and Abel story of irreconcilable hatred, this could be identified with political violence in the North. The history of Catholic and Protestant sectarianism, the slow movements of the peace process and idle attempts at reconciliation resemble the stages of Coleman and Valene's relation. Since most of Irish news abroad is related to this conflict, it is not surprising that it becomes the backdrop for many reviewers' interpretations of Irish drama. However, this political label threatens to limit the understanding of other interesting aspects of Martin McDonagh's drama.

This is clearly the case in *The Sydney Morning Herald*, which summarised *The Leenane Trilogy*, on tour in Australia, as a drama representing "The Irish Art of Hating". The playwright's grotesque style of storytelling is seen merely as "a cynical laughing despair over the entire trilogy, over the story that is Ireland". Moreover, it is an Ireland of "simple, ignorant people... as driven in their ancient prejudices as permanently warring New Guinean highland tribes". The reviewer James Waites also recognises in Maureen, the woman with the claim to the cynical title of *Beauty Queen of Leenane*, the epitome of the emerald isle itself, "isolated, impoverished and bitter as ever". McDonagh's cruel language and violent action, combined with a grim nihilistic mood, inspires the critic to the following conclusion regarding the playwright's message: "If the Irish are so good at playing war, why not try their hand at something new, or at least different: playing peace"?

These political interpretations of *The Leenane Trilogy* on the whole hinder a wider understanding and appreciation of McDonagh's writing and ignore the double edge of his grotesque irony. As John Peter has pointed out in *The Sunday Times*, there is a crucial distinction between drama that meditates on the state of Ireland, and universal drama that could not be set anywhere but in Ireland, such as McDonagh's trilogy. Restricting the value of *The Beauty Queen of Leenane, A Skull in Connemara* and *The Lonesome West* to a political commentary on the state of Ireland would be an immature view of Irish drama. Innovative art tends to the universal, and is supposed to subvert, to confuse, to pose questions. John Peter uncovers the intricacies as follows:

> All important drama bears the imprint of its nationality; but countries that are battered, colonised, exploited, corrupt or insecure (delete as appropriate) tend to produce plays of conscience and self-examination. Who are we as a nation? Have we an identity? Should we be proud of it? If not, are we to blame? Such plays are the opposite of patriotic reassurance: they are made up of guilt, pity, anger and subversion. That is why the plays of Synge and O'Casey were first greeted with such fury. There is now a new generation of Irish writers who have moved on.... This is the voice of a new Ireland that knows itself well enough not to be either guilty or completely self-absorbed.... (In the trilogy) you can see portraits of Ireland, but these pictures are neither parochial nor tribal; they would be understood all too well on several continents. This is a time of maturity.

Martin McDonagh is a playwright rooted in the same landscape, the same experience which inspired his dramatic precursors. His drama conforms to, but simultaneously subverts the canon of Irish drama. As such McDonagh confidently establishes his own gothic soap style which fuses the traditional and the radical. Zooming in so closely on the small, imagined town of Leenane, the trilogy transforms every detail into something very disproportionate, so that ultimately it acquires universal relevance. The microscopic picture of Leenane becomes the macrocosm of modern life, at once emblematic of modern Irish culture and representative of any unsettled nation torn between dreams and despair.

* I am very grateful to the staff of Druid Theatre Company, Galway, for the use of their theatre archive, and special thanks to David Chan, Kirry O'Brien and Dr. Lionel Pilkington for useful comments on this paper.

Works Cited:

McDonagh, Martin, (1997), *The Beauty Queen of Leenane* (London: Methuen)
------ (1997), *A Skull in Connemara* (London: Methuen)
------ (1997), *The Lonesome West* (London: Methuen)

Homo Fabulator: The Narrative Imperative in Conor McPherson's Plays

Scott T. Cummings

In Conor McPherson's *St. Nicholas*, a Dublin theatre critic stands on a bare stage and tells an audience about his harrowing experience one summer in the custody of vampires. His incredible story ends with his resolve to return to the life he left behind, a decision he makes with a smug sense of triumph. He anticipates "the fuss people were going to make of me", concluding his monologue with an almost fiendish glee: "I had my health. I had resolve. But most important. Over everything else. I had a story".

I have a story, therefore I am. This is the lifeblood and essence of McPherson's troubled heroes. Whatever misadventures overtake them and whatever ignominy or sorrow may come as a result, the fact of having a story and the act of telling it constitute a kind of redemption, a saving grace which imbues their profane lives with a touch of the sublime. McPherson's early monologue pieces, *Rum and Vodka*, *The Good Thief*, *This Lime Tree Bower*, and *St. Nicholas*, and his subsequent, more conventional plays, *The Weir* and *Dublin Carol*, all hinge on personal narratives, public confessions of private sins which provide first an entertaining evening and then, upon reflection, an investigation into the nature and function of story itself.

Conor McPherson has a story, too, more than one no doubt, but the one that first caught the public's attention concerns his swift rise at a young age to playwriting celebrity. At the time of his 25th birthday in August 1995, he was a promising but unknown playwright from the north side of Dublin with a degree in English and Philosophy from University College Dublin. He had won the Stewart Parker Award in 1994 but still had to form *Fly by Night Theatre Company* with his pals from UCD to get his work on in fringe venues around town. Just over four years later, as the new millennium dawned on January 1, 2000, the Royal Court's production of *The Weir*, which won the 1998 Olivier Award for Best Play, was still running in their temporary West End home at the Duke of York's Theatre. With much ballyhoo, his follow-up play, *Dublin Carol*, was selected to open the Royal Court's refurbished facility in Sloane Square. In New York, *The Weir*, on Broadway, and *St. Nicholas* and *This Lime Tree Bower*, off Broadway, all had had successful runs. His widely praised screenplay for Paddy Breathnach's offbeat gangster film, *I Went Down*, led to him directing his own first feature-length film, a version of *This Lime Tree Bower* titled *Salt Water*. He was fielding and rejecting lucrative offers from Hollywood. He interviewed Meryl Streep for

Harper's Bazaar. In London and New York, he was, before the age of thirty, Ireland's "latest literary giant" (Franks: 1999).

Throughout this heady rise to fame, McPherson was widely characterized in the press as a low-key, modest, almost self-effacing bloke with a wry sense of humour. James Christopher's description was typical: "With his tightly woven rug of red hair, apple cheeks, and studious-looking glasses, he could be any young Dublin bollix that wandered off the street". McPherson weathered the inevitable comparisons to Martin McDonagh, whose own meteoric rise came at the same time and whose public shenanigans made much more sensational news. In some interviews, McPherson deferred credit for his success to the cast of *The Weir* and its director, Ian Rickson; in others, he expressed some wish for the whirlwind of publicity, much of which he recognized as hyperbole, to die down. He seemed at moments to feel like one of his hapless characters, overcome by "the complete embarrassment of finding yourself in a position not of your own making. And it's your whole life" (White: 1994, xxx).

That's the way that McPherson, as early as 1994, described the narrator of *Rum and Vodka*, the first of the four monologue pieces which paved the way for *The Weir*'s astonishing success. However limited in scope or ambition, these early monologues may prove to be his most exciting work for the theatre. Each has an immediacy and a roughness, to borrow terms from Peter Brook, that makes it essentially theatrical. The immediacy comes from the simplicity of the monologue form: an actor stands onstage and talks directly to an audience for an hour or more. The total emphasis on narrative verges on the anti-dramatic. There is no theatrical fiction, no pretence that the stage represents an imaginary elsewhere. The time is now and the place is right here — in the theatre. The only character is the narrator — or narrators in the case of *This Lime Tree Bower* — and all he does is tell his story, without impersonating other characters or engaging in other physical histrionics.

The roughness comes from the substance of that story. Each one features a hopeless ne'er-do-well who, down on his luck and fuelled by alcohol, takes a reckless step and finds himself careening down a slippery slope headed for sure disaster. In *Rum and Vodka* (1994), a Dublin office worker with a wife, two kids, a drinking problem, and a house in Raheny is shocked at age 24 to realize that "this was as good as things were going to get". At lunch one Friday, he starts a weekend-long bender that has him stumbling in and out of pubs and parties all over town. In *The Good Thief* (1994), a small-time thug goes out on a job to rough somebody up for a racketeer and gets caught in an ambush that leads him to kill a couple guys on the spot, kidnap a mother and daughter, steal a car, and head for Sligo in an effort to escape both the authorities and the henchmen sent to silence him. In *This Lime Tree Bower* (1995), unusual for its use of three narrators, two brothers and their sister's boyfriend take turns describing their parts in the robbery of a bookie in a small seaside town. In *St. Nicholas* (1997), the aforementioned critic becomes obsessed with a beautiful actress named Helen and follows her to London, where he finds himself recruited to be the procurer of fresh victims for a household of polite and seductive vampires.

Each story gathers a precipitous momentum and contains sufficient danger that the hero's very survival would seem to be in jeopardy were he not right there as narrator telling his tale. As a result, the audience's concern shifts from 'will he survive?' to 'how will he get out of this?' In McPherson's stories, getting out of a predicament is tantamount to getting away with something, an indiscretion, a sin, a crime or just the obnoxious bravado of a drunk. His protagonists are, in plain language, shits and fuck-ups. When their behaviour is not outright criminal, it is still irresponsible to the point of being reckless, selfish to the point of being cruel. Neither proud nor apologetic, they recount their misdeeds with a detachment that is disarmingly blunt. Seemingly without scruples, they elicit a measure of sympathy in part because their devil-may-care attitude masks a brooding conscience. A smouldering mix of self-pity and self-loathing surfaces at moments in a way that activates an odd compassion. The audience may not approve of the hero's antics (or the values they imply), but if handled properly in performance, they will not disapprove of him getting away with it.

Nor will they disapprove of McPherson himself getting away with spinning an improbable yarn that strains credulity. There is a mischievous quality to McPherson's work, evident in such choices as writing an evening-length monologue about a theatre critic who consorts with vampires. His stories always begin in a world that is familiar and ordinary. Then, as the narrative gains momentum, they take advantage of the listener's initial trust, the proverbial willing suspension of disbelief. The situation goes to implausible extremes — of alcohol consumption, of ruthless crime, of supernatural occurrences. In *Rum and Vodka*, what starts off as four pints at lunch on a Friday turns into a weekend-long binge that defies human physiology. In *The Good Thief*, the title character makes "a pig's mickey" of his rough-up assignment and goes on the lam; when his boss finally tracks him down, his life is spared, but the woman and child he kidnapped and the entire family of his friend in Sligo who provided a hide-out are all killed. In *St. Nicholas*, after barging in late one night on a household of actors, the theatre critic goes on to spend a month cruising London bars for young people ready for an after-hours party and bringing them back to the vampires' wood-panelled home in the suburbs; they wake up in the morning hung over and short a few ounces of blood but none the worse for wear.

In each case, not only does the situation go from bad to worse, it goes from credible to incredible. As critics particularly of *St. Nicholas* observed, the stories have a playful shaggy-dog quality to them. Some even recognized that this is precisely the point. McPherson flirts with the improbable and the unbelievable first and foremost for the sheer fun of it and then as a way of drawing attention to the psychology of storytelling. When regarded collectively, his body of work demonstrates a self-consciousness about the mechanics of Mcpherson's craft that adds a meta-narrative dimension to his tall tales. They become, in part, stories about storytelling.

In the preface to the published edition of *St. Nicholas* and *The Weir*, McPherson tells a story about meeting a series of strangers, friends of friends, in the pub one Christmas and telling each of them a "big lie" about a violent encounter he had that day with a seagull on Dublin's Ha'penny Bridge. As he reports, "the first thing people would say after I'd said this was, 'Is that true?' Because although they didn't believe me, we live in a world where we don't expect complete strangers to lie to us. Not in pubs at any rate. But it's nice in the theatre" (Pref: *SN*: vii). The fictive environment of the theatre invites the audience to invest belief in what on another level they know to be an artistic fabrication. But McPherson's monologues, some of which were first performed in pubs, confuse this dynamic by presenting themselves as elaborate pub tales. Their simple, direct form, confessional nature, and implausible turns keep the question "Is that true?" alive in the mind of the spectator. S/he becomes an auditor in both senses of the term, listening with care and then auditing the narrative account from moment to moment for consistency, accuracy, verisimilitude.

This process includes perforce an assessment of the narrator's character. "Is that true?" quickly leads to "Can he be trusted?", which in turn raises questions about the speaker's identity and motive. The critic in *St. Nicholas* makes this dynamic explicit and self-conscious shortly after he describes his first encounter with William, the leader of the vampires. Interrupting himself, he says, "Mm. There's always going to be a smugness about you listening to this. As we all take part in this convention. And you will say, 'These vampires are not very believable, are they?'" With a rhetorical sleight of hand, he proceeds to argue for the reality of the vampires and the truth of his tale by differentiating between magical and scientific ways of thinking, concluding "We may know that the earth goes around the sun. And we may know that this is due to 'gravity'. But not one of us knows why there is gravity. So don't sit there and cast judgement on the credibility of what I say, when you don't even know why you aren't floating off your seats" (*SN*: 26).

Casting judgement on the credibility of what his narrator says is precisely what McPherson wants his audiences to do because it necessitates a more general judgement of the narrator's character. His deeds might incriminate him, but the audience's appetite for a good story leads them to let him off the hook, so to speak, of moral condemnation. As the one spoken of, the hero of the tale is undeniably in the wrong, but as the one speaking, the narrator of the tale elicits sympathy — through the charisma of the performer and the sheer desire for narrative itself. Just as McPherson did (or said he did) in the pub at Christmas time, his narrator tells a "big lie" and then defies the audience not to believe it. He activates and isolates the audience's (aesthetic) will to believe his story in order to secure their (moral) will to forgive his shortcomings.

In *St. Nicholas*, the critic describes the incident which finally motivated him to break free of the vampires' spell. One day, William told him a story, what amounts to a fairy tale about a woodsman who rescued an old man from the bottom of a well and received a watch as a token of thanks. Years later, he discovered that when he wound the watch backwards he could travel back in time accordingly. He never used his power because "everything he loved was in the present", but when his wife died and he got lonely, he would wind the watch back to a time when she was alive. Curious, he eventually wound his way back to when she was a child, before he knew her, at which point the watch broke. A sad old man watching his future wife play as a little girl, "he was stuck in the past". Desperate, panic stricken, he grabbed the screaming child and ran into the woods, where the townspeople caught him and beat him and left him for dead.

The critic in *St. Nicholas* responds to this story by asking the vampire what it means. When William has no idea, the critic is prompted to recognize the difference between humans and vampires: "We reflect. They don't.... The cunt wanted a conscience. He fucking regretted not being able to regret the things he did". The critic's revelation that man is the self-reflective animal, the creature who looks back, judges, and regrets, may strike some as forced, simplistic, or moralistic, but when seen as the direct result of a story-within-the-story, it takes on an added dimension. At one point, the critic describes the mysterious power of the vampires as "not the power to make you do what they want. But real power. To make you want what they want" (*SN*: 23). This, of course, is the power of the storyteller as well. McPherson clearly recognizes that a good story takes over the will of the listener and manipulates his feelings and responses. The story about the woodsman and the magic watch helps to restore the critic to his humanity as a creature of conscience, but the critic's London adventure and its conversion to narrative ("I had a story") turn him into a figurative vampire. The metaphor of the storyteller as vampire suggests something about his self-consciousness and possible ambivalence about his chosen craft. The monologue ends rife with irony. The critic, whose profession it is to attend and judge the stories of others, finally has his own tale to tell, and he revels in "the potential it gave me to bully sympathy out of everybody" (*SN*: 41).

As a storyteller, McPherson is out to do more than suck nourishment or bully sympathy out of people. Like the benign vampires in *St. Nicholas*, he offers audiences an evening's frolic that lets them wake up the next morning with nothing worse than a hangover. In the process, he celebrates the power and value of stories as a crucial form of human intercourse. Nothing makes this clearer than his first conventional play, *The Weir*, which demonstrates how stories create community and provide consolation for loss, loneliness, and regret.

Commissioned by Stephen Daldry, late in his tenure as artistic director of the Royal Court Theatre, *The Weir* is McPherson's characteristically cheeky response to the call for him to write characters who talk to each other instead of the audience. He has them tell stories. Moreover, he situates them — where else? — in a pub. The play takes place in a rundown pub in rural Leitrim, one inspired by places McPherson visited with his grandfather, whose death, according to the playwright, casts an influential shadow over the play's creation. Some commentators may have challenged the choice of setting as an Irish cliché, but given McPherson's preoccupation with narrative and the tricky intimacy of the pub, it was virtually unavoidable.

McPherson further flirts with stereotype by having the eccentric denizens of the bar gather to tell ghost stories on an unabashedly dark and stormy night in the west of Ireland. This gothic sensationalism is rooted in an otherwise forthright naturalism. In one uninterrupted scene that suggests real time, the play depicts an evening in the pub: the bartender sets up, the regulars arrive, followed by a special guest, they catch up on the news, buy a few rounds, and get acquainted with the stranger, and then go their separate ways. Small talk dominates the colloquial dialogue, which is spare and repetitive at the same time. Compared to the roller coaster of events described by McPherson's monologists, nothing much happens. The action is subtle, subtextual, and absolutely bound up with the sequence of stories told by four of the play's five characters.

The two regulars in Brendan's place are Jack, a crusty old bachelor who runs a small garage, and Jim, a grown-up country boy who still lives with his aged mother. Like Jack, both Brendan and Jim are single, which adds a particular energy to their reception of Valerie, an attractive Dublin woman in her thirties who, for unknown reasons, has just moved into Maura Nealon's old house nearby, empty for five years. She is being squired about this evening by Finbar Mack, the local real estate mogul who runs the hotel in town and has city airs. The bachelors three suspect that the sporty but married Finbar has designs on Valerie, and once the party of five has gathered, a neighbourly competition for the lady's attention develops: in succession, Jack, Finbar, and Jim each tell a ghost story designed to impress Valerie with local legend and lore.

Jack starts off with a story about how the house where Valerie is to live was supposedly built on "what they call a fairy road" (*Weir.* 66); around 1910, when Maura Nealon was a young girl, her mother got a terrible fright one night when there was a knock at the door and nobody was there. Finbar follows this with a tale about the night eighteen years ago that he went to the rescue of his neighbour Mrs. Walsh and her daughter, who claimed to see a ghost on the stairs after trying to raise the dead with a Ouija board. Jim, after awhile, launches into an account of the time he and Declan Donnelly took a job in a neighbouring town digging up a grave where a man was to be buried with his parents. Standing in the rain, sick with the flu and a bit drunk from Declan's poitín, Jim was approached by a man in a suit who said he was opening the wrong grave and directed him to a little girl's new grave. Jim later recognized the man as the deceased, who turned out to be a child molester, seemingly eager to carry on his perverted ways in the after-life.

From one story to the next, the presence of the supernatural becomes progressively more real, tangible, and ominous. In the first, the fairies are out there somewhere, unseen, knocking at the window or the door. In the second, Finbar admits to feeling a presence on the stairs which he could not bring himself to turn and face. In the third, Jim goes face to face with the ghost. In each case, the story hinges on a spirit figure who threatens a little girl. The story Valerie will tell features a little girl as well, as do all of the early monologues: the woodsman's girl-wife in the story-within-the-story in *St. Nicholas*; the girl who is kidnapped along with her mother in *The Good Thief*; a teenage girl who is raped in one strand of *This Lime Tree Bower*'s triple narrative. *Rum and Vodka* ends with the narrator sneaking back home in the middle of the night and sitting on the floor of his daughters' bedroom listening to them breathing as they sleep. The trope of a little girl in jeopardy and the recurring image of a sleeping female, child or adult, being watched by a man emerge in McPherson's work as symbols of vulnerability and innocence which are threatened but seldom violated.

As a newcomer and as a woman in a man's domain, Valerie has some of that same vulnerability. What starts off in the pub as a bit of craíc, the equivalent of telling spooky stories around the campfire, takes on subtle sexual undertones as one man after the other has a narrative go at the innocent female. She faces the same issues of trust as any auditor. Seemingly ruffled by what she has heard, Valerie excuses herself to go to the ladies room, leaving the men quarrelling about whether they went too far. This paves the way for what turns out to be McPherson's master stroke: reversing Valerie's role from listener to storyteller. More emboldened than scared by what she has heard, she returns and shares a story of her own, much more personal than the others, one that explains her presence there that night. She and her husband had a young daughter who was terrified of the dark and who one day was killed in a swimming accident at school. Months after the death, still mired in grief, Valerie got a phone call one morning and heard her daughter's voice at the other end of the line asking her to come and fetch her at her Nana's. Her husband, she concludes, "felt that I... needed to face up to Niamh being gone. But I just thought he should face up to what happened to me" (*Weir.* 85).

Compared to the standard-issue ghost tales of the men, with their graveyard settings, howling winds, and mysterious knocks at the door, Valerie's story registers as much more believable, even though it, too, deals with the restless souls of the dead. In shifting Valerie's position in the narrative dyad, McPherson shifts the question "Is that true?" more squarely onto the theatre audience, as in the monologues, all the more so because the men onstage react with a measure of doubt. After a compassionate pause, Jack, Finbar, and Jim all begin to debunk her story, offering rational explanations for what happened to her (a bad dream, her prolonged grief, a wrong number). Jim dismisses his own ghost encounter as a hallucination brought on by a high fever and too much poitín. All three men are caught between their sympathy for Valerie's terrible loss and their disbelief in the supernatural part of her story.

Brendan, silent but attentive to all their stories, leaps to Valerie's defence. "She said she knew what it was", he insists in a tone that brooks no challenge (*Weir.* 86). Conspicuously, Brendan is the only character in *The Weir* who does not tell a story. Over the course of the evening, all he seems to do is pour drinks and listen. This would reduce him to the conventional bartender cum therapist were McPherson not so accomplished in his focus on the dynamics of storytelling. Brendan transcends the stereotype and emerges by inference as McPherson's image of the perfect audience, the one who sacrifices doubt to compassion and accepts the experience of the aggrieved as given. The importance of this role was underscored in the original Royal Court production by the heralded performance of Brendan Coyle, who won an Olivier Award for best supporting player and inspired a 1999 *New York Times* feature article on current plays with crucial listening characters.

Having demonstrated the spontaneous community of feeling generated by stories and storytelling, a less daring playwright might have stopped with Valerie's sad tale and sent his characters tenderly into the night.

Ever one to go to extremes, McPherson includes a fifth story, one that suggests something about the beneficial effect of Valerie's presence this night. After Finbar and Jim head for home, Jack, Brendan, and Valerie settle in around the fire for one last round. Valerie asks Jack if he ever wishes he had married and had children, and he proceeds to tell the story of how as a young man he abandoned the love of his life and then resented it when she married another fellow. Full of pride and a defiant lack of regret, he attended the wedding in Dublin, only to find his future open up in front of him like a vast, empty desert, a feeling that recalls the dread and alienation of the narrators of the monologues.

Jack's story pivots on his brief anonymous encounter with a backstreet bartender ("Like yourself Brendan, ha? Businesslike, dutiful." (*Weir.* 93)), who after serving him a couple silent pints, asked him if he was all right and then made him a sandwich, a simple gesture of care so profound that it fortified Jack to face the lifetime of loneliness ahead. That bartender did not need to hear Jack's story to bear witness to it. Neither does Brendan for that matter, who hears it nonetheless, perhaps for the first time or the fortieth. "But I do be at this fella, don't I?" says Jack to Valerie at the end of his story, referring to Brendan and affirming one last time the quiet valour of the listener. There is a long pause before they grab their coats and head for the door.

This last story in *The Weir* contrasts with the others that precede it for its lack of ghosts, and at the same time it completes a pattern of experience for the audience aptly described by Ben Brantley in the *New York Times.*

> Then a moment arrives, and it's hard to say exactly when because you've shed all sense of time, when you realise that you have strayed into territory that scrapes the soul. Suddenly, the subject isn't just things that go bump in the night, but the loss and loneliness that eventually haunt every life. There's a new chill abroad, evoking something more serious than goose flesh, but there is also the thrilling warmth that accompanies the flash of insight…. Though a feeling of individual isolation in a baffling and often hostile world pervades *The Weir*, the stories woven by its characters become solid, if temporary, bridges among them. And if the disturbing mysteries of existence haven't been given explanations, they have been given forms, and that in itself is a victory.

In McPherson's plays and monologues, that victory, the imposition of narrative form on chaotic and troubling experience, can serve a variety of purposes. It can be a plea for sympathy, an act of expiation, an affirmation of sanity, an effort to conquer or seduce, or a confession. In each case, a past personal ordeal is converted into a kind of present public ordeal. That is, a previous test of character, one which often reflects unfavourably on the speaker, becomes the basis for a story which, however fantastic, through the symbiosis of telling and listening redeems the speaker. Even as his misfits reveal themselves as creatures of conscience, guilt, and regret, their storytelling restores to them a measure of lost innocence that can be had by no other means.

Works Cited:

Brantley, Ben, (1999), 'Dark Yarns Casting Light,' *New York Times* 2 April, E-1

Brook, Peter, (1968), *The Empty Space* (New York: Avon)

Christopher, James, (1998), 'The problem with Irish road movies is that you arrive too soon', *The Observer*, 25 January, xxx

Franks, Alan, (1999), 'Ireland's sober voice', *The Times*, 11 December, Features

McPherson, Conor, (1996), *This Lime Tree Bower: Three Plays* (London: Nick Hern Books)

------ (1997), *St. Nicholas* and *The Weir* (London: Nick Hern Books)

------ (1999), '24 hours with Meryl Streep', *Harper's Bazaar*, January, 124-7

Renner, Pamela, (1998), 'Haunts of the Very Irish', *American Theatre*, July/August, Vol. 15 no. 6, 20

White, Victoria, (1994), 'Love's small steps to ruin', *Irish Times*, 27 August, 14

------ (1998), 'Telling stories in the dark', *Irish Times*, 2 July, Weekend 4

Wolf, Matt, (1998), 'A darling of the critics who doesn't flatter them' *New York Times*, 15 March, II-8

------ (1999), 'They Also Act Who Only Sit and Listen', *New York Times*, 13 June, II-9

Biography of Contributors

Thomas Kilroy is an academic, novelist and one of Ireland's leading playwrights. He is best known for *The Death and Resurrection of Mr. Roche, Talbot's Box* and *Double Cross*. His most recent drama *The Secret Fall of Constance Wilde* played at the Abbey Theatre in 1997.

Declan Hughes founded Rough Magic with Lynne Parker, and directed sixteen of the company's productions. His plays include *I Can't Get Started, Love and a Bottle* (with George Farquhar), *Digging For Fire, New Morning, Halloween Night* (all Rough Magic); *Twenty Grand* (Peacock Theatre). His work has won the Stewart Parker Award and a Time Out Theatre Award. *Declan Hughes - Plays: 1* is published by Methuen.

Marianne McDonald is Professor of Classics and Theatre at the University of California, San Diego, a member of the Royal Irish Academy, and teaches yearly in Ireland at University College Dublin and Trinity. She is the founder of projects to computerize Greek literature (Thesaurus Linguae Graecae) and Irish literatures (Thesaurus Linguarum Hiberniae). Author of, among other books: *Terms for Happiness in Euripides; Euripides in Cinema: The Heart Made Visible; Ancient Sun/Modern Light: Greek Drama on the Modern Stage;* an English translation of Shinichi Hoshi's *The Cost of Kindness; Star Myths: Tales of the Constellations; Mythology of the Zodiac,* and *Sing Sorrow: Ancient Classics in Modern Opera* (to be published by Greenwood Press).

Lionel Pilkington is a lecturer in English at NUI, Galway and has published articles on Irish theatre and cultural history in *Graph, Modern Drama, TDR: the Drama Review, Éire-Ireland, Irish Review University,* and *Études Théâtrales/Essays in Theatre.* He is currently completing for Routledge a book-length study of theatre and politics in 20th century Ireland.

Anna McMullan is Director of the M.Phil. in Irish Theatre and Film at the School of Drama, Samuel Beckett Centre, Trinity College Dublin. Her book, *Theatre on Trial: Samuel Beckett's later drama,* was published by Routledge in 1993. She has co-edited with Caroline Williams the contemporary drama section of the Fourth Volume of the Field Day Anthology, devoted to Irish women's writing, which is forthcoming in 2001.

Fintan O'Toole is an *Irish Times* journalist. His books include: *The Politics of Magic: The Work and Times of Tom Murphy, A Traitor's Kiss: The Life of Richard Brinsley Sheridan, No More Heroes: A Radical Guide to Shakespeare, A*

Mass for Jesse James, Black Hole, Green Card and *The Irish Times Book of the Century.*

Bruce Arnold is Chief Critic of the Irish Independent, writing about Theatre, Literature, Art, Music and Politics. He writes a regular weekly political column each Saturday. He is the author of fifteen books, including a cycle of four novels, biographies of the painters, William Orpen, Jack Yeats and Mainie Jellett, and has written other works on art, politics and on James Joyce. His "The Scandal of Ulysses" describes the "Life" of the book in the twentieth century, and he is currently making a film on the subject. He is a film-maker and opera-librettist.

Ashley Taggart was born in Belfast and holds a PhD in modern drama from York University. He published in *Modern Drama* on Strindberg's *The Father* and in the *Modern Language Review* on Maeterlinck's *Les Aveugles*. He has also written several screenplays (3 produced) and has published short-stories. He is currently director of an American study abroad programme in Dublin.

Caoimhe McAvinchey was a Fulbright Scholar at Tisch School of the Arts, New York University. She is currently Artistic Director of the Lyric Drama Studio, Acting Programmer at the Old Museum arts centre and teaches on the new Drama Degree at QUB.

Joseph Long is Director of the Drama Studies Centre, National University of Ireland, Dublin. His most recent publication is an English language editon of *Three Plays by Armand Gatti*, which was published in March 2000 by Sheffield Academic Press.

Jocelyn Clarke is lead theatre critic with the *Sunday Tribune*. He has lectured at the Samuel Beckett Centre and the Gaiety School of Acting in Dublin. He has written adaptations of *Bob* – from interviews with Robert Wilson, Lewis Carrol's *Alice's Adventures Underground* for SITI (New York) and of *Alice's Adventure in Wonderland* and most recently, *Alice through the Looking Glass* for Blue Raincoat Theatre Company, Sligo.

Redmond O'Hanlon lectures in Drama at the Centre for Drama Studies, NUI Dublin. He has published internationally on modern drama and on the novel and he has broadcast internationally on the novel, drama and cultural affairs. He is a translator of modern poetry and drama.

Bernice Schrank is a Professor of English Literature at Memorial University of Newfoundland. Her research is primarily in the area of Irish drama. She has published extensively on the work of Sean O'Casey.

Declan Kiberd is Professor of Anglo-Irish Literature and Drama at National University of Ireland, Dublin. He is the author of *Inventing*

Ireland: The Literature of the Modern Nation, Synge and the Irish Language, Men and Feminism in Modern Literature and *Idir Dhá Chultúr*.

Anne F. Kelly is a lecturer in the Religious Studies Department at St. Patrick's College, Drumcondra, Dublin. She holds degrees in Religious Studies, Theology and Modern Drama. She is a regular contributor to journals, and her work has been published in a number of collections.

Terry Eagleton is the Warton Professor of English Literature at St. Catherine's College, Oxford. His books include: *The Idea of Culture, The Illusions of Postmodernism, Literary Theory: An Introduction, The Truth about the Irish, Marxist Literary Theory, Ideology* and *Saint Oscar and Other Plays*.

Akiko Satake is an Assistant Professor and teaches English (Language) at Rikkyo University, Tokyo. She is a member of IASIL. She has written articles on Shakespeare, James Joyce, Brian Friel, Tom Murphy, Denis Johnston, George Fitzmaurice. She holds an MA from the University of Tokyo.

Deirdre Mulrooney is a lecturer, journalist, and contributes to Lyric FM. Her "Orientalism, Orientation, and the Nomadic Work of Pina Bausch" is online at www.deir.ie.

Eamonn Jordan is a lecturer in Drama at the Sligo Institute of Technology. His book *The Feast of Famine: The Plays of Frank McGuinness* (Bern: Peter Lang) was published in 1997. He has also written two critical commentaries for the new Leaving Certificate: the first on Frank McGuinness' *Someone Who'll Watch Over Me* and the second on Arthur Miller's *Death of a Salesman*.

Christopher Murray is Associate Professor of English and is former Director of the Centre for Drama Studies at the National University of Ireland, Dublin. His book *Twentieth Century Irish Drama: Mirror up to Nation* was published in 1997. He has published widely on Irish Drama and has recently edited *Brian Friel: Essays, Diaries, Interviews, 1964-1996* (Faber and Faber).

Ger FitzGibbon is a senior lecturer in the Department of English, University College Cork and is Chair of U.C.C.'s Board of Drama and Theatre Studies. His current critical writing is in the area of contemporary Irish theatre — especially the work of Brian Friel, Tom Murphy, Frank McGuinness and Sebastian Barry. Recent publications include "Southern Voices: Traditionen und individuelle Talente" in *Irische Dramatiker der Gegenwart*, revision and updating of all the contemporary Irish entries in the current editions of *The Cambridge Guide to Theatre* and *The Concise Cambridge Guide to Theatre*, contributions to the *Oxford Companion to Irish Literature*, and a forthcoming article on Brian Friel due to be published in the *Hungarian Journal of English and American Studies*. He has written a number of plays, the most recent of which, *Sca* (based on Sheridan), premiered in Cork in 1999. His most successful play, *The Rock Station*, was premiered by Soho Theatre Company in London in 1992 and later adapted for radio production by BBC.

Riana O'Dwyer lectures in the Department of English, National University of Ireland, Galway. She has published on the drama of Tom Murphy and Frank McGuinness and on the fiction of James Joyce, John McGahern and Kate O'Brien. She is a contributor to the *Field Day Anthology of Irish Literature*, Vol. 4.

Martine Pelletier is a lecturer at the University of Tours and holds an M.Phil in Irish Studies from Trinity College Dublin. An updated English version of her 1997 book *Le Théâtre de Brian Friel* published in France by Septentrion is due out in 2001 with Maunsell. She has also written on Field Day and contemporary Irish drama for a number of French and international publications.

Melissa Sihra holds a Masters Degree in Modern Drama Studies from NUI, Dublin and is currently researching the plays of Marina Carr for a Ph.D at the Samuel Beckett Centre, Trinity College, where she is also a Teaching Assistant. She is a Script Reader for the Abbey Theatre and a Producer with Blue Rose Theatre Company.

Eric Weitz has just completed a PhD thesis on Humour in Performance. As a professional actor in the U.S. he worked on and off-Broadway and in regional theatres including the Guthrie in Minneapolis and the Arena Stage in Washington, D.C. He has directed at amateur, student and professional levels, and founded a small production company in Dublin under the name of Tricksters. He has taught in Dublin at Gaiety School of Acting, NUI, Dublin, TCD, and DIT.

Victor Merriman lectures in Drama at Dublin Institute of Technology, Rathmines Road. A member of An Chomhairle Ealaíon/The Arts Council from 1993-1998, he chaired the *Review of Theatre in Ireland 1995-1996*. He publishes regularly on contemporary Irish theatre, and on drama pedagogy. He is currently researching a PhD on 'Postcolonial desires and representations of subjectivities in contemporary Irish theatre' at the Institute for New Media and Performance Research, University of Surrey, UK.

Karen Vandevelde is a Ph.D student in Irish Theatre History at National University of Ireland, Galway. She has written on Children's and Irish Contemporary Poetry in the Flemish/Dutch journal *De Poeziekrant*, and articles on Irish Theatre at the turn of the century in *Ropes*, Ireland. She is also involved in translations of poetry (English-Dutch-Swedish) and has published in Sweden and Belgium.

Scott T. Cummings directs plays and teaches courses in dramatic literature, theory, and criticism in the Theatre Department of Boston College. His essay here is dedicated to the memory of Adele Dalsimer.

INDEX

A

Abbey Theatre, xi, xix, xxxii, 1, 2, 27, 28, 30-34, 47, 48, 63, 84, 87, 90, 92, 110, 123, 188, 190, 192, 210, 224, 225, 237, 239, 247, 249, 257, 264, 268, 278, 291, 294, 313, 315
Andrews, Elmer, 128, 129, 143
Anglo-Irish Agreement, 241
Arts Council, xi, 60, 92, 106, 237, 249, 281, 316
Auden, W.H., 149, 158
Audience, 95, 97-99, 103, 122, 138, 143, 144, 176, 177, 189, 248, 250, 251, 256-258, 262, 263, 267, 269-271, 273, 276, 278, 292, 293, 297, 298, 313-315

B

Bakhtin, Mikhail, xvi
Banville, John, 57, 163
Barabbas, xxviii, xxxiii, 89, 269-279
    Half Eight Mass of a Tuesday, 89
    The Whiteheaded Boy, xxxiii, 90, 269, 270, 271, 274, 278, 279
Barnes, Ben, xi
Barry, Sebastian, xi, xxx, xxxi, xxxviii, 54-56, 130, 221, 224-235, 238
    Boss Grady's Boys, xxx, 54, 224, 225, 232-235
    Fanny Hawke Goes to the Mainland Forever, 225, 235
    Our Lady of Sligo, xxx, 232, 233, 235

Prayers of Sherkin, xxx, 55, 57
Steward of Christendom, xxxviii, xxx, 224, 231, 232, 235
The Only True History of Lizzie Finn, 224, 230, 235
White Woman Street, xxx, 224, 228-232, 235
Barthes, Roland, 187
Bausch, Pina, 188
Beckett, Samuel, xxvii, xxx, xxxii, 5, 7, 50,72, 82, 83, 86, 93, 94, 146, 150, 158, 171, 177, 183, 184, 234, 237, 243, 248, 257, 263, 267, 293, 313-315
    Waiting for Godot, 42, 183, 259
Behan, Brendan, xxvii, 32
    The Quare Fellow, 183
Belfast Festival at Queens, 86, 87
Bell, Sam Hanna, 143
Ben Barnes, 63, 92, 96
Bickerstaffe Theatre Company, 92
Bloody Sunday, 68, 69, 122-125, 127, 138, 140-144, 194, 201-203, 207
Blue Raincoat Theatre Company, 92
Body, xxvi, 2, 19, 21, 42-44
Bogart, Anne, 104
Boland, Eavan, 169, 170
Bolger, Dermot, xvii, xxxi, xxxix, xli, 91, 249-256
    A Dublin Bloom, 249
    A Dublin Quartet, 250, 256
    April Bright, 249, 250, 253
    Blinded by the Light, 249, 250, 254
    Finbar's Hotel, 249
    In High Germany, 56, 250, 252
    One Last White Horse, 55, 56, 91
    The Holy Ground, 250, 252
    The Lament for Arthur Cleary, xxxi, 55-57, 91, 250, 251